Hitler
Homer
Bible
Christ

HITLER
HOMER
BIBLE
CHRIST

The Historical Papers of Richard Carrier
1995–2013

RICHARD CARRIER
Ph.D.

Philosophy Press
2014

TO LIFE

What a strange thing it is
to be alive and to acquire knowledge.
We struggle to see the truth
as the evidence of it dissolves
over time.

Our brains are the bits
of the universe struggling to know itself,
and often getting it wrong.

Hitler Homer Bible Christ
Copyright © 2014 Richard Carrier
Additional copyrights noted in the text.

All rights reserved.

ISBN: 1493567128
ISBN-13: 978-1493567126

Published by Philosophy Press
Richmond, California

www.richardcarrier.info

1. History (General).   2. Ancient History.   3. Greco-Roman World.
4. Public administration—Rome—History.
5. Rome—Politics and government—30 B.C.-284 A.D.
6. History—Methodology.   7. History—Philosophy.
8. Hitler, Adolf—1889-1945—Translations into English.
9. Homer—Criticism and interpretation.
10. Virgil—Criticism and interpretation.
11. Tso chuan—Criticism, interpretation, etc.
12. Heroism.   13. Soul.   14. Ghosts.   15. Coins, Roman.
16. Herod—I—King of Judea—73–4 B.C.
17. Civilization, Ancient—Extraterrestrial influences.
18. Jesus Christ—Date of birth.   19. Jesus Christ—Historicity.
20. Bible—New Testament—Criticism, interpretation, etc.
21. Josephus, Flavius— Criticism and interpretation.
22. Tacitus, Cornelius—Criticism and interpretation.

CONTENTS

Doing History

1	The Function of the Historian in Society	1
2	History Before 1950	11
3	Experimental History	15
4	B.C.A.D.C.E.B.C.E.	25

History Done

5	Heroic Values in Classical Literary Depictions of the Soul: Heroes and Ghosts in Virgil, Homer, and Tso Ch'iu-ming	31
6	Herod the Procurator and Christian Apologetics	71
7	Herod the Procurator: Was Herod the Great a Roman Governor of Syria?	83
8	On the Dual Office of Procurator and Prefect	131

Debunking the Bogus

9	Flash! Fox News Reports that Aliens May Have Built the Pyramids of Egypt!	143
10	Pseudohistory in Jerry Vardaman's Magic Coins: The Nonsense of Micrographic Letters	155

11	More on Vardaman's Microletters	163
12	Hitler's *Table Talk*: Troubling Finds	167

THE VEXED BIBLE

13	Ignatian Vexation	193
14	Pauline Interpolations	203
15	Luke vs. Matthew on the Year of Christ's Birth	213
16	Mark 16:9-20 as Forgery or Fabrication	231

THE TROUBLESOME EVIDENCE FOR JESUS

17	The Nazareth Inscription	315
18	Thallus and the Darkness at Christ's Death	327
19	Origen, Eusebius, and the Accidental Interpolation in Josephus, *Jewish Antiquities* 20.200	337
20	The Prospect of a Christian Interpolation in Tacitus, *Annals* 15.44	369

BOOKS AND CHAPTERS BY RICHARD CARRIER
(with common abbreviations)

HHBC = *Hitler Homer Bible Christ: The Historical Papers of Richard Carrier 1995-2013* (Richmond, CA: Philosophy Press, 2014).

NIF = *Not the Impossible Faith: Why Christianity Didn't Need a Miracle to Succeed* (Raleigh, NC: Lulu.com, 2009).

OHJ = *On the Historicity of Jesus: Why We Might Have Reason for Doubt* (Sheffield, UK: Sheffield-Phoenix, 2014)

PH = *Proving History: Bayes's Theorem and the Quest for the Historical Jesus* (Amherst, NY: Prometheus Books, 2012).

SGG = *Sense and Goodness without God: A Defense of Metaphysical Naturalism* (Bloomington, IN: AuthorHouse, 2005).

[*TCD* = John Loftus, ed., *The Christian Delusion: Why Faith Fails* (Amherst, NY: Prometheus Books, 2010).]

TCD$_s$ = Richard Carrier, "Christianity Was Not Responsible for Modern Science," *TCD*, 396–419.

TCD$_w$ = Richard Carrier, "Why the Resurrection Is Unbelievable," *TCD*, 291–315.

[*TEC* = John Loftus, ed., *The End of Christianity* (Amherst, NY: Prometheus Books, 2011).]

TEC$_d$ = Richard Carrier, "Neither Life nor the Universe Appear Intelligently Designed," *TEC*, 279–304, 404–14.

TEC$_m$ = Richard Carrier, "Moral Facts Naturally Exist (and Science Could Find Them)," *TEC*, 333–64, 420–29.

TEC$_s$ = Richard Carrier, "Christianity's Success Was Not Incredible," *TEC*, 53–74, 372–75.

[TET = Robert Price & Jeffery Lowder, ed., *The Empty Tomb: Jesus Beyond the Grave* (Amherst, NY: Prometheus Books, 2005).]

TET$_b$ = Richard Carrier, "The Burial of Jesus in Light of Jewish Law," *TET*, 369–92.

TET$_s$ = Richard Carrier, "The Spiritual Body of Christ and the Legend of the Empty Tomb," *TET*, 105–232.

TET$_t$ = Richard Carrier, "The Plausibility of Theft," *TET*, 349–68.

WNC = *Why I Am Not a Christian: Four Conclusive Reasons to Reject the Faith* (Richmond, CA: Philosophy Press, 2011).

DOING HISTORY

1

THE FUNCTION OF THE HISTORIAN IN SOCIETY

Originally published in The History Teacher *35.4 (August 2002): 519-26. Reproduced with permission.*

The public rarely understands what historians do or why they are necessary. We've often been asked, "What do you really *do*?" Inevitably, in the classroom or at a cocktail party, we hear the gibe, "You historians don't do anything important. You don't really produce anything. You don't save lives or contribute to the economy." However the question is worded or the idea implied, we are often asked what the point is of spending our energies or institution's money on historical study, teaching, and research, especially about events in the remote past. We also are often asked why anyone should bother learning, much less teaching, special skills only of use to historians, like heuristics or dead languages. "Hasn't everything been translated already? Isn't it all just opinion anyway? Does it matter what really happened in the past?"

Such attitudes would be merely annoying if they weren't so alarming. There is a memorable scene in the film *Schindler's List*, in which a Jewish historian is listed as "nonessential" and earmarked for an extermination camp until, passed off by Schindler as an expert polisher of artillery shells, he is saved and put to "useful" work. This example is admittedly extreme. But it hints at the frightening outcome of a society that has abandoned any value for real historians, trading them in for ideologues and pseudohistorians of the type that bolstered Hitler's Third Reich.

This essay will help forestall the naysayers and educate the naive, who believe historians have little social utility. It is hard to find anything that analyzes and explains, in simple terms, the vital functions a historian fulfills for the healthy society, functions only a skilled historian can fulfill. An approach is needed both expository and normative: describing what historians do, but also what they ought to do, in order to be of use to humankind. Here I shall try to tackle that task, hoping at least to inspire both students and teachers of history to reevaluate the positive roles historians play in our society.

A simple come-back to questions about our alleged uselessness is this: "Is your memory unimportant? Nonessential? A do-nothing? Would you really let anyone carve it out or, worse, transplant whatever memories they wish to put there?" Surely no one but a fool would say yes. A human is a useless cripple without a memory, and can become someone else's puppet when true memories are replaced with false. Society is no less dependent on maintaining its true memory, on not letting its memory vanish or become manipulated and eclipsed by others' fantasies, myths, or false memories. A society afflicted with Alzheimer's or troubled by a collective psychosis is just as doomed as any individual suffering the same ailments. Historians are the memory cells of the metaphorical "brain" that is the whole human race: it can no more do without them than you can do without the memory cells of your own brain.

To function as a society with an accurate memory requires an entire culture of historical study, teaching, and research. Good historians don't grow on trees. Nor do books spontaneously correct or update themselves. Nor can works of scholarship be interrogated or asked new questions without the efforts of trained historians. To put it another way, historians are the workhorses of long-term social memory.

Some aphorisms will hammer this home, carrying to fruition the analogy of your memory cells and the historian. To know who we are, we have to know who we were: what we used to be, how we got here, and the progress we have made, even the progress we haven't. We need to know what has and hasn't worked, what has and hasn't been tried, if we are to avoid past mistakes, benefit from past successes, and maintain a store of realistic models from which to draw and inspire new innovations and solutions to new problems. By removing the distorting lens of a single culture or time, historians help us to better understand humanity. To know what humans are really and truly capable of, the good and the bad, we need a continuous databank of human behavior, of our heroism, villainy, mediocrity. To know how things get done, and how they fail, the historian sets out to discover and record the most relevant and essential information. Mythology will not serve as a substitute: for to deal with reality, we need to know reality, not fantasies and idealizations. We want historians to be as truthful with us as we want our own memories to be, perhaps even more so. We cannot do without them.

The problem partly stems from people's uncertainty whether history is a science or an art. History sits on the border between the sciences and the humanities. Through art, thought, literature, and language, the humanities inform us about ourselves and equip us to better understand and communicate with each other. They educate us in human desires, perceptions, dreams, and nightmares. History does this, too, though in a different way. Through literature we understand fiction and the internal meaning of texts, but through history we understand fact and external cause and effect. Yet history informs the meaning of a text, even a fictional one, while literary analysis assists the historian in sorting fact from fiction and understanding just what past writers were trying to say. Ascertaining historical truth is a science, but interpreting it, and conveying it to society in an intelligible and engaging form is an art. So historians have as much to gain from understanding scientific rationalism as from the literary craft.

There are important differences between history and science. Through science we seek general truths by observing repeated cases, by isolating the object being observed, by controlling conditions as much as possible. Historians more usually seek specific truths about particular events, and rarely get to experiment. But the difference largely ends there. The underlying method is the same: historians try to sort out the false or subjective by employing the most proven means of distinguishing fact from opinion, evidence from argument, and using the most objective checks against error available. We seek to be precise in our terminology, and accurate and thorough in documenting and analyzing our evidence. Like scientists, we keep ourselves honest through peer review and public debate. Esoteric discussions of skepticism or "multiple subjectivities" aside, both the historian and the scientist seek to discover an objective reality. Nevertheless, because historians tend to work from incomplete information of varying or even uncertain reliability, making historical judgments is often as much art as science.

In the simplest of terms, when historians say "this happened in our past, but that did not," they are issuing a kind of prediction: if they could use a time machine to peek back at the moment they are describing they would find that what actually took place would correspond to what they said. But in more practical terms, if something happened as historians claim, then it will have had causal effects on the whole world, and traces of this will remain. Pieces of evidence will exist that would not exist if the event that brought them about never occurred. So it is naive to suggest there is no truth in history to be sorted from the myths, falsities, and errors that seem the bread and butter of human thought. There are claims that are more probably true than others, many that are most probably true, and many more that are most probably false, and in every case, it is the evidence that informs us and puts a check on human opinion and ulterior motive.

Of course there are ideologues, demagogues and mythmakers. There are pseudohistorians whose work mimics the work of true historians just as there are pseudoscientists whose work mimics that of true scientists. Fortunately there are ways to discredit them. Pseudohistorians will often fail to document key evidence they claim to interpret, or when they do they will fabricate it, or appear to provide it, but not really. They will omit evidence that might disprove their story. They will employ both classical and novel fallacies of all varieties in their reasoning. And they will avoid or dismiss the criticism of their peers by every excuse they can invent.

By contrast, true historians will identity every primary source, every shred of relevant evidence, so the reader will be able to check their claims. Where the evidence is incomplete and they have to speculate, they will admit it, keeping facts and judgment distinct. They seek to understand why things happened the way they did, and will openly use evidence to support their accounts, and by concealing nothing, and by not pretending their assumptions are facts, they permit the reader to reach his or her own judgment about the truth. Above all, they open themselves to the examination of their peers, and facilitate future scholarship by checking and correcting the claims of other historians. That is why their results are far more trustworthy, far more useful, than the products of dogmatists and demagogues.

We obviously do not want history in the hands of ideologues or mythmakers who don't care about facts, but who will simply make up whatever suits their particular agenda. We want history in the hands of skilled researchers held to high standards of evidence and argument within a widespread framework of expert peer review, criticism, debate, and openness to progress and admission of error. As in science, a willingness to accept and live with uncertainty and doubt is essential to progress toward truth in history: for you cannot approach the truth without being willing to abandon the false. Truth in history, no less than in science, is conditional on future discoveries, and is built on probability, not any sort of unachievable certainty. The dogmatists, demagogues, and mythmakers will mislead and manipulate us and try to confuse our memory, but the historians will try their best to keep our collective memory deep and accurate, and above all brutally honest. In other words, to have a sharp and reliable memory, and to enjoy its benefits, we need the scientific historian. It is essential. But not just anyone can do the job. To have such experts requires years of highly specialized training.

When we maintain a rich community of competent historians, the historical profession provides several unique benefits to society. Historians perform at least five services with direct or indirect social benefits, surveyed here in their order of importance:

1. Historians solve big problems of significant importance to our understanding of ourselves and our past, or correct or improve the solutions to those problems worked out by past historians. This is the plum of historical progress, and though not a routine product, it is a fundamental social benefit.

2. Historians master all the technical work generated in their field and convey to the public, in terms nonspecialists can understand, the fruits of all historical research to date. This is the ultimate end-product and most extensive social benefit of the historian.

3. Historians train future historians. History is one of those rare professions in which the professionals are both producers and teachers of the next generation of experts.

4. Historians teach what they know to a broad reach of students, who as citizens need an accurate knowledge of human history and a sense of historical method in order to become more informed and competent, essential to the health of a free democracy.

5. Historians solve small, esoteric problems and publish their findings in technical journals. This is the most

common labor in history and creates the incremental progress other historians need: the more small problems that are solved and published and filed away for others to consult, the easier it becomes to solve the big problems, and the more thoroughly and accurately histories can be written for the public, and the more ably students can be taught, whether training to be historians themselves or just well-informed citizens. It is also this task that hones and improves an expert's skills as a historian. There is simply no substitute for the long-term, technical, hands-on experience this provides. It improves, broadens, and deepens their understanding of the time and culture they study, making them more knowledgeable and insightful.

There is a sixth function for those historians who specialize in dead literate cultures, for these men and women are a vital resource in another unique respect: they can truly understand the old languages and thus connect us with the vast body of literature and human genius that would otherwise be lost behind meaningless symbols. It is truly naive to say, "it's all been translated," for it hasn't. Vast numbers of documents do not exist in any English version, or indeed any modern language, and we are always finding more. But more importantly, translations mediate the past to the present but do not always accurately convey the true meaning, much less the beauty, of the original. Every translation is flawed. Moreover, modern words convey additional meanings and associations that were not present in the original language—and vice versa—and thus true understanding of the text is only possible in its original language, and with a deep and accurate understanding of its original context: social, cultural, historical, political, economic, and religious. So historians must work from the original language if they are to discover past errors, or refine past interpretations, or identify new insights gained from new discoveries that illuminate other texts. And yet this is only possible if this subtle linguistic and contextual knowledge is mastered, stored, and passed on in an unending chain from master to apprentice. Without this expensive intellectual architecture within society, the vast majority of human memory would be lost.

Finally, the historian might on occasion take up the useful role of historical activist. Legislators and statesmen do not want to hear about the historical development of Ibo art, but they do want to hear about how the history of Nigeria explains current political and social problems in that country. It is only within the latter context that solutions to social problems are to be found, as well as warnings against self-defeating attempts at solving them. This does not mean that esoteric subjects are useless to society, but we should not confuse how we came to understand a culture with how that understanding informs our political advice to those in power. Since a command of history, especially the ability to explode myth, is key to fruitful political diplomacy and progress around the world, the historian is more important in our world now than ever before.

Some people might still question the value of the technical papers on obscure subjects, which are the most common material product of any working historian. This must be understood. The historian writes in two different genres with two different goals: the technical paper or monograph, and the popular history. The second is, or certainly should be, the ultimate aim for which all history is done, and this end product could be said to be the ultimate social purpose of the historian. But it would not be possible, or certainly not of much quality, without the first activity performed in spades. Technical papers and monographs are indeed the brickwork of history. They are produced to aid all researchers and historians in getting access to and evaluating important facts and theories. Solutions or surveys of hyper-specific problems are collectively employed as the matter for comprehending and composing popular historical articles and monographs. But even more than this, in the very act of producing them historians perfect their ability and their knowledge, and it is through this legwork that they become a priceless asset. A technical piece characteristically skips over basic material and works from standard assumptions that have been established as accurate or true to the general satisfaction of all peers, since all expert readers will know this material, while historians out of the field can get it by reading the introductory literature. By maintaining a focus and speaking in a precise language shared by other informed experts, technical work achieves the goal of an efficient and practical furtherance of historical understanding, one piece at a time.

However, popular books and articles are the most important function of history. These educate the public about what really happened in our collective past, and make historical facts and knowledge available and comprehensible to society as a whole. In this respect they must be entertaining, but also true and simple and readable by any educated person. By their nature they cannot be as exhaustive, precise or thorough as technical works, since breadth, readability, and brevity are key to their success. Thus, this product of the historian avoids all the aspects of technical work that render it inaccessible to lay readers, such as specialized language, background assumptions, or foreign languages. Since progress is continually made in history, popular history is never perfect and can become obsolete, so the historian's job is never done. Historians are ever at work refining and transmitting society's memory, performing an irreplaceable social function.

The conclusion is clear: the ideologue, demagogue and mythmaker are not historians, and pseudohistory cannot benefit society. But real history can, and it requires well-trained and experienced historians. One might try to push the benefits of pseudohistory, as Plato did in the *Republic*, but these are pipe dreams. As soon as our understanding of the past is divorced from facts and objectivity-fostering methods, all opinions become equal, and there will be no benefit from any one history, because there will be others that will wash out and cancel the effects of the one anyone may favor. As such a scenario develops, psuedohistorians wedded to a false past may become willing to resort to the use of force and intimidation to control the public mind, which is essentially the defining feature of a Dark Age. Then, society will not flourish, but will stagnate and devour itself, breaking into divided units set against each other, as people rally around that version of a pseudohistory that pleases them most.

A society gripped by pseudohistory is a victim of social psychosis. It will suffer a memory disorder that, as with an individual whose memory is wholly fictional, will lead that society to confusion, despair, and self-defeating behavior. This is why theology tends to create more and more schisms but science tends to create more and more agreement: in the one case we base our allegiance on opinion alone; in the latter, our opinions are checked by facts and objectivizing methods that we cannot simply wish away. And history applies the same scientific methods to literature and artifacts, as a corrective process that steers us toward what is true, and not what we merely wish to be true.

Even if all these difficulties could be overcome, pseudohistory only offers one supposed benefit to society: the ability to manipulate it, which is only of use to those in power. In contrast, true history offers several benefits of use to all people. We will know who we really are, not what someone else wants us to be. We will understand humanity outside the distorting lens of a single culture, a gain that pseudohistory often specifically aims to prevent. We will know what *actually* has and hasn't worked, what *actually* has and hasn't been tried, what humans are *actually* capable of, how things *actually* get done. Perhaps armed with that knowledge, we will be able to avoid past mistakes and recover past successes. Pseudohistory, in contrast, pays no attention to such realities and thus its results give us no such information about ourselves or the universe. It does not prepare us for the future. For that, you have to honor the historical craft, and fund the institutions that make its practice possible.

> For more on this topic, including improvements on some points and bibliographies for further reading, see Richard Carrier, *Proving History*, chapters 2–4.

2

History Before 1950

Originally published at Richard Carrier Blogs
30 April 2007. Revised. © 2003, 2007, 2014.

All too frequently I run into hacks inordinately fond of quoting obsolete historical scholarship, sometimes a hundred or more years old. I take them to task, for instance, in my summary critical review of the woefully unreliable work of Kersey Graves in my article "Kersey Graves and The World's Sixteen Crucified Saviors" (Secular Web 2003), whose infamous book is a fine example of how (with a few exceptions) antiquated historical scholarship is simply not to be trusted. Though I do not address there the few aspects of his work that actually have been vindicated by sound scholarship of later years, my generalized critique makes the point that it's only recent scholarship, pro or con, that is worth consulting. Graves shouldn't even be read, much less cited.

Among the many arguments I gave for this conclusion was one in particular about the history of history itself:

> Graves's scholarship is obsolete, having been vastly improved upon by new methods, materials, discoveries, and textual criticism in the century since he worked. In fact, almost every historical work written before 1950 is regarded as outdated and untrustworthy by historians today.

I was subsequently asked in feedback what I meant by that. Not, that is, in reference just to Graves, but in apparently condemning the whole field of history even up to the middle of the 20th century. As I have made the same point in many other contexts, I gave a detailed reply to this question years ago. I now realize this is well worth publishing here, since it applies far beyond the case of Graves and relates a point I will continue to make again and again.

So here it is, with some minor editing.

The first day I arrived in the office of my graduate advisor at Columbia University, Professor William V. Harris, a very distinguished scholar of ancient history, one of the first things he said to me is (paraphrasing, since I can't recall his exact words—this was now about ten years ago), "Don't rely on anything written before 1950 or so unless you can confirm what it says from primary evidence or more recent scholarship." Point blank.

I have since found that his advice was quite apt. That doesn't mean we don't consult such texts (many crucial references were produced in the 1920s and 1940s that have never been revised) but generally we only use them as a "guide" back to the primary evidence or to check against later scholarship, etc. Hence the biggest exceptions are works that do little but present primary evidence (e.g. collections of inscriptions, critical textual apparatuses, etc.). Though there are a few exceptions in historical scholarship—but very few. For example, Ronald Syme's *Roman Revolution* (1939) is practically required reading on the Roman Civil Wars. Yet even then no historian would ever use Syme as a source without backing up whatever claim he is relying on with primary evidence or more recent scholarship. As there has been a lot challenging even Syme on various points. And again, Syme is exceptional.

Generally, the reasons for our attitude toward such early historical work are many, but here are four major ones:

(1) Historians were often, for some reason, more textually naive before the 1950s, trusting what historical texts and primary sources said too much, and trying too hard to make the evidence fit them. The situation has reversed since then, and archaeology is now more important, and multiple corroboration, and other methodological approaches are required (e.g. showing how a claim fits general cultural knowledge, and conceding uncertainty more often than previous historians did, etc.). As a result, a lot of what was argued before 1950 has been refuted or heavily qualified or modified. So you have to check and see in any given case if a claim still stands.

(2) A lot more evidence has come to light. For example: new Arabic texts relating to the history of science; papyrological finds pertaining to the Hellenistic period in Greece, the origins of Christianity, Roman history and economics, Egyptian government and society under Greek and Roman rule, etc.; plus documents recovered from Pompeii and Herculaneum and the Dead Sea and Nag

Hammadi, and so on (heck, we're *still* recovering texts from Oxyrhynchus); etc. This evidence has often changed, sometimes radically, the findings of earlier decades. Since you cannot know in advance what has been revised in light of new evidence, you simply can't assume old works stand as written, and must check more recent work to confirm any conclusions.

(3) Social and cultural history were largely (though not completely) neglected before the 1950s, and when addressed, were approached with the less sophisticated tools of the time. Since then significant advances have been made in sociology, psychology, economics, and anthropology, which have changed the way we understand and study other cultures. This has made a significant impact on the study of the history of religions, of ancient economics, social relations and interactions, background assumptions and worldview studies, and so on. And since these things connect with and affect every historical event in some way, improvements in our understanding of culture and its various facets entail changes in the way we understand and interpret historical texts and events.

(4) Finally (though this list is not comprehensive) the methodology of historians has become more scientific after WWII. That is, historians have become more method-conscious, and more concerned about distinguishing opinion from fact, and causal theory from chronological sequence, and much more concerned with thorough documentation, relying as much as possible on primary evidence, and being very critical when forced to rely on scholarship instead. Citation of sources is more meticulous. For example, before the 1950s you will find a lot of historians making claims to fact that are really the opinions or theories of earlier historians—and often they won't even tell you that.

A really good example of these factors can be gleaned from reading my dissertation advisor's rather famous book (in *our* field, that is): William Harris, *War and Imperialism in Republican Rome: 327-70 BC* (1979, reprinted with a new preface in 1991). He basically shows how earlier historians were hugely wrong on this subject—which is really something, since political and military history was the major thing before the 1950s, so you would think that if they could get anything right, it would be that. But no—and precisely because the religious and cultural and economic contexts, for example, were not properly understood or properly taken into account.

Of course, Harris also refutes a lot of historians from the 60s and 70s, too, but how he does so is also what distinguishes this work (and most works of professional history today) from most pre-50s material: enormously copious (and meticulous) citations, references, and reliance on primary evidence, a careful distinction between fact and theory, and taking into account new discoveries and scholarship, especially (but not only) in the ancillary fields that study human nature and the nature of cultures and societies (psychology, sociology, economics, anthropology, etc.). Harris deploys the same superior methodology (and again refutes common conclusions of earlier eras) in his equally-definitive works *Ancient Literacy* (1989) and *Restraining Rage: The Ideology of Anger Control in Classical Antiquity* (2004).

And yet I still recall in high school, in the late 80s, being taught a theory of Roman imperialism that Harris had so soundly refuted in 1979 that his findings became the gold standard and remain unchallenged. And that wasn't the only thing I was taught in high school history classes that I later found out was not only false, but soundly refuted, by work well-predating my high school years. It seems that high school textbooks, and teachers, are still relying on obsolete historical scholarship. And that's a problem. But the solution is caution. Always double-check a claim or conclusion against more recent scholarship.

3

EXPERIMENTAL HISTORY

*Originally published at Richard Carrier Blogs
28 July 2007. Revised. © 2007, 2014.*

A few weeks ago I teamed up with my friend David Fitzgerald once again to talk about historical method for a gaggle of godless kids at Camp Quest West. David and I dressed up in silly costumes and did a skit or two. One girl loved my hand-made ivy crown so much I was happy to let her have it after the show, but sadly we were so busy we forgot to get any pictures. Oh well. Anyway, the gist of our presentation was that the scientific method also applies to the field of history, and in fact history is really just another science, with its own peculiarities like every other field.

In more "typical" sciences, people go to the lab and run experiments, or go out and make observations of the phenomena they want to document or explain. But history is all in the past, so you can't run experiments on it, or observe it anymore. So how do you apply the scientific method to it? Well, the same way, actually. Of course there are already explicitly historical sciences (geology, cosmology, paleontology, archaeology), so obviously "it's all in the past" hasn't stopped scientists before.

But human history presents its own peculiar problems. And yet, so does every science. Psychology faces completely different methodological challenges from particle physics, as particle physics does from zoological anatomy, and thus the actual methods in each branch of science will vary greatly. But they all share the same basic structure that I outline and discuss in my books *Sense and Goodness without God* (pp. 213-26) and *Proving History* (pp. 45-49, 104-06), and they share many common elements of method besides those. Ultimately, human history is closer to criminal forensics in scientific genre, though still a field all its own, certainly in terms of the methodological toolbox needed to "do history" scientifically.

In short, all a scientist really does is adduce a theory or hypothesis about what happened in any given case (an experiment, a daily observation, whatever), then deduces from that what else would be observed it if were true (and, just as importantly, what should *not* be observed if it is true, or in other words, what would be observed if it were *false*), and then we go out and make many more observations, and from all the evidence we get, we inductively determine the relative probability of the hypothesis being true. Then we subject our work to peer review and replication by other experts, to confirm our observations and conclusions are valid and genuine, until we develop a consensus of experts in the field. The whole process aims at reducing the probability of deception and error in our conclusions. And all the other little refinements in method or technique, at each step, in every distinct field, are directed to that same end.

History works the same way. A historical event, like an atom or magnetic field, can't be observed. We can only observe its effects, and then infer the underlying facts, more or less precisely and with more or less certainty, depending on how much information we have access to. Like atoms and magnetic fields, a historical event causes things to exist that would not have existed otherwise. Evidence is left behind or destroyed. The course of events turns out one way rather than another. By observing the effects of an event that survive (what we call "historical evidence") we can infer what caused that evidence, in other words, what happened in history.

Of course, the biggest difference is that in most history, especially ancient history, we have a lot less data than any other science enjoys access to, even the more historical of them (like geology or cosmology). But this only means we will be a lot less certain of the results, and must often be a lot less ambitious in what we can claim to know about our past, but once that caveat is embraced and understood, everything works out the same way. To claim that a certain collection of evidence does *not* prove a particular historical claim, is in effect to propose an alternative theory of how that evidence came to exist, just as in every other science.

The kinds of evidence available to historians vary in nature and reliability, from each other and from the kinds of evidence available in other scientific fields. I discuss this at a fairly basic level in *Sense and Goodness without God* (pp. 227-52) and at a more advanced level throughout *Proving History*. But just as "laboratory experiments" are what most people imagine when they think of the "scientific method," so "research" (literary and archaeological) is what most people imagine when they think of the "historical method." Yet in fact much of science is built on observations that cannot be controlled or reproduced in any lab. Astronomy, for example. Or geological theories about the formation of the Grand Canyon. Likewise, there *are* (more or less) controlled experiments in the field of history.

I'm going to talk about the latter here, giving more examples than I did at camp, because I've run into so many lately I just have to talk about them! In "experimental history" you basically recreate a historical circumstance and see what happens, and from that you can infer things about what happened in the past. This employs the same general principle that science also depends on: the argument from analogy. What works yesterday works the same today, what works on Earth works on Mars, what works in London works in Paris, what works today worked the same a thousand years ago. A physicist would not demand that Newton reproduce a demonstration of his laws of motion in Paris on the assumption that physics works differently in London, nor do we demand that Newton's experiments be replicated every morning on the assumption that the laws of physics can change any day.

We accept this because we have abundant reasons to believe such deviations are highly improbable. Sometimes, it is true, analogies don't hold. Yet because a violation of this rule is so rare, you need really good evidence to believe things were different or have changed *before* you can conclude that any given analogy doesn't hold. The rate of fall of dropped objects is indeed lower on Mars than on Earth, and the elevation of the planet Mars is indeed different in London than it is in Paris. Yet we've accumulated plenty of evidence confirming that the circumstances in these cases *are* relevantly different. In fact, once we add those differing circumstances into our calculations, the corresponding differences in result vanish, and the analogy holds after all. Newton's laws *are* actually the same on Mars as on Earth, and in fact this *explains* why objects fall faster here than there. And once we take into account the sphericity and rotation of the earth, the actual celestial declination of Mars turns out to be *identical* with respect to Paris or London. And so on.

So, too, in history. I have already discussed this in some detail (in my essay "What Can We Infer from the Present about the Past?" published on the Secular Web in 2006). So I won't belabor the point. Let's get to some examples of experimental history instead, since that's the interesting bit. Of course these all relate to my own field, ancient history, and ancient science and technology in particular, since that's what I know well. There are no doubt examples in other fields.

What the Hell is a Tettarakontareme?

At Camp Quest I opened with the example of the Trireme Project. Around the 5th century B.C. the Greeks invented the trireme, which revolutionized naval warfare and contributed to the rise of the Athenian empire, and the subsequent defeat of Persia, two events that were rather decisive for us secularists, since without them the Age of Greek Rationalism might never have happened, and the development of modern Science, Logic, Human Rights, and Democracy might have been delayed considerably, possibly indefinitely, since these all subsequently began and originally grew only in Greece.

But in all this lay a historical problem. No trireme has ever been recovered, and surviving depictions and descriptions of them from antiquity are frustratingly incomplete or imprecise. So what exactly *was* a trireme? We know the word means something like "three rower" and that triremes were propelled by 170 oarsmen and about 120 feet long and employed a ram as their principal weapon. From all this it was reasonably surmised that "trireme" meant there were three decks of oars, one above the other, with six rows of oarsmen in all.

But soon after that a naval arms race began. There is a lot of interesting stuff about that arms race, and the best scientific discussion of it all is in Vernard Foley and Werner Soedel's 1981 article "Ancient Oared Warships" in *Scientific American* 244.4 (April issue, pp. 148-63). But here the troubling problem was that bigger and bigger warships were built and fielded. First came the quadriremes (four-rowers), then the quinquiremes (five-rowers), then sextiremes (six-rowers), and on and on, all the way up to the monster of them all, the tettarakontareme, a "forty rower." What the hell!?

Obviously, the argument from analogy operates here well enough to conclude that there is no damned way they fielded a ship with 40 decks of oars. So if that's not what the "-reme" refers to, then are we also wrong about what a *trireme* was? And what, after all, is a *tettarakontareme*? Enter experimental history. First a hypothesis: the 1981 work of Foley and Soedel tentatively solved the problem by applying science to it and proposing (rather persuasively) what these ships really were like. But then how do you test it? Well, you build one.

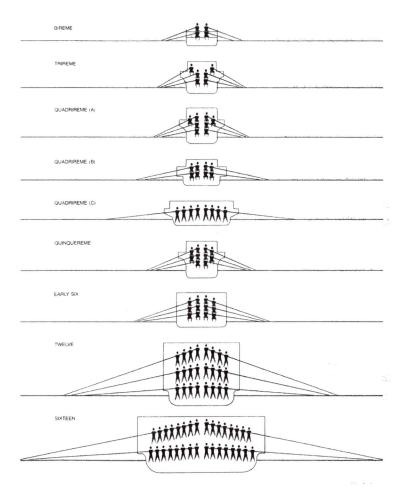

In the late 80s and early 90s the Trireme Project was launched, and hypothetical trireme designs were realized, actually built and sailed. This allowed historians to experimentally test a trireme's maneuverability, speed, weight, and other important data, and to rule out some things, and rule in others. Ultimately, the tests proved that the trireme probably did have three vertical banks of oars, but that adding any more banks would have been increasingly unmanageable and unlikely. Meanwhile, the theories of Foley and

Soedel made even more sense on the same evidence. So these experiments lent strong support for them.

Their solution was that after the trireme, larger ships kept the same basic structure of three decks of oars (which in a trireme were manned by six rows of oarsmen, one man to an oar), but then added rows of oarsmen.[1] So the quadrireme put two men per oar on the top deck, to give added power where it was most needed, then the quinquireme put two men per oar on the top *two* decks, and so on. All this increased the size of ship that could still be propelled at an effective ramming speed, which allowed larger complements of catapults and marines to be carried, and that changed the course of battles.

Then the largest ships started putting three men per oar, and then four, sometimes more, which mechanically required installing steps for some oarsmen to march up and down to work their end of an oar. With this information, historians took a second look at literary descriptions of the tettarakontareme and concluded it must in fact have been a giant war catamaran, with two hulls connected by a battle bridge, all propelled by three decks of oars on each side of each hull, up to eight men to every oar. This monstrosity never saw battle. Though it did see service, its function was more to serve as a deterrent: the fact that the king of Egypt had it was intended to scare the shit out of everyone else.

The Antikythera Computer

In 1900 sponge divers recovered the contents of an ancient shipwreck dating to the 80s B.C., whose cargo included crusted bits of geared machinery. This is in fact what my old blog avatar was an x-ray of (as I explained in "Why the Bizarre Avatar?" at Richard Carrier Blogs on 2 November 2006). But this also offers an example of experimental history: historians figured out what this machine was

---

[1] Images on this and preceding page depicting these oar arrangements (in cross section) are reproduced from Foley and Soedel's article in *Scientific American*. Images © 1981 by George V. Kelvin. Used with permission.

by building one. They observed the parts that were available (including Greek inscriptions on some of the parts, which turn out to have been something like an instruction manual) as data to infer or rule out hypotheses about all its surviving, broken, and missing parts, and their arrangement. Then they built some examples and experimentally confirmed what it had to have been: an astronomical computer for predicting solar and lunar eclipses, lunar phases, solar positions in the zodiac, and even the positions of the known planets. All with just an elaborate system of gears.

> (You can read all about this device and its construction and history in Jo Marchant's book *Decoding the Heavens: A 2000-Year-Old Computer—and the Century-Long Search to Discover Its Secrets*, published in 2009.)

Horse Shit

A lot of experimental history has been done with horse equipment. Two I know well are harness experiments and cavalry experiments.

In the first case, it had long been claimed (and is still, in the writings of historians not up on their game) that the ancient system of harness impeded economic and technological progress, because it choked horses and thus prevented the exploitation of the greater power afforded by them, over mules, donkeys, and oxen. Although it is often not mentioned that horses consume a lot more fuel than these, so the decision which to use did not simply hinge on harness technology. Nevertheless, the Romans have been called stupid for not having figured out the inefficiency of their harness, while the invention of the modern horse collar has actually been credited as an inevitable result of Christianity (I won't bore you with the twisted logic behind that one, but you can read more about it in my follow-up piece at Richard Carrier Blogs, "Lynn White on Horse Stuff," published on 3 August 2007).

Well, J. Spruytte figured this was so much armchair horseapples, and actually made an ancient horse harness and tested it. Turns out it doesn't choke horses and in fact does not impair their pulling power at all. Dr. Judith Weller gives a good online summary of this and other issues related to ancient harness in "Roman Traction Systems" (at www.humanist.de/rome/rts/dorsal.html). The horse collar may have afforded certain advantages, but none that would be at all decisive in the progress of civilization. Western history did not turn on its invention. So much for that theory.

In the second case, one question people often wonder at is how the hell the Greeks and Romans fielded such effective cavalry without a stirrup. The cavalries of Trajan or Alexander the Great, or even the Persians, were legendary, effective enough to decide an entire battle, and heavily relied on tactically for nearly a thousand years, before anyone thought, "Hey, you know what would be a good idea…?"

Lynn White, who also came up with the Horse Collar of Christ theory (and many other inept boners like it), also hugely exaggerated the importance of the stirrup in the course of Western history, assuming that somehow the medieval heavy cavalry that depended on it were somehow a miracle (again of Jesus, in a roundabout way) that were essential to the rise of the Western world. Scholars who know better have taken him to task for such an absurd claim. Indeed, if he had seen how easily heavy cavalry could be defeated by mere sticks in the movie *Braveheart*, he might have thought twice about his silly idea. The Romans had so decisively defeated waves of war elephants (a far scarier military unit than stirruped heavy cavalry) with the similar tactic of the caltrop, that the elephant ceased to be employed at all, ever again, in the history of warfare. I don't imagine the legions would have had any greater trouble with mounted knights.

Anyway, stirrupless cavalry were certainly effective, since evidence of their effective use in antiquity is quite extensive. Hey, I hear tell the American Plains Indians fielded formidable cavalries that kicked some major ass, without even *saddles*. Maybe had it not been for guns and germ warfare, things might have turned out differently for them? At any rate, the question remains: how much does not having stirrups affect a rider in combat, and what kinds of combat does this affect?

Well, Ann Hyland found out…by experimenting. She set a horse up with Roman gear and attempted various cavalry maneuvers with it and reported on the results. She found that a stirrup does afford some advantages, though not as many as once thought (and in fact it presented some disadvantages—like getting caught in them). Most importantly, she also tried out a Roman four-horned saddle we know from extant military reliefs had been invented by the early 2nd century A.D., and found something surprising: it negated almost all the disadvantages of fighting without stirrups.

Though it would not have helped mount a medieval-style heavy cavalry, it would have increased the fighting effectiveness of light cavalry to the same level the stirrup allowed. Thus, in fact, the Romans didn't need Jesus to invent an improved method of mounting cavalry.

And the Rest

I could add many other examples like this. In the 60s A. Gerhardt Drachmann built numerous ancient machines and instruments according to the available literary descriptions of them, in order to test their functions and properties, as well as the manufacturing knowledge and abilities of ancient scientists and craftsmen. Michael Lewis recently did the same for ancient astronomical and surveying instruments, ascertaining their accuracy, for example, and matching it with the known accuracy of Roman construction projects (such as some remarkably precise inclines built into aqueduct systems). John Riddle tested the efficacy of ancient drugs according to ancient pharmacological treatises, finding, for example, that they had in fact discovered several effective birth control drugs and abortifacients. John Healy tested some of the more suspect chemical claims in Pliny the Elder's *Natural History*, proving that, contrary to previous assessments, often enough Pliny actually knew what he was talking about.

Others have done something similar in the textiles industry, building various models of ancient looms and testing their products against surviving samples of ancient cloth, to ascertain what sort of loom technology they had, and perhaps even date its development. Recently I read a study of ancient wine technology in which historians reconstructed ancient wine production methods in an actual vineyard, according to surviving technical manuals from the time, and then ascertaining the productivity and efficiency and other features of these ancient practices. But one of the most interesting examples is an ongoing experiment in ancient shaft furnace design, in which ancient smelting technology is being tested for its production and efficiency attributes, teaching us things about the choices made regarding labor and economics in the Roman iron industry, and aiding in the interpretation of archaeological finds, such as determining the amount of waste slag produced per furnace. Students every year man the furnaces and smelt iron, accumulating more and more data. Fun!

Some cases can be rather fanciful. I saw an episode of *Myth Busters* where they tested, using only technology known to have been available at the time, whether Archimedes could have burned attacking ships with parabolic mirrors. Parabolic burning mirrors were well known at the time and scientific treatises were written about them and the scientific basis for their operation. Though the literary evidence already confirms that Archimedes' use of them as a weapon was a medieval legend, testing whether it was still possible by conducting experiments (in "Archimedes' Death Ray," airing in 2004) still qualifies as doing experimental history.

But my favorite example is an episode of *NOVA* ("Pyramid," which I believe aired in 1997). They went to Egypt with a bunch of historians and archaeologists to test their various theories of how the blocks were lifted into place, and all met with considerable difficulties, until an Egyptian stone mason walked by and was astonished at how silly their ideas were, and then showed them how it was done, blowing them away with a very simple, effective method.

Intriguingly, that might be somewhat moot now. It has recently been argued (now by two chemists, first Joseph Davidovits and then Michel Barsoum) that the pyramids were partly constructed from a pre-Roman form of poured concrete, and the evidence for this is somewhat impressive. I'll wait and see if this theory survives peer review and persuades the experts.[2] But one thing is certain: experiments will certainly play a part in confirming or refuting it, or fleshing it out.

---

[2] This theory was published under peer review in M.W. Barsoum, A. Ganguly & G. Hug, "Microstructural Evidence of Reconstituted Limestone Blocks in the Great Pyramids of Egypt," *Journal of the American Ceramic Society* 89.12 (2006): 3788–96. So far the only expert rebuttals I've seen are straw manning the argument, by testing the wrong stones, and mistakenly assuming the proposal is that *all* of a pyramid's stones were placed this way, which neither Davidovits nor Barsoum have ever claimed.

4

B.C.A.D.C.E.B.C.E.

Originally published at Richard Carrier Blogs
6 January 2012. Revised. © 2012, 2014.

You may know there are two conventions for representing historical years: the traditional A.D. and B.C., and the chic new C.E. and B.C.E. (if you don't know about that, Wikipedia will get you up to speed). People often ask me why I use one or the other, or what (as a historian) I think we should use. I always use B.C. and A.D. when I have a choice, and I believe we should only ever use that convention. The other should be stuffed in a barrel filled with concrete and tossed to the bottom of the sea. However, I don't always have a choice. When I publish with Prometheus Books (and so far that means five chapters in two volumes, *The Christian Delusion* and *The End of Christianity*, and the whole volume *Proving History*), I have to adhere to their editorial conventions, which include a requirement to employ the newfangled convention (so their copy editors always convert the abbreviations, which led to an error in *Delusion*, where a C.E. date was given as B.C.E., on page 413, which I'm told was corrected on a later printing). So sometimes you'll see me use one, and sometimes the other. That's why.

But why do I think C.E. and B.C.E. are dumb? Really dumb, in fact. The newfangled convention has been promoted in an idiotic and patronizing attempt not to "offend" non-Christians who have to use the Christian calender (yes, it's a Christian calendar, *full stop*). That's the same non-Christians who (we're to suppose) are still being regularly offended by having to call a day Saturday even though they don't worship the God Saturn. Christians don't get offended by naming a calendar day by a non-existent pagan god. So why should non-Christians get offended by naming a calendar year after a non-existent Christian god? Calling the sixth day of the week 'Saturday' (literally "Saturn's Day") does not entail embracing a Eurocentric worldview or belief in the God Saturn. It's just using the English language. So, too, the labels B.C. and A.D.

The new convention is even stupider than that, of course, because it's embarrassingly Orwellian. The traditional convention of B.C. ("Before Christ") and A.D. ("Anno Domini" = "In the Year of the Lord") is supposed to be improved by replacing it with the culturally neutral B.C.E. ("Before the Common Era") and C.E. ("Common Era"). But both indicate the same exact division, made by the same exact religion, for the same exact reason, to honor the same exact god. Either way, it's the same demarcation, which was the invention of Christians, and only makes sense as such. There is no other reason for starting "year 1" where it does, other than what Christians mistakenly believed to be the birth of their Lord and its cosmic importance.

Yes, mistaken. There is no evidence that Jesus (even if he existed) was born in 1 A.D. (much less on Christmas), and in fact all the evidence we have is against that. The only evidence there is (if it can be trusted at all) entails he was born either no later than 4 B.C. or no earlier than 6 A.D. (a contradiction that further entails at least one of those dates must be wrong). For a summary of the evidence on this point see my article "Luke vs. Matthew on the Year of Christ's Birth" (included in the present volume). Personally, I think it's more embarrassing for Christians if we keep the traditional terms, as that can only perpetually remind them of how fallible and silly they are. Whereas the new notation makes the rest of us look even sillier.

Anyway, point is, the only reason whatever for starting the calendar at year 1 in the B.C.E. / C.E. system is the wholly erroneous medieval belief that the god Jesus was born in that year. Changing the acronyms does nothing to conceal that fact and therefore serves no purpose, other than to please a pernicious form of liberalism that believes you can change what things are by renaming them. And like all stupid attempts to conceal what things really mean by renaming them, the B.C.E. / C.E. notation is less intelligible (era common to whom?), less explicable (why does the 'common era' begin in the year it does, instead of some other year?), less practical (repeating the same two letters in each designator slows visual recognition), and less efficient (using five letters to do the work of four). It's therefore just monumentally stupid.

As George Carlin once observed, our fear of facts often involves making our language more polysyllabic, confusing, and useless. That's how 'Shellshock' became 'Post Traumatic Stress Disorder'. As Carlin put it, "American English is loaded with euphemisms. Because Americans have a lot of trouble dealing with reality. Americans have trouble facing the truth, so they invent the kind of a soft language to protect themselves from it, and it gets worse with every generation." This 'Common Era' fiasco is a good example of that, although in this case foreigners are just as guilty of it, as if they want to hide from the fact that they were conquered or outdone by Christian imperialists and are now compelled by that accident of history to use their calendar instead of their own. Just deal with reality. It's much better that way. Trust me.

The bottom line is, the original notation is more familiar, more honest, more factual, more meaningful, less confusing, and easier to use. There is no good reason to change it.

History Done

5

Heroic Values in Classical Literary Depictions of the Soul: Heroes and Ghosts in Virgil, Homer, and Tso Ch'iu-ming

Originally published at RichardCarrier.info in 2013.
© 1997, 2004, 2013.

The following essay was my senior honors thesis at UC Berkeley for the awarding of the Bachelor's degree in History (minor in Classical Civilizations). It was originally written in 1997. In 2004 I reorganized and numbered its sections, updated its references, revised some sentences, and added some paragraphs, all with the intent to consider publication, but decided I was no longer confident in its core thesis. There are interesting insights and information here, but ultimately the evidence of afterlife beliefs and heroic ideals in ancient Greece, Rome, and China is a little more complicated than this. I provide it here only for the sake of what utility and interest it may have, but also to illustrate how historians reason and use evidence, and to show the importance of cross-cultural comparison to understand our own history. But I no longer fully endorse all of the conclusions here, and my treatment of the evidence is not adequately broad to be considered thorough. It's quite good as an undergraduate thesis. It probably won me my doctoral fellowship. But it meets only minimum standards for graduate level work. — Richard Carrier.

1. Introduction

How a society understands the 'hero' affects its understanding of the 'soul'. Eastern and Western views of heroism and the soul reflect this connection, while at the same time differing from each other in notable respects, allowing us to gain perspective on Greek and Roman beliefs when compared to Chinese parallels. The exploration of this phenomenon can in turn illuminate contemporary differences between Eastern and Western cultures, by tracing their ancient origins.

To this end we will examine three cultural classics, great works that lay at the origin and heart of the Chinese, Greek, and Roman cultures and thus reflect important fundamental differences among them. Western individualism is reflected, even exaggerated, in Homer, against an idealized Chinese communalism in the *Tso Chuan*. Yet Virgil's *Aeneid* reflects a middle ground of tension between both kinds of perspective. In many ways, Roman cultural ideals regarding the hero and the soul were somewhat more like the Chinese than the Homeric, exhibiting an early attempt to reconcile such different ways of viewing the world, presaging modern cultural struggles between materialistic individualism and social responsibility.

2. Why Focus on These Classics?

By "classic" I mean a literary work that is revered and identified as preeminent by the great majority of those who share a culture. It plays a central, universal role in education, becoming familiar to everyone, a treasury of shared analogies, idioms, and lessons, much like the Bible through the Middle Ages to the early 20th century, which still competed fiercely for this position with the classical tradition after the Renaissance, when "to no small extent knowledge of the classical world and acquaintance with the values communicated through the vehicle of classical education informed the mind and provided much of the intellectual confidence of the ruling political classes of Europe" (Turner 1981: 5).

The present state, of a Western culture lacking a universal classic, could be either part cause or symptom of a general state of confusion about our common identity, which has impaired our ability to communicate in a vocabulary of familiar themes, a point forcefully argued by Kopff (1999). Even if we disagree with him on the details, he is describing a real problem. Perhaps television and film are stepping up to fill this gap, however imperfectly—epic sagas such as *Star Wars*, *Star Trek* and *The Simpsons* have actually contributed to our dialogue a vocabulary and a plethora of allusions that is somewhat comparable to the effect the literary classics once had, but as such things are not shared equally by all generations or subcultures, a valuable continuity is being undermined. The present situation makes it difficult for many to comprehend the forceful relevance classics once had in every great culture.

There is no doubt that Homer's *Iliad* and *Odyssey* (written c. 8th century B.C.) were the defining classics of ancient Greek culture. Their central, even overwhelming role in Greek education is undisputed and well-documented (Cribiore 2001, 1996; Marrou 1948), as is the ubiquity of Homeric language, themes and idioms throughout the whole of Greek literature (MacDonald 2000: 4-6). As Hurwitt puts it, the Homeric epics were "storehouses of values and ethics and textbooks of conduct...full of information detailing what it was to be Greek" (1985: 106, 114).

The place of these epics in society was not the least bit undermined even when some elite attitudes regarding how to approach or interpret Homer changed. We can see the most radical examples of counter-cultural critique in Plato's *Laws* (4th century B.C.) and Plutarch's *How the Young Man Should Study Poetry* (1st century A.D.). But mass culture, even among elites, still took to Homeric values and ideals. Some modern interpreters have seen Homer as actually attacking the self-destructive values he is usually seen as glorifying. But Alexander the Great didn't keep a roll of the the *Iliad* under his pillow because he admired Homer's ironic criticism of martial valor. Nor is he likely to have cared much for the moral criticisms of Plato. The fact is, the values presented in Homer remained, in one form or another, dear to the heart of the average Greek. The Homeric epics might exaggerate into extreme relief ideas that were in practice more subtle and complex, but nevertheless pervasive. It is also true that cultures typically enjoy an active debate and a diversity of views, even when one set of ideas continues to signify the reigning zeitgeist. So the fact remains: Homer was everywhere. Even the illiterate heard him sung, or knew his stories by word of mouth and in public art.

Much the same can be said of the *Tso Chuan*, preeminent among the Confucian Classics, which had a central role in Chinese education from as early as the 2nd century B.C. (Cromer 1993: 114). Indeed, the Chinese classical tradition "had been institutionalized in a system of education and recruitment based on an orthodox classical curriculum that took as its core a series of so-called Confucian texts," which included the *Tso Chuan*, "Just as late modern Europe had accepted the centuries-old belief that a man had only to know Greek and Latin to be educated." In other words, "If the works of Homer and Hesiod helped to define what it was to be Greek, the *Songs*, *Documents*, and *Tso Chuan* played a similar role in China" (Keightley 1993: 13-15). These classics also played a key role in Japanese and Korean literate culture. The *Tso Chuan* in particular became "one of the cornerstones of a traditional education" having "an immense influence on later Chinese literature and historiography" (Watson 1989: xi).

And this can also be said of Virgil's *Aeneid* for a traditional Roman education in Latin after its composition in the first century B.C. This work was seen as a kind of synthesis of Homeric and Roman ideals, ripe for comparison and contrast (cf. Juvenal, *Satires* 6.434-56, wr. 1st century A.D.), and it was certainly regarded with the highest reverence as the pinnacle of Roman literature, having "achieved a pre-eminence in the Latin world that was scarcely inferior to the ascendancy of the Homeric poems among the Greeks" (Cary and Scullard 1975: 395). It was also used as a vehicle for spreading Latin culture abroad, justifying "the ways of Rome" to foreign subjects, and ultimately as a textbook for moral education and grammar (Morgan 1998; Gwynn 1926). Virgil consciously attempted to infuse Roman values into a Homeric model, but still could not completely escape the Homeric mind, nor did Homer's epics lose their attraction or educational role among the Romans, for whom a thorough familiarity with Greek was regarded as essential to the gentleman (Cribiore 2001; Morgan 1998).

As a result, Homer and the Greek mind have remained within the Western psyche to this day, even among those who have never read a word of it. Though perhaps this is becoming less so, still the fundamental mindset persists, and there are certain affinities between the way we think now, and the way Homer and his audience thought then, which do distinguish us from those raised within more "Chinese" cultures. Homer even underlies the Greek cultural springboard of the Western ideals of science: as we see in the *Iliad*, "The key words are competition, argument, persuasion, and peers—all aspects of what we mean by objectivity and, ultimately, science" (Cromer 1993: 74), and as we see in the *Odyssey*, "The sea is freedom, adventure, wealth, and knowledge—all factors important to the development of science," in fact "Odysseus has for almost 3,000 years epitomized the solitary adventurer. Washed naked onto the shores of Phaeacia, he must survive on his wits alone" (Cromer 1993: 75), a heroic theme that is ubiquitous in modern Western rhetoric, cinema, and literature today. Yet this stands in conflict with Eastern values. The Chinese culture "suppressed the very elements—the entrepreneurs and adventurers—who have been the instruments of change in the West" (Cromer 1993: 119; see also Lloyd 1990, 1996, 2002). These different approaches have had profound effects not only on our material culture, but our mental culture as well. The *Aeneid*, in contrast, in a sense dipped its toes in both ponds, attempting a synthesis. Modern multiculturalism aims at a similar target.

I have decided to credit the traditional authors here out of convenience, even though there is some dispute in the case of Homer and Tso Ch'iu-ming. The date and authorship of the *Tso Chuan* is even more disputed than the works of Homer (on Homer, see Nagy 1996 and Davison 1962; on the *Tso Chuan*, Cheng 1993 and Loewe 1993). But I shall attribute the *Tso Chuan* to the near-contemporary of Confucius, Tso Ch'iu-ming (c. 6th century B.C.), since it bears his name; and likewise to Homer, the *Iliad* and *Odyssey*. For these classics have paramount importance as portals into the cultures that produced and revered them, no matter who wrote them, as each was still a product of those cultures and a pervasive influence upon them.

Finally, it might be objected that Homer and Virgil were poets, and Tso Ch'iu-ming a historian, and thus their works cannot be compared due to differences in genre. But this difference is not of great consequence to this study. Each author treated values and beliefs, even regarding heroism and the soul, in the medium most appropriate to his own time and culture: oral drama for the Greeks, prose commentary for the Chinese, and patriotic verse for the Romans (Keightley 1993: 14-15, 37-40). The mode of writing has little bearing on the fact that all these works hold an analogous place to each other as the greatest classics of their place and time, and the primary engines of enculturation.

3. The Classical Hero

As we will see later, Homer depicts the soul as powerless and fleeting, while the author of the *Tso Chuan* portrays it as potent and energetic. Virgil, on the other hand, presents a soul that is partly both. All three authors accomplish this through descriptions of the actions of souls, through the vocabulary used to describe or define them, and through actual metaphysical statements about their nature. These differences correspond in some sense to how each author viewed the hero: for Homer viewed heroism as bodily perfection; Tso Ch'iu-ming, as cultural perfection. Virgil, however, imagined it as the mind overcoming and mastering the body in the service of national destiny—the bloody, senseless struggles that he saw in the world around him echo in his depiction of a corresponding inner struggle between body and mind, a conflict known in Western thought since Plato. Our first object, then, is to examine how these authors portrayed the hero, defined here as "a protagonist of exceptional courage and fortitude who engages in bold and significant actions" (Keightley 1993: 16), an actor who embodies the cultural ideal, someone whom readers are expected to praise or emulate.

As Keightley observes, "It is difficult to generalize about early Greek views of heroism because the subsequent elite culture appears to have been more pluralistic, more given to the preservation and transmission of conflicting views than the elite culture of early China was" or indeed the other more "Asiatic" cultures of the West, such as that of the Hebrews, which was transmitted through Christianity and thus came into direct conflict with the very different Greek culture (Keightley 1993: 23; MacDonald 2000). Once Christianity became ascendant on the coattails of Roman power it put Judaic and Hellenic cultural values into fierce conflict, and it took centuries to find even an uneasy synthesis. Nevertheless, Homeric thinking is always found, even when it is struggled against.

In contrast, early Chinese culture had only one major counter-culture, the intellectual currents of Taoism. But this was never as influential in elite government or education as its Confucian counterpart, and more importantly it "did not...provide an alternate model for social, political, and military action in the world," but rather called for inaction and retirement, for removing oneself "from the arena of action" (Keightley 1993: 25). Moreover, Taoism was itself a holistic, counter-individualist philosophy and thus was simply another expression of the same collectivist mindset. Indeed, Keightley continues, "the pluralism of the Greek views and the greater unanimity of the Chinese view is itself significant" as a distinction between the two cultures. Unlike

Chinese culture, a love of struggle and conflict is natural to the Greco-Western intellect, even indicative of it.

3.1. Homeric Heroism

In the case of Greece, the evidence begins with the word "hero" itself. It comes from the Homeric word *hêrôs*, "hero," used by Homer to signify a warrior who excelled in *aretê*, "excellence, manhood, valor, or prowess." These two words alone give some indication of the Homeric concept of heroism, and we should begin with an analysis of their meaning to Homer's audience. It is not necessary to establish real etymological links. Since we are dealing with the realm of ideas, it is sufficient, even more important, to know whether the ancients *thought* certain words were connected.

The word *aretê* is derived from *Arês*, the "god of war and slaughter, strife and pestilence," and an "appellation for war, battle, discord, slaughter, as well as warlike spirit" (Liddell and Scott 1996: 115, 116). In fact, several words denoting goodness in Greek contain the *ar-* root, "the first notion of goodness (*vir-tus*) being that of manhood, bravery in war," hence our own word *aristocracy*, "rule of the best," is derived from this. *Hêrôs*, in turn, may have connections with *hôra* (Schein 1984: 69), meaning "the prime of the year, springtime," and used metaphorically for "youth, prime of life," as well as "the part of the year available for war" (Liddell and Scott 1996: 906-7, I.2 and IV). Thus, we see that Western heroism is connected at its very root with martial valor and prowess, as well as bodily perfection, and this is manifest in the Greek fascination with athletics and physical training. Thus Nestor's speech (*Il.* 23.624-50) outlines the bodily expectations of Homeric heroism, which he tells us are lost in old age. Heroism is for the young, the strong, the quick, those who are handy with chariot, spear, or fist. Even outside the context of war, Laodamas tells Odysseus, "No greater is a man's glory so long as he might exist, than whatever he might bring about with feet and limb and hands" (*Od.* 8.147-8). And so, when Patroclus and Hector perish, their fleeing souls weep for the youth and manhood (*hêba* and *androtês*) they must leave behind (*Il.* 16.857, 22.363).

The *Iliad* in particular reveals the Homeric emphasis on the body as the symbol and vessel of heroism. We see this in the myriad ways wounds are graphically described, drawing our attention to the anatomy and how its beauty is marred. Yet, when Priam laments the thought of an old man being devoured by dogs, he contrasts this fate with a young warrior killed in battle, declaring that "it is entirely fitting for a youth, once slain in war, to lie stretched out, cleaved by sharp bronze: though dead, everything is beautiful no matter what may be seen" (*Il.* 22.71-3). Thus in Homer even the ugliness of a war wound is beautiful compared to destruction by scavengers, and this is truly revealed by the pervasive concern for preserving the corpse from mutilation by man or dog. The importance of this bodily beauty is so great that the gods go out of their way to preserve Hector's body, going so far as to close his wounds and wash away the bloodstains (*Il.* 24.410-423).

3.2. Chinese Heroism

The matter is quite different in the *Tso Chuan*. There is no word in Chinese that translates exactly as "hero," but the closest analogies are *chieh*, "of surpassing quality," and *chün*, "talented, eminent, great" (Karlgren 1957: nos. 284b, 468t), terms not generally associated with physique. In ancient China, the individual was defined more by their role within their culture than by their individual prowess or glory (Keightley 1990: 20, 1993: 49). Hence we may say that heroism in the *Tso Chuan* is "cultural" as opposed to physical, in that it does not require bodily perfection to obtain it. "Culture" heroes are heroes serving as cultural ideals, who understand and fulfill vital rituals, ethical customs, or social roles in an exemplary or model way, usually in the face of some challenge or difficulty forcing them to make a choice between the cultural ideal and themselves. And so, while Homer's heroes brag endlessly of their own martial prowess, the Chinese are chastised for such boasting (*Tso Chuan* 7.16.6 = Legge 1970: 397; Watson 1989: 133). Indeed, "Feats of strength…along with prodigies, disorders, and spirits…was one of the four topics about which Confucius…chose not to speak" (cf. *Analects* 7.20); "Homer, by contrast, sang of them all" (Keightley 1993: 26-7).

Instead, the heroic model that readers of the *Tso Chuan* are urged to emulate is summed up in the words of the warrior Lang Shen when he says, "He who dies doing what is not righteous is not brave," but "he who dies in the public service is brave" (6.2.1 = Legge 1970: 233). And so here the emphasis is on embodying a cultural rather than a physical ideal: not prowess or physical perfection, but loyalty and honorable action are the goals of the hero. Another exemplary case of this "cultural" heroism is the story of Hsieh Yang, a messenger who is captured by a rival king and condemned to death for refusing a bribe: "A minister counts it a blessing to die carrying out his orders," Yang tells his captor, for he would rather die "a faithful servant." His captor is also a model hero: beholding Hsieh Yang's heroism in simply saying this, he lets him go (7.15.2 = Watson 1989: 105; Legge 1970, 328). And in direct contrast to the treatment of Nestor in the *Iliad* (where Achilles declares Nestor too old, and Nestor agrees), when Mu ignores the advice of the aged Chien Shu for the same reason, he meets defeat (5.32.5, 5.33.8 = Legge 1970: 221, 225; Watson 1989: 68, 70). The obvious moral lesson is that one ought to listen to one's elders. But more important is that here the concerned and forthright advisor, Shu, represents the heroic ideal, not the war-eager Mu. Although elders in Homer are also respected for age and wisdom, they are just as often belittled by younger heroes and sometimes even themselves, in a way that is never found in the *Tso Chuan*. On this point, Falkner provides an in-depth analysis of the treatment of the elderly in ancient Greek literature, arguing with abundant evidence that there is clearly "an underlying disdain and even contempt for" old age in Homer (1995: 9-34). In China, we find precisely the opposite. Moreover, whereas war is the means of obtaining glory for Homer's heroes, for Tso Ch'iu-ming, in the words of the king of Ch'u, "the purpose of military action is to prohibit violence" (7.12.3 = Watson 1989: 99; Legge 1970: 320). Thus glory is won more by ending war than fighting it: in other words, by fulfilling one's cultural role as a capable and virtuous ruler or servant of the state, not by displaying martial prowess on the battlefield (Liu 1967; Kierman 1974).

This is confirmed in another Chinese classic, which has been called the closest parallel to Homeric epic poetry in China, the *Shih Ching*, an account of heroic kings and dukes who consolidated or governed the Chou empire. From an analysis of this and many other texts, Wang concludes that "The display of martial power (*wu*) is never as worthy as the exhibition of cultural eloquence (*wen*)." Indeed, in the *Shih Ching* itself, the two kings, father and son, are named Wen and Wu, and as one might expect the father is portrayed as a greater hero than the son who completes militarily what his father started culturally. For throughout the epic "the cultivation of *wen*, or cultural elegance, is emphasized," while "the martial-heroic spirit is kept muted" (Wang 1975: 27). Wen's virtue lies in his adherence to tradition and his humility and deference, and his corresponding perseverance under a tyrant. As Wang observes, "The wrath of Achilles that leads to heroic action finds no equivalent" in the *Shih Ching*, rather "the heroism of King Wen is in the governance by virtue, by meekness; providing the people with clearings for the growth of food; and standing in awe of his ancestors." Put simply, "He is pious." Even the more warlike Wu models this cultural heroism, for after Wu's conquest, he "ordered his subjects to suppress martial spirit and to cultivate cultural subjects, namely rites and music," he even ordered weapons to be wrapped and put away and war horses set free (Wang 1975: 28).

One point of sharp contrast between this Chinese ideal and the Roman is the role of warfare: for the Chinese elites, war was an unsavory and dirty business, to be undertaken by others and put aside quickly, never an object of praise or public glory. This does not mean the Chinese were more peaceful than other civilizations, but it was their perception of war. In contrast, the Romans were obsessively and openly militaristic in every aspect of their society. Members of the elite could not expect to gain any power or prestige unless they engaged in hands-on combat on an annual basis, while the highest public praise was reserved for military glory, as witnessed in the Roman "triumphal procession" for victorious generals and their armies. A martial character is evident in everything from their calendar to their political organization, even their religion (Harris 1979: 9-53). This is a very un-Chinese embrace of militarism, indicative of Rome's Indo-European roots. As we shall see, Rome's affinity with a Chinese mindset lies not in their attitude toward war, but in the more basic conception of the role and nature of the hero.

3.3. Roman Heroism

For Virgil, the hero is not an individualist, as in Homer, but one who, embodying the Roman virtue of *pietas*, "dutifulness" in the broadest sense, submits to and serves the national interest. But this is conceived not in terms of a particular ruler, as in the *Tso Chuan*, but in terms of the empire itself throughout all time (*Ae.* 1.279). Nevertheless, Virgil faces a Homeric tradition even among contemporary Roman views of heroism, and his vision competes with this, in the poem as in real life.

The evidence for this again begins with vocabulary. Virgil emphasizes *pietas* beyond any other concept as the defining characteristic of the hero: Aeneas, the principle hero in the epic, is associated with *pietas* or described as *pius* no less than thirty times (Wetmore 1911: 365, 366). Aeneas is compared to Hector, a Homeric hero, who was usually not as idolized as his nemesis Achilles. But it says a great deal that Virgil chose the filial hero of the *Iliad* rather than the more popular martial one. And yet Virgil goes further, telling us that although both Hector and Aeneas "were distinguished in courage and in being superior in arms, Aeneas was first in *pietas*" (*Ae.* 11.291-2).

There are also prominent examples of this *pietas* in the *Aeneid*. There is the famous symbolism of Aeneas first taking upon his shoulders his father, and later the shield representing the fate of Rome (*Ae.* 2.708, 8.731). There is his decision to place obedience to the gods and the destiny of Rome before his own love and safety in the arms of queen Dido (*Ae.* 4.393). There is also the melee with Lausus, where even that man, an enemy, displays *pietas* in rescuing his father from Aeneas, and Aeneas acknowledges this, even in mid-battle, as an act of heroic character (*Ae.* 10.824-6). All this suggests at least a partial rejection of the Homeric notion of the glory-seeking individualist, here replaced instead with the hero who puts obligations to others, and to destiny, before all else. This is not uniquely Virgilian, but a traditional Roman view of heroism, coexisting with a Homeric view emphasizing martial valor and glory: for just like Greek *aretê*, the common Latin word for heroic "virtue" was *virtus*, the root meaning of which is manliness and valor (Glare 1997: 2073; Lewis and Short 1995: 1997). This Homeric ideal creeps up even in Virgil's epic, as in the case of Lausus again, where Aeneas declares that his pitiful death would be mitigated by the glory of dying at the hand of "great Aeneas" (*Ae.* 10.830). And in contrast with the usual Roman admiration for the virtue of clemency, Virgil concludes the Aeneid with a very Homeric act of vengeful murder.

3.3.1. *Pietas* as the Essence of Roman Heroism

To understand the distinctions we must understand what this virtue meant to Virgil and his Roman audience. In general, *pietas* is the expression or embodiment of the *pius*, acting "according to duty," especially in reference to performing what is "due to the gods and religion in general, to parents, kindred, teachers, and country." Expanded in meaning, it can include being pious, kind, good, loyal, or patriotic, but always relates in some way to the proper handling of social obligations (Lewis and Short 1995: 1381, 1374; Glare 1997: 1378, 1384). Cicero wrote that *"pietas* is that through which benevolent duty and attentive reverence is devoted to one's country and those who are connected by blood" (Cicero, *De Inventione* 2.53.161). Servius, in his 4th century A.D. commentary on the *Aeneid* (1.378; Maltby 1991: 478), claims that the original meaning of *pius* was religious, referring to some kind of ritual purification from sin, and from there one who was *pius* was *purus*, "pure, clean, faultless," and *innocens*, "innocent, unselfish," and hence one who "abstains from every crime."

This is certainly not a virtue Homer praises his heroes for, yet it is clearly a prominent feature of heroes in the *Aeneid*. Not only is Aeneas routinely described as *pius*, but at key moments of action (e.g. *Ae.* 4.393, 10.826). The importance of this virtue is also established by the fact that when the ghosts of the dead visit the living in the *Aeneid*, it is not to beg for their own burial like Homer's Patroclus (*Il.* 23.71-2.), but to serve gods, fate, and family by giving advice. Creusa's ghost, for instance, concludes her visit by wishing her living husband well and urging that he preserve his love for their son (*Ae.* 2.789), both expressions of filial *pietas*. Likewise, in Virgil's elaborate vision of the afterlife, the hellish Tartarus is a place of the *impia*, while the *pius* go to blissful Elysium (*Ae.* 5.733), thus imagining his entire eschatology in the light of this one virtue. And while Homer lists three sinners being punished in the underworld, all of whom are guilty only of tricking or insulting the gods (*Od.* 11.576-600; w. 5th century B.C.: Pindar, *Olympian Odes*, 1; 2nd century A.D.: Pausanias, *Description of Greece* 2.5.1), Virgil adds numerous crimes punished there, which he calls "monstrous sins" (*immane nefas*: *Ae.* 6.624), all of which are in one way or another violations of *pietas*: hating one's brother, striking one's father, deceiving clients, not sharing wealth with kin, adultery, rebellion, selling out one's country, incest, and breaking a pledge with one's master (*Ae.* 6.608-627). This is not entirely an invention of Virgil's, but it is a reflection of a Roman tradition of elevating the role of *pietas* in the cosmic order of things, as we also see in the so-called "Dream of Scipio" in Book VI of Cicero's *De Republica*.

Pietas was seen as the essence of heroism by most Romans before and after Virgil. Cicero wrote that it was "the foundation of all virtues" (*Pro Cnaeo Plancio*, 12.29). The Elder Pliny (1st century A.D.) goes further, giving us examples demonstrating the pervasiveness of the Roman emphasis on *pietas* as the greatest of virtues, or at least the most Roman: "It is true," Pliny writes, "that countless examples of *pietas* stand out all over the world, but there is one at Rome with which all the others cannot be compared" (*Natural History* 7.121), revealing that Pliny believed *pietas* to be especially Roman, as does Virgil, who has Jupiter promise to his wife that she will see the Roman race "excel both men and gods in *pietas*" (*Ae.* 12.839).

Roman legends bear this up. When Pliny says the Romans exceed all in this virtue, he gives a legendary example from Roman folklore: a daughter visiting her jailed mother was searched to keep her from bringing food, yet she was caught nursing her mother from her own breast, the ultimate act of benevolent duty. This story is repeated, with even greater emphasis on *pietas*, by Valerius Maximus in his 1st century A.D. collection of memorable stories (5.4.7). As in the *Tso Chuan*, such a display of heroism is acknowledged and rewarded by those in power: the mother is released and both are granted a lifetime subsidy (a theme of the "recognized hero" that occurs in the *Aeneid* as well). A temple to the deified Pietas was even erected on the site of the prison to honor the event. Pliny provides other examples, such as the father of the famous Gracchii, who, when given a choice by an oracle between his life and the life of his wife Cornelia, chose to die himself, "to show mercy on his wife, and to consider the public interest" (for she might still bear children to serve the state: Pliny, *Natural History* 7.122). From Roman legend also comes the example of Coriolanus, who ceases his angry assault on Rome in response to pleas from his mother, wife, and children, a change of heart unimaginable for an Achilles (Plutarch, *Coriolanus* 36; Valerius Maximus also presents this as a model of *pietas*, 5.4). Thus, it is clear that *pietas* was viewed as a primary heroic trait in Roman culture generally, and not just in the eyes of Virgil (Saller 1994: 105ff.; Garrison 1992: esp. 263, n. 16; and Shelton 1998: 2-3, 294-6, 370).

3.3.2. The Role of Homeric Heroism in Virgil

In the *Aeneid*, Virgil does not depict Homeric heroism in a very good light. Individualistic heroes end up dead, usually as a direct result of their selfish glory-seeking. Virgil often uses for this lesson the theme of selfishly-sought spoils of war. In the case of Euryalus, his spoils give away his position and slow him down, resulting in his death (*Ae.* 9.364, 373-4, 384-5). Then there is Turnus, who "celebrates and rejoices" at taking the belt of the slain Pallas, but dies in the end for no other reason than this (*Ae.* 10.500-505, 12.945-948). In a rare narrator's voice, Virgil specifically denounces this looting, lamenting men who do not know "to maintain a proper measure when elated by success" (*Ae.* 10.501-2), a direct criticism of the Homeric hero, yet a sentiment that would be quite at home in the *Tso Chuan*. In a similar fashion, the arrogant and boastful Numanus gets himself killed by approaching the Trojan battle line to mock them with a classic Homeric taunt. Before meeting his fate, he declares the hero to be one who "is always delighted to collect the spoils and to live on plunder" (*Ae.* 9.612-3), but the real hero that lays him out (Ascanius) issues only a brief and unassuming retort, and "only this" (*Ae.* 9.636), displaying the un-Homeric sense of proper measure that Virgil later praises. A similar sequence occurs in the case of Camilla and Arruns (*Ae.* 11.780-794).

This departure from Homer is also revealed in Virgil's treatment of the body. Although there are echoes of Homer in the depiction of anatomy in battle scenes (e.g. *Ae.* 12.273-6, 306-8), a regular use of appellations of heroic handsomeness (e.g. *Ae.* 7.107, 1.588-593), and references to wounds defiling the body (e.g. *Ae.* 11.591, 848), Virgil parts somewhat from this Homeric emphasis, leaving these examples to represent conflict more than praise. For instance, there is no parallel in the *Aeneid* to what Laodamas tells Odysseus is the "greatest glory" for a man. The closest comment, issued by Jupiter, does not emphasize physical acts (*Ae.* 10.467-9). Likewise, there is no parallel to Priam's speech about a body slain in war being beautiful, and there is less focus placed on devouring by scavengers: there are two references (*Ae.* 9.485-91, 10.559-60.), but the gods do not go out of their way to preserve anyone's body to the extent they do for Hector, and Anchises once even declares, rather un-Homerically, that "the loss of a grave is easy" for him to bear (*Ae.* 2.646). In addition, while the dying souls of Patroclus and

Hector weep specifically for lost youth and manhood, in the parallel passages in Virgil, the deaths of Turnus and Camilla, their ghosts still flee, angered or indignant, but offended by exactly what is not specified (*Ae.* 12.951-2, 11.831), a conspicuous omission: Virgil went out of his way not to mention youth and manhood lost, an omission Tso Ch'iu-ming would surely appreciate.

3.3.3. The Context and Cultural Message of the *Aeneid*

The *Aeneid* was written in a period of history that is exceptionally well-documented, compared to the circumstances in which the *Tso Chuan* and Homeric epics were composed. This allows us to understand in good detail the context of the *Aeneid*'s formation. And as it represents an important example of a rising conflict between a Greek and a Chinese-like cultural ideal within the Western tradition, we will benefit from examining the historical context influencing its author.

Virgil was well aware of Rome's immediate history. The republic had ultimately been torn apart by individualism. Men in the 1st century B.C. like Caesar and Pompey, and Sulla and Catiline before them, were more concerned about their own personal honor and glory, and governed, or attempted to govern, through a privately cultivated network of favors, *gratia*, rather like ancient mobsters. Caesar himself wrote that his own reputation mattered more than life itself, and on that pretext refused to surrender his arms for the benefit of the state (Caesar, *De Bello Civili* 1.9.2 and 1.8.3), demonstrating that this kind of thinking was not aberrant, for if Caesar did not consider this a dignified argument he would not have made it. Cicero, of course, had criticized all of these men, and those like them, dubbing them the *audaces* (the reckless, the bold), and the enemies of the *boni*, the "good men." *Audax* and its cognates in Ciceronian political discourse referred to the "subverters of the republic" (*eversorum rei publica*e: Cicero, *Pro Sestio* 86) whose lack of moderation and bloated sense of self-importance would lead to the ruin of good government, and of society itself. Mark Antony would be seen in this role as well, in his selfish refusal to make a compromise for the benefit of the state, and, after Cicero's murder, Virgil would see this individualism culminate in the battle of Actium in 31 B.C. Cicero had, in fact, repeatedly charged Antony, a member of the *audaces*, with being *violentus*, "violent," immoderate, uncontrolled (Cicero, *Philippics* 2.28.68, 5.7.19, 12.11.26).

Virgil does not have much to say about Antony (he is mentioned only once: *Ae.* 8.685ff), though he does indirectly contrast him with Aeneas through the fact that Antony chose to stay with his Dido (Cleopatra) and led alien gods against his own country, while Aeneas rejected the allurements of a Dido for the national interest, and for the preservation of his own household gods. Nevertheless, the influence of Cicero on Virgil seems to be suggested by the retention of his terminology in reference to the principal villain of the *Aeneid*: Turnus. Turnus is specifically identified with the quintessential Homeric hero, Achilles (e.g. *Ae.* 6.89, 9.742), the man with whom Alexander the Great liked to identify himself (in contrast, Aeneas is identified with Hector, as noted earlier). Yet Virgil describes Achilles as the "subvertor of Priam's domains" (*Priami regnorum eversor*: *Ae.* 12.545), showing a hint of Ciceronian terminology. Turnus is also repeatedly described as *audax* (e.g. *Ae.* 7.409, 9.3, 9.126), associating him with Cicero's *audaces*. Finally, Turnus is attributed with *violentia* on numerous occasions (e.g. *Ae.* 10.151, 11.354, 11.376, 12.45, 12.9), completing the connection between Turnus and the Ciceronian view of men like Mark Antony.

Just as Cicero would see *furor* and *violentia*, as attributes of the *audaces*, bringing chaos and ruin, so apparently did Virgil depict the same thing in his *Aeneid*: the entire epic might be described as depicting a great conflict between chaos and order, the *audax* (Turnus) against the *pius* (Aeneas), on both a human and a divine scale, as is seen from beginning to end, from the role of Neptune as a representative of order (*Ae.* 1.131-56), to when the madness of Turnus, a representative of destructive chaos, persists even when he knows better, and for no other reason than because he does not wish to be seen disgraced (*Ae.* 12.666-8, 12.676, 12.678-680), the very reason Caesar gave for crossing the Rubicon.

In reaction to this villainy, this enemy of peace and order, Virgil apparently seeks to emphasize not the Homeric hero, but the Roman hero: the exemplar of *pietas*. In the process, Virgil's *Aeneid* acquires many similarities to the *Tso Chuan*, and the view of heroism therein. For instance, the role of boasts is similar: displays of arrogance, though not directly criticized by superiors, are nevertheless a sure sign of impending death, as shown in the cases of Numanus and Camilla. We also see a similar paradigm of "the recognized hero" in the case of Euryalus, who, similar to Hsieh Yang, is rewarded when he exhibits heroic *pietas*: before going on a risky venture, he asks the Romans to care for his mother when he is away, and this "image of *pietas*" inspires Iulus to promise that Euryalus' reward will go to his mother and family even if he fails (*Ae.* 9.294 and 9.301-2).

Even more similar is Virgil's expressed view of the purpose of war: as we are told in the *Tso Chuan* that "the purpose of military action is to prohibit violence," so we find Virgil stating, in the words of the prophetic soul of Anchises, that the task of Rome will be "to impose moral order upon peace, to spare the subject, and to subdue the proud" (*Ae.* 6.852-3, or with the possible emendation of *pacique* to *pacisque*, "to impose the custom of peace," cf. Williams 1992: xxxiii, 513). And, in the words of the god Apollo, "all the wars that are fated to come will grow calm with justice" under the Trojan line of Aeneas (*Ae.* 9.642-3, w. 9.259). Virgil also gives us a bold declaration of peace as the aim of the Roman empire, from the mouth of Jupiter himself: "fierce generations, their wars then put aside, will become gentle" (*Ae.* 1.291; see also 1.292-296). Then, in the words of Drances, Turnus' political opponent, we are told "there is no salvation in war" (*Ae.* 11.362). It would seem that Virgil's view of war is at least a bit more Chinese than Homeric.

We also see Virgil's view of heroism take shape in his treatment of the elderly. Unlike in Homer, where the elderly cannot be heroic however respected they may be, in the *Aeneid* they can be powerful exemplars of heroism, just as in the *Tso Chuan*. The parallel between Nestor and Entellus in the boxing match (*Ae.* 5.387-484), provides a prominent example of how Virgil uses the role of the elderly to invert the values of Homer, emphasizing his own view of heroism. In the *Iliad*, Homer depicts a boxing match between Epeius and Euryalus, two young men (*Il.* 23.660-99). Epeius boasts of being undefeatable in typical Homeric fashion, and then overwhelmingly defeats his opponent. In Virgil's boxing match, however, Dares is the parallel for Epeius, but faced against him is Entellus, an old man who, in direct parallel to Nestor, laments his own lost youth (*Ae.* 5.397-9). But the Homeric plot is reversed: Dares does not win. The old man, Entellus, although taking a fall like Euryalus (*Ae.* 5.446-9), returns with a fury and overwhelmingly defeats his foe, who is described in the same fashion as the defeated Euryalus in Homer: carried by his comrades and spitting out blood (*Ae.* 5.468-71 vs. *Il.* 23:695-9). Given that Entellus was driven to return to the fight (*Ae.* 5.455) by a sense of shame (*pudor*) and of valor (*virtus*), there may be an echo here of the Roman reaction to their catastrophic defeat before Hannibal at Cannae (3rd century B.C.), such resurgent invincibility being a symbol of Roman heroic character (as witnessed in their wars with Hannibal, Pyrrhus, Spartacus, etc.).

The contrasts continue. At the request of Aeneas, Entellus calms his fury and bows out, offering his reward as a sacrifice to Eryx, his god and teacher. After this fitting act of *pietas*, he lays down his gloves in retirement: a symbol of Anchises' entreaty that Caesar be the first to show mercy and "throw down his weapons" (*Ae.* 6.834-5): a prerequisite for any lasting peace, an act here portrayed as heroic. And so we see that Virgil's view of heroism is in some ways closer to what we find in the *Tso Chuan* than in the *Iliad* or *Odyssey*, although we still have remnants of an emphasis on martial valor and personal glory: Entellus, after all, is spurred on by a personal sense of shame and valor, and since he makes his pious sacrifice to Eryx by smashing in the skull of his prize bull with his fist (*Ae.* 5.468-472), we see he is not ashamed to show off his physical strength—though he directs this display to the public good. The Virgilian hero is thus more subtle and mature than the Homeric.

4. The Classical Soul

Having surveyed the cultural ideal of the hero within a vital Chinese cultural classic, in comparison with the messages of Homer and Virgil, it remains to contrast their visions of the human soul, by which I mean whatever it is that is believed to survive bodily death and to retain some trace of personal memory and identity. The differences in their views of such 'ghosts' reveal important parallels in their different conceptions of the hero.

4.1. The Portrayal of the Soul

The simplest evidence lies in how souls are shown to act, and what they are capable of. In Homer, souls don't seem capable of much at all. Although he describes the souls of the dead as appearing identical to the person when they were alive, thus retaining something of their individuality (*Il.* 23.107, *Od.* 11.36-43), they are unable to be touched or grasped (*Il.* 23.100-3; *Od.* 11.204-8) and lack the strength to grasp others (*Od.* 11.393-4).

The groaning hoard of phantoms creeping up to Odysseus to drink the sacrificial blood is the most moving example of the impotency of the Homeric soul (*Od.* 11.30-130). Most of the ghosts gain their wits only upon drinking the offered blood (thus requiring the aid of necromantic magic). Even then, the dead display no knowledge of the world above, much less the power to affect it, as they cannot even contest Odysseus' sword or work any other evils or blessings upon him. Sourvinou-Inwood (1995: 78) suggests that a statement by Achilles (Il. 24.595-6) suggests otherwise, but Achilles says "if only" the dead Hector might know what he was doing, thus it cannot be said Achilles believed Hector *would* know. Likewise, Sourvinou-Inwood suggests that the ability to keep the souls at bay with a sword "implies some sort of corporeal nature" (1995: 83), but this is not so clear: apart from the possible talismanic powers of bronze, if the dead do not have all their wits, then the fact that a sword can't harm them might never occur to them—they may be acting upon the same instincts they possessed when alive. Likewise that they "drink blood" need not entail physical lips and a digestive system in a world of magic, where the mere absorbing of blood's power (its essential life force) may have been imagined instead. And the evidence is otherwise clear: the dead are utterly bodiless and thus powerless and dumb.

Hence Odysseus does not fear the numberless dead approaching "with a confused and wondrous noise" (*Od.* 11.632-5) but only "the Gorgon head of a dreadful monster" that the goddess Persephone might send against him. And Elpenor does not threaten to "haunt" Odysseus (as Walter Shewring translates *Od.* 11.70, cf. Shewring 1980: 129), but merely warns that he might "become the cause of some wrath of the gods" against him (in a manner elaborated by Virgil for Elpenor's parallel, Palinurus: *Ae.* 6.376-83). Thus, in their actions alone, the souls of the dead are powerless in Homer. Indeed, they are the exact opposite of the living hero, just as we should expect if everything that makes a hero is tied to having a body.

In the *Tso Chuan*, however, the souls of the dead are quite potent, and more than capable of acting upon the world of the living. One ghost returns as a large boar, contributing to the assassination of his opponent (3.8.5 = Legge 1970: 82; Watson

1989: 19). In another story, the spirit of a murdered king turns into a yellow bear, which later torments the duke of Chin in his dreams while he his ill. Only sacrificing to the dead king's spirit cures the duke's sickness (10.7.4.3 = Legge 1970: 617; Forke 1962, I: 214). Even more vivid is the case of Prince Shen-sheng, whose ghost appears to his former carriage driver on the road and converses with him, then petitions "the Emperor of Heaven" to punish the reigning king (5.11.6 = Legge 1970: 157; Watson 1989: 28-29; Forke 1962, I: 203), entailing a much more active role in divine affairs than that of Elpenor. And the most startling tale of all is that of Po-yu, whose ghost goes on a killing spree until appeased (10.7.4.4 = Legge 1970: 618; Forke 1962, I: 208). Souls also return to aid the living, as in the story of one ghost tripping another man's opponent in battle (7.15.4 = Legge 1970: 328; Forke 1962, I: 211). This all makes sense because the body is not essential to the Chinese hero. What makes them great can transcend death, just as their living memory transcends it in the form and process of ancestor worship, a fundamental aspect of ancient Chinese religion.

In the *Aeneid*, we find a blend of what we might call Homeric and Chinese views of the soul. Virgil obviously makes a conscious effort to model his descriptions on the precedent set by Homer, as ghosts are unable to be touched or grasped (*Ae.* 2.792-4, 6.700-3), but he adds to this in several important respects. In Homer, we have only one case of a ghost visiting the land of the living: Patroclus, who only visits (in a dream) to beg for burial. In fact, the only reason he is still around in this world is because, lacking burial, he has not been admitted below (*Il.* 23.75-6). In the *Aeneid*, however, there are numerous visitations, by ghosts who never ask for burial, but visit solely to serve fate and kin. The ghost of Dido's murdered husband is the first mentioned (*Ae.* 1.353-9). Rather than asking for a funeral for his forgotten corpse, he urges her to flee to a new country, and reveals the location of a secret treasure, an "unknown hoard," to aid her journey (*Ae.* 1.358-9). This displays both the possession of esoteric knowledge (the location of an "unknown hoard") and an interest in Dido's future rather than his own burial (yet another example of *pietas*). Then the ghost of Hector visits Aeneas (*Ae.* 2.270-97). He, too, has come to urge flight, to protect the household gods of Troy, and displays supernatural knowledge of Aeneas' destiny. Shortly thereafter, Creusa's ghost visits her husband Aeneas as he is searching for her in flaming Troy (*Ae.* 2.771-94), and she also does not mention burial, but rather wishes Aeneas well and reveals secrets about his fate, including knowledge of his future kingdom along the river Tiber.

The most prominent example of this "spiritual activism" is the soul of Anchises. After his death and burial, his spirit visits his son Aeneas more than once (*Ae.* 4.351-5, 5.722-40; cf. 6.695), providing advice and urging him to continue on his fated mission, demonstrating knowledge of worldly affairs, and of the future— such as Aeneas' earlier conversation with Nautes (*Ae.* 5.728) and the coming war in Italy (*Ae.* 5.731-2). And when Aeneas visits him in the underworld, Anchises is as wise and cogent as Teiresias, but without any ritual of blood magic to regain his wits, and without any footnote about special gifts from the gods. Thus, the souls of the dead are not powerless in Virgil, though they do remain limited and insubstantial. Perhaps because Virgil sees two forms of heroism in conflict, the body-centered vision of Homer and the Roman notion of *pietas*, this conflict plays out in the potency of souls: they are still capable of heroic action, by performing acts of *pietas* from beyond the grave, but lacking bodies they cannot engage in matters of the flesh, such as fighting or loving embraces, a remnant of the Homeric conception of the soul.

4.2. The Vocabulary of the Soul

Having examined the actions of souls as portrayed by Virgil, Homer, and Tso Ch'iu-ming, we must now turn to how the actual vocabulary used to describe and define the soul reinforces their views. In Homer, the basic word for the soul is *psychê*, meaning "breath, life, spirit," derived from the verb *psychô*, "to breathe" (Liddell and Scott 1996: 903). Homer occasionally uses in place of *psychê*, no doubt by metonymy, the word *eidôlon*, "image, phantom, any unsubstantial form," from the adjective *eidos*, "that which is seen; form, shape" (Liddell and Scott 1996: 226, 227). He also compares it to a "shadow" (*skia*: *Od.* 10.495) or a "dream" (*oneiros*: *Od.* 11.222) or both (*Od.* 11.207). All of these words imply insubstantiality, or at most a fleeting corporeality, and Homer emphasizes this by calling souls "senseless" and "feeble."

For example, Homer once uses the phrase *nekroi aphradeës*, "the senseless dead" (*Od.* 11.475). Sourvinou-Inwood (1995: 80, 84) assumes Homer must mean "witless" in the sense of completely lacking mind or thought, and then shows that ghosts do not behave as if mindless, "proving" that Homer held two contradictory beliefs about the dead. But the dead do not have to be totally mindless to warrant this adjective, merely dull-witted, so "witless" is too extreme a translation of *aphradeës* in this context—or, of course, Achilles may be guilty of hyperbole (see below). Either interpretation is supported by Homer's use of the same word to refer to the living suitors, who clearly are not totally lacking minds (*Od.* 2.282). The word can be used for "insensate, reckless, senseless, lifeless," and typically indicates "lacking physical senses" or lacking the ability "to ponder, contrive, design" (Liddell and Scott 1996: 140; cf. also *phrazô*, 870, II), a clear reference not to mindlessness but to powerlessness. Even in Homer, its adverbial (*aphradeôs*) and verbal (*aphradeô*) forms do not entail a total lack of wits (cf. *Il.* 3.436, 9.32; *Od.* 2.282, 7.294).

Likewise, Homer often uses the elegant formula *nekyôn amenêna karêna*, "the feeble heads of the dead" (*Od.* 10.521; 10.536; 11.29; 11.49; etc.). Shewring gives a less literal but clearer translation as "the strengthless presences of the dead." The word *nekys* of course is literally the adjective for "dead" and thus means "dead body, corpse, spirit of the dead" (Liddell and Scott 1996: 528), while *karênon* means "the head" of the body, usually in the plural, employed like our phrase "many head of cattle," a common way of saying "persons" in Homeric idiom (Liddell and Scott 1996: 401). But the key word here is *amenênos*, which means "powerless, fleeting, feeble" (Liddell and Scott 1996: 43; cf. also *menos*, 498), and here in particular, "lacking in physical strength, force," again emphasizing the lack of heroic virtue, which is lost with the body.

The vocabulary used in the *Tso Chuan* is almost the exact opposite in its implications. Tso Ch'iu-ming employs two words for the disembodied soul without apparent distinction: *kuei* and *shen*. Contrary to modern findings by Arthur Wolf (Wolf 1974: 173-6), the distinction between *shen* as good spirits and *kuei* as bad spirits does not exist in the *Tso Chuan* (cf. Legge 1970: 616, 234; Ying-shih 1987: 380), nor even in the 1st century writings of Wang Ch'ung (Forke 1962, I: 191), so it must have been a later development.

Kuei means "ghost" or "spirit" (Schuessler 1987: 216.3). The word may have originated as the name of a "strange anthropoid creature" (Wolf 1974: 174) or some sort of demon mask (Cohen 1971: 34, n. 16; Chien-shih 1936; Suetoshi 1956), but was definitely used to mean "fear" or "something to fear" (Cohen 1971: 18; Ying-shih 1987: 379, n. 35). And so, as Wolf observes, "*kuei*, the name of a corporeal creature, was 'transferred' to represent the imagined appearance of a spiritual being, i.e., the ghost of the dead." (Wolf 1974: 174). Note how this etymology, and the latent meanings the word would then imply, contrasts with that of Homer's *psychê*: a *kuei* is associated with physical, fearsome things, not breath or fleeting images. This is reinforced by a passage in the *Tso Chuan* (which I'll soon discuss) stating that the *kuei* of a deceased person, if not appeased, can become *li*, "wicked, cruel" (Schuessler 1987: 374.12) or "biting, grinding, stinging, or vicious" (Cohen 1971: 19).

The other word used in the *Tso Chuan* for souls of the dead, *shen*, means "spirit, heavenly spirit, ancestral spirit" (Schuessler 1987: 534). Its phonetic element means "to stretch, prolong, continue" (Schuessler 1987: 533; Cohen 1971: 16-17) and it is related to the similar-sounding word for "body, person, physical self" (Schuessler 1987: 533; Ames 1984: 45). Furthermore *shen* is defined as "to extend" by the 1st century philosopher Wang Ch'ung, based on the idea that the spirit is an active principle that "fosters and produces things" (Forke 1962, I: 191). So *shen* also contains latent ideas of corporeality and potency. These implied connections would be on the mind of both author and reader of the *Tso Chuan*, and they make sense in light of their views about heroism and the soul. Other relevant vocabulary confirms this, as we shall see when we discuss the metaphysics of the Chinese soul.

Virgil's vocabulary, on the other hand, closely mirrors that of Homer. The basic word he uses for the soul is *anima*, "air, wind, breath of life, soul" (e.g. *Ae.* 3.67, 4.242, 5.98, 6.264, etc.), derived from the Greek *anemos*, "wind" (Maltby 1991: 36, 37; Lewis and Short 1995: 123; Glare 1997: 132), so it is effectively the Latin counterpart of *psychê*. And just as Homer also employs the word *eidôlon* for disembodied souls, so Virgil frequently uses the Latin equivalent, *imago*, "imitation, copy, image, likeness" (e.g. *Ae.* 1.353, 2.793, 4.654, 6.480, etc.) and its synonyms *simulacrum* (*Ae.* 2.772) and *facies* (*Ae.* 5.722). Virgil also likens disembodied souls to shadows (*umbra*: e.g. *Ae.* 4.386, 5.81, 6.264, 11.81, etc.), dreams (*somnum*: *Ae.* 2.794, 6.703), wind (*ventus*: *Ae.* 2.794, 6.703) and smoke (*fumus*: *Ae.* 5.740).

Although this vocabulary, as in Homer, implies insubstantiality, Virgil modifies its significance. To begin with, he does not use any terms like *aphradês* ("senseless") or *amanênos* ("feeble") to describe the souls of the dead, even though the latter is practically an idiom in Homer. Instead, the splendor of spirits is amplified, as in the case of Creusa's ghost, which is described as *nota maior imago*, "an image greater than usual" (*Ae.* 2.773). And the *felices anima*e, "happy souls" (*Ae.* 6.669), that Aeneas encounters in Elysium include his own dead father Anchises, as well as the *inlustris animas*, or "bright souls" (*Ae.* 6.758) of those awaiting bodies to participate again in the making of Rome's history. Likewise, reflecting a Roman element of ancestor worship, the deceased spirit of Anchises is hailed with the appellation *sancte parens*, "sacred father" (*Ae.* 5.80, 5.603) and even *divinus*, "divine, godlike" (*Ae.* 5.47; perhaps an allusion to the deification of Julius Caesar).

Virgil also employs an additional term for the soul, one that is traditionally Roman: *manes*, the "spirits of the departed," a word that does not easily translate (Lewis and Short 1995: 1108; Glare 1997: 1072-3). Though it is often rendered as "shade" without justification (it has no such connotation), it is most probably related to the archaic adjective *mânus*, "good" (Lewis and Short 1995: 1108, 1112; Glare 1997: 1078), although some ancient grammarians proposed other theories (Maltby 1991: 364, 367), such as a derivation from the verb *mano*, "to extend, spread, emanate, arise" (creating a rather notable parallel with the Chinese word *shen*) or *maneo*, "to remain, endure, await." The alternative hypothesis that *manes* is derived from the Greek *manos*, "few, scanty" (Liddell and Scott 1996: 487) cannot be credited, since the Latin equivalent of *manos* is *rarus*, not *manus*, the declension of *manes* is not what we would expect if it were merely a Latinization of *manos*, and there is no historical support even for a belief in such a connection.

Manes, therefore, is a term that calls to mind, among Roman readers, notions of moral or even physical potency: being good (or malevolent, if the appellation "good" is propitiatory), as well as arising, or extending, and enduring. It is also related directly to Roman ancestor worship, and the popular fear of malevolent spirits. This is revealed by the formula for warding off the angry souls of the deceased, *manes exite paterni*, "ancestral spirits, depart!" (Ovid, *Fasti* 5.443; 1st century A.D.), and by the popular practice of worshipping the dead collectively as the *Di Manes*, 'Divine Spirits' (e.g. in the injunction *Deorum Manium iura sancta sunto* in Cicero's *De Legibus* 2.9.22). In the *Aeneid* altars are erected to the *manes* as if to gods (*Ae.* 3.63, 3.304-7), the *manes* of individuals are called upon or invoked (*Ae.* 3.303, 5.98-99, 6.506, 10.524), and *manes* are capable of sending "false dreams" to the living (*Ae.* 6.896). Thus, Virgil follows the Homeric notion of the soul as incorporeal, but does not emphasize its powerlessness, but rather adds to it a spark of moral force and influence that is typically Roman, and un-Homeric.

4.3. The Metaphysics of the Soul

In addition to depictions and vocabulary, the nature of the soul is more or less stated explicitly by all three authors. Homer gives us three passages that make these metaphysical declarations about the soul. The first is the remark by Achilles, "Yea, indeed, something exists even in the house of Hades, *psychê* and *eidôlon*, yet the *phrên* is not at all present" (*Il.* 23.104). The word *phrên* literally means "midriff, heart, breast" (cf. *Il.* 16.481) but is used metaphorically to mean "the heart" as the source of thought or passion, or "mind, wits, will" (*Il.* 10.10, 22.296; *Od.* 6.147, 10.438; etc.). Most specifically, it refers to "the midriff, the muscle which parts the heart and lung from the lower viscera, the parts about the heart, the breast" and thus "the heart as the seat of passions, mind, wits, will, purpose," while its negation is frequently used in the same way as our phrases "out of his mind," "out of his senses," "out of his wits," etc. (Liddell and Scott 1996: 871; cf. *aphrôn*, 140).

This is the first indication that the souls of the dead lack, or are weak in, *phrên*. Sourvinou-Inwood again (1995: 78) takes this too far, regarding it as "mind" and arguing that Achilles is declaring that souls completely lack a mind, but this is not plausible. It is absurd to think that Achilles meant the mind of Patroclus was totally absent, after having just had a detailed conversation with him. Thus, *phrên* must mean something subtly different here. For instance, Hammond translates this phrase as "without real being at all" (Hammond 1987: 367). It is also possible that Achilles is guilty of hyperbole—the only two times such extreme views of the soul are offered, both are uttered by the same person: Achilles (see above). But lack of *phrên* does not always correspond to total mindlessness anyway, as we see in Hesiod's *Shield of Herakles* (89; 7th century B.C.), and its negative, *aphrôn*, usually means "crazed, frantic, silly, or foolish" (Liddell and Scott 1996: 140) which is not the same thing as a total lack of mind.

This concept is elaborated further in the encounter with the dead prophet Teiresias (*Od.* 10.490ff.), whose *phrên* is "steadfast" (*empedos*) since Persephone has furnished him with *noos* (= *nous*), "mind, perception, sense." Thus, we are told that "he alone is wise" (*oioi pepnysthai*). Since Homer offers Teiresias as an exception to the rule, we can infer that the *phrên* for the dead in general is not *empedos*—they do not lack *phrên* altogether, only a "steadfast" *phrên*—and that the dead lack wisdom and *nous*—not necessarily "mind" altogether, but a keen mind.

Last but not least, Odysseus gets a lecture on the nature of souls from his own dead mother, though only after she 'drinks' the sacrificial blood, temporarily regaining her wits according to the instructions of Teiresias (*Od.* 11.216-23). When Odysseus tries to grasp her and cannot, he asks if she is merely "some *eidôlon*" that Persephone has sent him. She responds:

> Persephone, daughter of Zeus, is not beguiling you in any way, but it is the very law of mortals whenever someone dies: for muscles no longer hold the flesh and bones, but the mighty rage of the blazing pyre overpowers these, as soon as life leaves white bones, and the *psychê*, like a dream, having flown away, flutters about (*apoptamenê pepotêtai*).

The closing phrase is very unusual both in its vocabulary and grammatical construction. Recalling that this is poetry, the conspicuously abundant "popping" sounds Homer creates with this phrase call up a link between the soul and the ashes produced by the crackling fire, which do in fact fly away and flutter about, reinforcing the idea of fleeting substance and powerless drifting. Thus, the soul in Homer's epics is fated to fly away and flutter about, with little more substance than a dream, as the body disintegrates from rot and flame, confirming the notion that the dead lose their heroic potency upon losing their body.

We can contrast this with a single passage on the nature of souls recorded by Tso Ch'iu-ming (10.7.4.4). This paragraph is relatively famous, and may be the most translated passage of the *Tso Chuan* in English. What follows below is an adapted translation stitched together from five different renditions (Legge 1970: 618; Ying-shih 1987: 372; Cohen 1971: 170-2; Forke 1962, I: 209; Smith 1958: 174), no one of them being completely clear or faithful to the original text. After having just appeased the murderous ghost of Po-yu, Tzu-ch'an, a philosopher-statesman of Cheng, had this to say:

When man is born, what is first created is called *p'o*, and when *p'o* has formed, its positive part is called *hun*. When a man is materially well and abundantly supported, then his *hun* and *p'o* grow strong (*ch'iang*), and produce spirituality (*ching-shuang*) and intelligence (*shen-ming*). Even the *hun* and *p'o* of an ordinary man or woman who has met a violent death can hang around the living and do vicious deeds (*li*)....The stuff Po-yu was made of was copious and rich, and his family great and powerful. Is it not natural that, having met with violent death, he should be a ghost (*kuei*)?

The most important point noted here is that a person's spirit can grow strong during life and that, as a result, it is "natural" that it should remain potent after death. This is an assumption wholly different from any in Homer, where spirits are enfeebled by the loss of a body, and drift off like dreams, even if the person dying has a "great and powerful" family, is "materially well" and "abundantly supported," and dies a "violent death." Instead, here, the conditions for generating a powerful spirit happen to be those that generate a potent culture hero: the proper and abundant use of things, and a role within a powerful family with many generations of properly conducted rituals. Likewise, to die a violent death upsets the natural order of things, leaving the hero with unfinished business, usually some offense against ritual or propriety left to be punished. The vocabulary used in this passage also reinforces the points made earlier: a person's spirit, far from being "feeble" and "senseless," is instead described with words like *ch'iang*, "strong, violent, energetic" (Mathews 1943: no. 608), *ching-shuang*, "lively, brisk in spirits" (Mathews 1943: no. 1149.10) and *shen-ming*, having "divine brightness, intelligence" (Mathews 1943: no. 5715.32).

Finally, we are left with the words *hun* and *p'o*, the two aspects of a person's soul. Both words in written form contain the character for *kuei* (ghost) as an element. *P'o* has been variously translated as "soul" or "animal soul" (Legge 1970: 618; Forke 1962, I: 209), "latent soul" (Cohen: 1971: 17), even "brightness of mind" (Legge 1970: 708; Ying-shih 1987: 371) and it also means "white, bright, or bright light," a meaning derived originally from the glowing light of the new moon, and so used in describing lunar phases (Ying-shih 1987: 370). It is also related semantically and phonetically to words meaning "residual, remain behind, cling onto" (Cohen 1971: 17), connecting it logically with *shen*. And so, again, we have latent connections to concepts of potency. And instead of being connected with darkness (like the "shades" of Homer in dim Hades), it is connected with lunar "brightness." Though the color white is generally associated in Chinese culture with death, in the same way that black is so associated in the West, *p'o* is associated more with an animate brightness. The same applies to the word *hun*, variously translated as "mind" (Forke 1962, I: 209), "conscious spirit" (Ying-shih 1987: 372), even "essential vigor" (Legge 1970: 708; Ying-shih 1987: 371). It includes the character for "cloud" (Cohen 1971: 15; Smith 1958: 168, 174), and may be related to the word for "whirling water" (Cohen 1971: 32-33, n. 7). So *hun* is also associated with energetic processes and forces of nature, rather than dreams, images, or shadows.

Virgil devotes an even larger passage in the *Aeneid* to a metaphysical explanation of the nature of the human soul. Here he knits together aspects of religion and philosophy from numerous sources in a total conception of the cosmos that is beyond the scope of this paper to examine (*Ae.* 6.724-51). For instance, reincarnation and the view of the body as a prison for the soul both derive from Orphic-style mystery religion via Platonism (Plato, *Cratylus* 400.c; *Phaedo* 66.b-68.e, 113.a-113.e; Herodotus, 2.123.2), while the idea of a world-soul, and the cosmic role of fire, derives from Stoic philosophy (Cleanthes, *Hymn to Zeus*). Both are Greek in origin (even if developed under the influence of Eastern religions), but notably counter-Homeric, and possibly not commonly believed among Romans generally. But how Virgil uses this novel construct is revealing.

The most important piece of the puzzle is the notion that the body is a burden to the soul, and that the soul is purer, even "better," without its body. Although this is coupled with the idea that the body is still necessary to participate in physical action, it is still a notion that stands in opposition to Homer's glorification of the body and diminishment of the soul. This, in fact, may explain in Virgil's mind, and in cosmic terms, the reason for the conflict between the two forms of heroism: the body is a necessary part of the order of things, but it impairs the soul with emotions and other burdens and thus gets in the way of the pure embodiment of *pietas*, which is the true expression of heroism. Such a view is similar to that of the New Testament, wherein the body is a burden and a source of sin, but the spirit can be pure and eternal.

For Virgil, the dissertation by Anchises about the nature of the soul is the most explicit demonstration of this view. He explains that in all living things—men, cattle, birds, fish—there is a "fiery force" that is of divine origin (*igneus vigor* and *caelestis origo*: *Ae.* 6.730.), at least "insofar as their harmful bodies do not slow them down and their earthly limbs and mortal members are not sluggish" (*Ae.* 6.731-2). To explain what this means, he continues:

> Because of this, men fear and lust, feel pain and joy, and, locked up in darkness, a blind prison, they do not see the light. In fact, even in the end, when life abandons the light, every evil still does not withdraw from the miserable, nor entirely do all the bodily plagues, for it is necessary that many things, compounded at length in astonishing ways, should implant themselves all through. (*Ae.* 6.732-8)

And thus these tainted souls go through a process of purgation, and after a period of time this "removes the compounded stain, and leaves clean the ethereal consciousness, and the fire of pure air" (*Ae.* 6.746-7). Recall above the ancient equation of *pius* with *purus*, here translated as "clean." The total message seems to be that the body, far from being the focus of the hero, is actually a burden that gets in the way; and the soul, rather than being a feeble vestige of a once-glorious life, actually represents something that is purer, more divine (as implied by the adjective *aetherius*, "ethereal, heavenly"), and it is associated more with fire and energy than dark, faint images. Virgil's cosmic scheme ranges far wider, including different and longer processes for the progressively more wicked, with a system of reincarnation for those too tainted to yet be purged, but the central notion of the body as burden, and the soul as something purer, stands out. Though providing a Hellenistic superstructure, Virgil is no doubt working from a native Roman belief, as seen earlier regarding the *manes*.

This conception of the soul is supported by other passages in the *Aeneid*. When Aeneas expresses amazement at the idea that the souls of the dead might actually desire new bodies in the scheme of reincarnation explained by his father, he asks if it must be believed that "souls would seek to return to sluggish bodies" (*Ae.* 6.720-1), again using the denigrating term *tardus* to refer to the body. Likewise, he earlier declares that "the spirit rules these limbs" (*spiritus hos regit artus*, *Ae.* 4.336), where the soul (*spiritus*) is treated as superior to the body, unlike in Homer where the seat of thought and will is associated with the body (per the physical associations of *phrên* noted above). Likewise, Virgil tells us that, when Aeneas is faced with Dido's protests, "worries are deeply felt in his great heart (*pectus*), but his mind (*mens*) remains unmoved" (*Ae.* 4.448-9; *pectus* is anatomically the Latin equivalent of *phrên*), conveying the idea that emotions are of the body, and get in the way of heroic conduct, while thought, and thus righteous action, are mental, and thus to be associated with the soul. Likewise, when Iris is sent to end Dido's life, her mission is to "free her struggling soul and her fettered limbs" (*Ae.* 4.695), another body-as-burden metaphor. An additional example, though less direct, is when Alecto's magic drives Amata insane: the terminology describing the progression of her madness emphasizes the body (*praecordia*, another Latin synonym of *phrên*: *Ae.* 7.347; *pectus*: *Ae.* 7.349; *ossibus*, "in her bones": *Ae.* 7.355), but her soul (here, *animus*, "intellect," a masculine cognate of *anima*) all the while does not yet perceive the fire raging through her heart (*pectus*: *Ae.* 7.356). Thus, Virgil's vision, in part reflecting his own time and culture, has departed from Homer, indeed even reversed the Homeric view, by portraying the body as getting in the way of man's better half: his soul.

Virgil's portrayal of the soul is far more complex than either that of Homer or Tso Chiu-ming. Souls are described as shadows and phantoms, yet they are not senseless, nor necessarily miserable. They cannot terrorize the living, except collectively, nor do they have the ear of the gods, yet they still play a vital part in the universe—indeed, they possess the ability to know about and influence the land of the living, just not physically. And though the soul is purer than the body and retains a certain vital energy, it is not powerful in the sense that the Chinese soul is seen to be. This complexity derives from the fact that Virgil views the body as a burden to the hero, though still an essential part of the working of fate toward a worldly destiny. Thus the dead gain in wisdom but lose the power to act in the physical world, a view that seems to find a middle ground between the extremes of the Homeric and Chinese views. Virgil's hero, in other words, is one who must overcome the body to be a hero, but who must have a body to be a primary actor in the making of history.

This represents an intellectual struggle that actually began in Classical Greece, gradually changing even the Greek perception of the dead (and the hero) toward more Virgilian lines a few centuries after Homer and before Virgil. As one might expect, this evolution has been traced as a result of increasing need for a more communal social cohesion (Johnston 1999). But this transformation still took place within the context of a Western mode of thought that could never really do away with its obsession with the physical and the particular, with individualism and glory-mongering, whose roots are exposed in Homer, and never really banished by Virgil. As in the *Aeneid*, only a compromise could be reached rather than a victory. Homer lurks still.

5. Conclusion — with Speculations from Cultural Science

Everything points to the same conclusion. Homer saw heroism as involving bodily accomplishment and perfection, which was also by and large the most popular view among the early Greeks, and remains to a lesser but still notable extent in modern Western culture. The two most idolized types in the West today are the celebrity and the athlete, who each achieve their status through physical beauty or prowess, while in film and fiction the ultimate hero is not the wise elder, but the handsome loner righting wrongs through gratuitous displays of righteous force. Homer would approve.

But Homer also perceived the souls of the dead as feeble and fleeting. And this idea was strongly connected with the lack of a body, even with words implying the opposite of "body," such as "image," "shadow," "dream," or the lack of *phrên*. Even exceptions—such as the land of Elysium (*Od.* 4.561-69), Castor and Polydeuces (*Od.* 11.300ff.), the sage Teiresias—occur rarely and only as special favors from the gods. This does reflect the Western obsession with individualism and materialism, and in Homer we see the exaggerated roots of this mindset. However, our modern view of the soul has followed more in the footsteps of Virgil. Most Westerners imagine the dead as 'better off', free from the travails of the flesh, their souls perfected in heaven. Yet, like Virgil's ghosts and unlike Chinese spirits, they are hardly able to meddle in earthly affairs.

In contrast, Tso Ch'iu-ming saw heroism as involving a "cultural" accomplishment and perfection rather than bodily perfection. He also perceived the souls of the dead as potent and energetic, an idea connected with the cultural role of the hero in his society, and his submission to communal duty. Thus, there is an evident connection in Homer and the *Tso Chuan* between the concepts of heroism and the soul. Even when other factors are at work, such as the ideology of ancestor worship in China (paralleled to a lesser extent in Rome), which logically entails a belief in the potency of departed spirits, we might expect a culture's view of heroism and the soul will approach a logical consistency.

Distinctive elements of contrast between the Western and Eastern mindset, as explored by contemporary cross-cultural psychology, might illuminate this finding (Shea, 2001; and Bower 2000, 1998, 1997; summarizing: Ji, Schwarz, and Nisbett, 2000; Nisbett, Ji, and Peng, 2000; Keller 1998; Kitayama, 1997; Heine and Lehman, 1997a and 1997b; Bond, 1996; Moser, 1996; Markus and Kitayama, 1991; Triandis, 1989; Hansen, 1983; Hsu, 1981; Nakamura, 1964). If we are willing to tentatively consider this possibility, we should first observe that these differences have ancient roots. Nisbett observes that "East Asian societies such as China's were until recently based on agricultural economies in which cooperation is crucial and hierarchical political organization requires obedience," eventually relying on large-scale irrigation works and command supply-management systems, whereas "European economies were based on hunting and herding to a much later period" (Nisbett, Ji, and Peng 2000: 953). For the early Indo-Europeans were nomadic warriors, not agriculturalists, and they influenced virtually all Western cultures, most of whom still speak derivations of their language, "and, uniquely among the great ancient civilizations, that of Greece was not based on agriculture but [primarily] on animal husbandry, fishing, and trade."

The Romans, in contrast, were always much more agriculturally oriented (Shelton 1998: 149, 160), so if the environmental thesis should turn out to be correct, we might expect early Roman culture to lean more toward Asian principles than Greek, although Rome's Indo-European roots, intense contact with Greek culture, and militaristic society would provide Roman culture with a more "Western" mind overall. (On Mesopotamia and Egypt, see Johnston 1999: 86-95). These Greek and Chinese differences in origin have been linked to different modes of thinking by several scholars, including Cromer (1993), Lloyd (1990), Witkin and Berry (1975), and Nakamura (1964). And there is some scientific support:

Cross-cultural research indicates that hunting and herding peoples, as well as people who live in the relative freedom of modern wage economies, emphasize autonomous functioning in child rearing and have a relatively loose social structure [whereas] sedentary agricultural groups stress interpersonal orientation and conformity in child rearing, and they have a tight social structure, in which group members need to accommodate each other and strive to regulate one another's behavior. (Nisbett, Ji, and Peng 2000: 953, in reference to Barry, Child, and Bacon 1959, and Whiting and Child 1953)

Furthermore, "Farmers, who are required to attend to the social environment, are more field dependent," that is, more holistically-minded, "than either hunters or industrialized peoples [who] are relatively free to focus on their own goals in relation to an object rather than having to coordinate their actions in relation to a complex social world" (Nisbett, Ji, and Peng 2000: 953), an idea well-argued by several others, including Keightley (1983, 1985, 1990), Hui and Triandis (1986), Witkin and Goodenough (1977), Berry (1976), and Berry and Annis (1974). All of this is relevant to modern cultures:

> Our Western conceptions of man and art, of the individual and the body, of the epic and heroic in both life and literature, and of man's place in the cosmos, still resonate, whether we like it or not, in sympathy with the powerful, imaginative creations of the early Greeks [while] early Chinese conceptions of man and art have stirred, with equal profundity, the elites of traditional China for a period of some two millenia. (Keightley 1993: 51)

In light of such research, from psychology and anthropology, the Chinese definition of the self in terms of the group rather than the individual, and the Chinese idea of substances as interpenetrating, rather than broken up into different pieces with different powers, may perhaps lie at the heart of the Chinese notions of heroism and the soul. Hence the body becomes irrelevant, and cultural perfection everything. In contrast, the Western definition of the self in terms of bodily attributes, individual goals, and physical achievements, and the Western propensity for division of substances, powers, and properties, might be connected to Homeric views of heroism and the soul. The body becomes preeminent, and materialism elevated.

This connection might also be argued in Virgil's *Aeneid*. For Virgil heroism is a form of cultural perfection, where a soul embracing *pietas* overcomes bodily desires and associations, which, being individualistic and near-sighted, do not see the big picture of cosmic destiny, thus leading to ruin and chaos. And so, the souls of the dead retain some power and importance by retaining their moral or intellectual potency, but not the ability to act in the physical sense—thus losing both the advantages *and* the burdens of a body. This is consistent with the fact that Roman ancestor worship was not as complete or as extensive as in China, yet still far greater than among Greeks, leading to a patriotic and religious vision in the *Aeneid* somewhere between the two.

Whether we accept the anthropological hypothesis or not, it is still apparent, and I will conclude with this, that Virgil perceived a conflict in his own day between Homeric and Roman heroism. He saw that a solution required a bigger vision encompassing and explaining both. This solution justified Virgil's very Roman ideas, as being aligned with fate and the divine order, while criticizing the Homeric view as near-sighted and disastrous. Yet it does not appear his message has quite transformed its audience. For the same ideological and metaphysical conflict, between individualism and obsession with the body on one side, and communal duty and praise of the mind on the other, persists within Western cultures even today.

Bibliography

Ames, Roger T. 1984. The Meaning of Body in Classical Chinese Thought. *International Philosophical Quarterly* 24(1): 39-53.

Barry, H, I. Child and M. Bacon. 1959. Relation of Child Training to Subsistence Economy. *American Anthropologist* 61: 51-63.

Berry, J. 1976. *Human Ecology and Cognitive Style: Comparative Studies in Cultural and Psychological Adaptation.* New York: Sage.

Berry, J. and R. Annis. 1974. Ecology, Culture and Differentiation. *International Journal of Psychology* 9: 173-93.

Bond, M, ed. 1996. *The Handbook of Chinese Psychology.* Hong Kong: Oxford University Press.

Bower, Bruce. 1997. My Culture, My Self: Western Notions of the Mind may not Translate to Other Cultures. *Science News* (18 October): pp. 248-9.

——— . 1998. Teens Put Cultured Spin on Friendship. *Science News* (8 August): 84.

——— . 2000. Cultures of Reason: Thinking Styles may Take Eastern and Western Routes. *Science News* (22 January): 56-8.

Cary, M. and H.H. Scullard. 1975. *A History of Rome Down to the Reign of Constantine*, 3rd ed. Hong Kong: St. Martin's Press.

Cheng, Anne. 1993. *Ch'un ch'iu, Kung yang, Ku liang and Tso Chuan. Early Chinese Texts.* Michael Loewe, ed. Berkeley: Institute of East Asian Studies. 69ff.

Chien-shih, Shen. 1936-7. An Essay on the Primitive Meaning of the Character [Kuei]. *Monumenta Serica* 2: 1-20.

Cohen, Alvin P. 1971. *The Avenging Ghost: Moral Judgement in Chinese Historical Texts.* Dissertation: University of California at Berkeley.

Cribiore, Raffaella. 2001. *Gymnastics of the Mind: Greek Education in Hellenistic and Roman Egypt.* Princeton, NJ: Princeton University Press.

——— . 1996. *Writing, Teachers, and Students in Graeco-Roman Egypt.* Atlanta: Scholars Press.

Cromer, Alan. 1993. *Uncommon Sense: The Heretical Nature of Science.* New York: Oxford University Press.

Davison, J.A. 1962. *The Homeric Question. A Companion to Homer.* A.J.B. Wace and F. Stubbings, eds. New York: St. Martin Press. 234-265.

Falkner, Thomas M. 1995. *The Poetics of Old Age in Greek Epic, Lyric, and Tragedy.* University of Oklahoma Press.

Forke, Alfred, tr. 1962. *Lun-Heng: Philosophical Essays of Wang Ch'ung.* New York: Paragon Book Gallery (unaltered reprint from 1907).

Garrison, James D. 1992. *Pietas From Vergil to Dryden.* University Park, Pennsylvania: Pennsylvania State University Press.

Glare, P.G.W. 1997. *Oxford Latin Dictionary.* Oxford University Press.

Gwynn, Aubrey. 1926. *Roman Education from Cicero to Quintilian.* New York: Russell and Russell.

Hammond, Martin, tr. 1987. *Homer: The Iliad.* London: Penguin.

Hansen, C. 1983. *Language and Logic in Ancient China.* Ann Arbor: University of Michigan Press.

Heine, Steven and Darrin Lehman. 1997a. The Cultural Construction of Self-Enhancement: An Examination of Group-Serving Biases. *Journal of Personality and Social Psychology* 72(6): 1268-83.

Heine, Steven and Darrin Lehman. 1997b. Culture, Dissonance, and Self-Affirmation. *Personality and Social Psychology Bulletin* April: 389-400.

Hsu, F. 1981. *Americans and Chinese: Passage to Differences*, 3rd ed. Honolulu: University of Hawaii Press.

Hui, H. and H. Triandis. 1986. Individualism-Collectivism: A Study of Cross-Cultural Research. *Journal of Cross-Cultural Psychology* 17: 225-48.

Hurwitt, Jeffrey. 1985. *The Art and Culture of Early Greece: 1100-480 B.C.* Ithaca, NY: Cornell University Press.

Ji, Li-jun, Norbert Schwarz, and Richard Nisbett. 2000. Culture, Autobiographical Memory, and Behavioral Frequency Reports: Measurement Issues in Cross-Cultural Studies. *Personality and Social Psychology Bulletin* 26(5): 585-93.

Johnston, Sarah Iles. 1999. *Restless Dead: Encounters Between the Living and the Dead in Ancient Greece*. Berkeley: University of California Press.

Karlgren, Bernhard. 1957. *Grammata Serica Recensa*. Stockholm: Museum of Far Eastern Antiquities.

Keightley, David N. 1983. *The Hero, Art, and Culture: Early China and Early Greece*. Unpublished manuscript.

———. 1985. *Dead but not Gone: Cultural Implications of Mortuary Practice in Neolithic and Early Bronze Age China, ca. 8000 to 1000 B.C.* Unpublished manuscript.

———. 1990. Early Civilization in China: Reflections on How it Became Chinese. *Heritage of China*. Paul Ropp, ed. Berkeley: University of California Press.

———. 1993. Clean Hands and Shining Helmets: Heroic Action in Early Chinese and Greek Culture. *Religion and the Authority of the Past*. Tobin Siebers, ed. University of Michigan Press.

Keller, M. et al. 1998. Reasoning About Responsibilities and Obligations in Close Relationships: A Comparison Across Two Cultures. *Developmental Psychology* 34(4): 731-41.

Kierman, Frank Jr. 1974. Phases and Modes of Combat in Early China. *Chinese Ways in Warfare*. Frank Kierman, Jr., and John Fairbank, eds. Cambridge, Mass.: Harvard University Press. 27-66.

Kitayama, Shinobu et al. 1997. Individual and Collective Processes in the Construction of the Self: Self-Enhancement in the United States and Self-Criticism in Japan. *Journal of Personality and Social Psychology* 72(6): 1245-67.

Kopff, E. C. 1999. *The Devil Knows Latin: Why America Needs the Classical Tradition*. Wilmington, Delaware: Intercollegiate Studies Institute.

Legge, James, tr. 1970. *The Ch'un Ts'ew with the Tso Chuen. The Chinese Classics: With a Translation, Critical and Exegetical Notes, Prolegomena, and Copious Indexes* 5. Hong Kong University Press (updated reprint from 1872).

Lewis, C. and C. Short. 1995. *A Latin Dictionary*. New York: Oxford University Press (reprint from 1879).

Liddell, H.G. and R. Scott. 1996. *An Intermediate Greek-English Lexicon*, 9th ed. New York: Oxford University Press (reprint from 1940).

Liu, James. 1967. *The Chinese Knight-Errant*. University of Chicago Press.

Lloyd, G.E.R. 2002. *The Ambitions of Curiosity: Understanding the World in Ancient Greece and China*. Cambridge: Cambridge University Press.

———. 1996. *Adversaries and Authorities: Investigations into Ancient Greek and Chinese Science*. Cambridge: Cambridge University Press.

———. 1990. *Demystifying Mentalities*. Cambridge: Cambridge University Press.

Loewe, Michael, ed. 1993. *Early Chinese Texts: A Bibliographical Guide*. Berkeley, CA: Institute of East Asian Studies.

MacDonald, Dennis R. 2000. *The Homeric Epics and the Gospel of Mark*. New Haven, CT: Yale University Press.

Maltby, Robert. 1991. *A Lexicon of Ancient Latin Etymologies*. Leeds, Great Britain: Francis Cairns.

Markus, H. and S. Kitayama. 1991. Culture and the Self: Implications for Cognition, Emotion, and Motivation. *Psychological Review* 98: 224-53.

Marrou, Henri. 1948. *Histoire de l'Education dans l'Antiquite*, 3rd ed. (tr. as: *A History of Education in Antiquity*, 1986. Madison, Wis.: University of Wisconsin Press).

Mathews, R.H. 1943. *Mathews' Chinese-English Dictionary*. Harvard University Press.

Morgan, Teresa. 1998. *Literate Education in the Hellenistic and Roman Worlds*. Cambridge: Cambridge University Press.

Moser, D.J. 1996. *Abstract Thinking and Thought in Ancient Chinese and Early Greek*. Dissertation: University of Michigan.

Nagy, Gregory. 1996. *Homeric Questions*. Austin: University of Texas Press.

Nakamura, H. 1964. Ways of Thinking of Eastern Peoples. Honolulu: University of Hawaii Press.

Nisbett, Richard, Li-Jun Ji, and Kaiping Peng. 2000. Culture, Control, and the Perception of Relationships in the Environment. *Journal of Personality and Social Psychology* 78(5): 943-55.

Saller, Richard P. 1994. *Pietas and patria potestas. Patriarchy, Property and Death in the Roman Family*. Cambridge University Press.

Schein, Seth L. 1984. *The Mortal Hero: An Introduction to Homer's Iliad*. Berkeley: University of California Press.

Schuessler, Alex. 1987. *Dictionary of Early Zhou Chinese*. University of Hawaii Press.

Shea, Christopher. 2001. White Men Can't Contextualize. *Lingua Franca* September: 44-51.

Shelton, Jo-Ann. 1998. *As The Romans Did: A Sourcebook in Roman Social History*, 2nd ed. New York: Oxford University Press.

Shewring, Walter, tr. 1980. *Homer: The Odyssey*. New York: Oxford University Press.

Smith, D. Howard. 1958. Chinese Concepts of the Soul. *Numen: International Review for the History of Religions* 5(3): 165-179.

Sourvinou-Inwood, Christiane. 1995. *'Reading' Greek Death to the End of the Classical Period*. New York: Oxford University Press.

Suetoshi, Ikeda. 1956. *Revue bibliographique de Sinologie* 2: no. 525.

Triandis, H. 1989. The Self and Social Behavior in Differing Cultural Contexts. *Psychological Review* 96: 506-20.

Tucker, T. G. 1931. *A Concise Etymological Dictionary of Latin*. Halle, Germany: Max Niemeyer Verlag.

Turner, Frank. 1981. *The Greek Heritage in Victorian Britain*. New Haven, CT: Yale University Press.

Wang, C.H. 1975. Towards Defining a Chinese Heroism. *Journal of the American Oriental Society* 95(1): 25-35.

Watson, Burton, tr. 1989. *The Tso Chuan: Selections from China's Oldest Narrative History*. New York: Columbia University Press.

Wetmore, Monroe Nichols. 1911. *Index Verborum Vergilianus*. New Haven, CT: Yale University Press.

Whiting, J. and I. Child. 1953. *Child Training and Personality: A Cross-Cultural Study*. New Haven, CT: Yale University Press.

Williams, R. D., ed. 1992. *The Aeneid of Virgil: Books 1-6*. Thomas Nelson and Sons.

Witkin, H. and J. Berry. 1975. Psychological Differentiation in Cross-Cultural Perspective. *Journal of Cross-Cultural Psychology* 6: 4-87.

Witkin, H. and D. Goodenough. 1977. Field Dependence and Interpersonal Behavior. *Psychological Bulletin* 84: 661-89.

Wolf, Arthur. 1974. Gods, Ghosts, and Ancestors. *Religion and Ritual in Chinese Society*. Arthur Wolf, ed. Stanford University Press. 131-182.

Ying-shih, Yü. 1987. 'Oh Soul, Come Back!' A Study in the Changing Conceptions of the Soul and Afterlife in Pre-Buddhist China. *Harvard Journal of Asiatic Studies* 47(2): 363-395.

6

HEROD THE PROCURATOR
AND CHRISTIAN APOLOGETICS

*Originally a work of educational humor
published at Richard Carrier Blogs on 6 January 2012.
Revised. © 2012, 2014.*

The Backstory…

Herod the Great (you know, that guy in the Bible who killed all those babies, but didn't really) was a procurator. (WTF is a procurator? Don't worry, I'll get to that.) In fact, Herod wasn't just any procurator. He was the chief procurator of the entire Roman province of Syria. Holy crap! That's amazing! Er…or totally, fantastically irrelevant and boring. One or the other, I'm sure. (Right?)

Who cares? Hardly anyone really. Why am I writing about this? Well, to be honest, because I had to at some point, and now is as good a time as any (more on that later). But kind of, also, because it's really interesting to ancient history geeks. And, strangely, Christian apologists. Why? Because they can argue from "Herod was the procurator of Syria" to "Luke and Matthew *don't* contradict each other on the year of Christ's birth, contrary to what all you mean atheist harpies keep saying." Yeah. It takes some twists and turns. But they make a good effort to get from A to B. Strangely, this point also connects to the debate over the existence of Jesus. No shit. Lotta twists and cul-de-sacs, but A gets to B on that one, too.

Even given that context ("Ooo! Christian apologetics? Now it's getting interesting!"), this is one of the most jaw-droppingly uninteresting bits of trivia you've probably come across in months. Or ever. I mean, there are mighty battles being fought elsewhere over very important issues. Sexism, slander, dumbassery, political murder, bad science, the Republican primaries, soda mice. (Among all of which you will learn that a new spell has been added to the Harry Potter lexicon: wave your wand and utter the words Rebecca Watson and a hoard of nitwitted sexist trolls are summoned; unfortunately they immediately attack the spellcaster so it's kind of a shit spell really.)

But here's the backstory. For my Master of Philosophy at Columbia University (aka M.Phil., a graduate degree between M.A. and Ph.D., sort of like what everyone else calls ABD) I completed a thesis in preparation for working up a prospectus for my dissertation. That thesis was never published, mainly because, though it is more thorough and meticulous than anything on its topic, someone I'd never heard of beat me to publication with their own paper arguing the same thesis (albeit a lot less comprehensively and in a more wishy washy way, but nevertheless, journals won't publish my work now because "it's already been done," as one editor directly told me). It's a mind-numbingly boring thesis. But I worked really hard on it and I'm sure someone will find it useful someday. So I updated it (even citing and incorporating that other guy's paper, as well as all the revisions asked for by my peer reviewers) and published it on my website for anyone crazy enough to read it (that article follows here).

It does have one interesting vibe to it. If you read it all through (you have to be kind of a little crazy to do that, but that can be in a good way; why, hey, the PDF edition is "only" 36 pages long), one thing you will learn, especially if you are not a professional historian, is how incredibly complicated doing history really is, and why expertise and training is so important for it. My thesis details all the actual steps that are involved in coming to a conclusion on any question (even one so seemingly simple as "Was Herod the Great really the procurator of Roman Syria?"), showing you all the sorts of things you have to know about and research, the process of reasoning and analysis you have to go through, and all that jazz. Usually you just see the end result, maybe a paragraph summary, and don't see all the messy, crazy shit that went on to produce that paragraph. Now you get to see Oz working the controls. Batshit crazy controls.

You'll also learn (especially if you read the most boring part) how translations, even by total bona fide experts, can screw up the original meaning of a text, and how beholden laymen are to what are really often very subjective translations hiding all manner of assumptions and agendas of the translator. Not just the Bible has this problem; all ancient books do. You'll also learn a bit about how determining what the original text said from existing manuscripts is no simple matter, either. And you'll learn some stuff about various languages, Roman provincial administration, and how Herod the Great and Emperor Augustus were such party buds I'd bet a sawbuck they high-fived over a shared a hooker or two.

(Not literally, of course; sure, everyone knows double-teaming hookers was invented in 1891 B.C., but the high-five is a 20th century invention; so, whatever the ancient Roman equivalent was. Yeah, I'd risk a tenner on that. Stranger shit has supposedly happened. Story is, emperor-to-be Titus banged two hookers over an open Torah scroll on the sacred sacrificial altar of the Jewish Temple just to flip the bird at the nutty superstitious Jews he'd just wasted several years of his life putting down a rebellion of. I remember the first thing I thought when I read that, "I hope those girls were paid well." Probably. Everyone says Titus was a real mensch. Anyway…)

So back to the Christian thing…

Okay, quick summary:

Matthew says Jesus was born a year or so before Herod the Great died, which was in 4 B.C.; Luke says Jesus was born when the Roman senator Quirinius became governor of Syria and conducted the first ever Roman census of Judea, which was in 6 A.D.; the contradiction (a ten year miss, even) proves the New Testament is, uhem, errant (oh, and BTW, notice that neither says it was 1 A.D.; and in fact that date is entirely impossible on either of their accounts…oops); "Oh, shit!" Christians say to themselves (probably not out loud, because that might anger their storm god); Christian apologists scramble for some way to fix this fiasco; they come up with a wild pile of bullshit; if you rummage around in that shit pile (like I did), you'll find this gem (I'm humorously paraphrasing, of course):

> "Well, see, Quirinius must have been governor of Syria twice somehow (*even though no one ever was a governor of the same province twice and we have zero evidence Quirinius was or even could have been*), and there must have been some other,

> earlier census of Judea, conducted by Herod (*even though that is illogical and impossible on every known fact of the matter*), and since the evidence says other guys were governing Syria at the time, not only was Quirinius twice governor, but he must have been co-governor with someone else (*even though no such thing as a co-governorship of a province existed in the Roman administrative system and in fact it would have been illogical and absurd*)."

When mean atheists like me point out the parenthetical points (put in italics above), Christians scramble for damage control, generally by making shit up or pretending at being historians, doing some embarrassingly incompetent amateur hatchet job with "facts" they tweeze out of modern translations of ancient books (unlike Muslims, who often insist on Arabic fluency and thus actually know how to read their scripture, most Christians never actually learn Greek and generally couldn't give a shit what the actual words in their inspired scriptures are) and/or antiquated, long-superseded scholarship (because when Christians can't find what they want in up-to-date scholarship they dig around for something written in the 19th century, back in those golden days before that Darwin dickwad ruined everything; because surely any history done then must be superior and more reliable than any done now…and they're, like, totally right).

Case in point: Josephus (and an occasional stone inscription) repeatedly says there were two governors of Syria. So there! Except he doesn't (nor do any inscriptions). Ah, those pesky translations. You see, what Josephus (and every other source from then) says is that every Syrian governor had a lieutenant, and they often hung out and did shit together. "But that's the same thing, right?" Uh, no. Because ancient Roman society didn't work like our modern American "classless" society. Technically we do have classes (e.g. lower, middle, and upper) demarcated by access to wealth and power, but in classical times classes were official matters of law, and one couldn't cross from one to the other just by getting rich or elected. You had to be officially recognized as of that class; and it took some hoodow to make that happen. And in the meantime, your career options were limited by what class you were in.

So we need a little intro to Roman social history.

It breaks down like this: the unwashed masses (actually, the Roman masses were often very well washed) were just "ordinary people" and couldn't hold any significant political or military office (didn't even qualify; couldn't even buy their way in…unless they bought their way into a higher social order); next in rank were the equestrians (literally "horsemen," so sometimes called "knights"; the term originally designated someone rich enough to buy and keep a horse, although that was an antiquated notion even by then…even the poorest Roman equestrian could buy and keep a small *shitload* of horses), who (unlike those below them) qualified for appointed administrative positions and could serve as something like NCOs in the military (or perhaps more analogously, low ranking officers, depending on what point of comparison you start with), but couldn't run for elected office and couldn't be a staff officer…unless they were at least 30 years old and met the multi-million-dollar entry requirement for the next class: the senators. To enter the senatorial class you had to prove you had millions of dollars in property and then (to be elligible to hold any office) you had to get elected to the entry-level position of quaestor ("treasurer"; yep, the bottom-ranking gig even then), which got you pretty much permanently into the Roman Senate, and from there you could run for higher offices (but always by ranks, i.e. you couldn't skip straight to Lord of All I Survey, you had to serve as quaestor, then praetor, then consul, and your social rank would always be based on how high you'd gotten, e.g. a consular senator outranked a praetorian senator, big time). Of course, kids of senators were automatically of the senatorial class, although they still had to get elected (or, if we set aside the Doublespeak, given the real nature of politics under the emperors, *appointed*) to a quaestorship to enter the Senate itself (and yes, that meant daughters could be of senatorial rank, but sadly, as they could never hold any office, they never became senators).

Okay. So? Well, because of the Roman constitution at the time, no one could govern a province who was not a consular senator. This is because the provinces were officially governed by the emperor (who had consular rank) or the senatorial consuls, and "governors" were just their stand-ins, but in an official government capacity, which meant they had to be of the same rank. Thus a praetorian senator was not of sufficient rank to govern a province and thus could not act in any other governor's stead. You had to appoint a senator who had served as a consul at some prior time and thus achieved consular rank. (There were a handful of weird provinces, called senatorial provinces, that didn't precisely fall under this rule, but Syria wasn't one of them so they're irrelevant for our purposes; one of the constitutionally relevant differences, BTW, was that senatorial provinces usually never had legions in them.)

Notice that *not even lower ranking senators* could govern a province, much less lowly equestrians, who couldn't even hold a real political office at all, much less govern a province. They weren't even *senators*. It would have been scandalously offensive (and indeed risked outright assassination or civil war) if an emperor were to openly flout the constitution and insult every upper class senatorial man in the empire by appointing a lowly equestrian to govern a province (case in point: Caligula is said to have almost appointed his horse, and they promptly killed him...and tried to damn his memory–literally: the senate proposed [and may have eventually passed] an official decree of *damnatio memoriae*; yeah, they had those). And certainly such a remarkable curiosity would make every history book of the time, as the weirdest thing to happen since someone discovered water could be turned into a white powder. Conversely, no senator (much less of mighty consular rank) would disgrace himself or his whole family's honor by ever deigning to lower himself to work in an equestrian post. That would be more unbelievable than a former U.S. President becoming a fry cook at McDonald's.

Now, governors of imperial provinces, who were always consular senators, and officially were high-ranking military officers, commanders of legions, obviously had a whole chain of command working under them, of lower ranking senatorial line and staff officers, as well as equestrian field officers and NCOs and bureaucrats. Thus, a governor could divide up his provincial command and appoint lower ranking officers to take care of business there, principally taking charge of any troops and enforcing the law. These were typically equestrians (because Roman paranoia prevented entrusting too many major provincial and troop commands to senators, who might have ambitions; whereas equestrians were generally locked in their low status and thus no threat, and in fact for that reason typically more loyal). These officers were called "prefects," literally "guys placed in front," in other words "dudes in charge." Prefects were always equestrians; senatorial officers had other ranks (namely, quaestor or praetor).

Now that you have all that background (and notice how there is no way a layman is likely to know any of this; there's a reason you need a Ph.D. to draw correct conclusions about the ancient world), you can get the punchline: Whenever we see mentions of governors and their lieutenants (as in Josephus, for example), it's always a consular senator *and his equestrian prefect*. Men who are not even of the same social class. You might already see where this is going. Quirinius is well established to have been a consular senator as of 12 B.C. We know all the consular governors of Syria from 12 to 3 B.C. He therefore cannot have been any of their "lieutenants," because those lieutenants were always prefects of the equestrian class, and he was way the hell higher ranking than an equestrian, in fact he held the highest possible social rank in the whole Roman empire: a consular senator. So much for the co-governor idea.

Enter Christian Logic.

Now that you are as bored as you possibly can be, it gets even more boring. Enter Herod the Procurator. The Christian's logic goes like this (and I've had versions of this argument sent to me in email over the years by a half dozen D-list Christian apologists). Pontius Pilate was the "governor" of Judea. Pontius Pilate was a procurator. Therefore a "procurator" is a "governor." Herod the Great was the Procurator of Syria. Therefore, Herod the Great (a foreigner) was the "governor" of Syria. Therefore the Romans played fast and loose with their constitution when it came to provincial government. Therefore they could well have had double governors or something. In fact when Herod was "governor" of Syria, we know another consular senator was governor of Syria, so bingo, there we have it, there were two governors of Syria!

This is all so fucked up it makes me want to cry. Okay. First. Judea was not a province. Thus Pilate was not "the [provincial] governor" of Judea. The governor of Syria was. Judea was then a district of the Roman province of Syria. Pilate was just the *prefect* assigned to govern that *district*. By the governor of Syria. And as you'd expect, Pilate was of equestrian rank. Thus no argument can proceed by analogy from the government of Judea to the government of Syria. Second. A procurator is not a prefect. To identify Pilate as "governor of Judea" is to identify him as a prefect, not a procurator. A procurator is not an administrative or military office. It's a private occupation. It means "business manager" (literally, "one given care of stuff," e.g. an agent, a manager, etc.). Thus in no sense does procurator ever mean "governor." Thus in no sense at all was Herod the Great ever "the governor of Syria." So, no playing fast and loose here. The Romans stuck to their constitution, or as near as could pass as plausible (in an Orwellian sense, if one examines how the emperors invented the entire office of emperor without actually, literally changing the constitution, which never mentioned any such office *per se*, by cleverly exploiting various loopholes in that constitution, but that's a whole other story, not relevant here).

So despite trying to rescue the big gaping historical error in the Gospels, the attempt to get from "Herod the Great was Procurator of Syria" to "the Bible is inerrant" is built on a pile of the hack mistakes of presumptuous Christian apologists who don't know their Roman social history for shit.

What does any of this long boring digression have to do with my thesis paper on Herod the Procurator? Well, among other things (like analyzing the evidence for Herod being a procurator of Syria at all), I document in it all the evidence and scholarship laying out the distinction between prefects and procurators. Which has another use, for those following the "did Jesus really exist?" debate…

That would be the question whether Pontius Pilate was a "prefect" or a "procurator."

A prominent defender of the thesis that Jesus is a mythical person (more now in the agnostic camp, but still) is G.A. Wells. And one argument he made, against the authenticity of a passage attesting to the existence of Jesus in the Roman historian Tacitus (writing around 116 A.D.), is that Tacitus there calls Pilate a "procurator" when in fact we know, from logic (given the above) and an actual stone inscription cut at Pilate's own direction, that Pilate was a *prefect*, not a procurator, which isn't even a government office. "Surely" Tacitus would not make that mistake (so the passage is a forgery) or "surely" Tacitus would not make that mistake if he was working from government documents (so he must be relying on an unreliable source, like a Gospel-reading Christian informant). Therefore the information is bogus. Therefore (given various other conclusions) Jesus didn't exist. Now, like many an unsound argument, the primary conclusion is true (Tacitus is almost certainly relying on a Gospel-reading Christian informant, and not any kind of government records), but the argument for it is not.

Tacitus almost certainly got this information from his good friend Pliny the Younger, who would have gotten it from his strong-arm interrogation of a Christian deaconess in 110 A.D.

(when Tacitus and Pliny were governing adjacent provinces in what is now Turkey, and carrying on a regular correspondence in which Tacitus evinces asking Pliny for information to include in the history books he was then writing). And she would certainly have gotten the information from the Gospels, many of which were surely being read in the churches of the time. So yes, Tacitus is in fact giving us useless evidence, since it is not independent of the Gospels (that's why his account contains nothing not in them, yet that would have been in an official government record, like Jesus' full name and crime). But Wells' argument to that same conclusion is incorrect, due to another oddity about the ancient Roman system that non-experts don't know about (and that even many experts don't know about, not having specifically studied the matter of imperial administration and economics).

In actual fact, Pilate was *both* a prefect *and* a procurator. An imperial procurator, to be precise. In fact this was true of all the prefects of Judea, and many other regional prefects, such as the prefect of Egypt, who governed that whole province directly for the emperor (Egypt never had a senatorial governor, its governorship was always officially held by the emperor himself, who never shared it, because Egypt was the breadbasket of the empire at the time and thus any senator allowed to govern it would be tempted to do the obvious…and they wouldn't have that uppity, smartypants Cleopatra gumming up their game, either). It was actually commonplace for prefects to also be procurators. Why? Well, I explain in my thesis (for those who only care about this topic, you can skip directly to the section on "The Procurator in the Time of Augustus").

Procurators were private agents. So, for example, if you were some rich guy and owned lands in several provinces, you obviously couldn't personally oversee their management, so you would hire someone as your *procurator* to go act as landlord for you. Pretty much any business, or property, or account of money that you had somewhere needed someone to manage it on your behalf. That someone was a procurator. The wealthy elite had armies of them in their employ. And the emperor was the wealthiest man in the Western hemisphere.

Another little known fact is that the emperors often compelled their vanquished opponents to sign treaties not with the Roman people (SPQR) but with the emperor himself and his private family estate. Annual tribute was then owed not to the Roman government, but directly to the Roman emperor's family estate. And in such cases lands seized were not the public property of Rome, but the private property of the emperor, taken as spoils (or as bribes, or simply bought outright, and just as often inherited, from people wanting to get their surviving family on the emperor's good side). This meant the emperor had tons of lands he needed to manage privately (not officially as a Roman statesman) and tons of cash that had to be collected every year and held in his name and managed at a profit, or delivered to him across regions and seas. And that meant the emperor had to employ thousands of procurators to act as his business managers for all this.

Well, who would make the best procurator? Or rather, the best *chief* procurator, who would look over and keep in line all the other procurators who were actually managing the individual landholdings, and collections, and stashes of banked cash? Why, who best to hire for that job than the chief of police? The very guy who governs the district and has charge of the courts and the law and cohorts of infantry and cavalry to enforce his will. Brilliant, eh?

And so it was. Every prefect of Judea was also the emperor's privately hired business manager, who ensured all the imperial procurators in their district behaved and did their jobs, and everyone who owed the emperor money (or had the temerity to sue him) was dealt with. In our modern democracy this would be perfectly appalling. It would be obvious corruption if the President hired the Secretary of the Interior to manage all of his private lands, and the Secretary of Commerce to run all of his private companies and businesses, and hired Superior Court Judges to manage the very private estates they passed judgments on in court (imagine suing someone and finding out that the judge deciding the case is the property manager of the very estate you are suing!). But the Roman empire had no such moral notions, and no laws on the books against it. To them it was just convenient.

But there were complaints. Although not necessarily of the kind you'd expect. One of the persistent drums Tacitus beats throughout his entire *Annals* is that it was shocking (why, just shocking!) that lowly equestrians were being given the official powers of senators. As business managers, procurators were only ever equestrians, or often even commoners or slaves; no senator would disgrace himself by taking such a servile job (again, imagine the President of the United States taking a job as a "common" real estate agent). But Tacitus was annoyed even by the idea of *prefects* running things. Procurators were just an even bigger insult. Since an imperial procurator was the legal agent of the emperor, he literally had power of attorney to represent the emperor in court and contracts. Which meant that in practice, lowly procurators could tell mighty consular senators what for. It's not like a senatorial governor is going to cross the emperor. Thus procurators often wielded *in effect* imperial-scale power. And that pissed off consular senators like Tacitus. His *Annals* is full of morality tales illustrating how so really disastrous and awful this was.

Which gets us back to that passage in the *Annals* where Tacitus says Christ was executed by Pontius Pilate "the procurator." Tacitus was a consular senator who had held many imperial provincial governorships and nearly every other office in the land. He knew full well that Pilate was a prefect. He would not have had to check any records to know that. He also knew full well that Pilate, like all district prefects, was the private business manager of the emperor, a lowly money collector and landlord, a filthy *procurator*. Assuming Tacitus really did write this passage (I suspect not: see the last chapter of this volume), he clearly chose to call Pilate a procurator here, and not a prefect, as a double insult: on the one hand, his aim was to paint the Christians as pathetically as possible, and having their leader executed by a petty business manager was about as low as you could get (and Tacitus would never turn down a good juicy snipe like that); and on the other hand, he was always keen to remind the reader of his persistent protest against granting equestrians real powers, and thus calling Pilate here a procurator does that, by reminding the reader that the chief of police who executes criminals in Judea is a "fucking business manager" ("and what the hell is he doing with judicial powers?"). The fact that Pilate was also a prefect and thus had real constitutional authority is the sort of honest detail that would screw up Tacitus' point. So he wouldn't take the trouble to mention it.

Okay. Right. Here we are now. Anyone who has actually read this backstory all the way to this point (I commend you, sir and/or ma'am!) will now be able to guess the conclusion of my thesis: Herod the Great was appointed by his good buddy Augustus to be his principal business manager in Syria. Wow. Amazing, right? That conclusion is going to haunt you for days. Life changing stuff. Just simply life changing. And so that you will have it with you always, I have now published my old M.Phil. thesis on Herod the Syrian procurator, which has sections on all this stuff (so if you want to cite evidence and scholarship at anyone in defense of these points, like about Pilate being both procurator and prefect, this is the paper for you), and other stuff besides (as I babbled on about in the earlier half of this chapter).

Enjoy. Or not. Anyway, here it is.

L'Chayim!

7

HEROD THE PROCURATOR: WAS HEROD THE GREAT A ROMAN GOVERNOR OF SYRIA?

Prepared by Richard Carrier as his M.Phil. thesis in 2000.
Revised and published at RichardCarrier.info in 2012.
© 2000, 2012.

Contents

1. Introduction to the Problem
2. The Text
3. The Translations
4. The Interpretations
5. The Meaning of 'Procurator'
6. Preliminary Conclusion
7. The Procurator in the Time of Augustus
8. The Grant of the Provincial Procuratorship to Herod

1. Introduction to the Problem

According to Samuel Sandmel, Augustus made Herod the Great "governor over part of Syria" around 20 B.C.[1] Though Sandmel has slightly misstated two passages in Josephus, what those passages mean has long been debated. In 20 B.C. Augustus toured the East, settling various affairs, finally landing in Syria, where he acquitted Herod of charges against him brought by the Gadarenes, and attached the territories of the recently-deceased tetrarch Zenodorus

---

[1] Samuel Sandmel, *Herod: Profile of a Tyrant* (1967), p. 179.

to Herod's own growing kingdom.[2] Then Josephus reports something quite astonishing: Augustus "mixed him in with those who were procurating Syria, ordering them to do everything in accordance with his judgement," or indeed, "he appointed him procurator of all Syria, so the procurators could manage nothing against his advice."[3] This has been variously interpreted, and variously translated, and as translations are themselves a form of interpretation, we will first deal with the text, then the translations, then the interpretations, followed by a new discussion of what it meant for Herod the Great to be, in effect, the procurator-in-chief of the Roman province of Syria in the time of Augustus.[4]

2. The Text

The texts of Josephus are not in a good state. Only one decent critical edition each of the *War* and *Antiquities* has ever been made, and that is already over a hundred years old, and much in need of revision. This edition, established by Benedict Niese between 1885 and 1895,[5] has been given too much confidence by later editors, and all other editions rely too uncritically on Niese's work, particularly Naber, which is inexcusable given their near-simultaneous publication.[6] Indeed, no less than sixteen mss. are known today that

---

[2] *BJ* [= *Jewish War*] 1.399-400, *AJ* [= *Jewish Antiquities*] 15.354-361; corroborated by Dio Cassius, *RH* 54.7.4, 54.7.6, 54.9.3, and partly by the *Res Gestae* 11, which notes the founding of the *Augustalia* in honor of Augustus' return from Syria in 19 B.C.

[3] *AJ* 15.360 and *BJ* 1.399.

[4] This problem was recently examined in Anthony Barrett, "Herod, Augustus, and the Special Relationship: The Significance of the Procuratorship," in David Jacobson and Nikos Kokkinos, eds., *Herod and Augustus: Papers Presented at the IJS Conference, 21st-23rd June 2005* (2009), pp. 281-302. The most thorough treatment of the issue of Augustan procurators, verifying the conclusions here to be drawn, is Peter Eich, *Zur Metamorphose des politischen Systems in der römischen Kaiserzeit: die Entstehung einer "personalen Bürokratie" im langen dritten Jahrhundert* (2005), esp. pp. 106-58; see also Werner Eck, *Rom und Judaea: Fünf Vorträge zur römischen Herrschaft in Palaestina* (Mohr Siebeck, 2007), pp. 24-48.

[5] Benedict Niese, *Flavii Josephi Opera*, 6 vols. (1887-1894).

[6] S. Naber, *Flavii Josephi Opera Omnia*, 6 vols. (1888-1896).

Niese never examined, and he disregarded on subjective grounds eight more as unworthy of consultation.[7] To what extent Nodet's work will remedy this situation remains to be seen in our present case.[8] Earlier editions by Dindorf, Hudson and Havercamp are now widely regarded as substantially inferior to Niese, and do not employ a critical apparatus of any substance.[9]

Other scholars have surveyed the situation but done little to improve it, and disagreements exist. Most important are the introductions by Thackeray. He remarks, for example, that

> The difficulties which confront the editor of Josephus arise from a comparative paucity of ancient mss., the inconstancy of some mss., which renders grouping uncertain, and the fact that corruption has often affected the text of all. Each variant is to be considered on its merits; and there is considerable scope for conjectural emendation, on which many eminent scholars have exercised their ingenuity.[10]

In Thackeray's opinion, Niese over-estimated the value of one mss. (the Codex Palatinus [Vaticanus] Graecus 14, which is the oldest extant mss., created in the 9th or 10th century),[11] and Naber "relied too exclusively" on the other mss., while Thackeray recommends his own combination of mss. that should be given priority. In contrast with this bleak opinion, Feldman defends Niese's text as sound, and claims no new edition is needed. And instead of what Thackeray saw as a frequently corrupt text, Feldman argues:

---

[7] For this and more detail on the current state of the manuscripts, though over-generous in defending Niese, see Steve Mason, ed., *Flavius Josephus: Translation and Commentary*, v. 3 (2000), pp. xxxvii-xxxviii (remarks by Louis Feldman).

[8] Etienne Nodet, *Les antiquités juives* (1992-2010), has not yet reached even book 12 of the *AJ*, and the apparatus is minimal and thus not encouraging.

[9] L. Dindorf, *Flavii Josephi Opera* (1865); J. Hudson & S. Havercamp, *Flavii Josephi Opera Omnia*, 1726, a revision of Hudson's earlier *Flavii Josephi Opera Quae Reperiri Potuerunt Omnia* (1720).

[10] H. Thackeray and R. Marcus, *Josephus in Nine Volumes*, vol. 1 (1926), pp. xvii-xviii (i.e. the Loeb edition).

[11] This is certainly correct, as proved by Niese's own extensive hyperbolic praise of it, as in his *praefatio* to the *AJ* text, pp. xx ff.

Since Greek was Josephus' third language (after Aramaic and Hebrew) it is not surprising that his knowledge of Greek grammar and idiom is sometimes deficient, and so his prose is difficult to understand. We should not assume that difficulties in the manuscripts result from copyists' errors.[12]

Feldman certainly knows his subject, though I myself have never found Josephus' Greek to be 'deficient' any more than merely *Koinê*, and usually a very nice variety. Indeed, we know that Josephus relied on expert secretaries to prepare his Greek text of the *BJ*, and yet its style does not notably differ from the *AJ*, so this destroys Feldman's entire reasoning here.[13] Difficulties are more the fault of our being non-native readers two thousand years removed than the outcome of any garbled use of the language by the writer, but this still leads to the same conclusion: we should not be hasty in proposing emendations for what merely seems awkward. Even so, Feldman and Thackeray remain at odds: while Feldman says "there have been few reasons for challenging" Niese's text, Thackeray says the mss. Niese relied on the most are "when unsupported...seldom trustworthy."

In our current case, Thackeray's caution is proved wiser than Feldman's confidence. Niese reads: *enkatamignusin d' autên tois epitropeuousin tês Surias enteilamenos meta tês ekeinou gnômês ta panta poiein (AJ*

---

[12] Mason, ibid. [n. 7].

[13] *Contra Apion* 1.50 (with *BJ* 1.pr.6): *chrêsamenos tisi pros tên Hellênida phônên sunergois houtôs epoiêsamên tôn praxeôn tên paradosin*, "I composed [the *BJ*] by employing some assistants in the Greek language." Cf. Per Bilde, *Flavius Josephus between Jerusalem and Rome: His Life, His Works, and Their Importance* (1988), pp. 132-3, 142-3. Josephus' remark in *AJ* 1.7 that "it was for me a slow and delayed process to translate so great a subject into a habit of speech strange and foreign to us" is the sort of exaggerated modesty occasionally found in historical prefaces of the time, and only refers to his translation of the Bible (1.5); a similar hyperbolic apology closes the *AJ* (20.263) where, after asserting his lengthy and diligent education in Greek language and literature, Josephus excuses himself for being unable to *pronounce* Greek with precision, not for being unable to write well (i.e. he is merely apologizing, possibly to audiences at his public readings, for having a Hebrew accent in his diction or a Hebrew style in his composition).

15.360); and *katestēsen de auton kai Syrias holēs epitropon ... hōs mēden exeinai dicha tēs ekeinou symboulias tois epitropois dioikein* (*BJ* 1.399). No variants for either passage exist in any of the extant mss., epitomes or Latin translations that were examined by Niese, but one: Codex Palatinus is alone among all nine mss. consulted by him in having the feminine pronoun *autēn* as the object of the *AJ* passage. This radically changes the meaning of the sentence in a way that contradicts the parallel passage in the *BJ*, and Niese is wholly unjustified in preferring this against all the others which read *auton*. This is a perfect example of what Thackeray warned against: Niese's excessive trust in the relatively untrustworthy Palatinus mss. Thackeray wisely rejected it, and adopted *auton* for the text of the Loeb edition, but still noting *autēn* as a variant in his apparatus.

Analysis of this question is key to revealing the sorry state of the texts of Josephus, proving the need is great for new critical work wholly independent of Niese. In his apparatus, Niese says that the reading of *auton* in all the other mss. is "hardly right; it seems a gap ought to be here" (*vix recte; lacuna statuenda vid.*). He does not say why he doesn't think *auton* can be correct, but the only reason imaginable is that it seems to state the impossible: a foreign client king being made governor of a Roman province. This must be Niese's reasoning, since there is nothing grammatically wrong with the reading of *auton* (obviously referring to Herod), in fact it is exactly what we should expect given what the *BJ* says, though it is strange that Niese offers no remarks or emendations for *that* passage, even though it says essentially the same thing. But supposing this was his reasoning, why did Niese think *autēn* was a better reading? Perhaps because the feminine would not make Herod the object of the sentence, but the territory he was being given (in the preceding passage). The sentence would then read "[Augustus] adjoined this [territory] to those who were procurating Syria, giving orders to do everything with [Herod's] judgement." This would make a nice solution: instead of giving Herod power over Syria, Augustus is merely loaning his personal agents in Syria to Herod, ordering them to also work for him in administering financial matters in his newly-acquired lands. This would be legally uncontroversial: the same men serving as employees of Augustus in Syria simply serve as employees of Herod in an adjacent section of Herod's kingdom. But this all falls apart when we compare this passage with the *BJ*, which definitely excludes this interpretation (even if we tried to emend the text in some plausible way), and the agreement of meaning between the reading of *auton* in the *AJ* and what is stated in the *BJ*, coupled with the noted unreliability of the Palatinus ms., and the universal agreement of all other mss. (and even Latin translations, which have *eum*), certainly excludes *autên* as an acceptable reading. However, it is not certain that this is even what Niese had in mind, since he apparently thought some additional text was required, which he then proposed had fallen out in copying, and therefore he believed the received text was in some sense illegible, but this removes any plausible support he could have had for accepting *autên* as the correct reading.

Through their distortion of Niese's original note later editors show that they never actually looked at the mss. themselves. As we saw, Niese's actual words were "*vix recte; lacuna statuenda vid.*" But Naber rewords Niese's comment to say "*lacunam notavit Ns.*," in other words, "Niese noted a gap," an ambiguous paraphrase that seems to assert rather than conjecture. Ralph Marcus reworded this yet again in the apparatus to the Loeb edition as "*post hoc verbum lacunam stat. Niese*," in other words, "after this word lies a gap [according to] Niese."[14] Thus, what began as a merely conjectured missing word or two became a mythical 'observed lacuna' in the text. This gives us little confidence that either Naber or Marcus actually examined the Palatinus manuscript for themselves (and one wonders if they examined any), and when we read Niese's own words we see there is no real gap in any of the manuscripts. Niese merely conjectured that *auton* was too incredible to be believed, and since Palatinus was known to contain several lacunae,[15] he could solve his dilemma by simply proposing a lacuna here. But this is groundless. It appears that there is no lacuna, and *auton* is clearly the correct reading. The text here is sound, independently corroborated by two different works, in numerous mss., and it makes perfect grammatical sense.

3. The Translations

The earliest translation of Josephus into English is that of Theodore Lodge, which renders the text as "Hee made him one of the

---

[14] Both taken from the apparatuses to the relevant passage in Naber [n. 6] and Marcus [n. 10].

[15] Cf. Naber's *praefatio* to the *AJ* text [n. 6].

governors of Syria also, commanding them to execute nothing without his advice," such that Augustus "made him ruler over all Syria and...commanded the governours to doe nothing without Herods counsell."[16] Then follows the Thompson & Price translation: "He likewise conferred on him a supreme authority over the governors of Syria, and directed that his orders and commands should be obeyed in every particular," and once Herod was thus "appointed governor of all Syria" Augustus "enjoined the governors to consult Herod in all affairs of importance."[17] Both of these translations take substantial liberties with the details, and incorrectly translate as "governor" the Greek *epitropos*, which actually means "procurator," a mistake not made at the time in the Latin translation of Havercamp & Hudson (following older Latin translations traced as far back as the 7th century), which correctly gives, e.g., "*quin et eum cum Syriae procuratoribus coniunxit; eisque, ne quid fine Herodis sententia facerent, imperavit*" for the passage in the *AJ*.[18] As will be demonstrated later, a procurator was in those days a private employee, not a government official.

Fortunately accuracy prevailed, and the still-popular translation by William Whiston, fairly loyal to the text, says "He also made him one of the procurators of Syria, and commanded that they should do every thing with his approbation," and "He also made him a procurator of all Syria…and this was so established that the other procurators could not do anything in the administration without his advice."[19] The Loeb edition employs the translations of Marcus & Thackeray, which matches the Whiston translation in meaning: "he also associated him with the procurators of Syria, instructing them to obtain Herod's consent to all their actions" and

---

[16] Theodore Lodge, *The Famous and Memorable Workes of Iosephus* (1632), p. 407 and 586.

[17] Ebenezer Thompson & W.C. Price, *The Works of Flavius Josephus* (1777), Vol. 1, p. 604 and Vol. 2, p. 238.

[18] S. Havercamp & J. Hudson, *Flavii Iosephi Hebraei Opera Omnia* (1782), Vol. 2, p. 610-1.

[19] William Whiston, *The Works of Flavius Josephus* (1839), Vol. 2, p. 544 and Vol. 3, p. 381. The *Complete Works of Josephus* (1924), a "new and revised edition based on Havercamp's translation," is actually a verbatim copy of Whiston, who employed Havercamp's text; cf. Vol. 2, p. 555 and Vol. 3, p. 464.

he "gave Herod the position of procurator of all Syria, for the (Roman) procurators were forbidden to take any measures without his concurrence."[20] This improves on Whiston in one important respect: whereas Whiston's rendering of the *BJ* allows that the advice merely needed to be sought, not necessarily followed, Thackeray correctly eliminates this interpretation (following the Greek). Nevertheless, this same error is repeated in many of the German and French translations (below).

Even the Penguin edition of the *BJ* by Williamson gets the office correct, though it is less loyal to the text, stating that "he made him procurator of all Syria, with power to veto any decision of the other procurators."[21] Unfortunately Feldman's translation and commentary has so far skipped book 1 of the *BJ* and only reached book 10 of the *AJ*.[22] And though Cornfeld's edition of the *BJ* gives a correct translation, it has a confusing and not very useful commentary (discussed below). Closely following Thackeray, he writes that Caesar "awarded Herod the position of procurator of all Syria so that other (Roman) procurators were forbidden from taking measures without his concurrence."[23]

These passages have fared worse in other languages in the last century. In German, the *AJ* passage is rendered by Clementz as "Auch brachte er ihn in nähere Beziehungen zu den Statthaltern von Syrien, denen er auftrug, nichts ohne des Herodes Zustim-

---

[20] The *AJ* passage was translated by Ralph Marcus and edited by Allen Wilkgren when Thackeray's death prevented its completion; here quoted from *Josephus in Ten Volumes*, Vol. 8 (1963), p. 175; the *BJ* passage was translated by Thackeray, here quoted from *Josephus in Nine Volumes*, Vol. 2 (1927), p. 189.

[21] G.A. Williamson, *The Jewish War* (1959), p. 74.

[22] Mason [n. 7]; this began with vol. 3 (out of sequence) in 2000, containing bks. 1-4 of the *AJ*, with tr. and commentary by Louis Feldman; other volumes have followed, unfortunately many still out of sequence, and the relevant books for our purposes have not been completed. In 2008, v. "1b" was published containing only bk. 2 of the *BJ.*; and the *AJ* has been brought up only to bk. 10 (in v. 5, released in 2005).

[23] Gaalya Cornfeld, *Josephus: The Jewish War, Newly Translated with Extensive Commentary & Archaeological Background Illustrations* (1982), p. 76.

mung vorzunehmen,"[24] "He also brought him into a closer relationship with the governors of Syria, instructing them not to act without Herod's approval," the key word here being 'Statthalter' which regularly means "governor" and thus repeats the old errors of Lodge, Thompson and Price. This error is repeated in his translation of the *BJ*, "ernannte er ihn sogar zum Statthalter von ganz Syrien, sodass die unter ihm stehenden Landpfleger keinerlei Anordnungen treffen durften, ohne vorher seine Zustimmung einzuholen,"[25] "He even appointed him governor [*Statthalter*] of all Syria, so that the ministers [*Landpfleger*] under him were not allowed to issue any orders at all without first seeking his approval." Thus, not only did he render *epitropos* as 'Statthalter', but *epitropoi* as 'Landpfleger', which literally means "Land-keeper" and usually refers to prefects (and in modern parlance "governors"), and here, as men giving orders, that is certainly what Clementz had in mind.

The *BJ* passage is given by Berendts & Grass as "Er setzte ihn aber über die Syrischen Gewalthaber und über alle Befehlshaber, auf dass nichts ohne seinen Befehl täten,"[26] "He even put him in charge of the Syrian leader and of all commanders, in that they did nothing without his command." The key words here, 'Gewalthaber' and 'Befehlshaber' mean, respectively, 'power-holder' and 'command-holder', neither of which correctly grasps the sense of a procurator, but instead entails actual political-military power. Strictly speaking this is a translation from the medieval Slavic version of Josephus, and though the authors extensively compare it against the Greek text, their German is intended to be loyal to the Slavic. Nevertheless, they claim in a footnote, without argument or explanation, that "the facts are better put in the Slavic" than in the *BJ* or *AJ*. But if they actually have done justice to the Slavic, this clearly is not so.

Michel & Bauernfeind also provide a translation of the *BJ*, writing "Er setze ihn aber auch…als Verweser über ganz Syrien ein, sodaß es den Prokuratoren nicht gestattet war, ohne vorherige Be-

---

[24] Heinrich Clementz, *Des Flavius Josephus Jüdische Altertümer*, Bd. 2 (1959; orig. 1900), p. 353.

[25] Heinrich Clementz, *Geschichte des Jüdischen Krieges* (1923), p. 114.

[26] Alexander Berendts & Konrad Grass, *Vom Jüdischen Kriege Buch I-IV* (1924), p. 138.

ratung mit ihm Anordnungen zu treffen,"[27] "He also appointed him as administrator over all Syria, so that the procurators could not act without first meeting with him for advice." Here the key word is 'Verweser' which refers to any kind of administrator, deputy or agent, and thus is a slightly better choice on account of its ambiguity. But this word has been used to translate other roles (besides procurator: *vicarius, curator, administrator, patricius, patronus, dioecetes*) including those equivalent to "governor" (*praetor, praefectus, legatus*).[28] So 'Verweser' is not a good choice here, especially when *epitropos* is already rendered 'Prokurator' when speaking of the other procurators, but not when translating the very same word as the office given to Herod, incorrectly implying that Josephus said something different here.

The most recent German translation of the *BJ*, by Hermann Endrös, is here the very worst of all, following Clementz a bit too loyally. He writes "machte er ihn sogar zum Statthalter von ganz Syrien, so daß es den einzelnen Statthaltern nicht möglich war, ohne Beratung und Frühlungnahme mit Herodes Verfügungen zu treffen,"[29] "He even made him governor of all Syria, so that it was not possible for the individual governors to make any provisions without consultation and prior contact with Herod." Here the only word used in both cases is the incorrect 'Statthalter', governor, in the singular and plural.

More confusion lies in the French translation of the *BJ* by Pelletier, which says "Il fit aussi de lui un préfet de toute la Syrie... puisqu'il interdit alors aux préfets de prendre aucune mesure sans l'accord d'Hérode,"[30] "He also made him a *prefect* of all Syria ... since he then prohibited the *prefects* from taking any action without the agreement of Herod." This splits the difference between governor (= legate = propraetor or proconsul) and procurator by translating *epitropos* as prefect, but this is still incorrect, since there were distinct differences between a prefect and a procurator, as we shall see. A correct translation in French would be *procurateur*. Thus,

---

[27] Otto Michel & Otto Bauernfeind, *Der Jüdische Krieg* (1960), p. 107.

[28] See "Verweser" in Jacob Grimm & Wilhelm Grimm, *Deutsches Wörterbuch* (1956), esp. §1 and §2a-c, for Latin equivalents and history of usage.

[29] Hermann Endrös, *Der Jüdische Krieg* (1964), p. 94.

[30] André Pelletier, *Josèphe: Guerre des Juifs* (1975), v. 1, p. 120.

Savinel renders the *BJ* quite rightly as "Il nomma Hérode procurateur général de Syrie, interdisant aux procurateurs de prendre une décision sans le consulter,"[31] "he named Herod procurator-general of Syria, forbidding the procurators to make a decision without consulting him." In contrast, the popular D'Andilly translation misses the mark, giving for the *AJ*: "fut d'ordonner aux gouverneurs de Syrie de ne rien faire que par son avis,"[32] "[Augustus] gave orders to the governors of Syria to do nothing but what was according to [Herod's] opinion"; and for the *BJ*: "défendit à tous les gouverneurs de rien faire sans le conseil d'Hérode,"[33] "[Augustus] forbade the governors to do anything without Herod's counsel." Both use the incorrect 'gouverneur'. Unfortunately the Nodet translation and commentary has not as yet reached book 15 of the *AJ*.[34]

In the end, the oldest 20th century French translation turns out to be the best, though still not as precise as Thackeray's English. This is the monumental edition by Théodore Reinach.[35] Later French translators in my opinion have not uniformly improved on it. Here, Joseph Chamonard gives the *AJ* passage as "Il décida, en outre, de l'associer à l'autorité des procurateurs de Syrie, auxquels il enjoignit de ne rien faire sans prendre l'avis d'Hérode,"[36] "He decided, in addition, to introduce him to the authority of the procurators of Syria, enjoining them to do nothing without getting Herod's advice," and René Harmand gives for the *BJ* "il nomma aussi procurateur de toute la Syrie…car il défendit que les procurateurs puissent prendre aucune décision sans son conseil,"[37] "He also appointed him procurator of all Syria…as he forbade the procurators to make any decision without his advice." Indeed, Chamonard even

---

[31] Pierre Savinel, *La Guerre des Juifs* (1977), p. 178.

[32] Arnauld D'Andilly (adapted by J.A.C. Buchon), *Histoire Ancienne des Juifs & la Guerre des Juifs contre les Romains 66-70 ap. J.-C.* (1973), p. 489.

[33] Ibid., p. 671.

[34] Etienne Nodet, *Les Antiquités Juives*, begun in 1992; v. 5 with bks. 10 & 11 was published in 2010.

[35] Théodore Reinach, *Oeuvres Complètes de Flavius Josèphe* (1900-1928).

[36] Ibid., v. 3 (1904), p. 347.

[37] Ibid., v. 5 (1912), p. 80. This was revised by Reinach.

appends a footnote to his translation of this passage making explicit the very distinction other translators have missed: "*epitropoi* designates, strictly speaking, the procurators, not the governor of the province," adding that "the way it is put in the *BJ* is most likely exaggerated," perhaps thinking along the same lines as Otto (below).

In conclusion, some confusion still exists about how to translate these passages, but the current English authorities are the most accurate, with whose meaning my own translation concurs. If the received text is correct, as it seems to be, in the *AJ* Josephus claims that Augustus "mixed" (*egkatameignumi*) Herod with those who were "procurating" (*epitropeuô*) Syria, and "commanded" (*entellô*) that they do "everything" (*ta panta*) "after" (*meta*) Herod's "opinion" (*gnômê*). In the *BJ*, clearly describing the same decision of Augustus, Josephus claims that Augustus had "appointed" (*kathistêmi*) Herod "procurator" (*epitropos*) of "all Syria" (*Syrias holês*), "so that" (*hôs* + infinitive = *hôste*) it would be "allowed" (*exesti*) to "the procurators" (*hoi epitropoi*) to "manage" (*dioikeô*) "nothing" (*mêden*) "contrary to" (*dicha*) Herod's "advice" (*symboulia*). The translation is straightforward and, apart from the surprising meaning, there is no obvious corruption of the text.

4. The Interpretations

This passage has garnered a lot of attention, but rarely more than cursory treatment.[38] Sandmel took it to mean something impossible to conceive, that a Jewish king was assigned a proconsular command over a crucial Eastern province (or perhaps the prefecture of part of it), by Augustus of all men, who was at the time still playing at having restored the traditional Roman republic. The Senate would have been shocked (and might have started sharpening some knives), and it is doubtful Augustus would have even considered something so insulting to the Roman political mind. Hence most scholars have rejected the notion that Herod was chief *procurator* over a whole province, much less governor. For instance, there is a footnote in Marcus' translation of the *AJ* stating that "according to

---

[38] I will address all distinct arguments forthwith, but some of them are discussed or repeated in other works such as W. Horbury et al., *The Cambridge History of Judaism*, vol. 3 (1999): pp. 118-122; or L.-M. Günther, *Herodes der Große* (2005): p. 135.

B.J. i.399, Augustus appointed Herod 'procurator of all Syria', which seems an exaggeration unless we read 'Coele-Syria' (*Koilês Syrias*) for 'all Syria' (*holês Syrias*),"[39] citing Walter Otto (discussed below), who actually rejects that emendation, but shared Marcus' astonishment that Josephus would say something so remarkable. This conjecture actually goes all the way back to Marquardt and is properly to be attributed to him, as we shall see.

Schürer, of course, is typically the first authority to consult on Judaean affairs. He remarks that:

> [T]he unbounded confidence which Augustus had in him is shown conspicuously in this, that he, perhaps only during the period of Agrippa's absence from the East…gave orders to the procurators of Syria (Coele-Syria?) to take counsel with Herod in regard to all important matters.[40]

Schürer plays down the text by suggesting that the appointment was temporary (a stop-gap for the absence of Agrippa), and as Marcus suggests, perhaps only relating to Coele-Syria. But he correctly characterizes the position as a rare honor, certainly a sign of astonishing trust on the part of Augustus. But Schürer still sees the office as merely an advisory one, contrary to the more adamant language of Josephus. In a footnote Schürer supplies his reasoning: Josephus' words are "somewhat obscure" and notably different in each passage, and…

> from the nature of the thing it cannot refer to a formal subordination of the procurators of Syria under Herod, but, as even the expression *symboulias* in the latter [*AJ*] passage shows, only to the fact that the procurators as finance officers for the province were told to make use of the counsel of Herod. Also it is probable that for *Syrias holês* (resp. *Syrias*) we should read *Syrias Koilês* [for this Schürer cites Marquardt (see below)—ed.] … One should not take the note too seriously, since it evidently comes from the glorifying pen of Nicolas of Damascus.

---

[39] Marcus, ibid. [n. 10].

[40] Emil Schürer, *A History of the Jewish People in the Time of Jesus Christ* (1890), eng. tr. by John MacPherson (1994), 1st div., vol. 1, p. 453.

Thus, Schürer believes that *symboulias* can only refer to Herod's acting as a *consilium*, a source of advice, without any formal authority, but this does not explain the way the word is used ("so the procurators can do nothing without his advice" does not sound like such an informal arrangement) nor does it address the fact that, following the *BJ*, Josephus apparently felt the word *gnômê* was synonymous in meaning here, a more forceful word that means judgement, opinion, will, and that can even be used for the resolutions of councils and verdicts of courts. Schürer also ascribes to the idea of a dropped *kappa* in the *BJ*, no doubt because this would make Josephus' statement somewhat less amazing in scale, but since there is little chance of an identical error simultaneously occurring in the *AJ* we cannot find solace in proposing such an emendation to the *BJ* simply because it looks tempting.

Schürer's one good argument is one that no one else has made a point of noting: Josephus' principal source for the reign of Herod in *AJ* books 14-17 (and presumably for the parallel material in the earlier *BJ*) is the *Histories* of Nicolaus of Damascus, a close friend of Herod, who in turn relied on first-hand knowledge and Herod's own *Memoirs*.[41] From our knowledge of Nicolaus as an unabashed apologist for his friend, Schürer dismisses the element of exaggeration in Josephus as coming from Nicolaus' "glorifying pen." But this argument cuts both ways. For there could be no more expert an authority on Herod's reign than Nicolaus, giving the report substantial authority. Moreover, this particular passage implicates Augustus and thus faced the danger of condemnation as an obvious lie from Rome, which Nicolaus was still keen to court as a supporter of Archelaus, Herod's successor. And Josephus was well-aware of Nicolaus's bias and sufficiently critical of it not to rely solely on him (cf. *AJ* 16.183-7 and 14.9). In fact, we know Josephus consulted Herod's memoirs directly, and "others" (*tois allois*) who wrote about Herod's reign (*AJ* 15.174), so we cannot be sure the passages that concern us come solely from Nicolaus or if they come from him at all. Finally, even granting that Nicolaus exaggerated, and Josephus accepted that exaggeration uncritically, we still cannot say just what the exaggerated elements of the story are. Schürer tries to hit upon them all, but this is *ad hoc*.

More recent scholars have not given the matter sufficient attention. Perowne garbles the details in the one sentence he de-

---

[41] Cf. *FGrH* §90, §236.

votes to the event, writing only that during Caesar's visit to Syria in 20 B.C. Herod "was made one of the procurators of Syria, and the Roman governors enjoined to act always with his advice,"[42] which is incorrect (only the procurators were so enjoined, not the "governors"). Zeitlin also softens the report considerably, along the same lines as Schürer and others, when he says "Augustus Caesar also appointed Herod a sort of counsellor to the procurators of Syria; that is, he gave Herod the privilege of counselling the procurators in all their actions, which was a substantial privilege for one of their client-kings."[43] Indeed it was, but Zeitlin does not explain why he reduces what Josephus actually says to a vague advisory role. And strangely, despite writing nearly 900 pages on Herod the Great, Schalit completely ignores these passages. He only mentions in passing the addition of the lands of Zenodorus, reported in the very same place in both the *AJ* and *BJ*.[44]

Between the works of Perowne and Zeitlin an article appeared by István Hahn whose title gave the appearance of addressing this very issue in substantial detail, but in fact Hahn devoted merely two paragraphs to it out of a staggering 18 pages (the rest dealing instead with Herod's two prior posts as *stratēgos*, which we will address later).[45] He repeats the common practice of downplaying the plain words of Josephus by saying instead that Herod was merely made an "advisor [*Rat*] to the procurators of Syria," and he errs in saying that "The legate [*Der Legat*] of the province was instructed to obey his counsel in every matter,"[46] whereas Josephus mentions only procurators, not the legate of Syria. Hahn also assumes without argument that Herod's prior positions as *stratēgos* of Coele-Syria in 47 and 43 B.C. were somehow related to the position

---

[42] Stewart Perowne, *The Life and Times of Herod the Great* (1959), p. 146.

[43] Solomon Zeitlin, *The Rise and Fall of the Judaean State* (1967), vol. 2, p. 43.

[44] Abraham Schalit, *König Herodes: Der Mann und sein Werk* (1969), p. 327.

[45] István Hahn, "Herodes als Prokurator," in Elisabeth Welskopf, ed., *Neue Beiträges zur Geschichte der Alten Welt*, Bd. II (*Römisches Reich*) (1965), pp. 25-43; presented at a conference in 1962. Only the first and last pages (25 and 35) address the appointment in 20 B.C., and only the last does so in any detail.

[46] Ibid., p. 25. (Translations from German/French throughout are my own.)

of *epitropos* given him by Augustus in the year 20 (based in part on his support of Marquardt's implausible 'Coele-Syria' conjecture), but as we shall see later, such an equivalence is neither logical nor implied by anything Josephus says.

Hahn tries to build this equivalence circuitously by proposing that in both *BJ* 1.399 and 1.225 the "whole Syria" could be a translation error from an Aramaic form for Coele-Syria in the 'original' *BJ*. This argument fails for two reasons: first, it has since been demonstrated through grammatical and thematic analysis that the *BJ* as we have it is not a mere translation as Josephus claims, but clearly an original Greek composition;[47] second, the *hapasês* in *BJ* 1.225 also appears in *AJ* 14.280 but is not associated there with *Syrias* but is matched in both passages with the cognates *epimeleia* and *epimelêtês* (see note below). Moreover, this proposed error would make little sense of *AJ* 15.360 since that was not even reportedly a translation from Aramaic or Hebrew (it was directly composed for a Gentile audience, as explained in *AJ* 1.pr.5-10) and no word corresponding to "whole" appears there.

Uncertain of this connection himself, Hahn concludes:

> Josephus provides the following information, which is by no means clear: when Augustus visited the province of Asia ten years after the conclusion of Actium (20 B.C.), he gave Herod the territories of Zenodorus and appointed him at the same time the *epitropos* of all Syria (*BJ*) or—according to the more careful formulation in the *AJ*—placed him among the procurators of Syria and ordered them to do everything according to his opinion. These passages contradict each other: if Herod was *epitropos* of all Syria, he could not be called *symboulos* of the current *epitropoi* at the same time!

Hahn confusedly sees a contradiction where there is in fact a corroboration: when all the procurators of Syria have to obey Herod, then Herod is *de facto* the procurator of all Syria. The *BJ*, as usual, merely compresses what is spelled out in the *AJ*. Contributing to Hahn's confusion is apparently the ambiguity of the word *symboulia*, which can mean simply *concilia*, but can also mean *gnômê* (and Jose-

---

[47] See Steve Mason, *Josephus and the New Testament* (1992), pp. 58-9, with Attridge and Bilde cited on p. 83.

phus clearly uses them as synonyms in his two versions of this event). Hahn continues:

> So the information Josephus provides can only be regarded as historically reliable if the allegedly "procuratorial" powers of Herod regarding "all Syria" consisted simply of the fact that the current Legates [*die jeweiligen Legaten*] of the province were obliged to seek his advice [*Rat*] in every important question. The word *epitropos* is thus not to be taken in the technical, legal sense. The right to be asked by the governors [*die Statthalter*] of Syria did not by any means extend whatever existing procuratorial powers Herod already had—it could not have provided this—but, surely, this was merely what Josephus understood about procuratorial powers. Given the expansion and political-military importance of this kingdom in the border region between the Roman and Parthian empires, a constant mutual contact [*Kontakt*] between the governors [*den Statthaltern*] of the most important eastern province and the most powerful client king could only be desired. As far as we know, it worked in reverse for Herod as well, so that in difficult diplomatic and family questions he had to consult the Legate [*den Legaten*] of Syria.

Hahn, like so many scholars who have examined this issue, clearly does not understand the legal distinction between legates and procurators, and consequently the above paragraph is full of confusions. Since Josephus does not mention legates, but specifically says only *procurators* had to obey Herod, Hahn's entire reasoning collapses: for instead of what Hahn sees as obscurity, it is because of the specificity of Josephus that we *should* take *epitropos* here in its technical, legal sense. Indeed, Hahn forces himself into an interpretation that is trite and trivial: he claims that Josephus merely meant that Herod and the governors of Syria had to confer with each other. But since that is obvious, and certainly had always been the case already, there could be no reason for Josephus to describe this general political reality in the specific and particular way that he does. It is clear that Herod is being appointed in 20 B.C. to a position with some real and notable authority, and that Josephus is not talking about a general arrangement of cooperation between Roman leaders and client kings.

Some years later, Michael Grant picked up the problem, concluding without argument that

> Augustus entrusted Herod with some sort of an appointment in connection with the province of Syria. Probably he was made financial adviser to the imperial agent (procurator) who stood second only to the provincial governor in a quasi-independent position; and his function may have included lucrative duties relating to the collection of taxes.[48]

Without stating his reasons, in two sentences Grant rejects what Josephus plainly says, that Herod was appointed (chief) procurator with supreme authority over all the other procurators of Syria, and proposes instead that he was made an "advisor" to the (chief) procurator of Syria, perhaps having something to do with tax collection. Grant is also wrong about the imperial procurator being in some sense "second" in command (as will be demonstrated later). His use of the vague word "quasi-independent" also dodges the question of what sort of power, official or otherwise, Herod had just received.

Smallwood gives the issue a sentence and a footnote, concluding that "Augustus appointed Herod financial adviser to the province of Syria with powers to supervise all actions by the procurators there; but what this amounted to in practice is obscure, as there is no record of his advice being either proffered or sought."[49] She thus shares the predominant view that it was merely an "advisory" role (or maybe "supervisory," whatever that would entail), but uniquely bases her reticence on the fact that we have no examples of Herod's acting in this capacity to judge from. In a corresponding footnote, Smallwood says that the *BJ* version "is clearly absurd," citing Otto (again as if he supports the theory when in fact he does not) that it is "possible" Josephus had actually written 'Coele-Syria', and thus only meant that "Herod was given some specific control over the Decapolis," similar to previous appointments of Herod as *stratêgos*. Smallwood elaborates, concluding that in 47 B.C. Sextus Julius Caesar had appointed Herod "to a post in

---

[48] Michael Grant, *Herod the Great* (1971), p. 149.

[49] E. Mary Smallwood, *The Jews Under Roman Rule: From Pompey to Diocletian (A Study in Political Relations)* (1981), pp. 87-8.

the direct service of the Roman government in Syria as military governor of the Decapolis and the city of Samaria, former Jewish possessions,"[50] a position later confirmed by Cassius.[51] This supposed parallel, also proposed by Hahn (above), will be addressed in detail later, but we have already noted that this 'Coele-Syria' conjecture is unacceptable from the start.

Though aware of Smallwood's opinion, Baumann, following Hahn, completely missed the distinction that must be made between 'procurator' and 'governor'. He, too, devotes a single sentence to the issue, which I translate here:

> In 20 B.C. Augustus made the Jewish king the 'advisor' [*der Berater*] to the governor [*der Statthalter*] of Syria; what real authority went along with this remains essentially unclear; one might imagine that in giving this 'role' [*Funktion*] to Herod, a constant contact [*ständiger Kontakt*] regarding all outstanding problems was meant to be established between the most powerful client-king in the East and the governor [*Statthalter*] of the most important eastern province.[52]

By mistaking Josephus as referring to 'the governor' of Syria, Baumann's conjecture is wholly moot, and his reduction of the text to meaning only an 'advisory' role unjustified. Ultimately, Baumann's (repeating Hahn's) interpretation is even more ambiguous than what Josephus actually says (e.g., what exactly does *Kontakt* mean?).

A year before Baumann's work came out, Cornfeld's translation of the *BJ* with 'extensive commentary' was published. He appends a confusing explanation of 1.399 in a sidebar [ibid., n. 23], stating that this meant Herod was made procurator of those provinces already formally annexed to his territory, which is clearly not what Josephus says. Cornfeld confusingly uses the word "province" as a synonym of "territory" throughout his commentary, rather than employing it in the formal Roman sense, a choice certain to confuse less expert readers, as when he says this procuratorial

---

[50] Ibid., p. 45, interpreting *AJ* 14.178-80 and *BJ* 1.212-213.

[51] Ibid., p. 47, interpreting *AJ* 14.278-84 and *BJ* 1.224-9.

[52] Uwe Baumann, *Rom und die Juden: Die römisch-jüdischen Beziehungen von Pompeius bis zum Tode des Herodes (63 v. Chr.-4 v.Chr.)* (1983), p. 213.

power extended over "the provinces south of Damascus up to the borders of Herod's kingdom." Finally, as Cornfeld puts it:

> Imperial procurators were high officials responsible mainly for the collection of taxes paid to Rome. Herod played a certain role in the administration of Syria after the year 20 B.C. (at the zenith of his rule) as a result of the decree of Augustus to the imperial procurators *in provincia* to permit him to take part in their deliberations and decisions.

We will seek greater clarity on this point later, but for now observe that, contrary to the picture painted here, procurators were not officials, but private employees, of widely varying rank and responsibilities, and as such there would have been no need of a 'decree' from Augustus to establish what Josephus describes: as his personal agents, no legal manoeuvre was needed for Augustus to tell them what to do.

Finally, Peter Richardson follows the trend in devoting a single sentence to the question, noting that "In a further mark of his esteem, Augustus gave Herod procuratorial responsibility in Syria, probably confined to border regions, though Josephus's description makes it sound more extensive and important."[53] Again without saying why, Richardson rejects what Josephus says and comes up with his own conjecture that the appointment only concerned "border regions" (probably following Marquardt's conjecture of Coele-Syria for "all Syria"), simply because what Josephus said entailed something "more extensive and important" than Richardson thought possible. Since then only Anthony Barrett has gotten close to a correct analysis of the matter, which corroborates what I will argue here.[54]

---

[53] Peter Richardson, *Herod: King of the Jews and Friend of the Romans* (1996), p. 234.

[54] See Barrett [note 4]. Though correct and valuable in his analysis, Barrett is hesitant to declare a certain conclusion because, I believe, he overlooks the fact that, as we shall see, in principle and in practice the same person could be appointed both procurator and prefect, and Josephus only says that Herod was appointed the one, not the other; by contrast, Eck [note 4], correctly detects the fact of dual appointment, but doesn't discuss Herod in this connection, as he only treats events after 6 A.D.

5. The Meaning of 'Procurator'

All this brings us back to Walter Otto, who writes that "Augustus instructed the officials [*den Beamten*] of the Roman government in Syria to handle affairs there solely in agreement with Herod, but of course gave no legal authority over the province to the vassal Herod, although a passage in Josephus seems to suggest this."[55] He then elaborates in a lengthy footnote what he means, the most anyone had ever written on the subject until Barrett. My translation of his note follows:

> The passages are obscure, and in the one from the *AJ* something is probably missing, but in any case it seems impossible to me to read *epitropos* here in the technical sense of *procurator*, not only because it is a Roman office, but simply the fact that Herod is being granted this title (just as, e.g., in Caesar's grant of such a position to Herod's father, Antipater, the word *epitropos* is not used by Josephus in its technical meaning, cf. *BJ* I 199: *pasês epitropos Ioudaias*; also *AJ* XIV 143 and 166). Naturally it is completely impossible to conclude from this, with Gardthausen, op. cit. I 818, that Herod was appointed chief tax-farmer of Syria [on which see below—ed.]. And it's undesirable to change *holês* in the *BJ* to *Koilês* (as suggested by Marquardt, Röm. St.-V.² I 408, 2, but he incorrectly assesses the whole position of Herod), so one must take the passage from the *BJ* as a huge exaggeration, since it results in the impossibility of putting the vassal Herod over an entire Roman province (cf. p. 19, where the same impossibility has already been rejected once), and instead base the facts on the passage in the *AJ* (particularly the word *gnômê*, the *symboulia* in the *BJ* representing yet another amplification). The emendation of the *holês* to *Koilês* in the *BJ* could well resolve the difficulty, if for instance one puts it on a level with information such as in *BJ* I 213 and *AJ* XIV 180 [where Sextus Julius Caesar, as governor of Syria, makes Herod *stratêgos* of Coele-Syria and Samaria in 47 B.C.—ed.]. Since, however, this emendation creates a contradiction with the passage in the received

---

[55] Walter Otto, "Herodes," *Paulys Realencyclopädie der Classischen Altertumswissenschaft*, Suppl. II (1913), p. 71.

text of the *AJ*, it seems to me that avoiding it is the better method.

Otto's conclusion is somewhat contradictory: he says Augustus instructed "the officials" to follow Herod's orders, but that this was not a legal authority over the province. It is hard to understand how these two states of affairs could be any different: the administration acting "solely" (*durchweg*) in agreement with Herod gives Herod *de facto* legal authority over the province. But Otto is correct that a "vassal" being given command of a Roman province presents an apparent contradiction, and he can only say that Josephus must be exaggerating.

It is strange that Otto never emphasizes that Herod's authority in both passages is specifically restricted to procurators. Josephus pointedly avoids mention of any actual government officials (neither prefects nor legates nor any military officers of any kind), and Otto's translation of *epitropos* as 'Beamte' has become obsolete and is now misleading, thus obscuring this fact further. Today 'der Beamte' usually means a local official, civil servant, or bureaucrat, while forty years ago its most basic meaning was any agent who handled money in trust—as Grimm & Grimm put it, Beamte most readily meant any *munere fungens*.[56] Hence the word might have been a natural choice for Otto, referring (we can suppose) to Caesar's private agents, but today that sense is almost totally lost. Even so, whatever he meant, Otto never points out the distinction Josephus was making, and seems to think (wrongly) that having authority over procurators was equal to having "legal authority" over Syria. Though Otto does admit the passages are not very clear, they are clearer than he makes them out to be.

Otto then gives his reasoning for regarding these passages as exaggerations. He remarks in passing that maybe something is missing from the text of the *AJ* (clearly echoing Niese's remark, discussed earlier). But apart from the incredible thought of a vassal king ruling a Roman province, he principally rejects taking *epitropos* as meaning simply procurator [*Prokurator* = one who has power of attorney] for two reasons: he assumes only Romans could be procurators, and that in a preceding parallel instance the term must have had a different meaning: Julius Caesar's making of Antipater

---

[56] Contrast "Beamte" in the *Oxford-Duden German Dictionary* (1990), with that in the *Deutsches Wörterbuch* (1956).

"*epitropos* of all Judaea." But Otto's reasoning is unsound. On the one hand, Herod was a Roman citizen,[57] and procurators were private employees (as we shall see), and thus there could be no objection to Augustus hiring Herod to manage affairs in Syria as a procurator. Even freedmen could hold that position, so it would not offend the sensibilities of the Roman elite to hire a foreign king to do the same job.[58]

In fact, the precedent Otto points to could well be a similar procuratorship—Otto certainly offers no good reason to think otherwise. This point needs closer examination, as it begins to explain the resolution of the entire difficulty. Josephus writes:

> Caesar declared Hyrcanus quite worthy of the high priesthood, and gave Antipater his choice of office. But Antipater put the choice of honor back on the honor-giver, and he was appointed procurator of all Judaea [*pasês epitropos Ioudaias*] and also received the task [*prosepitunchanô*] of rebuilding the walls of his country that had been torn down. [*BJ* 1.199]

> Caesar appointed Hyrcanus high priest and left it to Antipater to decide upon an office that he would take for himself, but he put the decision back upon Caesar, who appointed him procurator of Judaea [*epitropos tês Ioudaias*]. He also entrusted Hyrcanus with the task of raising up the walls of his country, since Hyrcanus had asked for that favor, for they had been in ruins since Pompey tore them down. [*AJ* 14.143]

These two passages together paint the following picture: Julius Caesar confirmed Hyrcanus in power (he was both king and high priest, which was usually the case until Herod's accession), and honored Hyrcanus' right-hand-man Antipater (Herod's father) with the official title "procurator of all Judaea." Then in the *BJ* Josephus says Antipater was also tasked with rebuilding walls, but in the *AJ* it

---

[57] Client kings usually were, and indeed Herod had inherited his citizenship from his father: *BJ* 1.194; *AJ* 14.137, 16.53.

[58] Freedmen as imperial procurators: P. R. C. Weaver, "Freedmen Procurators in the Imperial Administration," *Historia: Zeitschrift für Alte Geschichte* 14.4 (October 1965), pp. 460-69.

is Hyrcanus who receives this task, having asked permission for it. However, this apparent contradiction is easily resolved by examining exactly what Josephus says. For Hyrcanus could naturally deputize Antipater, now as procurator of Judaea, to actually do the work, and the use of the verb *prosepitunchanô* ("also hit upon, also stumble upon") in the *BJ* suits this interpretation perfectly. Indeed, it is possible that the rebuilding efforts were aided by funds supplied by Caesar himself, which would require a procurator to administer, making further sense of Antipater being given this title. But even absent that conjecture, as procurator of Judaea, Antipater would be the man in charge of any Roman money sent their way, to be used or kept in trust, as well of any lands or other property interests Caesar held in Judaea. Above all, he would be responsible for collecting and managing the tribute owed by Judaea to Caesar.

Alternatively, or additionally, the title of procurator may have meant here an agent of Hyrcanus, not of Caesar. In such a case, Caesar was merely confirming Antipater's position as Hyrcanus' deputy, using Roman legal terms, since both men were Roman citizens (see note above), and an exact title would matter under Roman law. Royal power was usually conceived as a private family affair rather than a public trust, so that, in contrast to a Republic, a *royal* procurator could be in all respects the same as a governor. This last possibility has one strong point in its favor: in *AJ* 14.127 Antipater is described as "the deputy-governor [*epimelêtês*] of Judaea [or 'of Jewish affairs'] by order of Hyrcanus." The title *epimelêtês* ("one who cares for") often refers to an official curator or deputy (and more commonly the holder of a public trust rather than a private employee). So this can refer more easily to a governor or even a general, than can *epitropos* ("one who is entrusted with"), but otherwise these terms are similar in meaning.[59] It makes sense that Caesar simply conferred upon Antipater the position he already had by order of Hyrcanus, but now in Roman terms, and with Caesar's sanction, thus securing Antipater against any changes of mind that might strike Hyrcanus. This would have ample precedent in the conduct of affairs in Hellenistic kingdoms, where kings would put all the money in the hands of agents who accompanied their generals, thus hindering their generals from hatching designs of their

---

[59] E.g. Josephus uses them interchangeably of the men who supervised the money of priests: *BJ* 2.123-135.

own.⁶⁰ It also makes sense of later passages where Antipater is clearly building his power base by collecting and spending the king's revenues (e.g. *AJ* 14.163-4). Consequently, we have no reason to conclude with Otto that "the word *epitropos* is not used by Josephus in its technical meaning" in this instance.

Otto has also plainly misread the meaning of *AJ* 14.166, which he also offers as evidence for his position. There, Josephus writes, in the words of Antipater's wealthiest subjects (complaining to Hyrcanus), "for Antipater and his sons are not procurators [*epitropoi*] of your affairs now, don't let that idea into your head at all, but have obviously conspired to be despots," and as evidence they offer the fact that Herod had conducted illegal executions. It seems Otto took this to be evidence either that Antipater was not a procurator (though in fact it proves he was, since the meaning of the passage is that he has overstepped his role as procurator), or that Josephus was here using the term without its technical meaning (though there is no particular reason to think so). But even if Josephus was here using the term metaphorically, it does not mean he has done so elsewhere, particularly since this is not Josephus speaking, but a rhetorical speech put in the mouth of advisors to Antipater, where the employment of such a metaphor would have made the chastising remark all the sharper ("these guys aren't acting like procurators, but despots!").

When we examine all uses of *epitropos* by Josephus we find that he was not very inclined to use it non-technically or metaphorically. In pre-Roman contexts it often referred to a king's steward,⁶¹ except when used as part of the periphrastic title "steward of the kingdom" (*epitropos tês basileias*) or "steward of the empire" (*epitropos tês archês*) which referred to a regent.⁶² Again, given the private, family nature of royal power, in contrast to the distinctions made between public and private rights in Roman law, a king's procurator could effectively be a governor, but this concept would not translate into an Augustan context. When the term did not

---

⁶⁰ On both the private nature of royal wealth and the division of military and finance officers (*stratêgoi* and *oikonomoi*), cf. Peter Green, *Alexander to Actium: The Historical Evolution of the Hellenistic Age* (1990), pp. 187-200.

⁶¹ E.g. *AJ* 7.268, 18.194 (a slave as king's steward); *VJ* 126; *BJ* 1.487.

⁶² E.g. *AJ* 10.5, 12.360, 15.65, 20.31; *BJ* 1.209.

mean steward or regent, it was used for a variety of official deputies (in the Davidic kingdom, for example) that resembled Roman procuratorships, and is typically distinguished from offices of real power. For instance, in *AJ* 7.369 Solomon places *epitropoi* in charge of certain treasuries, villages, fields, and beasts, while *other* men are appointed governors (archons), generals (hegemons), centurions (hekatontarchs) and platoon commanders (taxiarchs). The role of *epitropoi* is typically financial,[63] and distinguished from military or judicial power.[64] Even a king's son could have one,[65] or a Roman emperor's mother.[66] Only once does Josephus use the concept in a clearly non-technical way.[67]

In strictly Roman contexts, Josephus appears to always use the word in its technical sense. Josephus never uses it for a person of senatorial rank. He describes Herennius Capito as a procurator of the particular town of Jamnia, demanding the payment of tribute owed to Caesar (*AJ* 18.158); and Sabinus as "Caesar's procurator of Syrian affairs" overstepping his authority by persuading soldiers to help him seize money owed to Caesar, forcing the governor to intervene (*AJ* 17.221ff.; *BJ* 2.16ff.). Josephus also refers generally to Caesar's *epitropoi* as men who collected money (*AJ* 16.26.). There is one notable exception: he often uses the word in reference to the prefects of Judaea,[68] and one might infer from this that Josephus is using the term loosely as synonymous with prefect. However, this equation has no other precedent in his writings. Since these prefects were also procurators (as we will see later), Josephus could still be using the term accurately, with its technical meaning. Though it is significant that Josephus thinks of them primarily as procurators, this may have more to do with the theme of his history (e.g. the oppressive abuse of Roman taxation, and the inap-

---

[63] E.g. *AJ* 8.59, 8.162; *BJ* 2.14.

[64] E.g. *AJ* 9.247, 11.61, 12.221; in *CA* 1.98 having the powers of an *epitropos* is distinguished from "all the other authority of a king."

[65] *J* 17.69; *BJ* 5.592.

[66] *J* 19.276 (a slave steward of Antonia, mother of Claudius).

[67] *AJ* 10.278, where the verbal form is used to refer to divine providence (via God's stewardship of the universe).

[68] *AJ* 15.360, 17.221, 20.107, etc.; *BJ* 1.538, 2.16, 2.117, etc.

propriate Jewish response to this) than with him using 'procurator' as synonymous with 'prefect'. For Josephus otherwise distinguishes *epitropoi* from hegemons (which generically encompassed all governors, including prefects) and military officers,[69] and the previous evidence supports the notion that Josephus always had such a distinction in mind. It is also clear that Josephus knew the procurator of Judaea had special powers beyond a mere procuratorship: he knew the Judaean procurator was also called a prefect or a governor,[70] and when the office began under Coponius in 6 A.D., Josephus introduces it in the *AJ* as one "governing Judaea with authority over everything" rather than as a procuratorship,[71] and in the *BJ* he says Coponius was sent as a procurator "who also took from Caesar the authority to kill," i.e. he was *also* made a proper prefect with *ius gladii*,[72] hence Josephus did not assume that procurators had such powers otherwise.

There are two other points made by Otto. First, Otto rests his case that "putting the vassal Herod over an entire Roman province" is an "impossibility" on an earlier parallel conclusion. The event in question is the assignment to Herod in 43 B.C. of a position of power in Syria, with a substantial army and navy, by Cassius and Brutus as they went to face Octavian (the later Augustus) and Marcus Antonius in the Roman civil war. But Otto's disbelief is not that justified. The situation of these men was desperate, they had to resort to extreme measures to cover the Eastern frontier and maintain a source of supplies while they brought the bulk of their forces to fight for control of Rome, and consequently it would not be surprising in this instance if they gave excessive and overreaching powers to an allied king-to-be. Whereas, in contrast, the situation of Augustus in 20 B.C. was the normative behavior of a proconsul in peacetime acting legally (or at least wishing to appear as such) within a unified Roman empire. This still produces an *a fortiori* argument: if it was an amazing action for Cassius and Brutus, one could conclude, as Otto does, that it was a truly inconceivable one for Augustus. However, this argument does not actually

---

[69] E.g. *AJ* 18.170, 19.292; *BJ* 6.238, 7.9.

[70] I.e. *eparchos*: *AJ* 18.33, 19.363; *hêgemôn*: *AJ* 18.55.

[71] I.e. *hêgêsomenos Ioudaiôn têi epi pasin exousiai*: *AJ* 18.2.

[72] I.e. *mechri tou kteinein labôn para Kaisaros exousian*: *BJ* 2.117.

apply to the action of Augustus, since Cassius and Brutus made Herod the *epimelêtês* of all the forces remaining in Syria (*BJ* 1.225; *AJ* 14.280), as *stratêgos* of Coele-Syria (*AJ* 14.280), not an *epitropos*, the latter being a substantially different and certainly less significant position.

Josephus does appear to say that this special appointment by Cassius and Brutus made Herod "deputy-governor" (*epimelêtês*) of "all Syria" (*Surias hapasês*) in the *BJ*, but, unlike our present case with Augustus, the passage in the *AJ* expands and clarifies the brevity of the *BJ*: it says Herod was given the "whole care" of the "army" in Syria (*straton...tên epimeleian hapasan AJ* 14.280), not a formal position of deputy-governorship of all Syria (that is, as an administrative province with legal jurisdiction over Roman citizens), and thus *epimelêtês* is probably used non-technically here. Smallwood proposes that (in the *BJ*) *Syrias hapasês epimelêtên* "is probably an error" for *stratêgon Koilês Syrias* (the exact words of the *AJ*),[73] but it seems more likely an error (or a deliberate metonymy) for *tên epimeleian hapasan*, since the two key words here are nearly the same and appear adjacent to eachother in both the *BJ* and the *AJ*. It is remotely possible that Josephus originally wrote, or intended to write, *Syrias hapanta epimelêtên*, "the whole caretaker of Syria," since a scribal mistake of *-anta* for *-ês* is not only feasible, but here likely, by confusion with either the proximity of *Syrias* or the *-ês* termination on the otherwise masculine *epimelêtês* (and indeed taking *hapanta* with *epimelêtên* is the more difficult reading). But such an emendation is not needed, since the received text can already be read as having the same meaning. Smallwood's argument about two different positions being implied here is thus moot: Josephus is talking about a single state of affairs in both cases, not two separate offices. The term *epimelêtês* in the *BJ* merely picks up the non-technical *epimeleia* in the *AJ*, as a description of the *consequences* of making Herod the official *stratêgos* of Coele-Syria at that time.

Thus, this does not serve as a parallel for *epitropos*. For *epimelêtês* is not a technical word for a Roman office anyway, thus leaving Josephus greater license for its use: it can describe a prefecture (*AJ* 18.89) or a governorship (*AJ* 17.6) on the one hand, or a property manager on the other (*BJ* 2.123, 129, 134), even those whom King David appointed to build the temple (*AJ* 7.364) or take care of city walls (*AJ* 7.67). And unlike this case under Cassius and Bru-

---

[73] Smallwood, op. cit. [n. 49], p. 47, n. 8.

tus, in the Augustan case both the *AJ* and *BJ* completely agree on the term used and Herod's apparent powers. It is important to note the fact that *epitropos*, and its verbal cognate *epitropeuô*, always carry the forceful if not official connotation of taking charge, whereas *epimeleia* first and foremost means just "care bestowed upon, attention paid to," an informal notion, and *epimelêtês*, though it can refer to military commands, often denotes a financial role (as seen above). In the same way, Herod's vast benefaction of grain to all Judaea and neighboring territories during a famine is called an *epimeleia* (*AJ* 15.315), as is Agrippa's appointment by Claudius to the task of refurbishing the Temple (*AJ* 20.222), and also the Jews' custody and care of the priestly vestments (*AJ* 18.90). Thus, Herod's position in Syria "as a whole" under Cassius and Brutus may have been one of controlling funds and supply lines, or providing for the military defense of all of Syria from his official strategic position in only Coele-Syria. This is implied by what Josephus says in *BJ* 1.225, where Herod's role in providing *tas chreias* ("useful things," possibly equipment and supplies) is stated as the reason for giving him this *epimeleia* in the first place. He might command an army to that end, but not hold supreme military command in Syria, and thus Josephus may simply be saying that Syria was then *de facto* protected solely by Herod's forces (Roman legions having to be posted elsewhere).[74] The financial connotations, and the theme of "care" that Josephus' words promote, suits such a role. The specific mention of Coele-Syria also supports this interpretation, since this was a precious source of supply for the armies of Cassius and Brutus, and a region none were better positioned to defend and man-

---

[74] On the Roman use of client kings and their armies in this way (and Herod in particular) see Denis Saddington, "Client Kings' Armies under Augustus: The Case of Herod," in David Jacobson and Nikos Kokkinos, eds., *Herod and Augustus: Papers Presented at the IJS Conference, 21st-23rd June 2005* (2009), pp. 303-23.

age at that time than the Hasmoneans.[75] And since this appointment sounds a lot like the one made by Sextus five years earlier (see above), it is reasonable to take this as simply a confirmation of Herod in an office he already held. Hahn equates this with a *strategia* established in the area by previous Hellenistic kings, and argues that the position given to Herod in 47 and 43 B.C. was just a carryover of this.[76] I think this connection is inconclusive, and the point not very helpful, since the Romans could have modified the powers or borders involved and thus little can be established by seeking an analogy with Greek practice in this case. But if Hahn is correct, this also supports the view that the positions in 47 and 43 were identical and plausible. Therefore, we cannot say from this instance that Josephus tended to overstate the powers given to Herod by Romans, certainly not in a way that would undermine what he says Herod received from Augustus in 20 B.C.

Nevertheless, Otto argues that this action of Cassius and Brutus could not have happened because Appian says otherwise. Appian reports that "Cassius left his nephew (*adelphidoun*) in Syria with one legion (*enos telous*) and sent his cavalry in advance into Cappadocia" (*Civil War* = *BC* 4.63). Otto believes this refutes Jose-

---

[75] What was Coele-Syria? Smallwood, op. cit. [n. 49], p. 45, n. 4, makes a case that Josephus can only mean by 'Coele-Syria' in this case (though not in every case) 'Decapolis' for three reasons (see also Barrett [n. 4], p. 283): (1) this equation had wide precedent (cf. Abraham Schalit, *Scripta Hierosolymitana* 1 [1954], pp. 64-77; Smallwood also suggests that extant coinage, and Claudius Ptolemy, *Geog.* 5.14, 18, corroborate this); (2) it was made by Josephus elsewhere (*AJ* 13.355-6, 192; 14.79; 16.275; and *BJ* 1.103, 155); and (3) it is required here by the fact that the Lebanon-Antilebanon valley also given this name was at the time ruled by the Ituraean king Ptolemy. Though 'Coele-Syria' could also mean all Syria and Palestine together, this meaning is impossible here, for that would put Herod above Hyrcanus, who was then king of Judaea, and the term would also already encompass Samaria, making specific mention of that territory redundant in the earlier parallel assignment to Herod of the same command by Sextus in 47 B.C. (*BJ* 1.213 and *AJ* 14.180). Samaria is also adjacent to the Decapolis, making a command of "Samaria and Coele-Syria" quite logical if "Decapolis" was meant. Hahn argues against this equation on various grounds (op. cit. [n. 45], pp. 28-31), and he favors the Lebanon-Antilebanon valley. Both are vital production centers key to the success of any military campaign. I do not intend to resolve this dispute since I do not believe it is relevant to what happened in 20 B.C.

[76] Hahn, op. cit. [n. 45], pp. 26-28.

phus, but Appian is not referring to the same event. Cassius left a legion with his nephew, according to Appian's narrative, before Cassius reduced Asia and Rhodes, and thus well before he marshalled everything he had for the great confrontation at Philippi. In contrast, Josephus is reporting that Herod was given command in Syria as Cassius and Brutus left for Macedonia, and thus *after* the actions in Asia and Rhodes. There certainly were no Roman legions in Syria at that time: all were going with Cassius, if they had not been sent ahead already, and the dispositions in Syria had already changed even before that (cf. e.g. *BC* 4.74). Nothing can be inferred from Appian's silence regarding Herod, since Appian never mentions the affairs of Herod. In the whole surviving corpus of Appian, a mere five words are devoted to the king: *idoumaiōn de kai samareōn hērōdēn*, when Antony marched east against Parthia, he made "Herod [king] of Idoumaia and Samaria" (*BC* 5.75). This is simply one item in a quick list of the kings set up by Antony in various places at the time, and is not well informed (it fails to mention the more important fact that he was made king of Judaea, and still had to win his kingdom by the spear). Thus, Appian clearly had no detailed sources on Herod. Since Appian is notorious for just this sort of patch-work source-dependency,[77] Otto is quite wrong to regard him as a better authority than Josephus on this point.

Finally, Otto confusingly draws exactly the opposite conclusion from Schürer regarding the relationship of the two words *gnômê* in the *AJ* and *symboulia* in the *BJ*. Whereas Schürer thought *symboulia* entailed a merely advisory role (thus implying that *gnômê* was the exaggeration), Otto thinks *gnômê* justifies the weaker conclusion of a non-official relationship and that *symboulia* is the exaggeration. I think if any such argument is to be advanced, Schürer's is the correct one, for *gnômê* is stronger, having readier official implications than *symboulia*, which has readier links to the informal concept of *concilia*. However, if Otto instead had his eye on the *dicha* in the *BJ*, which does unambiguously assert what the *meta* in the *AJ* implies, then his view (perhaps like Chamonard's, above) might make sense, since he clearly wants Josephus to say that they merely had to seek, not necessarily follow, Herod's advice, though that is not what Josephus is saying. Even the *meta…gnômês* of the *AJ* must be strained to bring out such a weaker idea, and the *BJ* outright ex-

---

[77] Cf. Gregory Bucher, "The Origins, Program, and Composition of Appian's *Roman History*," *TAPA* 130 (2000), pp. 411-458.

cludes it. We should sooner regard Josephus as intending the same meaning in both passages, and merely varying his idiom. Although it remains possible that he took the opportunity to correct in the *AJ* some such mistakes made in the *BJ*, the meaning of these two passages is simply too close to imagine such a correction here.

Otto also rejects the conclusions of Gardthausen and Marquardt, which we will now examine. About Gardthausen there is not much to say, since he gives no argument, but simply asserts that Augustus "gave explicit orders to his officials [*seinen Beamten*] in Syria, when dealing with important questions, to put themselves in agreement with the king, whom, as Josephus reports, he made the chief tax farmer [*General-Steuerpächter*] of the whole province of Syria."[78] Gardthausen makes it seem with this remark that this is what Josephus said, when in fact it is mostly Gardthausen's conjecture. Josephus does not overtly limit Herod's influence to "important questions," and it is not *immediately* obvious that Herod was made 'chief tax farmer' of Syria by being in charge of Caesar's 'agents' there (though that is a far more sensible conclusion than Otto claims). It is notable that, unlike Otto, Gardthausen uses *"his* officials" thus preserving some sense of the private vs. official nature of their position.

Marquardt says even less, simply noting that Caesar had once made someone with a royal title a procurator of Caesar, if we take *epitropos* to have that meaning in regard to Herod. To this remark he appends a footnote that the *BJ* passage (translating his German) "only seems correct if we read *Koilês* instead of *holês*, because Josephus mentions a *stratêgos tês Koilês Syrias* already" as we've seen earlier, "and Herod had never had anything to do with the true Syria before." He then proposes that Herod was given the procuratorship of the territory previously given to Cleopatra by Antonius. But here Otto is correct in dismissing Marquardt as badly confused about the situation, although Hahn makes a much clearer case along similar lines.[79] The only argument of Marquardt's that is worth attention is that Herod had been *stratêgos* of Coele-Syria before, and had never had any power over all Syria, "therefore" Josephus must have meant a similar position again, and this (he sug-

---

[78] V. Gardthausen, *Augustus und seine Zeit*, T.1 Bd.2 (1896), p. 818.

[79] Joachim Marquardt, *Römische Staatsverwaltung*, Vol. 1 (1881), p. 408 (1975 Arno edition); cf. Hahn, op. cit. [n. 45].

gests) would fit the fact that the loss of a single *kappa* in the *BJ* is plausible. However, as we've already noted, this emendation does not make sense of the parallel passage in the *AJ* where no equivalent error is likely, and making Herod an *epitropos* in peacetime holds no parallel at all with making him a *stratēgos* in wartime. And last, but not least, the fact that Herod had never held any position over all Syria before does not exclude the possibility of being given his first such role in 20 B.C.

6. Preliminary Conclusion

All the many attempts so far to explain or dismiss what Josephus meant in this case are in varying degrees incorrect, incomplete, or not well-founded. From a plain reading of the text, what Josephus describes as happening in 20 B.C. bears no relation at all to any prior *strategia* assigned to him, and cannot be emended or interpreted to have such a connection. Nor was it a description of a merely advisory role or of a general state of formal cooperation between the Roman and Jewish government. It was an appointment to a specific office with some sort of real authority. According to Josephus, Herod was not appointed as *stratēgos* in wartime, but *epitropos* in peacetime, and not of Coele-Syria, but of all Syria. Likewise, Josephus says nothing about Herod's role being temporary or limited only to important matters, nor is there any reason to suppose he means *epitropos* in some non-technical way. Indeed, far from being obscure, Josephus is explicit in identifying Herod's new position as a *procurator* with authority over other *procurators*, and not as having anything to do with Roman magistrates, officers, judges, or any of their representatives governing Syria, and thus Josephus is certainly not describing any sort of authority related to the dissemination of justice or control of the military. In short, Josephus did not say Herod was made a Roman governor of Syria.

Moreover, the two versions Josephus gives of this event do not contradict each other, nor is one an exaggeration of the other. Rather, as is usually the case, the *AJ* merely expands the compressed account of Herod's rise to power in the *BJ*. The *AJ* says those acting as *procurator* in Syria (and this entails *all* Syria) had to follow Herod in every matter, and this entails that Herod was put in command of all the Syrian *procurators*. Thus, when the *BJ* says he was made procurator of all Syria, it is certainly stating the obvious—if not an actual office that the *AJ* version describes without naming. Moreover, the appearance of *symboulia* in the *BJ* cannot be read as referring to an informal *concilia*, because the construction Josephus uses disallows such a meaning, stating quite the opposite: the procurators were not allowed to act *against* his *concilia*, and thus the *BJ* is describing just what the *AJ* says, real and final authority over the Syrian procurators. Josephus does not say the procurators had to consult Herod but didn't have to follow his advice, for he does not say they were "not allowed to act" *without* his advice (e.g. *ater*), but that they were "not allowed to act" *against* his advice (*dicha*). Moreover, the *AJ* makes absolutely clear that the former is not what Josephus meant, and the *BJ*'s use of the phrase "procurator of all Syria" also contradicts such a reading. Finally, we are left with no *plausible* explanation for how or why Josephus would make this up or exaggerate the truth (on two different occasions no less), and thus we have no particular reason to disbelieve it. The only thing that is obscure in all this is just why Augustus did this or how Herod was intended to use this position or how he actually did so. But some reasonable conjectures on these points will be advanced below.

Central to this conclusion is an understanding of a clear and crucial distinction between procurators (*epitropoi*) as private employees, and magistrates (propraetors, proconsuls, quaestors, etc.) and their official appointed representatives (prefects = *eparchoi*). The fact that this distinction has eluded almost all of the many scholars who have addressed this event indicates that it cannot be assumed. Therefore, a demonstration of this distinction will follow, and finally an examination of what it really meant for Herod to be procurator of all Syria.

7. The Procurator in the Time of Augustus

The term *procurator*, from *curator pro*, "one who cares for," means someone who takes care of something on someone else's behalf, for which the best English translation is usually "manager" or "agent." It was never an official term for any magistracy or promagistracy in the Roman constitution.[80] The word referred instead to anyone who managed someone else's property, in a relationship

---

[80] On this and following points see the extensive study of the imperial procuratorship by Eich, op. cit. [n. 4]], pp. 85-188 (and on this point specifically, also Eck, op. cit. [n. 4]).

like an apartment manager to a landlord or collection agent to a creditor, or anyone having anything akin to a "power of attorney." In the Republic and well into the Imperial period it was a private, non-governmental civilian office, and is equivalent to a role that would be filled today by, say, the U.S. President's private estate lawyer: certainly a man with great influence, but no more official legal or military power than any other citizen.[81]

As Cassius Dio puts it, speaking of the pre-Claudian administration, "In those days those who managed the emperor's money were not allowed to do more than collect the customary revenues, and in the case of disputes to accept judgment in court, according to the laws on an equality with private citizens."[82] His remark suggests things had changed by the time of the Severans, and in regard to certain civil cases it appears they had (as we'll soon see). But Dio's observation accords with the picture painted by Tacitus, who claims that adherence to proper legal processes was a prominent feature of the reign of Augustus and only began to deteriorate later in the reign of Tiberius.[83] Likewise, the Younger Pliny praises the fact that, in contrast to the abuses of Domitian, procurators in his day (under Trajan) had to face uncorrupted courts to win disputes, and even lost cases.[84] Though procurators occasionally overstepped their authority, this was illegal, and such overzealous procurators were typically punished. The most prominent case is that of "the procurator of Asia, Lucilius Capito" whom Tiberius claimed had only been given "authority over his personal slaves and money" and if he had "usurped the power of a praetor and deployed troops" he must be condemned. He was.[85] This appears to have been the normal reaction of the emperors at least into the reign of

---

[81] For this and what follows, the classic references are A.N. Sherwin-White, "Procurator Augusti," *Papers of the British School at Rome* 15 n.s. 2 (1939) and H.-G. Pflaum, *Les procurateurs équestres sous la Haut-Empire romain* (1950), though the more recent work cited below qualifies and improves upon these.

[82] Cassius Dio, *RH* 57.23.

[83] Tacitus, *Annals* 4.6.

[84] Pliny, *Panegyricus* 36.

[85] Tacitus, *Annals* 4.15. In fact Cassius Dio's comment (see note above) was made in the context of this trial.

Tiberius, and, as further evidence shows, even into the time of Caracalla and perhaps Severus Alexander.[86]

In other words, procurators in Augustan times did not have any legal or military authority: they did not hear cases or lead troops, and in fact when faced with any dispute they had to appeal to the courts as any other private citizen would. They were subservient to all the laws and legal authorities, and were certainly not "second only to the provincial governor" in any provincial administration. They were not even a formal part of the administration, though they were certainly intimately involved with it. Also, procuratorships were only held by persons of the rank of knight or lower, and often included freedmen (who weren't even full citizens). Like all salaried jobs, the position was looked down upon as a subservient and distasteful occupation by the more aristocratic elite, and no one of senatorial rank (much less proconsular rank) would ever allow himself the disgrace of holding such a position (and no one would insult them by offering it). Even so, a procuratorship was no doubt lucrative, since imperial procurators usually handled large sums of money.

The role of procurators could be much greater than we would imagine given our experience with government, since the Romans were long accustomed to contracting out tasks, like collecting taxes or building public works, to private citizens (the *publicani*), and by Augustan times it was routine for countless public duties to be carried out with private funds, since the emperor had more land and money than the government did—thus, e.g., we know hundreds of tons of silver and gold were spent out of Augustus' own pocket to pay and feed the army, to buy up land to retire them on, and even to pay the taxes in arrears for whole provinces or dole out grain to millions of people, to build countless public buildings, maintain public roads, and just about every conceivable thing we would expect only a government to pay for.[87] The vast sums and innumerable projects involved meant that a huge staff of managers was needed to oversee and pay for it all. Moreover, by right of conquest, as well as outright purchase, not to mention countless inheritances, the emperor was the largest landholder

---

[86] Millar, op. cit. (1965) [cited in note 89], p. 365. The case of Sabinus, related by Josephus (as mentioned earlier), came to the same conclusion.

[87] Augustus, *Res Gestae* 1, 3, 5, 15-24.

in the Western world, and someone had to manage all those properties and collect the rents. In all these cases, the task fell to the procurator, whom the emperor hired as a private employee.

Their specific responsibilities could vary immensely, however. Jones distinguishes two general types: "the procurators of provinces, who handled all the emperor's financial affairs within each, and the lesser procurators who were bailiffs of individual estates which the emperor owned in a private capacity."[88] Millar seeks greater specificity, and identifies five distinct categories: (1) "Procurators governing small provinces," which were "originally called *praefecti*" though in fact these were always prefects, some merely holding the procuratorship at the same time (a point I shall return to); (2) "Procurators of imperial provinces governed by *legati*" who were in charge of "the collection of tribute from their provinces, the payment of troops and so forth," although this would only be true insofar as Caesar's own money went to these ends (and not state money from the SPQR); (3) "Procurators with a variety of functions in Rome, Italy and the Provinces" such as those in charge of "libraries, imperial games, roads, indirect taxes (as opposed to tribute) and so forth," perhaps in many cases even as private contractors handling public money; (4) "Procurators of *senatorial* provinces" who were in charge of "imperial properties in these provinces" as a whole (such provinces otherwise being governed by the Senate and not, at least officially, the emperor); and (5) "Procurators of [individual] Imperial properties (estates, villas, mines, quarries, etc.)."[89]

In general, there were procurators of relatively high rank, assigned to and serving entire provinces, to whom many more procurators of various lesser ranks would be subservient. Among the latter, there were procurators who engaged in collecting moneys, and others who engaged in spending them. In the first of these two groups, some collected tribute payments (those promised by treaty to the emperor personally rather than the SPQR, and sometimes

---

[88] A.H.M. Jones, "Procurators and Prefects in the Early Principate," *Studies in Roman Government and Law* (1960), p. 123.

[89] Fergus Millar, "Some Evidence on the Meaning of Tacitus *Annals* XII.60," *Historia: Zeitschrift für alte Geschichte* 13 (1964), pp. 180-7, supplemented with even more evidence in "The Development of Jurisdiction by Imperial Procurators: Further Evidence," ibid. 14 (1965), pp. 362-7. His treatment is already extensive, but Eich, op. cit. [n. 4], even more so.

also taxes owed to the state, in which case acting as public contractors on behalf of the SPQR), others collected rents on properties owned by the emperor. In the second, some paid soldiers or bought their grain, while others handled more specific tasks like building roads or putting on games.

Needless to say, these duties insinuated procurators into the practical functions of government at all levels and thus, despite their constitutionally private status, they could appear to be *de facto* members of the provincial administration, especially at times by wielding (or threatening to wield) their influence on their employer (the emperor himself). Indeed, their private financial role did not preclude being given a bodyguard to protect the goods and money in their care, and no doubt these troops could be employed as a press gang when a procurator could get away with it.[90] But the sources clearly suggest that such extra-legal activity among procurators was frowned upon by Tiberius and certainly Augustus, and punished when found out.

The procurator is particularly to be contrasted with the *praefectus*, or prefect, "one put in charge of." This was primarily a military term, though of course in Augustan times there was little distinction between the government's administration and the military (nor had there ever been—the Roman state was fully militarized from as far back as records attest).[91] The office of prefect had a definite place in the Roman constitutional tradition, as an officer delegated by a magistrate to be his official deputy, with real military and police authority, and sometimes even judicial authority. This post was ordinarily only held by knights, and always military officers of non-senatorial rank, and certainly never by freed slaves, who, as only partial citizens, would not have been legally eligible for the delegation of *imperium*. Senators who were delegated authority by higher-ranking magistrates were granted the more prestigious title of *legatus* ("legate"), a general term usually entailing a *propraetor*

---

[90] E.g. Pliny, *Epistles* 10.27, where an imperial procurator, a freedman of Trajan, is given soldiers for his task of buying up grain for the army. Jones and Millar [n. 88, 89] give many more examples (the Sabinus episode in Josephus being another).

[91] For the thoroughgoing militarization of the Roman Republic from its earliest days, where no real distinction existed between public administrators and military officers, see William V. Harris, *War and Imperialism in Republican Rome: 327-70 B.C.* (1979).

or *proconsul*—if they had achieved the relevant rank: i.e. any senator who had held the supreme post of consul (of the empire) was thereafter eligible to serve as *proconsul*, "on behalf of the consul," whereas any senator who had only obtained the rank of praetor, or who was acting on behalf of a praetor, would serve as *propraetor*, "on behalf of a praetor." Roman provinces were governed first and foremost at the end of a spear, for military power was synonymous with keeping order. Thus, when a province or regional command was too small to be governed by any of these senatorial legates or magistrates, it was governed by a prefect, a distinctly lower-class officer deputized to act in their name.

The lines later blurred between prefects and procurators, hence many prefects in later sources are referred to, seemingly interchangeably, as procurators, and one possible reason for this is not hard to guess at. As the empire became more and more like an undisguised monarchy, and the public and private treasuries more and more blurred, the power of procurators became more and more real—even when still informal, their authority could be hard to challenge. Disobeying a procurator surely became in due course synonymous with disobeying their employer—who happened to be the emperor, and (as one might say) you didn't take the emperor to court. So it would not be surprising if we found, well after the Julian period, imperial procurators sharing the emperor's status in being above the law. That was a view of the emperor's legal status that was certainly post-Augustan. But there is a more demonstrable reason for the lines to be blurred at this level of the Roman government: it was often practical to simply hire an existing prefect as a procurator, since his private role as financial agent of the emperor would then be immediately backed up by his formal constitutional power as a prefect.

We have evidence of this practice already in the Republic. As Jones puts it, "it was apparently not unusual for proconsuls to grant prefectures (including command of troops) to the procurators of important persons, in order to give them power to collect their principals' debts."[92] He cites many examples from Cicero, who thought the practice was a bit fishy (*ad Att.* 5.21.10, 6.1.4-6, 6.2.8, 6.3.5-6). As we might expect, this was done to facilitate even the *publicani* collecting taxes (2 *Verr.* 3.75). In seeking imperial examples Jones may be speculating too far when he sees this practice in cases

---

[92] Jones, op. cit. [n. 88], p. 124.

like that of Capito (cf. note above), for had he been a prefect his actions would not have been illegal (as we're told they were); or in cases like that of Catus, procurator of Britain, who had a large contingent of troops with him including centurions (Tacitus, *Annals* 14.31-2), for the presence of *centurions* could easily suggest instead that he was merely being *assisted* by a prefect (and thus not necessarily one himself).

Even so, the practice of appointing procurators as prefects, or vice versa, is well attested. In the reign of Augustus, the supreme example is the prefect of Egypt, who was also the procurator of Egypt.[93] Egypt is an excellent example of the strange (to us) character of ancient government: all land in Egypt was originally owned by the kings. Upon his victory over Queen Cleopatra, all of Egypt became the private possession of Augustus, and he kept it that way to prevent any senatorial upstarts from using it as a base to launch another civil war. Thus, all "taxes" in Egypt were technically paid directly to Augustus and not to Rome as such, and hiring the prefect of the province to be chief procurator as well would be too convenient to pass up.

It is also fairly certain that all the prefects of Judaea were also procurators. For example, under Tiberius, Pontius Pilate was, besides the prefect of Judaea, also procurator there.[94] Pilate clearly engages in actions related to collecting and spending imperial money, suggesting procuratorial duties, though of course his actual *legal* powers would stem solely from his attested position as prefect.[95] But the decisive evidence is the contemporary Philo, who reports that "Pilate was one of the prefects appointed procurator of Judaea" (*Leg. ad Gaium* 299); Josephus also calls Pilate a procurator in *BJ* 2.169. Josephus, in fact, routinely calls the prefects of Judaea procurators (as noted earlier), and their activities often clearly involved financial matters. Upon the removal of Archelaus in 6 A.D. all the king's land and property no doubt became the private

---

[93] Philo, *in Flaccum* 3-4; cf. Jones, op. cit. [n. 88], pp. 120-2.

[94] Josephus, *AJ* 18.60, *BJ* 2.175, etc. Using many other sources (including papyri) further examples adduced by both Eich and Eck [n. 4] are quite numerous.

[95] An inscription confirms that Pilate was the *prefect* of Judea: cf. V. Ehrenberg & A.H.M. Jones, *Documents Illustrating the Reigns of Augustus and Tiberius*, 2nd. ed. (1976), §369.

possession of the emperor, and tribute previously paid directly to the emperor continued to be so, making the role of the Judaean procurator of sufficient gravity that prefects had to be assigned the duty.[96]

There is no evidence that any province, no matter how small, was ever governed by a procurator lacking a prefecture. In the words of Jones, "two emperors so careful of constitutional proprieties as Augustus and Tiberius" would not have made mere procurators provincial governors, "and a careful examination of the evidence has made it very improbable that they did," noting that inscriptions from the period always describe small-scale governors as *praefectus*—or *praeses* or *pro legato* (which mean essentially the same thing).[97] Jones believes that this began to change in the reign of Claudius, but his evidence is re-examined and the conclusion refuted by Millar.[98] In general, Jones' contrary evidence is either ambiguous as to whether attested procurators were in fact also governors, or fails to account for procurators acting illegally, procurators who were also prefects, etc. In the latter category are some cases where the men in question are referred to in sources by the lesser title only by way of abbreviation, or perhaps covert social commentary, as when Tacitus describes Pilate as a procurator in his account of Christianity in the context of the Neronian fire (*Annals* 15.44); for we know in fact (from epigraphic evidence) that Pilate was a prefect, and Tacitus (as a consular senator) would know that, but Tacitus would surely have found it more suitably embarrassing to say that Christ was executed by a procurator, which fact also

---

[96] Of course, after the Jewish War, *all* Judaea became the emperor's property by right of conquest (*BJ* 7.216).

[97] Jones, op. cit. [n. 88], p. 117; epigraphic evidence is discussed pp. 124-5, showing that this attention to constitutional accuracy extended even to the reign of Trajan if not beyond. Further evidence is provided by Millar, op. cit. (1965) [n. 89], pp. 364-5.

[98] Jones, op. cit. [n. 88], p. 125, also pp. 118-9; both of Millar's works on this, cited in note 89, address the issue in detail. See also the more recent and quite thorough analysis in Eich [n. 4].

played into Tacitus' running theme throughout the *Annals* that procurators were being given more authority than they ought.[99]

Millar could not find any evidence before Severus of procurators exercising jurisdiction, and abundant evidence that emperors actively opposed procurators assuming such powers.[100] Millar discovered that "The legal evidence shows clearly that procurators never had a recognised right to exercise criminal jurisdiction,"[101] though beginning some time late in the 2nd century procurators gradually acquired the right to judge certain *civil* cases that concerned them. Of course, this may have simply been another convenient abuse of the constitution, this time taking advantage of the fact that any citizen (perhaps even freedmen) could be appointed *iudex* (not a magistrate, but only a judge hearing specific cases), which is an extension of the same device as appointing a procurator *prefect*. This is the more likely explanation of the acts of procurators of large imperial estates who, though only beginning under Claudius, may have been given some sort of seigneurial authority on the private property of the emperor, allowing them to act in the place of the emperor when dealing with tenants, workers and other inhabitants on the emperor's own land, as Millar argues.[102]

Brunt challenged this conclusion, but somewhat unsoundly in my view, and I suspect they were both overlooking the real explanation.[103] Brunt makes the correct observation, but overlooks its importance, that many of these procurators may in fact have also been prefects, citing inscriptions naming some of them

---

[99] See Tacitus, *Annals* 4.15, 12.49, 12.54, 12.60 (on which see below), 14.32, 14.38-39, and of course 15.44 (frequently identifying prefects only by their concurrent position as procurator, and calling attention to the resulting injustice). On such methods in Tacitus see the analysis of T. J. Luce, "Tacitus on 'History's Highest Function': *praecipuum munus annalium* (Ann. 3.65)," *Aufstieg und Niedergang der Römischen Welt* II.33.4 (1991), pp. 2905-27 (supplemented by *Ann.* 16.16 and 4.33).

[100] The evidence is collected by E. Beaudoin, *Les grand domaines dans l'Empire romain* (1899), pp. 178ff.

[101] Millar, op. cit. (1965) [n. 89], pp. 364-5.

[102] See Millar, op. cit. (1964) [n. 89], p. 187, regarding Tacitus, *Annals* 12.60.

[103] P. A. Brunt, "Procuratorial Jurisdiction," *Latomus* 25.3 (July-September 1966): 461-89.

"procurator and prefect" as their full title.[104] So in the same fashion the others may have been appointed *iudex*. Brunt himself finds examples of this clearly being the case.[105] So even the Claudian act may simply have formalized the practice, which had already been normalized, of the emperor simultaneously appointing prefects to be his procurators—and now perhaps appointing other of his procurators to be judges over their own cases (which Tacitus suggests might already have happened on isolated occasions before). There is no evidence of it being otherwise.

We know Tacitus had a bee in his bonnet over the granting of imperial powers to procurators (as noted earlier) and thus had every reason to be overly rhetorical in emphasizing what annoyed him about this. The passage in dispute by Millar and Brunt is a rant against appointing knights to government (a privilege which, Tacitus laments, had used to be reserved for senators). He begins with the general complaint, that Claudius often said *parem vim rerum habendam a procuratoribus suis iudicatarum ac si ipse statuisset*, "that his own procurators ought to have the same judicial power as if he himself were speaking," and that the Senate passed a decree confirming this *plenius quam antea et uberius*, "more fully and broadly than before." Reading between the lines, the actual Senate's decree may have simply assigned the office of *iudex* to imperial procurators (while limiting their jurisdiction to civil courts, and even then only to cases involving imperial property—judging from the later epigraphic evidence collected by Millar and even Brunt). But Tacitus gives as his first example (of what he is saying was then expanded under Claudius) the Egyptian "procurator" being given judicial powers by Augustus, and we know this was accomplished by appointing that agent prefect, and not by simply granting judicial power to procurators. Tacitus then names other examples of (what in fact were) knights being appointed simultaneously as procurators *and* prefects (a detail Tacitus elides so as to make the facts seem more shameful). So when he closes this rant with the quip that *Claudius libertos quos rei familiari praefecerat sibique et legibus adaequaverit*, "Claudius even made the *freedmen* who governed his private estates equal to himself

---

[104] Brunt [n. 103], p. 463, n. 2.

[105] Brunt [n. 103], p. 469. It should be noted that apart from my mild critique, the evidence and analysis of Brunt and Millar are not only correct but essential reading for any question concerning imperial procurators, though their evidence and analysis has been perfected and expanded by Eich [n. 4].

under the law," Tacitus is most likely (and intentionally) glossing over the actual fact of the matter: that Claudius was appointing his procurators to be prefects (these would almost certainly have only been knights) or in some cases simply *iudices* (judges), so they could simultaneously make and adjudicate their own claims (and it is here that freedmen would be involved).

Even if we take Tacitus more literally, Millar's conclusion then prevails: the only freedmen procurators Tacitus mentions being given judicial powers are those in command of his private estates. And yet I doubt this was accomplished in any other way than simply declaring them civil *iudices* with confined jurisdictions. All the other procurators were equestrian prefects. But however one reads Tacitus on this point, he still says that this development only began under Claudius. In the time of Augustus it is clear that procurators *in and of themselves* were nothing more than the private employees of the emperor, and had no more formal legal authority than private citizens.

8. The Grant of the Provincial Procuratorship to Herod

Ten years after Actium, Augustus set about putting the provincial affairs in order, beginning with Sicily, then working his way to Greece, and via Samos to Asia, and finally to Syria before returning to Rome. In the spring of 20 B.C. Augustus left his winter quarters on Samos and came to Asia, going as far as Bithynia. He doled out money here and there, raised the tribute owed from various places, set up or put down various local laws, and punished municipalities for abusing Roman citizens. He intimidated or negotiated with the Parthians to retrieve some lost legionary standards. But he waged no campaigns. He also reorganized and divvied up various border lands among loyal allied kings, among whom was Herod, who received the lands of the just-deceased tetrarch (and his rival) Zenodorus.[106] When he arrived, Augustus was also approached by representatives of the Gadarenes charging Herod with being violent and tyrannical. Josephus suggests that they were attempting to get their territory taken away from him and annexed to Syria, where (it was thought) Roman governance would be more tolerable (*AJ* 15.354-356). They charged Herod with "wanton acts of violence, robberies, and destruction of temples" (*hybreis kai harpagas kai ka-*

---

[106] Cassius Dio, *RH* 54.7-10.

tuskuphus hierōn), but then, predicting after only the first day of the trial that Caesar was going to rule for Herod, they committed suicide instead, leaving Caesar free to acquit Herod of all charges (*AJ* 15.357-358). Josephus then describes Herod as having reached the pinnacle of good fortune, being held in the highest possible esteem by both Augustus and Agrippa (*AJ* 15.361).

It is in this context that Augustus appoints Herod chief procurator of all Syria. As we've already demonstrated, this did not mean he was governor of Syria. He had no judicial, magisterial, or military powers there. But his position can be considered akin to the procurators of Judaea and Egypt *without* the powers of a prefect, and thus more like the procurator of Asia, whom we know (from the case of Lucilius Capito discussed previously) had the charge of the emperor's own slaves, funds and properties. In the categorization of Jones, Herod was *procurator Syriae*, the highest ranking procurator who handled all the emperor's financial affairs within Syria, and, as Josephus explicitly states, was in charge of all the lesser procurators in that province—an estate manager on a grand scale. In Millar's more precise scheme, Herod was a procurator of Type 2, whom we know from other evidence would have managed the collection of tribute from all Syrian towns and regions owed to Caesar directly (as opposed to SPQR), and spent some of that revenue in the payment of troops and other tasks (such as, perhaps, constructing aqueducts or other public works, as we know Pontius Pilate arranged in Judaea). He would presumably also be in charge of collecting rents and handling other affairs in respect to the emperor's private landholdings in the province. As a mere practical matter he could not have micromanaged every procurator in Syria, but (if we accept the appointment as genuine) he certainly had supreme authority over them and set the agenda for how things would be done. And lacking evidence to the contrary, we can assume he held this job until his death.

There is no doubt that this was a prestigious and rare, if not unique, honor to be won by a foreign king. But there was no one more able or likely to have won it than Herod. Augustus heaped good fortune upon him and gave him little trouble to his dying day. Legally there could be no objection, for Herod was a Roman citizen, and the job was suitable even for freedmen. Socially there would be little protest, for even so high a position as *procurator provinciae* was so far beneath a senator that it was only held by knights and freedmen. Herod was an extremely wealthy and Hellenized king of renowned competence and loyalty to Rome, who ruled over both Jewish and Gentile territories. For him to assume a job on a par with imperial freedmen would be regarded by some as befitting a foreign but respectable potentate, and whoever would be bothered by it would not be able to stir enough outrage to deter Augustus from hiring him, as we might infer from the sorry case of the Gadarene accusers. (Herod would not have been of senatorial rank, of course, because although he certainly would have met the wealth requirement, he never won formal election to the senate. His formal status would have been that of a knight.)

The case of the Gadarenes may also illuminate the emperor's motives. No doubt the complaints of the Gadarenes were based on Herod's notoriously harsh exactions of tribute, and possibly extralegal actions to that end. Soldiers requisitioning taxes could be no different in appearance than bandits looting a town or temple. That Caesar so obviously favored Herod in this case as to drive the accusers to suicide might suggest that he approved of Herod's efficiency in securing the one thing Romans wanted most from their provinces: profit. After income, security took a close second, glory a distant third, as a reason for bothering to have provinces in the first place. It is possible that Augustus was sufficiently impressed with Herod's ability to organize and extract revenues that he decided not only to annex the lands of Zenodorus to Herod's kingdom, but even to put Herod in charge of exactions and financial affairs in the neighboring province of Syria, leaving all the emperor's employees there at his disposal. This action also makes sense in the context of the Gadarene case for another reason: Josephus argues that one of their motives was to have their lands transferred from Herod to Syria to escape his harsh methods. But by putting Herod in charge of exactions in Syria as well, the emperor would have completely thwarted this ulterior motive, ensuring no such cases would arise again. The message thus sent was that subject peoples in Syria-Palestine could no longer escape Herod's methods of tax collection.

From this position, if we accept it (and I don't see any reason not to), Herod would surely skim a sizeable bounty off the top and profit immensely from the Roman peace. It might not be coincidence that it is shortly after this year that all of Herod's most ambitious building projects began. At the same time he would have a positive interest in keeping that peace to ensure the steady flow of revenues from provincial economic success, while the emperor would benefit from Herod's apparent financial genius and general ruthlessness. Augustus would not have been the first to see Herod's potential in this regard: Cleopatra had previously hired Herod to do much the same for her holdings in Arabia (*AJ* 15.96ff.). Herod was still legally subject to all Roman magistrates, legates, and prefects in Syria, and technically (whatever actually transpired in practice), as an ordinary citizen there, he would have had to fight and win all relevant disputes in the courts. And nevertheless, though not a governor of Syria, Herod must have had substantial influence on Syrian affairs as Caesar's chief financial manager in that province.

8

ON THE DUAL OFFICE OF PROCURATOR AND PREFECT

Originally published at RichardCarrier.info
© 2012.

This brief essay summarizes the evidence and scholarship backing my analysis in the previous article ("Herod the Procurator"), which shows that from the time of Pontius Pilate to the time of Tacitus, equestrian governors of Roman provinces were both prefects and procurators.

The common practice throughout the early Roman Empire was not to defy established constitutional offices by creating new ones or radically changing their powers, but by accumulating offices and thus accumulating the powers already constitutionally provided. This is how the principate (the office of "emperor") was created: in terms of legal authority it was not a new office, but an accumulation of existing offices (tribune, censor, consul, proconsul, *princeps senatus*, various priesthoods, and so forth), which traditionally were not held by the same one person. (And *then* these offices were subject to minor tweaks over time that just stretched the constitution ever more slightly.)

Likewise all other changes in legal authority under the empire were accomplished by using constitutional offices in similarly novel ways. This is why procurators were empowered not by just "giving them" constitutional powers, but by appointing them to offices that already held those constitutional powers. This is how emperors avoided the appearance of being a dictator just "tossing out" the constitution, but could claim instead to be someone who respects and thus is preserving the constitution and is just using it to its maximum potential "for the good of the empire." This is precisely why Augustus did not simply claim supreme power (a perpetual dictatorship) as Julius Caesar did, but instead gave himself supreme power *constitutionally* by stacking up offices upon himself. Provincial governance must be understood in this context.

The Analysis of Fergus Millar

Fergus Millar wrote two important articles on the subject that remain fundamental to the field of Roman administration.[1] He found several different types of procurators, all of which were private financial occupations and not (in themselves) official government offices. For example, he concluded that "the legal evidence shows clearly that procurators never had a recognised right to exercise criminal jurisdiction."[2] He does discuss illegal or extralegal actions by procurators (which do not represent their actual official powers) and the slow expansion of their legal powers in the late second and third century, but neither pertains to the official nature of provincial administration in the first and early second century (when, for example, Tacitus and Josephus wrote).

Millar also shows that when procurators did exercise judicial rulings, they did so by *also* being appointed judges (*judices*), thus adhering to standard constitutional practice: giving procurators powers by appointing them to actual constitutional offices having those powers (and not just "giving them" the powers without the office).[3] Over the course of the second and third centuries the office of governor for small provinces grew more commonly to be called *praeses*, "the man sitting in front, superintendant," a more general term encompassing prefect (*praefectus*, "the man put in charge") as well as other positions of assigned governance. Other legal phrases meaning the same thing as prefect were *pro legato*, "[acting] on behalf of the legate," and v.a.l., *vices agens legati*, "interim agent of the legate," in either case the "legate" being someone above them of

---

[1] Fergus Millar, "Some Evidence on the Meaning of Tacitus 'Annals XII'. 60," *Historia: Zeitschrift für Alte Geschichte* 13.2 (1964): 180-187 and "The Development of Jurisdiction by Imperial Procurators: Further Evidence," *Historia: Zeitschrift für Alte Geschichte* 14.3 (1965): 362-667.

[2] Millar 1965, pp. 364-65.

[3] Millar 1965, p. 364.

senatorial rank (often the governor of a larger province). Occasionally reference to the phrase *ius gladii* ("the right of the sword") was used to the same effect (referring to the actual powers of the office of prefect). When reading letters, inscriptions, and legal documents it's important to understand these all refer to the same constitutional office, more commonly just called "prefect," someone officially selected by a legate (or the emperor directly) to act on their behalf. Even in the Republic men of equestrian rank were appointed to prefectures and could thus use the powers of a senatorial office on a senator's behalf (like the modern concept of a deputy sheriff).

Millar found no one on record who was definitely a procurator *and* a governor of a province (with judicial and military powers) without holding *both* titles of procurator *and* prefect (or equivalent, per above). Even as late as the third century, in full official contexts their title was not "procurator" but, for example, "procurator and praeses" (in modern parlance a *presidial procurator*), hence even at that late date the powers of a governor were not assigned to procurators except by *simultaneously* appointing them to the constitutional office of "legal deputy" (the office of prefect or *praeses*). As Millar says, inscriptions even at that late date "call equestrian governors '*proc[urator] Aug[usti] (item) praeses*' or '*proc[urator] et praeses*' rather than just 'procurator'."[4] Millar likewise points out that even as late as the third century procurators could only appoint judges to cases if they were *also* holding the office of *praeses*; and procurators could only judge cases themselves if they were also a *praeses* or officially appointed to the office of *iudex* (meaning "judge").

Millar concluded after his second study: that (1) only from "the early second century onwards" were procurators ever "exercising legal powers within imperial estates" (a far cry from governing provinces); that (2) procurators sometimes acted outside the law; and (3) the earliest evidence of their ever holding legal powers outside of ruling on property disputes within imperial estates dates to the third century, and even then this evidence still only concerned property cases. There is no evidence of any procurator governing any province, without also holding the office of prefect or its equivalent (*praeses, pro legato, v.a.l.*).[5] There are examples of gover-

---

[4] Millar 1965, p. 366.

[5] Millar 1965, p. 367.

nors being referred to as only prefect *or* procurator (when in reality we know they were both, as for example the prefect of Egypt), but there is little chronological consistency to this practice (for example, presidial procurators are sometimes called just "prefect" or "praeses" even after Tacitus, and are sometimes called just "procurator" even before Claudius), except that "procurator" becomes more common (but not exclusively so) as the centuries go by. But this still only reflects customs regarding which title to mention, not which titles were actually held. The evidence shows clearly (as Millar documents) that both titles were actually held by provincial governors of equestrian rank into the third century.

In his previous paper Millar noted that the procurators of provinces had held imperial powers since the time of Augustus (well before Pilate took office) and no change in this fact occurred under Claudius or at any time before Tacitus ("there is no evidence that there was a change in the judicial powers of these procurators").[6] He notes in fact that "their criminal jurisdiction is sufficiently well illustrated by the history of Judaea in the [whole of the] Julio-Claudian period," meaning all the prefects of Judea since the beginning (including Pilate) *were procurators*. Thus when he says they were "originally called *praefecti*" he doesn't mean *instead* of procurator; he means that it became more common (contrary to the usual practice before Augustus) to refer to them by their title of procurator rather than prefect, even though they were both. His remarks have since been misinterpreted as saying the name of the office was changed by or after Claudius. But that is specifically what Millar is saying there is no evidence of: Claudius made no change to these facts at all. Claudius only altered the powers of procurators of imperial estates (not provinces), and even that was likely accomplished only by appointing them to the constitutional office of *iudex*, and not by creating a new constitutional office.

The Analysis of A.M.M. Jones

Millar cites for this point the work of A.M.M. Jones, "Procurators and Prefects in the Early Principate," *Studies in Roman Government and Law* (1960). It is instructive to read what Jones actually says. Jones remarks (quite rightly, and in line with my opening point) that "it seems very improbable that two emperors so careful of consti-

---

[6] Millar 1964, p. 181.

tutional proprieties as Augustus and Tiberius would have given the title 'procurator' to provincial governors, and a careful examination of the evidence has made it very improbable that they did."[7] The same argument holds for Claudius in comparison with the Flavians, Antonines, and Severans: if the latter dynasties (who were far more distant from Tiberius and Augustus and certainly more profligate in tinkering with the traditional constitution) maintained the requirement of simultaneously appointing provincial procurators to the office of *prefect* or *praeses* in order to grant them judicial and military powers, we must conclude Claudius made no change to that practice. And there is no evidence he did. Moreover, since this procedure worked perfectly well, there would have been no reason at all for Claudius to have changed it.

To demonstrate the point, Jones presents inscriptions showing governors still being called prefects in the subsequent reign of Nero.[8] And even later, towards the end of the first century, when the Alpine provinces of Raetia and Vindelica were combined, we have an inscription identifying its governor as *procur[ator] Augustor[um] pro leg[ati]*, in other words he was a prefect of the legate *and* a procurator of the emperors (*ILS* 1348). It's worth pointing out that this is exactly when Tacitus was serving as a consul and provincial legate himself (his political career began under Titus in 80 or 81 and he was made consul under Nerva in 97), so he would certainly be well aware of the fact that provincial prefects were also imperial procurators, and vice versa. For that is exactly what the inscriptions show was the case precisely when Tacitus was advancing in imperial offices and provincial commands. Similarly, Jones demonstrates that this fact had long been so well known that the Jewish ambassador Philo, even before the reign of Claudius, knew that Pontius Pilate was *both* a procurator *and* a prefect, as he tells us Pilate was "one of the prefects [*hyparchoi*] appointed procurator [*epitropos*] of Judaea."[9]

Jones concluded, from all the evidence available to him (and this already before Millar, who read Jones and left this point unchallenged), that "procuratorships and prefectures may nevertheless not always have been kept strictly apart," showing that appoint-

---

[7] Jones 1968 (a Basil Blackwell reprint of the 1960 text), p. 117.

[8] Jones 1968, p. 118.

[9] Jones 1968, p. 119; Philo, *Embassy to Gaius* 38, §299.

ing one man to both is a practice in evidence even during the Republic. He points out that we have abundant evidence that this was in fact true of the prefect of Egypt, and "the same was probably true of all prefects of provinces."[10] He adduces more examples under Vespasian (for Sardinia) and Trajan (for Mauritania), and so on. (Again, Tacitus knew Vespasian personally, and wrote during the reign of Trajan.) Jones concludes his analysis with the remark that perhaps Claudius dispensed with this practice, but his own evidence abundantly contradicts that, and Millar subsequently demonstrated that Jones was misreading Claudius on this point.

Thus even Jones' one suggestion that perhaps there was a "change in title" for provincial governors, which even Jones' own evidence refuted, Millar specifically and extensively refuted again in his following two papers, finding instead that the development under Claudius that Tacitus refers to was the assignment of limited judicial powers to the procurators of private imperial estates; and again, even that was probably accomplished by simultaneously appointing them to the constitutional office of *iudex*, and thus not really a change in the legal authority of the procuratorship by itself.

The Analysis of P.A. Brunt

In this context we can now read the somewhat confused thoughts of P.A. Brunt, who attempted something of a rejoinder to Millar.[11] Brunt is the one who erroneously says:

> From Claudius' time these equestrian governors, outside Egypt and at times Sardinia, bore the title of procurators. But earlier they seem to have been called prefects, an appellation accorded even in the Republic to equestrian officials in the service of the state ... [and] these prefects, or presidial procurators, commanded troops and performed all the tasks that fell to a governor.[12]

---

[10] Jones 1968, pp. 123-24.

[11] P.A. Brunt, "Procuratorial Jurisdiction," *Latomus* 25.3 (July-September 1966): 461-89.

[12] Brunt 1966, p. 463.

But Brunt then cites evidence that this was not actually a change of title, but only a change in preference for which title to refer to them by, *as they had always held both offices*. For example, Brunt cites an inscription for the Sardinian procurator that reports his office as *proc[urator] Aug[usti] et praef[ectus]* (and in later centuries, *proc[urator] Aug[usti] et praes[es]*), thus illustrating the fact that they were both, and remained both, from Augustan times to well past the era of Trajan. Similarly, Brunt shows that the governor of Mauretania was a *proc[urator] Aug[usti] pro leg[ato]*, which again is just another way of saying he was procurator *and* prefect.[13]

Brunt claims one inscription identifies a governor of Noricum solely as procurator (*ILS* 1349), but he's wrong: it does not say the man in question (Gaius Baebio) *governed* Noricum, only that he served as procurator *in* Noricum (literally *in Norico*), having previously been the prefect *of* Moesia and the Maritime Alps. Baebio thus had governed Moesia and the Maritime Alps; but he did *not* govern Noricum. He merely held a procuratorship there (and not even the principal procuratorship, since he wasn't the provincial procurator but merely one of many procurators in the province).

Otherwise, Brunt agrees with Millar that the decree of Claudius mentioned by Tacitus "conferred then *no new powers* on presidial procurators, previously called prefects" (emphasis added), but that it had only related to other procurators (Brunt is unsure whether Millar is right that it only referred to procurators of private imperial estates, but he nevertheless agrees it had nothing to do with provincial procurators).[14] In other words, Brunt is not saying Claudius changed the name of the office of prefect to "procurator." He just repeats what Millar said, that presidial procurators were once exclusively called prefects. And then Brunt mistakenly assumes Millar said this change had occurred during the reign of Claudius, but that is not in fact what Millar said, and there is in fact no evidence that ever happened, and plenty of evidence it very definitely did not.

Brunt otherwise verifies the general point that powers were conferred on procurators by appointing them to constitutional offices (thus concurring with my opening point, as both Jones and

---

[13] Brunt 1966, pp. 465-66.

[14] Brunt 1966, p. 466.

Millar do). For example, he argues extensively that procurators had no constitutional legal powers well into the second or even third century *except* when they were actually appointed to the office of *iudex*, prefect, or *praeses*. For example, he remarks that when we find them exercising the power to judge cases, "the procurator was also a *iudex*."[15] The same would have been true, for the same reason, and as demonstrated by the same kind and quantity of evidence, for procurators exercising *imperium*: in order to constitutionally exercise that authority, they would also have been a *praefectus* or *praeses*.[16]

Conclusion

The abundant evidence adduced by Jones and Millar, and even Brunt, sufficiently confirms this. And not only confirms it, but confirms it had been that way in the time of Jesus (when Pilate

---

[15] Brunt 1966, p. 469 (in context: pp. 468-77).

[16] Examples adduced to the contrary are insufficient to prove otherwise. For instance, an inscription that mentions a military roads project built through the assistance of "Tiberius Julius Justus, procurator of the province of Thrace" (*ILS* 231) does not clearly mean the governor of Thrace, it could simply mean the procurator assigned to manage funds in Thrace, who might not have been the governor; and even if he was, he is here being referred to in his capacity as the manager of money and lands (for the building of roads), not in his capacity as the Thracian judicial and military authority. Thus we cannot conclude from this inscription that he was not also the prefect of Thrace. Similarly, we cannot know whether Claudius Paternus Clementianus (under Trajan) was a governor of the provinces of Judaea, Sardinia, Africa, and Noricum (*Corpus Inscriptionum Latinarum* III 5776) or only a procurator in them (see K. Kraft, *Münchner Beiträge zur Vor- und Frühgeschichte* 7 [1964]: 71-74). Even if he was their governor, the fact that the governorship of Sardinia is well documented through two whole centuries as being a dual-appointment (procurator and prefect), and thus was certainly so in his time, we can conclude he was both a procurator and a prefect and only chose to mention the former on inscriptions. We otherwise have several examples of inscriptions for other equestrian governorships all the way through the second century mentioning both titles being held by them (using one appellation or another), as well as inscriptions that mention only one or the other, demonstrating both were not always stated even when both offices were held: see H.-G. Pflaum, *Les carrières procuratoriennes équestres sous le Haut-Empire romain* (1960-1961), vol. 3, pp. 1044-99. Of course it should again be noted that some of the inscriptions that say only "procurator" may only be of procurators who never served as governors.

governed Judaea, he was, and was known by his peers to be, both a prefect *and* a procurator, even if that fact was not always mentioned) *and* in the time of Tacitus (as inscriptions of his time attest), and in all years in between. And thus nothing had changed, except at most the frequency of which title was mentioned when mentioning only one.

Debunking the Bogus

9

FLASH! FOX NEWS REPORTS THAT ALIENS MAY HAVE BUILT THE PYRAMIDS OF EGYPT!

Originally published in *Skeptical Inquirer* 23.5
(September-October 1999), 46-50.
Minor revisions © 2014 by Richard Carrier.
Original © 1999 by *The Skeptical Inquirer*.
Reproduced with permission.

Pseudoscience as news? The Fox Network's handling of its prime-time special "Opening the Lost Tombs: Live from Egypt" raises ethical questions.

I couldn't believe my eyes. It was a Sunday night, on the ten o'clock news. Right between a report on Y2K and another on a fine against a local construction company, *Fox 5 News* in New York saw fit to give us a "special report" on who built the pyramids. The graphic behind the announcer, on a backdrop of the Gizeh pyramids, asks the question: "Alien Architects?" The announcer plugs the upcoming Fox television network special "Opening the Lost Tombs: Live From Egypt," then segues into the story with the campy introduction, "There are many mysteries in Egypt, like the pyramids. Who built them and how did they do it?" With that she introduces *Fox News* correspondent David Garcia, who begins his voice-over to video of the pyramids: "The ancient future, a civilization of contradiction." Immediately we hear another voice in an Arabic accent, "a pyramid was a tomb," followed immediately by another similar voice, "the pyramid has never been a tomb."

This is how it begins, and it only gets worse. Besides the ramifications of this news report for the whole field of journalism—the way it was conducted, and the shoddy journalism it represents—there is the then-upcoming special that this "news report" was plugging, which aired the following Tuesday (March 2, 1999). Although that show might be excused as "entertainment," when the same thing is done on a regular news hour, amidst real news, such an excuse is inadequate. And as I eventually discovered, it would even be ethically questionable for Fox to call its live special "entertainment." One scholar who participated in it told me he agreed to take part in the show for no fee, on the basis that it was a "news" program. "They certainly used the word 'news'," he told me, "using that as the reason why 'no one' who was interviewed was getting paid." If that is true, and if Fox does claim the show was entertainment, then it is pulling a fast one.

Questionable Sources

On the ten o'clock news, after we are told that the pyramids have never been a tomb, correspondent Garcia continues, "Still, modern day scholars debate not only what they are, but why they are—who, or what, built them?" He treats both claims as if they are exemplary of real scholarly debate. Does Garcia really think that? He could not be reached for comment. Then we see a man identified onscreen as "Fadel Gad, Egyptologist." What news does he have for us? Why, just this: "Were the Egyptians thinking of UFOs at that time? Yes! A very sophisticated, highly intelligent species that had intercepted this planet Earth and had caused the evolution and the exploration of the human consciousness."

A real Egyptologist is saying this? This is what *Fox News* is reporting. Though I later found that Mr. Gad has extensive field experience and a master's degree in Egyptology, he has authored no known publications, and is not a member of the International

Association of Egyptologists.[1] But there is one more thing: Fadel Gad just happens to be a co-executive producer of "Opening the Lost Tombs." This is not mentioned in this news report. Here is a real blurring of the line between news and entertainment, with producers being portrayed as unbiased experts on news stories to drum up interest in their future entertainment programs.

The thrust of the report was definitely not skeptical. Garcia tells us that "traditional Egyptologists" consider "even the mention of UFOs or other-world intelligence [as] heresy," as if this were about opinion and dogma, with rival opinions as good as any other, instead of being about facts and evidence. The only skeptic presented was Zahi Hawass, "Undersecretary of State," a truly renowned Egyptologist, widely published in the field, with a Ph.D. from the University of Pennsylvania (all far more than Fadel Gad can claim). But Dr. Hawass was not listed as an Egyptologist—instead, he was identified as an establishment bureaucrat (though it wasn't mentioned, he would also be involved in the upcoming special).

Hawass explains, "People like to dream. If you meet someone who is not an archaeologist, they love to dream." Recounting the claims of aliens, he concludes, "That's a dream! My job is to let you dream, but you have to know a little bit about reality." That is all Hawass gets to say against the ideas of Mr. Gad. No other experts or information are presented on this matter. This furthers the impression that the debate is about opinions, not facts, about heretics fighting the establishment and being arrogantly dismissed as dreamers.

Eventually, Garcia tells us, "also preserved are records, etched in stone, supporting evidence not of this Earth." This is a tacit approval of the alien hypothesis by a mainstream journalist on a

---

[1] Fadel Gad was in 1999 the president of Joy Travel International (11600 Washington Pl., Suite 209, Los Angeles, CA 90066). He was traveling and could not be reached for comment. His resume cites official posts, from Inspector of Antiquities to Director of Excavations at Saqqara, excavations from 1973 to 1980, and a master's degree in Ancient Egyptian Art and Archaeology from Cairo University, 1981. He runs tours for organizations as diverse as The Institute of Noetic Sciences and the University of California, and works a lecture circuit on "Egyptian mythology." I contacted many people who met him, and all praised him as an ethical businessman and all-around nice guy. Online, you will find mostly New Age references to Fadel and his unusual teachings.

major network's regular ten o'clock news hour. This is not a tabloid; this is supposedly a mainstream source. Yet there is no hint of skepticism.

What is this "supporting evidence" not of this Earth? Gad again: "The records indicate that we came from another place, we came from the stars." Do they? A picture is then shown of some Egyptian hieroglyphs resembling rings, and we hear Gad declaring "they look like flying saucers!" Then comes a picture of a carving of an Egyptian in a ceremonial headdress, followed by Gad's voice again: "They are showing figures with antennas on their head. Very mysterious." No other interpretation is offered, no one is given the chance to rebut Gad's reading of these glyphs.

Garcia finishes with a sappy catch-phrase ending, typical of this brand of TV journalism, "A higher intelligence, or merely dedicated hard work? Which theory is correct? Neither is proven. It is the mystery of Egypt," an overt declaration that the aliens theory is just as good as any other, that it hasn't been "proven" that the pyramids are man-made. If the Fox network can be this gullible, or this incompetent, or this shifty, on a subject where information and experts abound, how can anyone trust anything else they report?

By now I was dreading the Fox special. I had already found the Fox website [www.foxnetwork.com/egypt] promoting all kinds of pseudoscience, uncritically, from mummy curses to aliens to psychics. No real journalism appears on the website at all, virtually no skepticism, and no references or authorities. Statements are made as if they were facts. The Titanic was sunk by a mummy's curse; the pyramids may have been built to signal space travelers; the fifty-year-old predictions of "the celebrated American psychic" Edgar Cayce suggest the pyramids were built ten thousand years ago; that the Sphinx shows damage from the Great Flood; and a secret hall of records from Atlantis would be found under it in the late 1990s—conveniently, the very time that Fox planned to explore, live on television, new shafts opened up "beneath" the Sphinx (not exactly—more like behind it).

"Forget about everything you've ever seen or heard about" the Sphinx and the pyramids, Maury Povich says as the show begins. Then there's a cheesy voice-over, asking the questions that set the tone for the rest of the show. "Are there clues to man's destiny? Was it Atlantis that taught Egypt how to build? Are we the descendants of astronauts from another world?" The entire two-hour show is littered with New Age authors pushing their theories, interspersed with more interesting archaeological tours led by Zahi Hawass. Hawass is a wonderful scientist, and clearly loves his job. He embodies the excitement of archaeology, and is eager to share it with others. Around this backbone of "reality," which included the new, "live-on-TV" discovery of an intact mummy, the exploration of an unused tomb, and the first-ever public viewing of the Tomb of Osiris, the content is entirely lopsided in favor of the "heretics." But the "reality" aspect of the show is also suspect; much of it seemed staged. It was apparent that Hawass had explored many of these sites before, identifying art and translating inscriptions, in preparation for the show (and then, perhaps, "setting them up" by covering them with sand). Moreover, many archaeologists, whose comments can be read in the ANE Digest archives, note that Hawass was providing a very bad example of how to conduct a dig. Some even said they would use the video to instruct students on what *not* to do.[2]

A Parade of Paranormal Purveyors

We are given a tour of all the outlandish theories at the start of the program, with longer, corresponding monologues popping in and out as the show progresses, apparently to fill dead time between setting up archaeological sites for the TV cameras. In each case an author pitches his theory, with the title of his book appearing on screen. We are thus led through the entire gamut of "heretical" Egyptology today. The narrative quaintly portrays these guys as the "doubters" and "skeptics" who are challenging supposedly tired, old views.

About these theorists, who posit lost civilizations and alien visitors, Povich tells us, "their ideas, or at least some of them, are not quite as wacky as you might suspect." Indeed, "they are vigorously challenging mainstream archaeologists like Zahi Hawass." When at last we get some comment from Hawass, sanity is championed, though not permitted a fair fight. He is only given time to say the obvious: "There is no evidence at all, existing in any place in Egypt, about this lost civilization."

---

[2] There was much discussion about this Fox special: you can peruse the ANE Digest archives online around the date of broadcast (http://oi.uchicago.edu/research/library/ane/digest).

So who are these purveyors of the strange? First, the views of Edgar Cayce, the deceased psychic mentioned in the website, are espoused by John Van Auken of the Edgar Cayce Foundation. He tells us we will be enlightened by the discovery of the secret hall of records containing the truth about our past. Then there is Richard Hoagland, author of *The Monuments of Mars*. We are descended, he says, from Martian refugees who settled at Gizeh. Robert Bauval is there, author of *The Orion Mystery*. The three pyramids of Gizeh were built thousands of years earlier than we think, according to him, since they must have been aligned with the Orion constellation, which was only possible in 10,500 B.C. We get to hear from John Anthony West, author of *Serpent in the Sky*. The Sphinx, he insists, must have been built in 12,000 B.C. in order for so much erosion to have occurred (and, of course, the fact that the head was refashioned is to him further proof of its fantastic antiquity). Graham Hancock, author of *Heaven's Mirror*, makes an appearance. He believes, among other things, that "an earlier civilization" that emphasized the soul rather than technology was destroyed in a great flood, and the survivors settled in Egypt. He says we are "technologically brilliant" but "spiritually barren" and so we should look to this ancient civilization for guidance.

Who gets to speak on behalf of the real scholars? Several—but none of them are asked or allowed to comment on any of the other theories being touted on the show. Among the genuine experts, who give brief talks on ordinary facts and theories not related to the New Age claims, are Bob Brier, an Egyptologist from Long Island University; Dieter Arnold from the Metropolitan Museum of Art; Gaballa Ali Gaballa, Secretary General of the Egyptian Antiquities Council (actually the Supreme Council for Antiquities), and, though it is not mentioned (as in the case of Hawass in the previous Sunday's news report), a leading Egyptologist with a Ph.D. from Liverpool University; Aidan Dodson, an Egyptologist (now at the University of Bristol) commenting on the King Tut dig; and Nicholas Reeves, author of *The Complete Tutankhamun*, who talks about how good forensic evidence suggests the boy king was murdered (Dr. Dodson weighs in on this one, too).

Mixing and Matching Expert Theories

The only credible expert with unorthodox ideas was Robert Schoch, author of *Voices of the Rocks*. Though not mentioned in the show, he holds a Ph.D. in geology and geophysics from Yale and has been a faculty member at Boston University since 1984. But the way his testimony is treated is part of a worrisome trend. By interweaving comments by both Schoch and West, Schoch's geological observations are depicted as supporting West. But Schoch only dates the *core body* of the Sphinx to around 5000 B.C. (as opposed to 2500 B.C. as is normally believed, or 12,000 B.C. as West argues), based on his estimation of the rates of rain erosion.[3]

Schoch told me he did not see the show, so could not comment on how his views were portrayed. But as far as I can tell, he certainly does not advocate West's theory, and it seems a bit shifty to present them as if they are a tag team supporting a common view. But Schoch's claims very specifically do not encompass the head or hind quarters of the Sphinx, and he also notes that his dating falls within the period of known megalith civilizations (the walls of Jericho, for example, were built around 8,000 B.C.). But this is not the theory presented on the show. Instead, the scene turns on two occasions to Schoch to argue about water erosion data, during the monologue of John Anthony West, who argues "if the water-weathering theory is correct" then there was "a very ancient and highly sophisticated" (stone carving is "highly" sophisticated?) "civilization existing at a time when no civilization is supposed to have existed." When? In 12,000 B.C. Povich then says this may be the "last monument" of a vanished civilization. When he rhetorically asks if there is further evidence, he turns immediately, not to any archaeologist or historian, but to Edgar Cayce—the psychic.

But that is not the most disturbing part of this story. Schoch is shown arguing that "there were moist periods, rainy periods, in Egypt that clearly predate the modern Sahara desert." Then at once we see West, who follows, "this kind of a rainy period prevailed in

---

[3] See R.M. Schoch, "Redating the Great Sphinx of Giza," *KMT: A Modern Journal of Ancient Egypt* 3.2 (Summer 1992): 52-59, 66-70; T.L. Dobecki and R.M. Schoch, "Seismic Investigations in the Vicinity of the Great Sphinx of Giza, Egypt," *Geoarchaeology* 7.6 (1992): 527-44; R.M. Schoch, "L'Age du Sphinx de Gizeh: Vers Une Revision Dechirante?" *Kadath: Chroniques des Civilisations Disparues* 81 (Winter 1993-1994): 13-53.

Egypt around from the time when the last ice age broke up," and thus the Sphinx had to have been built around then. There is no qualification or distinction made here between the two views. Schoch is very plainly being presented as if he is West's co-theorist. Lest we be mistaken, Povich introduced the whole segment by saying "as we have seen, many suspect ancient Egypt was influenced by a vanished genius culture. For one group, the rock of the Sphinx speaks the truth." But wait, isn't Schoch's book called *Voices of the Rocks*? This seems an almost deliberate attribution of West's odd theory to Schoch, as if his book argues for a lost civilization (it does not—it isn't even about the Sphinx, although it briefly mentions it). We are led here to believe that Schoch and West are the "one group" Maury is talking about. This is a dangerous license to be taken with serious scholarship.

There were other "experts" as well. Christopher Frayling, listed as a "popular culture historian" and author of *The Face of Tutankhamun*, tells us that "the most convincing explanation of the curse" of King Tut is that "some energy" of some kind was pent up in the tomb and released, affecting all who were associated with it. Fortunately, Dr. Aidan Dodson's account at least lets us judge for ourselves, since he reports how Lord Carnarvon died from an infected mosquito bite that was cut while shaving—a more plausible account, at least of his death. We are not told about any of the other "dozen" (Maury Povich) or "thirty-five" (Fox website) people who died under "mysterious circumstances," so Fox does not help us decide what to believe here.[4] The way Dodson's narrative is abused, however, pushes ethical boundaries yet again. Interspersed with his otherwise historical account we hear others interject fantastic comments: Povich tells us that "at the precise moment of [Lord Carnarvon's] death" there was a blackout in Cairo, and Frayling adds that Carnarvon's pet howled and died in England. Are we being led to believe that Dodson endorses this account?

When asked, Dodson said he could not confirm any of the claims inserted into his monologue. However, he doubted that there were a "dozen" mysterious deaths, and added that Cairo's power system is so notoriously bad that a blackout would not be a supernatural coincidence. Is it ethical to splice factual statements

---

[4] See David Silverman, "The Curse of the Curse of the Pharaohs," *Expedition* 29.2 (1987): 56-63.

when the speakers do not share each other's views? This is the very same thing done to Schoch. I asked Dodson if he would have liked to respond on TV to any of the claims made on the show (not just those littering his own segment). He said he would, but "with such off-the-wall ideas, it's almost impossible to even try to rebut them. There's just no point of connection between reality and fantasy!"

This abuse is matched by yet another example. Povich introduces the "monuments on Mars" theory again later in the broadcast, adding that "recent exploration suggests it may be so." Immediately we hear a replay of a real news report, over the sight of a rocket launch. The news anchor's voice declares, "All the talk tonight is about Mars and whether American scientists have the proof that life once existed on that planet." Immediately, we move to Richard Hoagland again, and Viking orbiter images of the "face" on Mars. But wait...are we being told that there was a real news story about this, that "American scientists" were really asking whether this was proof of life on Mars? The recording sure sounded to me like a report on the evidence of microbial fossils in a Martian meteorite, but I have no way of knowing, because that part was cut out. If this is what they did, isn't this dishonest? This seems a serious ethical question.

Eventually we get to the expected tie-in with the previous Sunday's news report. Besides being told repeatedly that the Egyptian constructions were "seemingly supernatural" in their technical perfection,[5] the hieroglyphs that "prove" our extraterrestrial origins are shown again. This time, Hoagland is our interpreter, despite the fact that even Fox won't stoop so low as to claim he has any expertise in this matter. We are shown a wall inscription, which Hoagland says has pictures of "high-tech things" like "helicopters and land speeders and spaceships and the Millennium Falcon." To prove his point, the Fox production team overlays video of an Apache helicopter to show the similarity. According to Ms. Griffis-Greenberg, an Egyptologist [then] at the University of Alabama at Birmingham, who saw this broadcast, this interpretation is absurd, but not new to her—it has cropped up

---

[5] The pyramids are still made of the most primitive of permanent construction materials (stone) and no super-technological cutting tools have been found. See also Robert Bianchi, "Pyramidiots," *Archaeology* 44 (November-December 1991): 84; and Daniel Boorstin, "Afterlives of the Great Pyramids," *The Wilson Quarterly* 16 (Summer 1992): 130-38.

on the Usenet so many times she is tired of answering it. But she was glad to explain yet again, and referred me to more credible sources.

I spoke to several other Egyptologists who were amazed that this was being done on television, although one said to me that he expects this sort of thing now, "It is just what TV does." But what do the experts say about this "helicopter" glyph? This will serve as an example for all the rest: the "helicopter" is in fact the Abydos palimpsest. A palimpsest is what is created when new writing is inscribed over old. In the case of papyri, old ink is scraped off, but in the case of inscriptions, plaster is added over the old inscription and a new inscription is made. The image described as a helicopter is well known to be the names of Rameses inscribed over the names of his father (something Rameses was known to do quite frequently). A little bit of damage from time and weathering has furthered the illusion of a "helicopter."[6]

What we should ask is why no Egyptologists were questioned about this, something well known in the literature? As one of them said to me, "We don't live under rocks!" It would not have been hard to get an expert to clarify the meaning of the "helicopter"—they had several experts on camera already. Hawass is heard saying the claim of aliens coming from space and building the pyramids "is nuts," but he is never asked to comment on any specific details of the arguments being made. This is a very one-sided investigation. The people are not being fairly informed.

The show did conclude on an encouraging note, however. West's theory was tied to Cayce's claim of a lost hall of records beneath the Sphinx, and when the Tomb of Osiris is being explored with Hawass, he is asked his opinion of the Cayce theory. His response? "It's a myth...but to be fair," he adds with a humorous tone, "I did not excavate this tunnel yet," pointing down a shaft perhaps leading in the direction of the Sphinx, "then really I don't know." Hopefully the audience will catch his sarcasm.

Hawass was also given (almost) the last word: "People like to dream. And I like to let them dream. But my show gives them a

---

[6] See www.bibliotecapleyades.net/egipto/abydos/abydos03.htm, with Juergen von Beckerath, *Handbuch der aegyptischen Koenigsnamen* [*Muenchner aegyptologische Studien* 20 (1984)], pp. 235-37; Omm Sety and Hanny El Zeini, *Abydos: Holy City of Ancient Egypt* (1981), p. 187; and Shafik Farid, ed., *The Temple at Abydos* (1983), p. 8. I would like to thank Ms. Griffis-Greenberg for her help.

little of reality. I believe that all that we found today, this is the reality." And indeed he is right—for despite all the "wacky" theories, the only real facts that were exposed on the show were of that very reality: the pyramids were tombs built for mummified corpses buried only thousands, not tens of thousands, of years ago. The pyramids were built without secret history or technology; no Atlantis; no aliens; no amazing hall of records. Just an exciting, fascinating, thoroughly human, and definitely Egyptian, historical reality.

10

PSEUDOHISTORY IN JERRY VARDAMAN'S MAGIC COINS: THE NONSENSE OF MICROGRAPHIC LETTERS

Originally published in the *Skeptical Inquirer* 26.2
(March-April 2002), 39-41, 61.
Minor revisions © 2014 by Richard Carrier.
Original © 2002 by the *Skeptical Inquirer*.
Reproduced with permission.

An archaeologist claims to find hundreds of microscopic letters on ancient coins and inscriptions that completely rewrite history. Conclusion: bogus.

Jerry Vardaman, at one time an archaeologist at the Cobb Institute of Archaeology at Mississippi State University, claims to have discovered microscopic letters covering ancient coins and inscriptions conveying all sorts of strange data, which he then uses to assert the wildest chronology of ancient events imaginable, particularly for Jesus. For instance, these "microletters" allegedly prove that Jesus was born in 12 B.C. (instead of 6 A.D., which is the most credible year to date), Pontius Pilate actually governed Judaea between 15 and 26 A.D. (instead of 26-36 A.D.), Jesus was crucified in 21 A.D. (instead of in the 30s according to mainstream scholarship), etc.

Vardaman's evidence is incredibly bizarre and can best be described as pseudohistorical. Certainly, his "evidence" is not accepted by any other expert in ancient coins to my knowledge. It has never been presented in any peer-reviewed venue, and was totally unknown to members of the American Numismatic Society until I brought it to their attention. Several specialists there concurred with me that it was patently ridiculous. Nevertheless, Vardaman's conclusions keep turning up matter-of-factly in more mainstream sources, so an investigation is warranted.

Vardaman's chronological arguments, and the use of his pseudo-evidence, appear in print in only three publications. The first, Vardaman's "Jesus' Life: A New Chronology," appears in Jerry Vardaman & Edwin Yamauchi, eds., *Chronos, Kairos, Christos: Nativity and Chronological Studies Presented to Jack Finegan*, published in 1989 by the small biblical studies press Eisenbrauns of Winona Lake, Indiana. The second is Vardaman's own *Chronology and Early Church History in the New Testament*, a series of typed and photocopied lectures delivered to the Hong Kong Baptist Theological Seminary in 1998. Only a few cheaply bound copies of this exist. Though I was based in New York city, I had to acquire mine on loan from the Southern Baptist Theological Seminary of Kentucky. The third item is in *Chronos, Kairos, Christos II: Chronological, Nativity, and Religious Studies in Memory of Ray Summers*, edited solely by Vardaman and published by Mercer University Press of Macon, Georgia, in 1998. In this, the evidence is not argued at all, but is simply taken for granted. This is true of Vardaman's "A Provisional Chronology of the New Testament: Jesus Through Paul's Early Years" (313-20)—which doesn't even mention the evidence on which the chronology is based—and of a chapter contributed by Robert Smith, "New Evidence Regarding Early Christian Chronology: A Reconsideration," (133-39), who takes all of Vardaman's claims about microletters for granted, based solely on his drawings.

Nevertheless, Vardaman's "conclusions" are cited without a single sign of skepticism by several people, including John McRay, who says in his 1991 book *Archaeology and the New Testament*, "Jerry Vardaman has discovered the name of Quirinius on a coin in micrographic letters, placing him as proconsul of Syria and Cilicia from 11 B.C. until after the death of Herod" (154). McRay cites a manuscript Vardaman sent him, which has never been published, though a similar claim appears in one of Vardaman's lectures delivered in China in 1998. That Vardaman had this theory at least since McRay wrote in 1989 and yet has never published it in any peer-reviewed journal (but instead made a significantly different claim in an isolated foreign seminary lecture eight years later) demonstrates that Vardaman either realizes he cannot convince any real experts on the subject, or was told so by independent reviewers.

I am not surprised. For what Vardaman means by "micrographic letters" (he usually calls them "microletters") are tiny letters so small that they cannot be seen or made without a magnifying glass and could only have been written with some sort of special diamond-tipped inscribers. He finds enormous amounts of this writing on various coins, supporting countless theses of his. He also claims that he and Oxford scholar Nikos Kokkinos discovered microletters on coins in 1984 at the British Museum, though Kokkinos has not published anything on the matter. Nevertheless, Vardaman tells us that some coins "are literally covered with microletters…through the Hellenistic and Roman periods" and that "whatever their original purpose(s), the use of microletters was spread over so many civilizations for so many centuries that their presence cannot be denied or ignored" (1989: 66, 67). Such confident assertions for an extremely radical and controversial theory that has not been proven to the satisfaction of anyone else in the field gives the impression of a serious loss of objectivity.

Vardaman cites one authority in support of his thesis that does not in fact support him, yet he fails to qualify this citation for readers but acts as if this makes his theory mainstream. He refers to "hand-scratched microletters" noted by E.T. Newell in volume 46 of the *American Journal of Numismatics* (1912: 112), yet Newell only shows evidence there of graffiti on coins: one or two letters, roughly scratched by hand with an ordinary object, and quite visible to the naked eye. This phenomenon is in fact well known and not unusual. But these are not "microletters" in Vardaman's sense: they are neither microscopic nor do they literally cover coins with added information, but only a few letters at most. Moreover, their date cannot really be established, since the scratchings could have been made decades after the coins were minted. In contrast, central to Vardaman's thesis is the claim that most of these inscriptions were created by the minters and thus reflect official records.

Needless to say, this is totally unattested as a practice in any ancient source and none of the relevant tools (magnifying glasses and diamond microcutters) have been recovered, or ever heard of from ancient times.[1] But there are even more concrete reasons to

---

[1] A few years after writing this I found evidence that the Romans did have primitive magnifying glasses and produced microsculptures, but no tools of the kind that would work on coin dies (or be effective on minted coins).

regard Vardaman's theory as crackpot. First, it is extremely rare to find any specimen of ancient coin that is not heavily worn from use and the passage of literally thousands of years, in which time the loss of surface from abrasion and oxidation is inevitable and significant. Even if such microscopic lettering were added to these coins as Vardaman says, hardly any of it could have survived or remained legible, yet Vardaman has no trouble finding hundreds of perfectly legible words on every coin he examines. Second, to prove his thesis, Vardaman would at the very least be expected to publish enlarged photographs of the reputed microscopic etchings. Yet he has never done this. Instead, all he offers are his own drawings. Both of these facts are extremely suspicious. Finally, the sorts of things Vardaman finds are profoundly absurd, and rank right up there with Erich von Däniken's *Chariots of the Gods*. Figure 1 is a typical example.

Figure 1. "Microletters" on a Roman coin as seen by Jerry Vardaman.

Notice that this is merely a drawing, not a photograph, and that Vardaman gives no indication of scale (1989: 70, 71, shown above in reversed order, and reduced). He never even properly identifies the coin type, and though he quotes the British Museum catalogue regarding it, he gives no catalogue number or citation, so readers are unable to hunt down a photograph of it or to estimate its size. I eventually found it on my own, in A.M. Burnett's 1992 catalogue of *Roman Provincial Coinage*, where it is listed as item 4797. There we discover that it is only 26mm in diameter. Yet his drawing of it has a diameter of 4.75 inches (about 120mm) for a scale of well over 4:1, and his blow-up is a little over three-times that, for at least 14:1 (see Figure 1). That means that his letters, drawn at around a quarter inch in size (around 6mm), represent marks on the original coin smaller than 1/50th an inch, less than half a millimeter. It would be nearly impossible to have made these marks, much less hundreds of them, and on thousands coins, at minting or afterward. Indeed, even the number of men and hours this would require would be vast beyond reckoning, considering the thousands of coins minted yearly, though Vardaman insists most of the marks were made in the dies from which the coins were cast (1989: 67), which entails a quality of die casting all but unimaginable for the ancient world. And though it would be entirely impossible for these marks to have survived the wear of time (see Figure 2), Vardaman sees them clear as day.

When we look at an actual photograph of this coin (here shown enlarged—Vardaman's drawings reproduce the coin's reverse, shown bottom), we see at once that Vardaman's claims are hopelessly untenable.[2] To begin with, his representation of this coin is very misleading: his drawing includes all sorts of crisp details that imply a coin in a near-flawless condition, like the facial features of the goddess and veins in the laurel leaves along the bottom left edge (nearest the

Figure 2. Photo of cast of coin in Figure 1, no microletters visible.

---

[2] The image in figure 2 is actually a photo of a plastercast of the coin (from Burnett), which reproduces relief details but not micro-details (the evidence of wear etc. is thus preserved, though micro-cracks and pits are not). In the next chapter I discuss photographs of the actual coin itself.

blow-up section), yet these are entirely a product of his imagination. It is quite clear that the coin has been worn so smooth that the face of the goddess is completely rubbed away, and the laurel leaves themselves have almost been obliterated—there are certainly no remaining details like the veins. We can also see that this wear has rubbed smooth the very region in which Vardaman finds the most microletters: there is nothing there. Even had there been something, it could not possibly have survived the wear endured by more robust features like the face and leaves. If Vardaman is reading anything, it can only be random scratches and pits, the byproduct of two thousand years of abrasion and oxidation.

There are flaws here even more fatal. Just as Vardaman says, this coin was minted by the city of Damascus in the reign of Tiberius, and the coin itself bears the legend "Λ HKT ΔAMAΣKΩN" or "Year 328 of the Damascenes," referring to its re-establishment as a Greek city by the first Seleucus, in the last years of the 4th century B.C. Coins minted in Eastern Greek cities did not use Latin letters or words, they used Greek—one can see even from Vardaman's drawing that the *real* letters on this coin are Greek, spelling Greek words—yet almost all of Vardaman's "microletters" for some strange reason appear in Latin. Second, and quite humorously, all the Latin letters for "J" appear, as Vardaman reproduces them, as modern J's, yet that letter was not invented until late in the Middle Ages. If his J's were genuine, they should appear as the letter I. This alone proves his claims are bogus.

But Vardaman doesn't stop there. The microletters tell him all sorts of new "facts" about the ancient world. Most bizarre of all:

> The most important references on this coin are to "Jesus of Nazareth." He is mentioned frequently, often in titles and phrases found in the New Testament, for example, "Jesus, King of the Jews," "King," "the Righteous One," and "Messiah." Reference to the first year of his "reign" is repeated often...for example, "Year one of Jesus of Nazareth in Galilee [*sic*]." (1989: 72)

The absurdity of all this, officially and microscopically inscribed on every coin by the royal mint of the King of the Nabataeans in 16 A.D., stands without need of comment.

In addition to coins, Vardaman also "sees" microscopic letters on stone inscriptions—even though stone, by its roughness and exposure to weathering, would be even less likely to preserve such markings if they had ever been made. Indeed, large stones of the day were not polished, making it quite impossible for microscopic letters to be inscribed on them in any visible way. For the stone would more often than not simply chip, while natural pits and cracks would obscure anything that took, and the rest would be worn away by time. Yet he finds these tiny letters on numerous stones, including the famous *Lapis Venetus* inscription (a badly damaged stone now in the Vatican). In an unnumbered page appended to his 1998 lectures, entitled "The Problem of Theudas and Microletters on the Lapis Venetus," he says microletters on this stone declare that the Jewish rebel Theudas was king of the Scythians! This was a people living on the Russian steppes, a thousand miles from Judaea. I suppose Vardaman imagines him as a latter-day Spartacus of some sort. But common sense leads me to conclude that this is all nonsense on stilts.

Now for the punchline. There is no Quirinius coin. McRay's reference is to an unpublished paper that no doubt comes up with more complete nonsense about Quirinius in the reading of random scratches on some coin or other. But Vardaman hasn't even published this claim. Instead, almost a decade later, when he did present a lecture on the matter, his paper on the dating of Quirinius, though over 20 pages in length, never mentions this coin that apparently McRay read about. Instead, a date of 12 B.C. is arrived at using nonexistent microletters on a stone inscription (the very same *Lapis Venetus*). Hopefully this pseudohistory can be seen for what it is. Any claim based on this work must be held in the highest suspicion.

11

MORE ON VARDAMAN'S MICROLETTERS

Originally published in the Skeptical Inquirer
26.4 (July-August 2002), 60-61.
Minor revisions © 2014 by Richard Carrier.
Original © 2002 by the Skeptical Inquirer.
Reproduced with permission.

Several observations must be communicated regarding my previous article "Pseudohistory in Jerry Vardaman's Magic Coins."

First, Vardaman passed away in November of 2000. I directed my work at his claims, still appearing in print (both John McRay and Lee Strobel cite him), not at the man, whom I believed was never challenged while alive. But it appears he was once, in a less-known antiquities journal (David Hendlin, "Theory of Secret Inscriptions on Coins is Disputed," *The Celator* 5.3 [March 1991], 28-32). Sent to me by a kind reader, this included a response by Vardaman in which he added still further references to evidence of ordinary graffiti or inscriptions as "support" for his thesis, an argument I refuted. The rest of his response was mere challenge and assertion. Hendlin, for his part, corroborates some of my observations, and adds some of his own, drawing on his vast experience in numismatic science. And he had the benefit of interrogating Vardaman. His article is an excellent addition to mine.

Second, several letters from readers unfairly questioned Vardaman's credentials. According to the Gale Database of Contemporary Authors he received a Ph.D. from Baylor University in 1974, after a Th.D. from Southwestern Baptist Theological Seminary in 1958 (he was an ordained Baptist minister). He was a genuine field archaeologist and held a professorship in religion at Tarleton State College in Stephenville, Texas, followed by instructorships at two Baptist seminaries, before receiving his position at Cobb in 1972.

Third, Joe D. Seger, current Director of the Cobb Institute of Archaeology (as of 2002), wishes to clarify that the "professional staff and colleagues of Vardaman at the Institute had fully disassociated themselves from his micro-letter theories long before his retirement in 1993." Though I made no claims or inferences about their views or involvement in this affair, it should be noted that Seger's statement is not backed up by any public document to my knowledge, and when asked for articles where Institute scholars criticised or disavowed Vardaman's theory, none were provided. I also received a private communication from Professor Stephen Williams, author of *Fantastic Archaeology* (1991) and a Harvard emeritus, who apparently was one of a few outside experts called in by MSU in the 1970s to evaluate Vardaman's claims. The consultants gave a resounding condemnation, but the only action taken appears to have been the removal of Vardaman as director of the Cobb Institute in 1981. He remained a professor there, and nothing was published on the matter. All this was in essence confirmed by Seger. It would appear that MSU was embarrassed by Vardaman but was happy to sweep the whole affair under the rug.

Fourth, the curators of the British Museum informed me that many of the plates in Burnett were made from plastercasts, not genuine photographs. So on a recent trip to England I studied the coin in question and arranged for new photographs. As I would not want to mislead anyone, it is fitting to present what I can personally vouch for as a genuine photo, remarking on what I observed under a magnifying glass and digital microscope. I can confirm there

Figure 1. Photograph of the actual Damascene coin. © The British Museum. As appearing in *Skeptical Inquirer* by permission.

are no "microletters" on the coin (Figure 1). The photo used in my original *Skeptical Inquirer* article faithfully indicates the nature and extent of the coin's wear, but it is clear from the new photograph how a delusional mind could be led to see microletters in grit, oxidation and numerous cracks and abrasions. Indeed, I observed the coin to be heavily patinated. Most of the scratchy lines and squiggles visible here are the green patina of oxidized bronze, not a part of the original coin as cast.

Blow-up A.

I took great care under high magnification to try and see how Vardaman's letters might be interpreted, but to no avail. There is nothing even resembling what he claims, despite ample fuel for the imagination. All the observations made in my original article remain correct, including the fact that the key area of the coin is completely smooth from wear, and thus could not have microletters even if they were once there (Blow-up A).

To be fair, elsewhere on the coin there is the clear appearance of the letter "M" ("W" was not invented until relatively recent times), a crack filled with bright green patina (Blow-up B). This is the only thing that looks like a letter and that Vardaman did indeed represent in his drawings as a vague squiggle. So Vardaman's drawings were indeed based on a photograph or personal viewing of the coin, and not just wholly fictional. But this "letter" is an irregular zigzag, a random crack carved out by rust, a common outcome of impurities in the coining process permitting accelerated oxidation (rampant rust-based cracking is pronounced on the coin's other face).

Blow-up B.

It is certainly not part of any word, and there is nothing like this anywhere else that accords with Vardaman's drawings.

Finally, many wrote me to ask whether my claim that 6 A.D. for Jesus's birth "is the most credible year to date" was a mistake for 6 B.C., as most references claim a date of 4 B.C. But experts have long known the Gospel of Matthew sets the date around 6 B.C. (or no later than 4 B.C.), while Luke sets the date at 6 A.D. However, if either Gospel contains any history, it is far more likely Luke than Matthew, for a number of reasons, not the least being that Luke alone writes like a historian and actually attempts to date events by reference to office-holders, while Matthew does not, but instead litters his account with fantastic stories begging credulity. So an objective assessment of the two conflicting sources leads us to Luke, not Matthew. The reason Matthew is ever preferred is largely ideological, not historical: it is impossible to fit Matthew's story to Luke's chronology, but possible (if you invent some external facts) to force Luke to fit Matthew. Thus, to preserve Biblical consistency one must side with Matthew. But the premises here are that the Gospels cannot contradict each other and do not contain false data, premises no skeptic can accept. Abandon those premises, and the most credible date for the nativity is A.D. 6. [Although I am certain even that is a fiction.] For more than you ever wanted to know about this, see my article "Luke vs. Matthew on the Year of Christ's Birth" [Chapter 15].

12

HITLER'S *TABLE TALK*:
TROUBLING FINDS

This article was first published in
German Studies Review 26.3 (October 2003): 561-76.
Minor revisions & new afterword © 2014 by Richard Carrier.
Original © 2003 by the German Studies Association.
Reprinted with permission from
Johns Hopkins University Press.

Hitler was passionately hostile to Christianity: "I shall never come to terms with the Christian lie... Our epoch will certainly see the end of the disease of Christianity. It will last another hundred years, two hundred years perhaps. My regret will have been that I couldn't, like whoever the prophet was, behold the promised land from afar." He accepted a broadly Nietzschean account of Christianity as a conspiracy of Jews for a slave revolt against their Roman conquerors: "Christianity is a prototype of Bolshevism: the mobilisation by the Jew of the masses of slaves with the object of undermining society."

— Jonathan Glover[1]

This is a claim often made, employing the same or similar quotations. But the quotations are largely false. Hitler did criticize priests and the Church and certain Christian dogmas quite a bit, but so do god-fearing Christians. Hitler never went quite as far as

---

[1] Jonathan Glover, *Humanity: A Moral History of the Twentieth Century* (New Haven: Yale University Press, 1999), pp. 355-56.

these statements imply. Has Glover been duped by a sham document? His source is Hitler's *Table Talk*, a curious text whose story remains to be adequately told by historians of the era. The need for further research will be emphasized by the findings presented here.

What is the Table Talk?

The *Table Talk* is purportedly a transcription from notebooks written in shorthand by at least two secretaries to Hitler, Heinrich Heim and Henry Picker, who were instructed by Hitler's right-hand man Martin Bormann to record for posterity whatever Hitler said in his bunker in Berlin [*actually not there but the one in Poland*], usually during meals or tea. In addition to official matters, they recorded things he said off the cuff, each logged by date and time (like "morning," "afternoon," or "evening"). So far all accounts agree.[2] Beyond this is some confusion that an enterprising historian will some day have to sort out. That may be difficult, since much is said by Genoud and Trevor-Roper without a word as to how they know it. No sources or documents are cited.

---

[2] Apart from still more changes of title, publisher, and publication date than are noted here, the following survey exhausts all major variants I know: First appeared the German version of Henry Picker in 1951 (1st ed., with Gerhard Ritter; 2nd ed. with Percy Schramm in 1963; 3rd ed. in 1976) entitled *Hitlers Tischgespräche im Führerhauptquartier, 1941-42* (1st ed.: Bonn: Athenaeum-Verlag; 2nd & 3rd eds.: Stuttgart: Seewald). In 1952 came the French version of François Genoud, *Libres Propos sur la Guerre et la Paix: Recueillis sur l'Ordre de Martin Bormann* (Paris: Flammarion). Then in 1953 arrives the English version edited by H.R. Trevor-Roper, *Hitler's Table Talk, 1941-1944* (London: Weidenfeld and Nicholson), also published as *Hitler's Secret Conversations, 1941-1944*. Reprinted many times (e.g. 1961, 1988), a new (2nd) ed. was issued in 1973, and a 3rd ed. in 2000 [*and in reaction to this article, a 4th ed. was released in 2007 with a new preface by renowned Hitler historian Gerhard Weinberg acknowledging the findings of this article*]. In 1980 came the most important edition of all: Werner Jochmann, *Monologe im Führerhauptquartier 1941-1944: die Aufzeichnungen Heinrich Heims herausgegeben von Werner Jochmann* (Hamburg: A Knaus). I have also stumbled across I.M. Fradkin's 1993 translation into Russian of Picker's version, entitled *Zastolnye razgovory Gitlera* (Smolensk: Rusich). Gitta Sereny, "The Truth Is, I Loved Hitler," *The Observer* (28 April 1996) mentions a serialization of the original German of Genoud's manuscript in an unnamed German magazine sometime in the 70s, which I could not confirm.

One might readily question the authenticity of such a text, given the conflicting versions and questionable chains of custody in this case and the abundance of other forged works purporting to reveal the secret thoughts or plans of Hitler. But it is likely the notes were real. There are two completely independent manuscripts, and a fragment of a third; and all agree in such a way as to corroborate the existence of a genuine original. The fragment consists of forty-two typed pages in the Adolf Hitler Collection at the U.S. Library of Congress, which are probably authentic.[3] Scribbled in handwriting atop the first page of these is the brief remark: "Found by Mr. Jos. Schrasberger,[4] München, Herzog Wilhelm Straße 4." This is probably part of the lost copy of the Bormann manuscript (discussed below). Finally, Werner Jochmann's edition of the text includes an introduction citing notes and letters confirming the *Table Talk* was indeed being made and collated during the war.

Picker, of course, was an eyewitness to this affair, and says in his first introduction (33-34) that Heim had been authorized by Bormann to go beyond his official duty to transcribe Hitler's spoken orders and decisions and to include whatever else interested him, and this authority passed to Picker during Heim's brief

---

[3] Cf. Gerhard Weinberg, *Guide to Captured German Documents* (Maxwell Airforce Base, Alabama: Human Resources Research Institute, 1952). On p. 55 it is noted that "Safe 5" contains item 6, a "box of miscellaneous Hitler items" including sub-item 4: "Führerhauptquartier, Jan 18, 1942, abends, 4 pp.," which "concerns German domestic politics;" "Führerhauptquartier, Jan 24, 1942, abends, 2 pp.," whose contents aren't described; and item 8, "Typed copies of the utterances of Hitler, 1942, under item 6 above" (file no. 52-178). In fact, item 8 contains copies of everything in item 6, plus: Jan 8/9: 9 pp.; 16/17: 14 pp.; 17/18: 3 pp.; 18/19: 2 pp.; 19: 3 pp.; 20: 2 pp.; 22: 2 pp.; 24: 2 pp. (all from 1942). I did not attempt a systematic collation, but I noticed many handwritten corrections aligning what was typed to what appears in Jochmann or Picker. [UPDATE: *The authenticity of these pages may come into question upon completion of Prof. Nilsson's research, which should be consulted in future. See following note.*]

[4] The letter "a" in Schrasberger is unclear—it could be another vowel. [UPDATE: *The name is actually Joseph Ehrnsberger. I had indeed misread the handwriting. But the reading was corrected and the man subsequently identified by Professor Mikael Nilsson as a German civilian employee of the American Central Collecting Point in Munich, hired in 1945 as a gallery assistant. See afterword to this article (pp. 188-90) for more on Nilsson's research.*]

absence. Picker says Hitler actually looked over his record on occasion and approved it as accurate, yet didn't realize how often these notes were being taken. He also reports that the official notebooks collated by Bormann were lost in the "confusion of the surrender." These would turn up a year later in Genoud's possession, and some pages from a copy of this apparently ended up in the Library of Congress. But Picker retained his own original notes and those made by Heim before him.

Trevor-Roper's edition claims to be working from a version of the notebooks extensively edited and collated by Martin Bormann, called the *Bormann-Vermerke* ("Bormann Notes"), which until recently existed only in the private collection of François Genoud. Genoud relates in his 1952 preface that the thousand-page monstrosity had a note at front in Bormann's handwriting: *Bitte diese—später äußerst wertvollen—Aufzeichnungen sehr gut aufheben*, "Please preserve with the greatest care these notes of a capital interest for the future" (Jochmann publishes a facsimile of this note opposite his title page). According to Jochmann's introduction, these were to be the "official" notebooks, collated and edited from the originals by Bormann and published as a definitive party manifesto for the victorious Reich. Unlike Picker's, the Bormann text continues to 1944. Since Picker received his copy of the notes from Heim upon replacing him until Heim returned, he did not have access to the remaining notes taken after this tenure.

Jochmann and Trevor-Roper (in the preface to his third edition) both relate (among many other details) that the *Bormann-Vermerke* was sent piecemeal from Bormann to his wife Gerda. Another copy reportedly went to an office in Munich, which was likely destroyed by allied bombing, apart from the pages recovered by Schrasberger [*i.e. Ehrnsberger*]. Gerda fled to Italy with her collection of the notes in 1945 and died there in a detention camp in 1946. A local Italian official then acquired the manuscript, which he sold to Genoud around 1948.[5] That manuscript is the basis for Jochmann's text, as well as Genoud's and Trevor-Roper's translations.

---

[5] Cf. Sereny, "The Truth."

Which Version Should We Trust?

There are so many published versions and editions of these notes I gave up attempts to track them all. In general, there are four major versions, each with its own advocate: Henry Picker (1951, 1963, 1976), François Genoud (1952), H.R. Trevor-Roper (1953, 1973, 2000), and Werner Jochmann (1980). Of these only two offer the original German (Picker and Jochmann). Genoud, a Swiss banker and lifetime Nazi, offers his own French translation. Historian Trevor-Roper presents the English translation of R.H. Stevens and Norman Cameron.

From the isolated comparisons I made, Trevor-Roper's English appears to be an almost verbatim translation of Genoud's French. Yet the title "Hitler's Table Talk" is a direct English translation of Picker's title, not Genoud's,[6] and Trevor-Roper's preface claims the translation was made from the German original of Martin Bormann. Genoud's version ends in 1942 (his preface declares an intent to publish the rest in a second volume, which never transpired), as does Picker's (who did not have any material beyond 1942), while Trevor-Roper and Jochmann continue with entries up to 1944.[7]

Assuming any published text is a genuine copy of these notes, Picker's edition (especially where it agrees with Jochmann) carries the strongest claim to authenticity. It contains the actual German, and was the first to be published, a year before Genoud, and though Genoud procured a lengthy but essentially trivial preface from Robert d'Harcourt of the Académie Française, Picker had the involvement and auspices of a major university and Hitler

---

[6] A full translation would be "Hitler's Table Talk in the Central Headquarters." Genoud's title translates "Candid Remarks on the War and Peace: Collected by Order of Martin Bormann." A handwritten title page attached to item 8 in the Library of Congress reads "Hitler Privat-Gespräche," which appears to be a reverse translation of Trevor-Roper's alternate title (each entry has a similar handwritten cover sheet identifying the corresponding pages in an unspecified edition of Trevor-Roper).

[7] The later entries were recorded by Heim upon his return, though several were recorded by Bormann himself. Jochmann's edition does not include any of the entries personally made by Picker, between March and August '42, due to a copyright dispute—on the other hand, Jochmann includes many entries in '41 and '42, presumably made either by Heim or (more likely) Bormann, that do not appear in Picker.

historian: "Arranged on behalf of the German Institute for the History of National Socialism, initiated and published by Gerhard Ritter, professor of history at the University of Freiburg."[8] Moreover, Picker was one of the actual stenographers (from 21 March 1942 to 2 August 1942), and thus transcribed many of the notes himself in the very presence of Hitler, making him an eyewitness with access to the notebooks of his predecessor Heim, which he says he acquired directly, bypassing the editing of Bormann.

Picker's second and third editions also contain several testimonials to the text's accuracy and authenticity by fellow bunker officers, including Gerhard Engel, and also a testimonial by historian Walter Mediger who checked the first edition against Picker's own transcripts and "made corrections" accordingly, testifying to the accuracy of the new edition in relation to those notes. Picker asserted in his first edition that [translating Picker's German] "a sufficient number of the staff at the FHQ lives to be able to testify to the authenticity of the recordings of the table discussions, since Hitler spoke rarely at table on military affairs," and to demonstrate his personal knowledge he gives a detailed description of the bunker and meeting room, and who was present on Hitler's staff at the time. Adding further credibility, Picker's text reads like a quick stenograph, with some things missing between entries, which are often short, with no time for any explanation or context (which Bormann on occasion added). Even the sentences themselves are often concise and sometimes missing simple words like pronouns.

Finally, Jochmann presents the text of the Bormann manuscript employed by Genoud and (supposedly) Trevor-Roper's translators, and it agrees with Picker and the pages recovered from Munich to such a detailed extent that we can be assured all three texts have a common ancestor, which must be the actual bunker notes themselves. Nevertheless, even at best, they are the hasty notes taken on the fly by a second party, not necessarily a true verbatim record of what Hitler said (all the editors underplay this fact, except Jochmann, who emphasizes it).

---

[8] From the title page: "Im Auftrage des Deutschen Instituts für Geschichte der nationalsozialistischen Zeit geordnet, eingeleitet und veröffentlicht von Gerhard Ritter, Professor der Geschichte a. D. Universität Freiburg."

The work of Werner Jochmann presents not only some sound scholarship on the *Table Talk*, but an important version of the text. The differences from Picker are mostly minor variations in wording that have no substantial effect on meaning, though some deviations are more significant (e.g., sometimes one text contains entire entries lacking in the other). Jochmann supports his text's authority by including photocopies of typed pages, as well as handwritten notes by Heim and Bormann, and other items. Jochmann also relates his own version of events regarding how the notes came to be made, and other details, though unlike Picker, who draws on his own recollections, or Genoud and Trevor-Roper, who cite no sources at all, Jochmann reconstructs events from letters and documents. How successfully or judiciously he accomplishes this I did not attempt to judge, but no one else has done as much.

Jochmann seems convinced that the *Bormann-Vermerke* contains the Heim originals, and thus it is Picker who was careless whenever they disagree. But since Picker's second edition was independently checked and certified, against notes direct from Heim, while Jochmann is working from later drafts that had passed through the editing of Bormann and his secretaries, it does not seem plausible that Jochmann's text can claim greater accuracy than Picker's. But I will leave this debate for others to resolve.

What Jonathan Glover didn't know is that the anti-Christian quotes he used only appear in Genoud's French and Trevor-Roper's English, not the German, except one that appears only in Jochmann. Yet Picker and Jochmann present the untranslated German, and from independent manuscripts. Indeed, Jochmann reproduces the very manuscript used by Genoud and (ostensibly) Stevens and Cameron. So whose version are we to trust?

Given certain blatant distortions in Genoud's French, it appears some shameful mischief has been done by Genoud, while Stevens and Cameron are equally guilty of some incompetence or dishonesty—at least, if they claimed to have translated the *Bormann-Vermerke* but in fact merely translated Genoud's French. In the preface to his third edition, Trevor-Roper describes the bitter copyright battle between Picker and Genoud, which is supposed to explain why Genoud didn't allow the actual *Bormann-Vermerke* to be published until 1980, and then only after decades of insistent cajoling by academics. One might wonder if Genoud was also trying to conceal his crime.

There may be a clue on the website of the controversial historian David Irving.[9] He relates how Genoud attempted to hoax him in the 1970s with what appeared to be a forgery of "Hitler's Last Testament," which Genoud published earlier.[10] Irving even claims he got him to confess to forging this "testament," Genoud declaring in his defense "But it's just what Hitler would have said, isn't it?" Irving's story throws a lot of suspicion on Genoud as a man willing to perpetrate a hoax, thinking it permissible to fabricate the words of Hitler if it was what he believed Hitler "would have said." Such a man would likely have no scruple against altering and inserting words and remarks into the *Table Talk*.

Further study of Genoud's history and motives, and the nature of the distortions he introduced into the record, would be worthwhile. He appears to have been a very strange man with a colorful history: a Swiss banker and Nazi spy who laundered money for the Third Reich, a self-professed neo-Nazi right up to his suicide in 1996 (though never an open supporter of the holocaust), a voracious purchaser and profiteer of Nazi archives,

---

[9] David Irving, "The Faking of Hitler's 'Last Testament'" (www.fpp.co.uk/Hitler/docs/Testament/byGenoud.html); this is part of Irving's "International Campaign for Real History," Focal Point Publications (www.fpp.co.uk/docs/Irving/FPhistory.html). Irving [*says he*] does not deny the Holocaust happened, only that Hitler knew of it [*among other things*]. His account of Genoud's involvement with him [*at any rate*] is first person and credible.

[10] François Genoud, ed., *The Testament of Adolf Hitler: The Hitler-Bormann Documents, February-April 1945* (London: Cassell, 1961 [also Icon Books, possibly others]). This was republished in 1978 (Los Angeles: World Service) with an introduction by L. Craig Fraser. It also appeared originally in French as *Le Testament politique de Hitler* (Paris: A. Fayard, 1959) with a preface by H.R. Trevor-Roper and commentary by André François-Poncet. On the questionable nature of this document, see Albert M. Beer, *Hitlers politisches Testament: Die Bormann-Diktate vom Februar und April 1945: eine Fälschung? Überarbeitete Fassung eines Vortrages auf der Tagung der Zeitgeschichtlichen Forschungsstelle Ingolstadt am 10. Mai 1986*. In a letter to me of 17 October 2002, Trevor-Roper reports being undecided about its authenticity. He claims Genoud would have nothing to gain by forging it, but [*that*] it could have been forged by one "Hans Rechenberg."

and an admitted financer of terrorists.[11] But I will leave it to more able historians to explore the facts of his life. Whatever Genoud's motivation for doctoring the text, the fact that Stevens and Cameron's English translation matches Genoud's falsified French (as we shall see), and not the actual *Bormann-Vermerke* published by Jochmann, leaves many questions unanswered. Were they lazy? Duped? Accomplices in crime? Whatever the case, the Trevor-Roper edition is to be discarded as worthless.

One might find fault in Trevor-Roper's excuse, at least in his first preface, for not comparing the two editions of Genoud and Picker: that Picker's text was not organized chronologically. Picker's first edition did organize the notebook entries by subject, but each entry was still precisely dated, and it would have been little trouble to manage a comparison. And this problem was corrected in Picker's second edition anyway, which restored the chronological order, leaving Trevor-Roper no reason not to demand a collation. Yet he sponsored two more editions since without comparing the texts or assessing the troubling discrepancies. Nor before releasing his third edition did he check the Stevens-Cameron translation against the German edition of Jochmann, which would have revealed the hoax, since here was their very source.[12] Or so he believed.

---

[11] Cf. Sereny, "The Truth"; Ben MacIntyre, "Swiss Banker who Worshipped Hitler Commits Suicide," *The Times* (4 June 1996); David Lee Preston, "Switzerland is Urged to Open its Files on Nazi who Financed Terrorists," *Philadelphia Inquirer* (19 March 1997). See also Pierre Péan, *L'Extrémiste: François Genoud, de Hitler à Carlos* (Paris: Fayard, 1996); Karl Laske, *Le Banquier Noir: François Genoud* (Paris: Editions du Seuil, 1996); Karl Laske & Maria Hoffmann-Dartevelle, *Ein Leben zwischen Hitler und Carlos: François Genoud* (Zurich: Limmat, 1996).

[12] However, Trevor-Roper, now Lord Dacre, has since come to suspect just what I argue: that Stevens and Cameron translated from the French, and poorly at that. In a letter to me of 17 October 2002 he reports recently discovering a mistranslation in the Stevens-Cameron text only explicable as a mistake in translating Genoud's otherwise correct French (they render *confus* as "confused" when the German and the context clearly indicate the connotation "embarrassed"), though he could not remember the exact passage (he is now nearly ninety, in poor health and, in his own words, "very blind"). He also heard that Richard Evans noted some questionable passages, in a brief for David Irving's defense in a "recent libel action."

Case Study: The Glover Quotes

At the conclusion of a two-page entry for the afternoon of 27 February 1942, the Trevor-Roper text reads as follows:

> If my presence on earth is providential, I owe it to a superior will. But I owe nothing to the Church that trafficks in the salvation of souls, and I find it really too cruel. I admit that one cannot impose one's will by force, but I have a horror of people who enjoy inflicting sufferings on others' bodies and tyranny upon others' souls.
>
> Our epoch will certainly see the end of the disease of Christianity. It will last another hundred years, two hundred years perhaps. My regret will have been that I couldn't, like whoever the prophet was, behold the promised land from afar. We are entering into a conception of the world that will be a sunny era, an era of tolerance. Man must be put in a position to develop freely the talents that God has given him.
>
> What is important above all is that we should prevent a greater lie from replacing the lie that is disappearing. The world of Judeo-Bolshevism must collapse.

But Jochmann and Picker both have a very different text here:

> Ich bin auf Grund höherer Gewalt da, wenn ich zu etwas nötig bin. Abgesehen davon, dass sie mir zu grausam ist, die seligmachende Kirche! Ich habe noch nie Gefallen gefunden daran, andere zu schinden, wenn ich auch weiß, dass es ohne Gewalt nicht möglich ist, sich in der Welt zu behaupten. Es wird nur dem das Leben gegeben, der am stärksten darum ficht. Das Gesetz des Lebens heißt: Verteidige dich!
>
> Die Zeit, in der wir leben, ist die Erscheinung des Zusammenbruchs dieser Sache. Es kann 100 oder 200 Jahre noch dauern. Es tut mir leid, dass ich wie Moses das gelobte Land nur aus der Ferne sehen kann.
>
> Wir wachsen in eine sonnige, wirklich tolerante Weltanschauung hinein: Der Mensch soll in der Lage

sein, die ihm von Gott gegebenen Fähigkeiten zu entwickeln. Wir müssen nur verhindern, dass eine ne-ue, noch größere Lüge entsteht: die Jüdisch-Bolschewistische Welt. Sie *muss* ich zerbrechen.[13]

My translation (here and hereafter with the assistance of Reinhold Mitschang):

> I am here due to a higher power, if I am necessary for anything. Leave aside that she is too cruel for me, the beatifying Church! I have never found pleasure in maltreating others, even if I know it isn't possible to stand your ground in the world without force. Life is only given to those who fight for it the hardest. It is the law of life: Defend yourself!
>
> The time in which we live indicates the collapse of this idea. It can still take 100 or 200 years. I am sorry that, like Moses, I can only see the Promised Land from a distance.
>
> We are growing into a sunny, really tolerant worldview: Man shall be able to develop his God-given talents. We must only prevent a new, even greater lie from arising: that of the Jewish-Bolshevist world. That's what I [must] destroy.

There are many significant discrepancies here. Compare the two versions above and we see some sentences radically changed in meaning. Yet there is no doubt that both are derived from a common source. Given the greater credibility of Picker and Jochmann, the sham is almost certainly in Trevor-Roper's edition, the result of trusting Genoud.

In particular, the anti-Christian sentiment exhibited throughout the Genoud/Trevor-Roper version is largely lacking in the German. There is no "disease of Christianity" that Hitler wishes dead, but the expediency of his own Nazi-enforced Social Darwinism. So

---

[13] This is from Picker's 2nd edition (correcting several errors in the 1st), which agrees with Jochmann in every detail but one: Jochmann reads *einsehe* where Picker reads *weiß*, but these have essentially the same meaning. The concluding *muss* is italicized in Picker, presumably indicating the word is missing from his actual notes and was restored to complete the sense.

the version of this quote used by Glover is false. Hitler's only genuine anti-Christian remark here is against the cruelty of the Catholic Church specifically, with his sarcastic play on *die alleinseligmachende Kirche*, the idea of a "one true church" that alone grants salvation.

We also find clues here to what seems to have happened: Stevens and Cameron made a mistake, not in translating the German, but Genoud's French! For here is the same passage as it appears in Genoud:

> Si ma présence sur cette terre est providentielle, je le dois à une volonté supérieure. Mais je ne dois rien à cette Eglise qui trafique du salut des âmes, et je la trouve vraiment trop cruelle. J'admets qu'on ne puisse s'imposer que par la force, mais j'ai horreur des gens qui ont le goût de faire souffrir les corps et de tyranniser les âmes.
>
> Notre époque verra sans doute la fin de la maladie chrétienne. C'est une affaire de cent ans, de deux cents ans peut-être. Mon regret aura été, à l'instar de tel prophète, de n'apercevoir que de loin la terre promise.
>
> Nous entrons dans une conception du monde, qui sera une ère ensoleillée, une ère de tolérance. L'homme doit être mis dans la situation de développer librement les talents qui lui sont donnés par Dieu. Ce qui importe avant tout, c'est que nous empêchions un mensonge plus grand de se substituer à celui qui disparaît. Le monde judéo-bolchevik doit s'effondrer.

My translation:

> If my presence on this earth is providential, I owe it to a higher will. But I do not owe anything to this Church that tampers with the salvation of souls, and I find it really too cruel. I admit that one can assert oneself only by force, but I detest people who have a taste for torturing bodies and tyrannizing souls.
>
> Our time will undoubtedly see the end of the Christian disease. It is a matter of a hundred years, two hundred years perhaps. My regret will have been, fol-

lowing the example of such a prophet, to see the promised land only from afar.

We are entering a conception of the world, which will be a sunlit era, an era of tolerance. Man must be put in the situation of freely developing the talents that are given him by God. What is essential above all is that we prevent a larger lie from replacing that which disappears. The Judeo-Bolshevic world must be crushed.

Apart from the obvious fact that this is almost exactly what the Trevor-Roper translation says (and not what the *Bormann-Vermerke* says, per Jochmann), among many clues two particular details are most curious:

First, the English of Stevens and Cameron uses the word "trafficks" precisely where Genoud uses *trafique*. But though *trafique* sounds like *traffick*, it actually means "toy with, tamper with, to doctor," *not* traffick ("to sell, deal with, trade in"). This makes their translation seem rather amateurish, as well as patently from the French, not the German, which doesn't really suggest such a word.

Second, Stevens and Cameron have Hitler saying "I admit that one cannot impose one's will by force, but…" which seems unintelligible. In the German and the French we see at once that Hitler's "but" makes sense because he just admitted that one cannot impose one's will *except* by force, hence the logic of his ensuing qualification. Why is Hitler denying this in Trevor-Roper when he asserts it in all other versions (Picker, Jochmann, *and* Genoud)? Most likely it is because Stevens and Cameron missed the *ne que* idiom used by Genoud, unique to the French language: the phrase does not mean *not*, as the *ne* alone would otherwise suggest, but *only* ("I admit that one can assert oneself *only* by force"). Thus, Stevens and Cameron made a mistake here that only makes sense if they are translating from Genoud's French, not the original German. They clearly weren't ignorant of the idiom, since they got it right when Genoud uses it in the following paragraph. They simply overlooked its use here.

Then there are crimes of omission. In Picker's and Jochmann's text, earlier under the same entry, Hitler says "Das, was der Mensch vor dem Tier voraushat, der vielleicht wunderbarste Beweis für die Überlegenheitd es Menschen ist, dass er begriffen hat, dass es eine Schöpferkraft geben muss!" ("What man has over the animals, possibly the most marvelous proof of his superiority, is that he has understood there must be a Creator!" [lit. "Creative Power"]). Such a clear assertion of Hitler's belief in God is not in Genoud or the Trevor-Roper text at all. As the table on the following page shows, the whole paragraph is missing in both texts, and the preceding paragraph radically altered. Again the English is clearly from the French. Why? How many other omissions are there? These are important questions requiring investigation.

Compare:

Trevor-Roper:	Picker:	Genoud:
In the trade union formed by the Church, many of the members have tangible interests to defend and see no further. A given set of grimaces, certain people identify them with true religion. After that, let's express surprise that these cynical exploiters of God are the true purveyors of atheism. Why should men fight to make their point of view triumph, if prayer should be enough? ...	In dem Verein ist ein Teil (die katholische Priesterschaft) an der ganzen Geschichte interessiert. Wie ist das aber, wenn ein so selbstsüchtiger Verein auf solche Weise die Schöpfung verhöhnt. Ein Götzendienst, der geradezu entsetzlich ist. Das, was der Mensch von dem Tier voraushat, der vielleicht wunderbarste Beweis für die Überlegenheit des Menschen ist, daß der begriffen hat, daß es eine Schöpferkraft geben muß! Man braucht nur durch ein Teleskop oder durch ein Mikroskop zu sehen: Da erkennt man, daß der Mensch die Fähigkeit hat, diese Gesetze zu begreifen. Da muß man aber doch demütig werden! Wird diese Schöpferkraft mit einem Fetisch identifiziert, dann bricht die Gottesvorstellung zusammen, wenn der Fetisch versagt. Warum überhaupt kämpfen, wenn es mit Gebet zu machen ist? ...	Dans ce syndicat constitué par l'Eglise, beaucoup des membres ons on des intérêts tangibles à defendre et ne voient que cela. Ces certains les identifient la vraie religion. Etonnons-nous après cela que ces exploiteurs cyniques de Dieu soient les vrais pourvoyeurs de l'athéisme. Pourquoi les hommes lutteraient-ils pour faire triompher leur point de vue si la prière devait suffire? ...

Though Picker originally omitted sentences, he corrected these and other mistakes in his second edition. One example appears in the same dated entry and contains another of the three quotes used by Glover, here expanded from Trevor-Roper:

> I realise that man, in his imperfection, can commit innumerable errors—but to devote myself deliberately to error, that is something I cannot do. *I shall never come personally to terms with the Christian lie. In acting as I do, I'm very far from the wish to scandalise. But I rebel when I see the very idea of Providence flouted in this fashion.* It's a great satisfaction for me to feel myself totally foreign to that world. But I shall feel I'm in my proper place if, after my death, I find myself, together with people like me, on some sort of Olympus. I shall be in the company of the most enlightened spirits of all times.

In Picker's first edition the sentences I have italicized above do not appear. The text simply runs from the preceding material to the following without stop. One might think they are spurious interpolations in Genoud (repeated in Trevor-Roper), except that Picker's second edition, corrected by Mediger against the original notes, has restored them as follows (my italics again):

> Ich weiß, dass der Mensch in seiner Fehlerhaftigkeit tausend Dinge falsch machen wird. Aber entgegen dem eigenen Wissen etwas falsch tun, das kommt nicht in Frage! *Man darf sich persönlich einer solchen Lüge niemals fügen. Nicht weil ich andere ärgern will, sondern weil ich darin eine Verhöhnung der ewigen Vorsehung erkenne. Ich bin froh, wenn ich mit denen keine innere Verbindung habe.* Ich fühle mich wohl in der geschichtlichen Gesellschaft, in der ich mich befinde, wenn es einen Olymp gibt. In dem, in den ich eingehe, werden sich die erleuchtetsten Geister aller Zeiten finden.

My translation:

> I know that humans in their defectiveness will do a thousand things wrong. But to do something wrong against one's own knowledge, that is out of the question! One should never personally accept such a lie. Not because I want to annoy others, but because I recognize therein a mockery of the Eternal Providence. I am glad if I have no internal connection with them. I

feel good in the historical society I am in if there is an Olympus. In the place I'm entering will be the most illuminated spirits of all times.[14]

Again we see reckless distortion. The overwhelming anti-Christian sentiment is gone. In fact, the sentence "I shall never come personally to terms with the Christian lie" would not even fit here, and is thus more evidently an interpolation. In contrast, "One should never personally accept such a lie" fits perfectly, carrying over and completing the thought of the previous sentence.

The lie Hitler was really talking about was not Christianity, but any dogma contrary to what one knows to be true. The Catholic idea of a "one true church" was such a lie in his view, though, for he had just finished arguing for *absoluten Toleranz* of alternative paths to salvation. But there is no attack on Christianity *in toto* in Picker, only certain dogmas, such as exclusivism. It is again clear that another of the three Glover quotes is false.

The restoration of the missing sentences also corroborates the reality of the *Bormann-Vermerke*, since Genoud could not have toyed with sentences that did not appear in Picker. He must have had on hand in 1952 a genuine, independent manuscript agreeing with Picker's. There are many other corrections made by Picker that show counterparts in Genoud's earlier edition, making a strong collective case for the authenticity of their independent manuscripts.

---

[14] I have said there are minor discrepancies between Jochmann and Picker, demonstrating they employed separate manuscripts, though with a common origin. This will serve as an example: here, where Picker reads *dem eigenen Wissen* ("against one's own knowledge") Jochmann has *meinem Wissen* ("against my own knowledge"), and Jochmann ends the sentence *das mache ich nicht* ("I do not do that") instead of *das kommt nicht in Frage* ("that is out of the question"). Following the same theme of converting the impersonal to the first person, Jochmann then reads "I personally will never accept such a lie" (*Ich persönlich werde mich einer solchen Lüge niemals fügen*) instead of "One may never personally accept such a lie." The rest of the material is identical to Picker, with the exception of one substitution of a *dass* for a *wenn*. In short, none of the variations change the meaning in any significant way, and therefore Jochmann typically supports Picker. Most trivial variations from Picker in Jochmann might be explained as Bormann's handiwork, as here Bormann probably converted Heim's impersonal tone to the first person to match the context.

We see still more evidence here that the Trevor-Roper translation is from Genoud's French and not the German of the *Bormann-Vermerke*. Genoud reads:

> Je n'ignore pas que l'homme, dans son imperfection, peut commettre d'innombrables erreurs—mais m'adonner consciemment à l'erreur, céda je ne le puis. Je ne m'accommoderai personnellement jamais du mensonge chrétien. En agissant comme je le fais, je suis fort éloigné du désir de scandaliser. Mais je m'insurge quand je vois bafouée de la sorte l'idée même de la Providence. C'est une grande satisfaction pour moi de me sentir totalement étranger à ce monde. Mais je me sentirai à ma place si, après ma mort, je me retrouve, avec des gens de mon bord, dams quelque olympe. J'y serai dans la compagnie des esprits les plus éclairés de tous les temps.

My translation:

> I am not unaware that man in his imperfection can make innumerable errors—but to give in consciously to error, I will never succumb to that. I personally will never accommodate myself to the Christian lie. In acting as I do, I am extremely far from the desire to annoy. But I rebel when I see ridiculed in this way the very idea of Providence. It's a great satisfaction for me to feel myself totally foreign to that world. But I shall feel I'm in my place if, after my death, I find myself, with people of my kind, in some Olympus. I shall be in the company of the most enlightened spirits of all times.

We see again the translators continued to mimic Genoud's French, using the same word order and sentence breaks, and employing obvious cognates, e.g. *innombrables erreurs* becomes *innumerable errors*, while *scandaliser* becomes *scandalise*, even though this is less natural a word in English for the context ("anger," "annoy," or "shock" are all acceptable translations of *scandaliser* that make more sense and are closer to the German).

The last of the three Glover quotes brings up a new problem. This falls under a different entry, that for 19 October 1941 (evening), where Trevor-Roper's text contains the sentence "Christianity is a prototype of Bolshevism: the mobilisation by the Jew of the masses of slaves with the object of undermining society." Picker has no entry for this date at all. But Jochmann's does, and it agrees with Genoud and Trevor-Roper: *Das Christentum war der Vorbolschewismus, die Mobilisierung von Sklavenmassen durch den Juden zum Zwecke der Aushöhlung des Staatsbaues*, "Christianity was the Proto-Bolshevism, the mobilization of the enslaved masses by the Jew for the purpose of undermining the state" (my translation). This just after comparing Christianity to syphilis, as the two diseases that destroyed Rome (the context seems to be an indictment of the Vatican).

Further study is needed to ascertain if this is genuine. Why does Picker's version of Heim's notes lack this entry? Jochmann's text indicates that the following entry (for 21 October) was made by Bormann, also not in Picker. Is it possible that Bormann also made the 19 October entry without noting it? Certainly, in-depth research of the whole *Table Talk* is needed, to establish not only how credible entries like this are, or who wrote them (might they even have been forged by Genoud?), but what Hitler meant in the *Table Talk* when he used various recurring words and themes, or indeed what he really believed, at least what we can reconstruct from the *Table Talk*.

It is especially curious that this paragraph under 19 October appears remarkably similar to another paragraph under 13 December, which appears in all editions and translations. There, Picker has this:

> Christus war ein Arier. Aber Paulus hat seine Lehre benutzt, die Unterwelt zu mobilisieren und einen Vorbolschewismus zu organisieren. Mit dessen Einbruch geht[15] die schöne Klarheit der antiken Welt verloren. Was ist das für ein Gott, der nur Wohlgefallen hat, wenn die Menschen sich vor ihm kasteien?

My translation:

---

[15] Jochmann has the past tense (*ging*) which is grammatically more correct, so I follow his reading in my translation.

Christ was an Aryan.[16] But Paul used his teachings to mobilize the underworld and organize a proto-bolshevism. With its outbreak the beautiful clarity of the ancient world was lost. What kind of God is it who is only pleased if humans chastise themselves before him?

Here, Hitler's position is more subtle. First, Hitler does not deny Christ but claims Christ for himself (Jesus was an Aryan and therefore his noble predecessor), and attacks not Christianity but the elements of Church doctrine (beginning with Paul) that are procommunist and antifascist, and thus hostile to Hitler's capitalist-authoritarian program. Hitler later goes on to question Christian dogma, but implicitly accepts the existence of God and the authority of Christ, a very different impression than we might get using isolated quotes like those from 19 October. In fact, this passage is very similar to that one. In both paragraphs Hitler refers to the *antike Welt* as *schön* and, using different words, refers to its breakdown, and in both we find the word *Vorbolschewismus* and a cognate of *Mobilisierung*. Is the entry for 19 October something Bormann reconstructed from a faulty memory of what was actually said three weeks later? Or is it an attempt by Genoud to fabricate a new text drawing on 13 December? These are the sorts of questions historians need to answer. For now, this third Glover quote must be regarded as either suspect or out of context.

There is another popular sentence under 13 December 1941 that, though not used by Glover, should be addressed here, as it presents a third problem. Again, it is a sentence restored in Picker's second edition, proving Genoud was working from an independent source. Trevor-Roper reads: "But Christianity is an invention of sick brains: one could imagine nothing more senseless, nor any more indecent way of turning the idea of the Godhead into a mockery" (matching Genoud almost verbatim: "Mais le christianisme est une invention de cerveaux malades: on ne saurait rien imaginer de plus insensé, ni une façon plus inconvenante de

---

[16] That is, not a Jew. A footnote in Picker indicates the basis for this belief: Hitler, and other Nazis, believed Jesus was indeed fathered by a Roman legionary (a story that dates back at least to the second century A.D.) and therefore a member of the master race.

tourner en dérision l'idée de la divinité"). But in Picker's German this sentence is somewhat different: "Das Christentum (lehrt 'die Verwandlung,' das) ist das Tollste, was je ein Menschengehirn in seinem Wahn hervorgebracht hat, eine Verhöhnung von allem Göttlichen,"—"Christianity (teaches 'Transubstantiation,' that) is the maddest thing ever concocted by a human brain in its delusion, a mockery of all that is godly."

The difference in meaning here is radical, and again shows how Hitler's words may have been distorted. However, the problem grows deeper here: Jochmann omits the material Picker placed in parentheses (Jochmann also replaces *was* with *das* but that has no effect on the meaning). Picker does not say why he placed parentheses around these words, but they are clearly meant to be incorporated into the sentence. Without them, the sentence does say "Christianity is the maddest thing that a human brain has ever concocted in its delusion." However, all versions follow this with a sentence attacking the absurdity of transubstantiation, as if that was indeed what Hitler meant. Such discrepancies between Jochmann and Picker thus present yet another problem for anyone aiming to get at what Hitler actually said.

Conclusion

All this is not to say that Hitler doesn't criticize Christianity even in Picker's and Jochmann's version of the *Table Talk*. For instance, again on 13 December 1941, Hitler argues against the idea of a physical resurrection and in favor of a spiritual one, and there and elsewhere he takes a very cynical view of Catholicism, voicing many of the same criticisms one might hear from a candid (and bigoted) Protestant. Yet even there he makes it clear that he believes in God, Christ, the immortality of the soul, and divine providence. Confirming this picture are recent studies of the religious beliefs of Hitler and the Nazi party by Bärsch and Steigmann-Gall.[17] As Jochmann himself concludes after surveying

---

[17] Richard Steigmann-Gall, *The Holy Reich: Nazi Conceptions of Christianity, 1919-1945* (New York: Cambridge University Press, 2003); Claus-Ekkehard Bärsch, *Die politische Religion des Nationalsozialismus: die religiöse Dimension der NS-Ideologie in den Schriften von Dietrich Eckart, Joseph Goebbels, Alfred Rosenberg und Adolf Hitler* (Munich: W. Fink, 1998), esp. 286-300.

Hitler's remarks on religion in the *Table Talk*. "Hitler was by no means unreligious" (*Hitler keineswegs areligiös war*, p. 31).

The matter is complicated by the interfering hand of Bormann himself. As an editor he had a tendency to make Hitler sound more like a Deist than he might have been, as for example in the entry for the night of 11/12 July, 1941, where he inserts a note into Hitler's speech, defining God as "the reign of natural law throughout the universe" (*das Walten der Naturgesetze im gesamten Universum*). Apart from this interpolation, and despite significant differences between the Picker-Jochmann and Genoud-Trevor-Roper editions, in the actual German of this entry Hitler does attack the Church, Christian dogma, and institutional religion, while promoting personal religion and religious tolerance. And while he talks of Christianity introducing lies, he still denounces atheism (e.g. "*zum Atheismus wollen wir nicht erziehen*" ["we do not want to promote atheism"]). In another entry Hitler talks of Christianity becoming obsolete while, again, denouncing atheism (14 October, 1941, midday).

Hitler's position appears to resemble Kant's with regard to the primacy of science over theology in deciding the facts of the universe, while remaining personally committed to a more abstract theism. But I won't argue for any particular construction of Hitler's religious views here. It is sufficient to note that, whatever his beliefs were, they are distorted in Genoud, and these distortions among many others were retained in the text of Trevor-Roper. Yet that is the only English translation of the *Table Talk* in print, and few know how worthless it is.

There is need of much more work on this source before it can be used in any way by competent historians. At the very least we need a complete investigation of the manuscripts on which they are based and the persons who have claimed to have them, their motives and capabilities, and a collation of all versions and editions with commentary on all the discrepancies, with a new English translation based on a critical edition of Picker and Jochmann.[18]

---

[18] This article was completed with partial funding from the Freedom from Religion Foundation. All of my translations from the German were completed with the assistance of Reinhold Mitschang, for whose help I am most grateful.

....

Afterword — State of Affairs at the Dawn of 2014

After this article appeared in *GSR* ten years ago, it inspired Dr. Mikael Nilsson, professor of history at Stockholm University (Sweden) to produce a detailed study of the *Table Talk* manuscripts. I have been happily consulting for him, and I can report that his research has already uncovered so many startling and curious facts that I am certain his eventual publications on the matter will be the definitive work on the subject.

My article has also broadly affected Hitler studies altogether, being cited now in leading monographs that rely on the *Table Talk* (such as Steigmann-Gall's *The Holy Reich*, who was able to read a proof of my article before publication) and acknowledged in the latest edition of the still-only English translation.

The Freedom from Religion Foundation deserves our thanks for starting this chain of events, which has already changed the way this text is used in Hitler studies and will conclude in a thoroughly researched and much-needed history of the *Table Talk*.

Since my article first appeared I have received requests to comment on other quotes used to "prove" Hitler was an atheist, in the *Table Talk* and elsewhere. All fall to one of the same faults identified in my article: either the German doesn't really say that, or the text is suspect (being either not in all versions or showing the meddling of Bormann or possibly Genoud, or otherwise not coming from Hitler), or the quotation is out of context.

Hitler was most definitely a devout Christian. But not in the way often assumed. Despite being publicly Catholic, Hitler's view of Christianity in the original German of the secret diatribes recorded in the *Table Talk* consistently reflects what was called at the time Positive Christianity—on which, besides Steigmann-Gall's *The Holy Reich*, see also Susannah Heschel's *The Aryan Jesus: Christian Theologians and the Bible in Nazi Germany* (Princeton University Press: 2010); for a primary source, the central text outlining and defending Positive Christianity (as a more patriotic and 'scientific' evolution of Lutheranism) was Alfred Rosenberg's *The Myth of the Twentieth Century* (1930).

Hitler clearly believed in Heaven and Providence and a Creator God, and that Paul corrupted the true teachings of Christ (producing the "madness" of the Catholic Church), and that Hitler himself was chosen by God to fix the world. He abhorred atheism just as much as sectarian Christian dogmas that he regarded as an "insult" to God (like exclusivism and transubstantiation). Many of his remarks about "Christianity" are in fact about Catholicism specifically. And *all* his remarks sound uniformly so similar to standard teachings of Positive Christianity that we can be sure he was secretly an adherent of that sectarian view.

Other quotes I am often asked about include, "There is something very unhealthy about Christianity" (*TT* 9 April 1942, dinnertime), where in fact the German says, "Here, as in so much in the Church, the reasoning is obviously incorrect," referring to a contrast Hitler made between Japanese paganism, which reveres state-serving heroes, and the Catholic "Cult of Saints" worshipping what Hitler regarded as do-nothing losers, "which reasoning is obviously incorrect." Hitler thus agreed with contemporary American "patriotic" Christianity, which echoes similar sentiments. Likewise, Hitler once compares "Christianity" to a drug or a cancer (*TT* 13 December 1941, midnight), but the context is an attack on the "religion" of Italians and Spaniards, and he explicitly identifies the Vatican as the target of his remark. The same follows for many other quotes, which additionally are not even found in Picker's edition, and thus whose authenticity is also suspect (*TT* 11-12 July 1941, night; 10 October 1941, noon; 14 October 1941, noon; 21 October 1941, noon; 14 December 1941, noon).

One of those reflects nearly every problem at once. Where Hitler says "Paul distorted the teachings of Jesus" (*TT* 21 October 1941, noon), that is exactly the view espoused by Positive Christianity. But the passage is also not present in Picker, and thus is suspect; in fact it is even explicitly identified as an entry made by Bormann. And as if that wasn't enough, the Trevor-Roper edition inaccurately translates this line as Paul effecting a "falsification of Jesus' doctrine," incorrectly rendering *verfälschung* as "falsify" (an amateur mistake, simply translating the word as it sounds rather than as it is actually used), when in fact it means "distort, misrepresent." And in context, Hitler is referring to Jesus being an Aryan rebel against Jewish greed, atheism, and superstition. Hitler approved such lessons as serving God vs. mammon, paying dues to Caesar, and clearing the money changers, viewing them as appropriately anti-Jewish. Hitler illogically despised the Jews for being both capitalists *and* communists, but that's a Nazi for you.

Other quotes adduced to "prove" Hitler's atheism come from elsewhere, but are likewise misreported or taken out of context. Joseph Goebels supposedly said in his diaries (which, incidentally, were also owned and published by François Genoud) that Hitler was an atheist. In fact, what Goebels wrote (in 1939) was that Hitler was "deeply religious" but "anti-Christian" because of its "elaborate Jewish rites," a remark that can *only* refer to Catholicism. Protestant Christianity generally does not have "elaborate rites," much less any that could be accused of being crypto-Jewish. Goebels' remark was thus not about Christianity as a religion, but Catholicism as a sect. There is a similar remark in the memoirs of Traudl Junge, which again in context clearly refers to *institutional* Christianity (sectarian Churches and priesthoods), not the Christian faith—Junge simply says Hitler "thought Christian sects were outdated, hypocritical institutions." Although she also claimed Hitler "was not a member of any Church," which suggests she did not really know him very well, since he was in fact a prominent member of the Catholic Church the whole of his life, so her information on his religious views is perhaps just as unreliable.

Yet another claim sometimes made is that Wilfried Daim once produced a photograph of a document purportedly signed by Adolf Hitler in 1943 that declared the abolition of Christianity. In actual fact, that document (even assuming it's authentic) calls for the "abolition of all religious *denominations* after the final victory," not the abolition of *religion*, and for the specific aim of unifying the world under a common banner of (in effect) Positive Christianity, by acknowledging Hitler as the "new messiah" and "God's emissary," very definitely *Christian* concepts. Similar views were reported by Albert Speer in his memoirs, where he remarks that Hitler thought Christians could learn a thing or two from Muslims about battle-readiness, and that he dreamed of one day uniting all the sects of Christianity under a common banner.

None of this is evidence Hitler was an atheist. In fact, it generally confirms his belief and devotion to Christianity.

The Vexed Bible

13

IGNATIAN VEXATION

Originally published at Richard Carrier Blogs
1 October 2008. Revised. © 2008, 2014.

In 2008 my fans funded a $20,000 research grant for me to produce an authoritative work on the historicity of Jesus. Thanks to them, that project culminated in two volumes, *Proving History: Bayes's Theorem and the Quest for the Historical Jesus* (published under academic peer review by Prometheus in 2012) and *On the Historicity of Jesus: Why We Might Have Reason for Doubt* (published by Sheffield-Phoenix, the publishing arm of the University of Sheffield, in 2014).

The project thus took six years to complete. I definitely put a great deal of work into it. But some of the hurdles I faced I couldn't even realistically overcome, leading me to vent my annoyance with the field of Biblical Studies. I quite agree with the broadside against that whole field launched by professor Hector Avalos in his marvously destructive book *The End of Biblical Studies* (Prometheus 2007). But my complaints were even more specific. This is one of them…

During my research for this two-volume project I ran into several muddles in New Testament studies that I thought had been reasonably resolved by now. Many issues I thought were cut-and-dried are actually mired in complexity, and my research in these areas has absorbed far more time than it should have.

The two most annoying examples of this (though not the only ones) are in dating the contents of the New Testament and identifying their authorship and editorial history. There is no consensus on either, even though standard references (like *Eerdman's Dictionary of the Bible*, *The Oxford Dictionary of the Christian Church*, and *The New Interpreter's Bible*) tend to give the impression there is. Even when acknowledging some disagreements, they do not accurately convey the sheer number of disagreements and the complexity of determining their relative merits.

In other words, not only is there no consensus, but there are dozens of positions, and arguments for each are elaborate and vast. It was only after over a month of wasting countless hours attempting to pursue these matters to some sort of condensable conclusion that I realized this was a fool's errand. I have changed strategy and will attempt some sort of broader, simpler approach to the issues occupying my chapter on this in *OHJ*, though exactly what that will be I am still working out. It *will* involve, however, a return to what historians *actually* do in other fields, which New Testament scholars seem to have gotten away from in their zeal to make sense of data that's basically screwed in every conceivable way. For when it comes to establishing the basic parameters of core documents, I have never met the kind of chaos I've encountered in this field in any other subfield of ancient history I've studied. Elsewhere, more often than not, either the matter is settled, or no one pretends it is.

It would bore me (and you) to attempt a thorough account of all I encountered on this subject of late. So I'll just walk you through one tiny example of the countless annoying paths I ended up on. And that only as briefly as I can (which is not very brief at all), since even this one story would bore the bristles off a boar if recounted in detail. It's probably boring enough as it is.

In most standard references or scholarly discussions, it's routinely claimed that the early Christian martyr Ignatius quotes the Gospel of Matthew in his letters, and Ignatius wrote those letters in the year 107 A.D. (or so), therefore Matthew was written before 107 A.D. That would be a fine example of establishing what we call a *terminus ante quem*, "point [in time] before which," the latest year a particular document could have been written. If either premise were a settled fact, that is. Unfortunately, they aren't. Yet typically this little problem isn't mentioned or explained, and these premises are declared in some form as if no one doubted them.

Already I encountered a general muddle even before getting to this particular vexation. In any other field, when historians don't know the exact year a book was written, they determine a *terminus post quem* ("point after which," also written *terminus a quo*) and a *terminus ante quem* ("point before which," also written *terminus ad quem*) and then conclude the book was written sometime between those two years. And they admit they can't know any more than that, which is something New Testament scholars tend to gloss over, often wanting to fix the year more exactly than the evidence actually allows, and then browbeat anyone who disagrees with them. In other areas of history we don't try that. If the terminal dates for *On Playing with Small Balls* (an actual book written by Galen, no kidding) are "between A.D. 150 and 210" then we accept that *On Playing with Small Balls* may have been written at any time within that sixty-year span. We don't scoff at someone who suggests it could have been written near the end of the author's life, nor claim as if it were a decided fact that it was written at the start of his career instead. Either is possible.

But in New Testament studies, the fact that the evidence only establishes *termini* for Matthew between A.D. 70 and 130 isn't something you will hear about in the references. Indeed, I say 130 only because the possibility that the earliest demonstrable *terminus ante quem* for Matthew may be as late as 170 involves a dozen more digressions even lengthier than this entire post. Because all the relevant issues of who actually said what and when remains a nightmare of debate so frustrating that I actually gave up on it mid-research, seeing it would take months to continue to any sort of conclusion, and not even a clear conclusion at that. Mind-numbing, truly.

But what about Ignatius? First of all, the year he wrote is not actually known. He doesn't say (which is always odd of Christian letters—real ancient letters were typically dated). And there is no consensus now, either. Dates from 102 to 117 are still defended by well-qualified scholars, and from what I can tell, any of these are possible. Normally that entails a *terminus ante quem* of 117, not 107. Until possible dates later than 107 are conclusively refuted, we must accept that the *termini* for Ignatius are from 102 to 117, so if Ignatius mentions Matthew, that sets a *terminus* for Matthew of 117, not 107. Because any date up to 117 is possible.

But no, it can't be as simple as that. For yes, of course (as if you didn't see it coming), there is still contention as to whether the letters of Ignatius are even authentic, or which ones are authentic, or whether they have been edited or interpolated, or whether the one datable reference in them (to the reign of Trajan) is inauthentic (and thus Ignatius actually wrote in a different, later reign—many scholars argue the Ignatians date to the 140s or even 160s), and on and on. The concerns are not crank. But sorting through and assessing them all would take months of research. And that's just on this one, entirely, mind-numbingly peripheral issue of the authenticity of the current text of the relevant epistles of Ignatius, all just to establish a *terminus ante quem* for just one book, Matthew!

Okay, but just for instance (just one point among a great many): Some scholars argue that the context of the Ignatian letters makes exactly zero historical sense. Ignatius is supposed to have been arrested and sent to Rome on a crime of illegal assembly (as a Christian), and on his journey to court his Roman jailers willingly take him to visit community after community of felonious illegal assemblies, and to meet with them and write letters to them and generally continue to flagrantly commit the capital crime for which he was arrested, in the presence of entire communities of fellow Christians also flagrantly committing that same crime, and in fact actively promoting the commission of that crime across half the Empire, and his Roman jailers don't mind. Not only do they not report any of this illegal activity, but they even aid and abet it at every step, taking him from church to church, allowing him ready access to his fellow criminals, a regular supply of papyrus and ink, and interfering not one whit. That sure is odd. Don't you think?

Now, let's suppose there is some brilliant response to this observation that explains everything and makes historical sense of these letters again. To find it and evaluate it—not just all the evidence and merit opposing this perplexing observation but supporting it as well, to give each side of the debate a fair shake—is a time-consuming task of no small order. And that's just one of literally dozens of objections to the authenticity of the Ignatian letters. But if they aren't even authentic, their date is no longer secure (even if it ever had been).

We could still argue for a *terminus ante quem* for these letters if they are all forgeries (since it wouldn't matter if they were, as a forged quotation of Matthew is still a quotation of Matthew) by observing that Polycarp, at some unspecified time in his life, wrote his own letter as a preface to the entire collection of Ignatian letters (because we have that letter), and Polycarp was martyred sometime between 155 and 168. Or so we think. In actual fact the evidence is problematic and some scholars argue his martyrdom could even have been as late as 180. Again, resolving that issue would require mountains of research (which, I must keep adding, might not in fact resolve the issue at all but merely demonstrate conclusively that it cannot be resolved on present evidence). And all that just to establish a *terminus ante quem* for the introduction of Polycarp, just to establish a *terminus ante quem* for the letters of Ignatius, just to establish a *terminus ante quem* for the Gospel of Matthew. (Oh, and remember, that's just one Gospel. Multiply all this by Mark, Luke and John…and then the two dozen other books in the New Testament…and you will only begin to touch the depths of my vexation in all this).

Okay. That's all just for the *first* problem with the Ignatian *terminus* for Matthew. The date. It gets worse when you start on the *second* problem: Did Ignatius even quote Matthew? Now things get extraordinarily annoying. Most scholars agree only some of his letters are authentic and that several were definitely forged, and that even the 'authentic' ones were expanded by forgers later on—we *think* we have the earlier, undoctored versions, simply because we have shorter, unembellished versions, although there is no secure reason to be certain these shorter versions aren't just longer redactions of even shorter but now lost originals…which we might even have in Syriac translation (and so on and so on and so on). But all that aside (Really? Can we just throw all that aside?), in his supposedly "authentic" letters (which ones are those again?), Ignatius definitely shows he knows of various stories peculiar to Matthew (like Matthew's nativity story), and he appears to quote Matthew verbatim a few times, and vaguely many times more.

Case closed, yes? Well, no. First, just because Ignatius knows the Matthaean nativity story doesn't mean Matthew preceded Ignatius. That would follow only if you assume (and note this) that Matthew invented that story. Now, that's a rather damning assumption. But if you reject it, then you can no longer conclude that Ignatius knows that story from Matthew. For he might know it from the same source Matthew learned it from. In which case, Matthew could possibly have written *after* Ignatius (indeed, he might even have taken details he learned *from* Ignatius and embellished them into his story). Again, resolving this, one way or another, takes considerable work, since the scholarship isn't entirely decisive or in agreement on these things. The problems are typically glossed over, as if there were no ambiguities or uncertainties here. Yet dig a little, and that's all you find.

Here's an example of what I mean:

> Now the virginity of Mary was hidden from the Prince of this world, as was her offspring, and the death of

> the Lord; three mysteries of renown, which were wrought in silence by God. How was He manifested to the world? A star shone forth in heaven above all other stars, the light of which was inexpressible, its novelty struck men with astonishment. And all the other the stars, with the sun and moon, formed a chorus to this star, and its light was exceedingly great above them all. And there was agitation felt as to whence this new spectacle came, so unlike everything else above. Hence every kind of magic was destroyed, and every bond of wickedness disappeared, ignorance was removed, and the old kingdom abolished, when God appeared in a human form for the renewal of eternal life.
> — Ignatius, *Letter to the Ephesians* 19

Ignatius is supposed to be attesting here to his knowledge of Matthew. Hey, sure, right? Matthew talks about a nativity star. Bingo! Often scholars or reference books will simply assert this as a given. Yet clearly Ignatius knows a completely different story. Ignatius does not appear to know Matthew's star story *at all*. He makes no reference to Magi, nor any moving star rising in the east and settling over the manger, no Herod, no Bethlehem. And in Matthew the star is but a sign, not the Savior Himself.

Instead, Ignatius knows some completely different star story, one that arguably conflates (or more likely lies behind, as more original) the nativity stories that found their way into Matthew and Luke (e.g. Luke mentions a chorus of angels in heaven, but no star, Matthew mentions a star but no chorus, while Ignatius knows about a chorus of stars in heaven). As far as Ignatius appears to know, the star was the arrival of Jesus himself (not a mere sign of his birth or birthplace), it was brighter than even the sun, all the stars in heaven sang, and *the whole world* was astonished and agitated by all this. Clearly, Ignatius has some other Gospel in mind. Or stories that precede all the Gospels we have. Or neither (because, remember, this letter could be a fake). But just as clearly, there is no evidence here that Ignatius knew the Gospel of Matthew.

Well, what about the exact quotes, and the paraphrases? Surely that's conclusive! I wish. Annoyingly, much of this evidence seems to imply the opposite: that Ignatius had no knowledge of Matthew's Gospel at all. For on several occasions when Ignatius is supposed to be "quoting" Matthew he uses the material in a completely unrelated context, as if he never knew how Matthew used it or even that he did. Problem number one. Ignatius also never mentions that he is quoting anyone (much less a Gospel, and much less a Gospel attributed to anyone named Matthew) or even indicates that he *is* quoting. Problem number two. In any other field, those two facts, combined with the first fact that Ignatius appears only to employ phrases and wording and concepts found in Matthew, would indicate that Matthew borrowed *from Ignatius*, not the other way around. Or does it? Again, there are arguments pro and con from here. And again, they are elaborate and vast. Time sucks down a rabbit hole.

Once again, I'll just give you one single example among several: Ignatius quotes verbatim Matthew's phrase "He who can receive it, let him receive it" (in *Smyrnaeans* 6:1). But in Matthew's Gospel (Matthew 19:12) Jesus utters this phrase about castration, becoming a eunuch for Christ, while Ignatius uses it in reference to receiving salvation. Ignatius says:

> The things in heaven, and the glory of the angels, and the rulers, both visible and invisible, if they believe not in the blood of Christ, shall, in consequence, incur condemnation. He who can receive it, let him receive it.

It is inconceivable that Ignatius would quote what Jesus said about accepting castration in a line about angels and demons accepting the salvation of Christ. One would sooner expect that Ignatius had no idea this line was ever used about men cutting their balls off. Hence this "exact" quotation would seem to suggest Ignatius *didn't* know Matthew, but knew a common stock of phrases and idioms *shared* by Matthew. But again, one could argue the point, and resolving any such debate is arduous.

Oh, by the way, did I also mention the manuscripts even of the "authentic" letters of Ignatius don't agree with each other, often containing entirely different sentences or even radically altered paragraphs? And that there may be evidence of retroscription? (That's later scribes correcting "inaccurate" quotations with "correct" quotations, a phenomenon that is definitely found in the manuscripts of Irenaeus, for example, thus calling into question any reliance on Irenaeus for the original readings of biblical passages, hence it might be circular to say Irenaeus confirms a biblical reading…yeah, because medieval sneeks rewrote his text to, but I digress). If we can't even know for sure what the original text of Ignatius's letters said, you can only imagine how much more this multiplies the task of sorting out issues of quotation or paraphrase.

And then there is the question (frequently overlooked) as to why Ignatius would rely on Matthew *at all*. For his soteriology is exactly the contrary of Matthew's and agrees instead with Mark's. For instance, Ignatius rails against the idea that Christians must obey Torah laws, but Matthew's entire Gospel was written to defend that position as endorsed by Christ (whereas Mark's entire Gospel was written to defend the position held by Ignatius), yet Ignatius supposedly repeatedly quotes and relies on Matthew (the Gospel of his enemies) without having any idea that Matthew copied from Mark, the very Gospel Ignatius would surely have preferred. How can Ignatius not know Matthew had doctored an earlier Gospel in order to advocate the very doctrines Ignatius opposes? Why doesn't he throw that in the face of Matthew-quoters, instead of inexplicably becoming a Matthew-quoter himself? Sorting *these* questions out is yet more time consuming madness.

And that's just trying to date Matthew by dating Ignatius. Ignatius also "supposedly" quotes or draws from Luke, or even John. Two more rabbit holes of confusion and unresolved debate. I won't even begin to bore you with that.

Now sure, everything above can be debated endlessly. But an endless debate on one detail, multiplied by a dozen details, multiplied by a dozen problems, multiplied by a dozen documents (since the Gospels aren't the only vexations among early Christian documents, not by a longshot), you end up with nearly two thousand endless debates. Even supposing you can fit an eternity into a day and thus nail a conclusion on any one point in under ten hours, ahem, two thousand days still works out to more than seven years (as you'll surely be taking weekends off at least—to drink yourself into a stupor, if nothing else). And at the end of it, you have perhaps only a few pages to show for it all, since that's all that will be needed to sum- marize your conclusions regarding the basic facts of your evidence before moving

on to the actual topic of your book. A handful of pages. Which took seven years of soul-crushing tedium to compose.

No thanks.

The field of New Testament studies needs to get its house in order. Until it does, I'll have to do *without* what I can normally rely upon in other fields: well-supported conclusions (or a ready consensus on the range of conclusions possible) on the most fundamental issues of evidence.

14

PAULINE INTERPOLATIONS

Originally published at Richard Carrier Blogs
1 June 2011. Revised. © 2011, 2014.

In the New Testament, at least two passages have been interpolated into the letters of Paul: 1 Thessalonians 2:14-16 and 1 Corinthians 14:34-35. Here I'll present the evidence for this conclusion that most experts have long known about, but most layfolk never hear.

For those not savvy to the study of ancient manuscripts (called textual criticism), an "interpolation" is a word or passage that was added to a text after it was written and disseminated, added of course by someone *not* the author, who wished to pass off that "interpolated" text as being *by* the author (or, often times, this insertion happens by accident—as I'll discuss in Chapter 19—but that didn't happen here). We have hundreds and hundreds of examples of interpolations in the Biblical manuscripts (most of which you don't hear about because they are so obviously interpolations that they aren't in your bibles but were deleted by modern scholars, or never got in because our bibles came from only one of many lines of the textual tradition, each line interpolating its own words and passages like crazy). For examples and discussion (and books to consult) you can review my PDF slideshow for the Carrier-Holding debate.[1] And for the most egregious examples, see my work on Mark 16:9-20 [Chapter 16].

It was in that debate with J.P. Holding that I cited as examples of clear interpolations that we don't have manuscript evidence of (because they occurred long before any extant manuscripts were produced) these two passages in Paul. Holding, of course (like most fundamentalists, despite his protestations to the contrary)

---

[1] www.richardcarrier.info/NTReliabilitySlideshow.pdf.

can't have these be interpolations (as that would require admitting the New Testament texts are hopelessly corrupt, because any passage you care to name could be another interpolation), so he argues against them being so, as have a few devout scholars.

In the debate I chose not to waste time pressing the issue so I could make other points instead, and for purposes of answering the point under time I simply noted that scholars do not agree with each other here (and most scholars do not agree with Holding), which proved one of my key opening debate points that the text of the New Testament is a product of disputable, fallible, human opinions (and therefore cannot be in any sense infallible, and hardly by any reasonable standard reliable enough to base your life on). I secured that argument quite thoroughly in the debate and Q&A, as you can tell by watching the video, where you can see why it's no trivial point to make.[2]

But I did have slides ready refuting his claims regarding the two passages I cited. And that information is worth having, since this is generally not easily accessible to everyone, being buried in esoteric journals and commentaries. So I provide it now, for reference and edutainment…

1 Thessalonians 2:14-16

This is where Paul refers to the end of the Jewish nation and its national cult, even though that occurred at least a decade after he is supposed to have died. In this passage Paul is made to say:

> …in Judea…the Jews killed both the Lord Jesus and the prophets, and drove us out, and pleased not God, and are contrary to all men; forbidding us to speak to the Gentiles that they may be saved, to fill up their sins always: but the wrath has come upon them to the uttermost.

Most scholars have concluded this was never written by Paul. The arguments are many, and accumulate to a conclusive case:

- Paul never blames the Jews for the death of Jesus elsewhere.

---

[2] www.youtube.com/watch?v=lOz8CpfR_lw.

- Paul never talks about God's wrath as having come, but as coming only at the future judgment (Romans 2:5, 3:5-6, 4:15).

- Paul teaches the Jews will be saved, not destroyed (Romans 11:25-28).

- Paul was dead by the time the "wrath had come upon them to the uttermost" (the destruction of the Jewish nation and temple in 70 A.D.).

A very good discussion of this passage and the "best" attempts to "rescue" it as authentic has been assembled online by Vridar.[3] He nevertheless sides against authenticity, with good reason, but he shows how some scholars do attempt to insist it's what Paul wrote. Though most scholars agree it's not: see Birger Pearson, "1 Thessalonians 2:13-16: A Deutero-Pauline Interpolation," *Harvard Theological Review* 64 (1971): 79-94; and G.E. Okeke, "1 Thessalonians 2.13-16: The Fate of the Unbelieving Jews," *New Testament Studies* 27 (1981): 127-36.

So was 1 Thessalonians 2:14-16 interpolated? Now, I'm open to the possibility of experts being wrong—because they often are. That they all disagree about a thousand things pertaining to the text of the New Testament entails every expert *is* wrong about quite a lot of things, because their pervasive disagreements entail they can't all be right about everything (that's a logical impossibility), and statistically no one of them can be right about everything anyway (nor have we any way to figure out which scholar is the magic infallible bean in that motley bag, even if there were such an impossible creature). Which means if experts can't agree and all are wrong about many things (as must they be), then we can't trust their reconstructed text either (since it's a product of the same fallible opinions and meets with all the same disagreements), except with varying shades of probability, none of which is enough to overcome any natural probabilities (so you can't use any New Testament passage to prove a miracle occurred, because textual corruption for any key phrase cited as evidence is *always* more probable).

---

[3] vridar.wordpress.com/2010/01/05/taking-eddy-boyd-seriously-3.

But in the case of 1 Thessalonians 2:14-16, attempts to defend its authenticity simply make no sense. They require us to believe too many improbable things. Which is exactly what a delusional person finds convincing, but not an objective critical mind. The passage is *very unusual* in several ways. Not in any of Paul's 20,000 words, and dozens of discussions of the Jews, is anything like it. That immediately casts it into doubt. Paul blaming the Jews for the death of Jesus is simply unprecedented. Paul also never talks about the Jews as if he wasn't one of them (compare Galatians 2:15; 1 Corinthians 9:20; Romans 9:1-5, 11:1; Philippians 3:4-5). And Paul acknowledged Jews as members of his own church, so he wouldn't damn them as a group like this, and never does (compare 1 Corinthians 1:24, 12:13; 2 Corinthians 11:12; Romans 9:24, 10:12; Vridar's analysis also shows how this interpolation is undeniably antisemitic—which is not at all characteristic of Paul).

Instead, Paul says things like, "Did God cast off his people? God forbid! For I also am a Jew, of the seed of Abraham, of the tribe of Benjamin" (Romans 11:1); and "Are they Hebrews? So am I. Are they Israelites? So am I. Are they the seed of Abraham? So am I" (2 Corinthians 11:22). That Paul actually taught the Jews would be saved, not damned, is clear throughout his letters, for instance in Romans 11:25-28:

> For I would not have you ignorant of this mystery, lest you be wise in your own conceits, that a hardening in part has befallen Israel, until the fulness of the Gentiles be come in; and so all Israel shall be saved: even as it is written…and as touching the gospel, they are enemies for your sake: but as touching the election, they are beloved for the fathers' sake.

That Paul believed God's wrath would come *only* at the future judgment is likewise a constant drumbeat for him (Romans 2:5, 3:5-6, 4:15; even 1 Thessalonians 1:10).

So let's look at the questionable passage again in context:

> For you, brethren, became imitators of the churches of God **which are in Judaea** in Jesus Christ, for you also suffered the same things **from your own countrymen** as they did **from the Jews** who both killed the Lord Jesus and the prophets, and drove us out, and pleased

not God, and are contrary to all men, forbidding us to speak to the Gentiles that they may be saved, to fill up their sins for evermore—but the wrath has come upon them to the uttermost.

Paul is writing to pagan converts (see verse 1:9) being persecuted *by pagans*, not by Jews (this is what he means in the authentic part of verse 2:14, highlighted above), so why would he suddenly break into a tirade against "the Jews" here? This makes no sense in context and violates the entire thread of his argument, that the Thessalonians are awesome for having withstood a *pagan* persecution.

The passage also says God's wrath has come upon the Jews "to the uttermost" (literally "to the end" / "with finality"). Attempts to reinterpret this as not meaning "with finality" is simply trying to get a word to mean the exact opposite of what it actually means. More importantly, the remark unmistakably refers to something that affected the Jews *in Judea* ("For you became imitators of the churches of God which are *in Judaea* ... for you also suffered the same things of your own countrymen as *they* did of the Jews who [killed Jesus and the prophets *in Judea*, and drove us *out of Judea*, etc.]..."), so the attempt to claim it refers to an earlier expulsion of Jews from Rome is a complete non-starter. That was a purely temporary and isolated event (and thus not by any stretch of the imagination "final"), and hardly anything one would call the wrath of God (unless you think God is really lame—as if the worst he could do to display his "ultimate wrath" is force some Jews living in pagan Rome to go back to the Holy Land), and in any case only affected Jews *in Rome*, not Jews *in Judea* (so how could God's wrath have been visited on the Jews of Judea by punishing Jews in Rome?).

So "reinterpreting" the passage to mean some other event (or even something "unobservable" like some sort of spiritual abandonment) simply makes no sense whatever of the passage's obvious meaning. The only thing a "final judgment" on "the Jews" in "Judea" can possibly be is the end of Judea itself (as a province) and the end of the Jewish cult (in the destruction of the Temple), universally recognized by Christians as God's final abandonment of the Jews. No other event makes any sense. And Paul was dead by then. So it's an interpolation. Which is obvious to anyone of sense.

1 Corinthians 14:34-35

Most experts again believe this is an interpolation. This passage has Paul command:

> Let the women keep silence in the churches: because it is not permitted for them to speak; but let them be in subjection, as also the law says. And if they would learn anything, let them ask their own husbands at home: for it is shameful for a woman to speak in the church.

We know this wasn't written by Paul because it directly contradicts what Paul says in the very same letter, where he actually gives rules *for when women speak in church* (in 1 Corinthians 11). So we can be sure someone else wrote this passage, probably influenced by the forgery of 1 Timothy 2 (where we find this misogyny repeated; notably in the authentic letters of Paul, such misogyny does not appear—it was a feature of later Christianity).

Everyone concurs that the passage contradicts Paul's teachings in the very same letter. So the only rebuttal fundamentalists have is that Paul must be quoting his opponents here, and arguing against it, not actually issuing this command himself. They do this with a raft of special pleading. Here is the whole passage in context, here using the ASV translation, but parsing the paragraph according to the argument made for these verses' authenticity (1 Corinthians 14:29-40):

> Let the prophets speak by two or three, and let the others discern. But if a revelation be made to another sitting by, let the first keep silence. For you all can prophesy one by one, that all may learn, and all may be exhorted; and the spirits of the prophets are subject to the prophets; for God is not a God of confusion, but of peace, as in all the churches of the saints.
>
> **Let the women keep silence in the churches: for it is not permitted unto them to speak; but let them be in subjection, as also says the law. And if they would learn anything, let them ask their own husbands at home: for it is shameful for a woman to speak in the church.**

> What!? Was it from you that the word of God went forth? Or came it unto you alone? If any man thinks himself to be a prophet, or spiritual, let him take knowledge of the things which I write unto you, that they are the commandment of the Lord. **But if any man is ignorant, let him be ignorant.** Wherefore, my brethren, desire earnestly to prophesy, and forbid not to speak with tongues. But let all things be done decently and in order.

The argument is that the material in bold is a quotation of his opponents and that Paul is denouncing the statement. But this is illogical in several ways, not least being the fact that he doesn't denounce the statement. If he were denouncing it, he would specifically say the statement is wrong or command them to let women speak in due order. No such remarks are present (obviously, because the interpolator intended us to think this was *Paul's* commandment, not that of his opponents).

It's rather lamely said the exclamation "What!?" alone constitutes a denunciation of the statement, which it is not (any author of the period would follow such an exclamation with a declarative sentence were that the case). Moreover, that exclamation is not actually in the Greek. It's a modern translator's conjecture. So no argument can stand on its presence here. The word that's actually there is simply "or" (and it is exactly so translated everywhere else in Paul's corpus). Nor is indirect speech indicated here, as the argument requires it be: there is simply no grammatical structure indicating Paul is quoting his opponents, unlike *other* passages where he *does* (1 Corinthians 7:1, "concerning what you wrote…"; 15:12, "some among you say…"; and 15:35, "some say…"; note that in 6:12 he's not quoting his opponents but himself: see 10:23 in light of 8:1-9:1 and 9:20-22).

Therefore the "quoting others" argument has no basis in the text itself and in fact goes against all the grammatical and rhetorical practices of the period generally and Paul specifically. To the contrary, we can be sure the original reading of 1 Corinthians 14:31-37 was:

> For you all can prophesy one by one, that all may learn, and all may be exhorted, and the spirits of the prophets are subject to the prophets, for God is not a

> God of confusion, but of peace, as in all the churches of the saints. [——] Or did the word of God originate with you, or come only to you? If any man thinks himself to be a prophet, or spiritual, let him take knowledge of the things which I write unto you, that they are the commandment of the Lord.

In other words, Paul is simply concluding the argument of the entire chapter, that they can't gainsay what he has just said "as if the word of God came only to them" because what he is saying is the definitive and universal commandment of God. The digression about women doesn't even fit here.

Of course, we also *know* this is how the passage originally read because in some manuscripts *this is exactly what Paul says*: the insertion about the women is moved to the end of the chapter. Which means (a) it was understood to be a separate unit (in thought and meaning, grammatically and rhetorically) and (b) the "challenge" question (what some bible translations render as beginning with the exclamation "What!?") was understood by many scribes and readers as directed at those promoting "confusion" rather than "peace," *not* the issue of letting women speak. (Thus Paul responds to the challenge question by declaring his rule *does* come from God and *is* found in all the churches, so Corinthians can't act like they received special instructions from God on any of these matters.)

In other words, the version I have just proposed, of what Paul originally said and *what it meant*, is exactly the version we find in some actual manuscripts of the Bible. The final clincher is that we know there were once manuscripts that didn't contain the interpolated verses *at all*, which confirms they were interpolated. This evidence is presented in Philip Payne's article "Fuldensis, Sigla for Variants in Vaticanus, and 1 Cor 14:34-5" in *New Testament Studies* 41 (1995): 240-50. I only just learned this the day before my debate with Holding (when I finished my complete literature search in preparation), which illustrates (a) how hard it is to claim you know what the original text said when you can't possibly have studied all the literature on every single verse! and (b) interpolations were once proven by manuscripts we no longer have (a crucial point we ought never forget), and (c) there is evidence even now in known manuscripts that scholars still have yet to discover (the manuscript evidence Payne reported in 1995 had been available to scholars for over a hundred years, some of it in fact over a thousand years; how much else is just sitting there unnoticed?).

Payne shows that scribal marks in one of our earliest manuscripts of this letter indicate the passage was known not to appear in some manuscripts available to the copier (manuscripts that must have been transcribed no later than the 3rd century), and that we have an explicit representation of this knowledge in a later manuscript prepared and supervised by Bishop Victor of Capua in A.D. 546, who ordered a rewrite of this section to omit verses 34-35, in the bottom margin of Codex Fuldensis. Bishop Victor's other corrections of the text in Codex Fuldensis routinely reflect his awareness of manuscripts with the readings he advised. Therefore Victor knew of a manuscript lacking vv. 34-35. So there once were manuscripts proving vv. 34-35 an interpolation, including some that must have been composed in the 3rd century, before almost all of the manuscripts we even now have.

Conclusion

There can be no doubt that these passages are interpolations (1 Corinthians 14:34-35 and 1 Thessalonians 2:14-16). This proves Christians had no problem doctoring the letters of Paul to make him say things he didn't say. And if they did this in these two cases, how many other passages in Paul are inauthentic? Remember, we caught these cases because we got lucky (the interpolators were sloppy, they just happened to pick things to say that contradicted Paul, and we just happen to have some telltale evidence in the manuscripts). Most interpolations won't have left such evidence—most will not so blatantly contradict Paul, and most of the ones, like these, that were inserted before 200 A.D. won't have just by chance left any evidence in the manuscripts. It is therefore necessarily the case that there are three or more interpolations in the letters of Paul that we don't know about. Because statistically, if *most* won't be evident, and two are evident, then there must be *at least* three not evident. Would you ever bet your life on which passage isn't one of them?

15

LUKE VS. MATTHEW ON THE YEAR OF CHRIST'S BIRTH

Originally published at ErrancyWiki.com.
Writing funded by ErrancyWiki.
Revised. © 2006, 2014.

Contents

1.1 Introduction
1.2 Author Qualifications
1.3 Background to the Problem
1.4 FIRST ATTEMPT: Looking in Luke for a Different Date
1.5 SECOND ATTEMPT: A Second Governorship for Quirinius?
    1.5.1 The *Lapis Tiburtinus*
    1.5.2 The *Lapis Venetus*
    1.5.3 The Antioch Stones
    1.5.4 The Vardaman Coins
    1.5.5 Sub-Commander Quirinius?
    1.5.6 Co-Commander Quirinius?
1.6 THIRD ATTEMPT: A New Date for Herod's Death?
1.7 FOURTH ATTEMPT: Another Census?
    1.7.1 Luke Meant "Before Quirinius"?
    1.7.2 Romans Subjected Allied Kingdoms to a Census?
    1.7.3 Jesus Born During Census of 8 B.C.?
    1.7.4 Herod's Census?
    1.7.5 Herod's Oath?
1.8 Conclusion

1.1 Introduction

It is widely acknowledged that Quirinius became "governor of Syria" in 6 A.D., only then conducting a census of Judaea, and that Herod the Great died in 4 B.C., ten years before. Since Matthew indisputably claims Jesus was born while Herod the Great was still alive, while Luke indisputably claims Jesus was born when Quirinius was governor of Syria during a census of Judaea, Luke and Matthew are clearly in contradiction regarding when Jesus was born. They disagree by at least ten years, which entails one of them has made a historical error (or both have).

Because this contradiction is so clear and certain and strongly backed by evidence, inerrancy proponents have invented a dizzying array of attempts to remove this contradiction by reconciling the details in Matthew and Luke. I have examined and researched these efforts in thorough detail, perhaps more than anyone. I have found all of them unsuccessful, even ludicrously so. Consequently, the primary importance of this contradiction is that it is one of the clearest and most irrefutable examples of historical error in the Bible, which is perhaps why it has generated so many desperate attempts to wiggle out of it.

And that is the second reason this error is so important: short of the vast and diverse "Bethlehem Star" literature (now superply dealt with by Aaron Adair in *The Star of Bethlehem: A Skeptical View*), there is probably no other biblical error for which so many false, groundless, or implausible arguments have been contrived to "invent" or "revise" the historical facts of the ancient Roman world. As a teacher and a scholar, I find all this disinformation and wanton invention about the period I study quite appalling. And because there are so many such contrivances, relating to technical details of the social and political history of Rome that are difficult if not impossible for the average layperson to investigate, duty demands that some impassioned expert do all the necessary research and make it available to the common reader. Otherwise, all those false claims might simply be believed and eventually become common assumptions.

1.2 Author Qualifications

Christian apologists often try to dismiss findings they don't like by attacking not the evidence and argmuments, but merely the qualifications of the messenger (qualifications that, ironically, the apologists often don't have themselves—so they will insist conclusions are to be rejected from anyone ill qualified, and then, being ill qualified, don't reject their own conclusions…seriously). So let's get some things clear from the start.

I am a published author, philosopher, and historian with considerable qualifications in the study of ancient history and languages, which should give my findings a sufficient weight of authority. I have a B.A. in history and classical civilizations from UC Berkeley, and an M.A., M.Phil. and Ph.D. in ancient history from Columbia University. In qualifying for my doctorate I formally studied ancient Greek for over seven years, including papyrology, linguistics, and paleography. And I have published several papers in peer reviewed academic journals on similar matters.

Regarding the date of Jesus' alleged birth, I thoroughly document all the arguments and evidence relating to the discrepancy in an extensive article at the Secular Web, "The Date of the Nativity in Luke" (6th ed., 2011) at:

www.infidels.org/library/modern/richard_carrier/quirinius.html

I will provide here only a summary of the major conclusions of that article, along with some of the most relevant evidence. But if you want to see more citations and discussion, you will find it there.

Invariably people write to me proposing some "new" argument, without having bothered to read the expanded article at the Secular Web, only to learn that their "new" argument is in fact "old" and already refuted there. I have received countless such emails to date, over several years, and have yet to hear of any fact or argument I haven't already addressed. I advise all challengers to read that original article in its entirety before proposing to challenge the fact that Luke contradicts Matthew on the year of Christ's birth.

The present summary is no substitute for that, and is only provided here to conveniently summarize the current status of this biblical error for readers not intent on gainsaying what they don't like to hear.

1.3 Background to the Problem

The Gospel of Luke says (2:1-6) Jesus was born during a census, which the historian Josephus records took place after Herod the Great died, and after his successor, Archelaus, was deposed after a ten year reign (*Antiquities of the Jews* 17.342-55, 18.1-2, 18.26). But the Gospel of Matthew says (2:1-3) Jesus was born when Herod the Great was still alive, possibly two years before he died (2:7-16), and before Archelaus even took office (2:19-22). On a plain reading of the Bible, this is a contradiction. Someone erred.

Efforts to challenge this conclusion fall into three general categories: either Luke meant something other than his words actually say, or Josephus failed to mention some "other" time that Quirinius was governor and a census made of Judaea, or Josephus erred in dating relevant events. A fourth option, of arguing Matthew meant something other than what he said, is blocked by the absolute clarity with which he said it. There is no rational way to argue that Matthew was referring to the political situation anywhere near 6 A.D. Not only does Matthew's narrative make this clear, but the physical evidence from coins of the region leave little room for disputing that Herod ceased his reign in 4 B.C., Archelaus then succeeded him, then ceased his own reign ten years later in 5 A.D., and Roman control of Judaea began in the year 6 (the year the earliest Roman coins struck for Judaea begin).[1] These facts are also recorded by Josephus (who is generally quite reliable on matters of public chronology) and partly corroborated by another historian, Cassius Dio (e.g. *Roman History* 55.27.6).

Consequently, to this day no one has attempted to argue that Matthew was describing an event of 6 A.D. Instead, all efforts are directed to arguing that Luke was describing an event five to twelve years earlier than we think, either by trying to harmonize such a reading of Luke with Josephus, or by attacking the accuracy or alleged omissions of Josephus. However, all such attempts have required inventing or distorting socio-political facts of the period, or twisting Greek grammar or vocabulary beyond anything that would be recognizable to an ancient reader. Allowing either tactic would permit us to prove that no text ever written in human

---

[1] See the relevant entries in Burnett's *Roman Provincial Coinage* (1992), including the supplemental volume with corrections.

1.4 FIRST ATTEMPT: Looking in Luke for a Different Date

Some observe that Luke says John the Baptist was born during the reign of "Herod the King" (1:5) and appears to have Jesus born less than a year later (1:22-24, 1:31-36, 1:80, 2:1, 2:40-42), which appears to agree with Matthew. However, Matthew does not mention or date the birth of John, and despite the impression given by English translations, Luke is unclear how much time actually passed between his birth and that of Jesus. More importantly, Archelaus was also called Herod (even on his own coins) and even Josephus calls him a king (*Antiquities of the Jews* 18.93). Unlike Matthew, Luke provides no detail indicating either he or his source meant anything other than Herod Archelaus when dating the birth of John. Therefore, unless we assume Luke is contradicting *himself*, we can't assume he dated either the birth of John or Jesus to the time of Herod the Great. So there is no case to be made from verse 1:5 that Luke agreed with Matthew.

Likewise, when Luke dates the start of John's ministry to 28 A.D. (3:1) and then over twenty verses later says Jesus began his own ministry at "about thirty" (3:23) some assume the two ministries began the same year, which would place the birth of Jesus at "about" 3 B.C. which for a "rough" estimate is close enough to fit Matthew. But Luke never says the two ministries began the same year, and for various reasons it's unlikely they did. Luke clearly didn't know the year Jesus started his ministry, since he didn't know how old he was, despite claiming to know exactly when he was born. Luke also claims to know the precise year John's ministrty began…yet doesn't claim to know the precise year Jesus' ministry began.

Since "about" thirty can be off by at least four years (26-34), and since Luke clearly believed some unknown time had passed between the start of John's ministry and his baptism of Jesus, and since scholars agree Jesus could have begun and ended his ministry anytime between 28 and 33 A.D., we are left with a window between 7 B.C. to 7 A.D. for his birth, far too wide to pin down. So there is no good case to be made from Luke 3:1-23 that he agreed with Matthew.[2]

1.5 SECOND ATTEMPT: Inventing a Second Governorship for Quirinius

Even fishing a different date out of Luke would leave a contradiction *within Luke*, since the only chronological detail about Jesus that Luke is absolutely clear on is that he was born during "the first census when Quirinius was governing Syria" (2:2). All evidence confirms that Quirinius first became governor of Syria in 6 A.D. and the first Roman census of Judaea occurred at that time, and Luke clearly says this was a *Roman* census (2:1-6). So Luke didn't leave much room to maneuver. To reconcile Luke with Matthew, one must invent two facts nowhere in evidence: some *other* Syrian governorship for Quirinius *and* some other census affecting Judaea, both before Herod the Great died.

But trying to invent an earlier Syrian governorship for Quirinius is a lost cause. Not only is there no evidence of it, and not only does it go against a plain reading of all the evidence we do have, but it's essentially impossible. No one ever governed the same province twice in the whole of Roman history. So the claim that Quirinius was the sole known exception is so extraordinary it certainly can't be maintained without evidence. Such an astonishing and unique honor could not have been omitted by Josephus or Tacitus (*Annals* 3.48), yet both describe his career without any mention of it. Historical evidence also confirms other men governed Syria between 12 and 3 B.C., so Quirinius could *not* have

---

[2] For more on the basic problem and these date-fishing efforts see "The Basic Problem" in my complete Secular Web article (quirinius.html#I). Backing my analysis is Mark Smith, "Of Jesus and Quirinius," *The Catholic Biblical Quarterly* 62.2 (April 2000): 278-93. It has also been argued that the entire line about the census in Luke is a later scribal interpolation [Jacques Winandy, "Le recensement dit de Quirinius (LC 2,2): une interpolation?" *Revue Biblique* 104.3 (July 1997): 373-77], although as I explain online (quirinius.html#1.1) the argument for that conclusion is not sound. But Luke could certainly have fudged or disregarded historical facts that weren't convenient for him [Robert Smith, "Caesar's Decree (Luke 2:1-2): Puzzle or Key?" *Currents in Theology and Mission* 7.6 (December 1980): 343-51].

been governor then, and he was not qualified to hold that office before the year 12.³

Stymied by all these facts, inerrantists have resorted to everything from fabricating evidence of dual governorships or other fictional offices Quirinius is supposed to have held, to changing the year of Herod's death. None of this is even remotely reasonable, and most of it is based on the fantasies of amateurs or the abandoned conjectures of long dead historians. First, the alleged physical evidence:

1.5.1 The *Lapis Tiburtinus*

This is a headless (and thus nameless) inscription that the Vatican has taken the liberty to "restore" with the name of Quirinius. It is then "interpreted" as saying he governed Syria twice. But the actual inscription does not say anyone governed Syria twice, nor does it belong to Quirinius. Scholars now believe it belongs to Lucius Calpurnius Piso, since it fits what we know of his career very well, while no basis exists for claiming it belongs to Quirinius. And even if it did, it doesn't say anything about governing Syria

---

³ Marcus Titius from 12 to 9 B.C., Sentius Saturninus from 9 to 6 B.C., and Quintilius Varus from 6 to 3 B.C., each serving a typical three year term; and both historians and inscriptions confirm Quirinius did not achieve consular rank until 12 B.C. Under Roman law and principle, such a rank was a political prerequisite for holding a provincial proconsulship (see discussion in Chapters 6 and 7). For previous governors: Josephus, *Antiquities of the Jews* 16.270-81, 16.344, 17.6-7, 17.24, 17.57, 17.89-133, 17.221-23, 17.250-98; Josephus, *Jewish War* 1.577, 1.617-39, 2.66-80; Strabo, *Geography* 16.1.28; Velleius, *Compendium of Roman History* 2.117.2; Tacitus, *Histories* 5.9.2. Coin evidence also exists for their terms, though often without precise dates, but all the evidence is collected and analyzed in Edward Dabrowa, *The Governors of Roman Syria from Augustus to Septimius Severus* (1998), where pp. 17-35 surveys the evidence and names of all the governors of Syria from 25 B.C. to 25 A.D. The consulship of Quirinius is reported in surviving consular lists etched in stone (see the entry for him in Pauly, Wissowa, and Kroll, *Realencyclopädie der klassischen Altertumwissenschaft*) and by Cassius Dio, *Roman History* 54.28.2 For more on the problems of inventing a new governorship for Quirinius see "Was Quirinius Twice Governor?" in my Secular Web article (quirinius.html#II).

twice. It says the honoree "received the governorship of Asia and again of Syria."⁴

1.5.2 The *Lapis Venetus*

This is an inscription that really does mention Quirinius. It is the epitaph of Aemilius Secundus and reports he helped Quirinius conduct a census when the latter was governing Syria. So this inscription confirms that a census was taken of Syria when Quirinius was governor of Syria. It does not give a date, either for the census or the inscription itself. But there is no reason to believe this is a reference to any other census under Quirinius except the only one we know of, that of 6 A.D. Several inerrantists have simply "invented" early dates for this inscription, and then used these fabricated dates to claim this inscription as proof there was an earlier census under Quirinius. It proves no such thing.⁵

1.5.3 The Antioch Stones

These are two stones commemorating the offices of Gaius Julius Caristanius Caesiano, both mentioning that he shared the deputy management of a city duumvirate held by Quirinius. The date is unknown but probably before the year 1. Conjuring various fantasies, inerrantists finagle this city office into evidence of an earlier governorship of Syria, but no rational argument can produce that

---

⁴ For more (including a complete translation of the inscription, citation of scholarship, and relevant analysis of the Latin grammar) see "The *Lapis Tiburtinus*" (quirinius.html#Tiburtinus).

⁵ For more (including a complete translation of the inscription) see "The *Lapis Venetus*" (quirinius.html#LapisVenetus).

conclusion. First, a duumvirate is a city office and has nothing to do with a provincial governorship. Second, this duumvirate was held in Galatia, not Syria.[6]

1.5.4 The Vardaman Coins

Jerry Vardaman claimed to have discovered microscopic letters literally covering ancient coins and inscriptions conveying all sorts of strange new facts, which he used to completely rewrite history. One of these amazing new "discoveries" was evidence Jesus was born in 11 or 12 B.C. Needless to say, Vardaman's claim constitutes fringe quackery that has gained no respect in the academic community. I inspected one of these coins myself under a magnifying glass and a digital microscope at the British Museum and found none of these amazing microscopic letters. Case closed.[7]

1.5.5 Sub-Commander Quirinius?

Since none of this evidence supports an earlier governorship for Quirinius, and all other evidence makes such a thing virtually impossible, only two strategies remain for the inerrantists: either Quirinius held some other "special command" in Syria and wasn't governor *per se*, or Quirinius held an unrecorded "dual-governorship" with some other governor. Neither of these proposals makes any sense in the context of Roman politics or historiography.

First, the "sub-command" thesis. Luke's choice of vocabulary is somewhat imprecise, using a word that can refer to many different positions of command. Seizing on this, inerrantists argue that Luke meant "when Quirinius was holding *a* command in Syria," and not "when Quirinius was *governing* Syria." But stretching the word like this requires ignoring the grammar. Luke says "of Syria," not "in Syria," and thus he could not have been referring to some command *in* Syria but only a command *of* Syria. Even if we ignore Luke's grammar, the only real "command" anyone can find for Quirinius is a war he fought in Galatia, probably between 6 and

---

[6] For more see "The Antioch Stones" (quirinius.html#Antioch).

[7] For a full account see Chapters 10 and 11 of the present volume (only summarized online at quirinius.html#Vardaman).

1 B.C. But there is no logical way Luke would refer to a census in Syria by referencing a war in Galatia, and no one would ever write or read "governing Syria" as meaning "fighting a war in Galatia." Unless Luke was a profoundly stupid man, or erred in his historical facts, he would have named the *actual* governor of Syria who oversaw a census in Judaea, not some unrelated officer in a faraway province.[8]

1.5.6 Co-Commander Quirinius?

A completely different tactic, to get around the problem that all the governors of Syria between 12 and 3 B.C. are already known, is to claim Quirinius was holding a dual governorship with one of those other governors. Not only does this still require claiming Quirinius governed the same province twice, an oddity never before recorded in the history of Roman politics, but it also requires completely inventing the idea of a "dual governorship." Since there is no evidence in all of Roman history of any province assigned two governors at the same time, this is another extraordinary claim that requires evidence to be believed. Since there isn't any, inerrantists invent some.

Josephus is cited as saying "Saturninus and Volumnius were in charge of Syria" (*Antiquities of the Jews* 16.280) which is said to "prove" Syria was special enough to be assigned two governors. But Volumnius was not a governor. He was a prefect (Josephus, *Jewish War* 1.538), an office held only by men of fundamentally inferior rank, who were not even qualified to hold the office of a provincial governor. Conversely, a Roman who had achieved senatorial, and even consular rank—like Quirinius—would never deign to accept such a humiliating office as prefect. Socially, this would be as unbelievable as a United States president taking a job as shift manager at a local McDonald's. In Roman society, this would be so remarkable and unprecedented that, again, Josephus and Tacitus would not have omitted it from their accounts of his career (see my discussion of the social reality behind all this in Chapters 6 and 7, regarding Herod's position as a procurator).

The same error is made using an inscription reporting that two "deputies," Rutilius Gallicus and Sentius Caecilianus, were assigned

---

[8] For further analysis see "Was Quirinius a Special Legate in B.C. Syria?" (quirinius.html#legate).

to the province of Africa. But this inscription clearly states that one of them was a praetor, and thus *not* of consular rank. So again, what we have here are not two governors, but a governor and his subordinate. Neither example supports even the *conjecture* that Quirinius *could* have held a dual-governorship, much less that he ever did so—or that anyone ever did. It would also make no logical sense for Luke to name a governor's *subordinate* rather than the actual governor of Syria.[9]

So there is no basis for this claim, either. Since Josephus records and thus confirms an actual census under Quirinius in 6 A.D. when Quirinius was, in fact, the governor "of Syria," all exactly as Luke says, there is no plausible case to be made that Luke had any other event in mind. All the evidence we have corroborates this conclusion, and none supports any alternative or renders any even remotely plausible.

1.6 THIRD ATTEMPT: Inventing a New Date for Herod's Death

Since there is no reasonable way to get Quirinius to be governor of Syria anytime before 3 B.C., the natural last-ditch resort is to argue that Herod didn't really die in 4 B.C. Since there is no clear evidence who was governing Syria after 3 B.C., or where Quirinius was in those years, inerrantists fantasize that their imaginary "earlier governorship" of Quirinius fell around then and simply failed to be mentioned. This still doesn't avoid all the problems noted before—from a total lack of evidence to the extraordinary implausibility of a second governorship. But it also requires rewriting history.

Josephus already says Varus, not Quirinius, was governing Syria when Herod died (*Jewish War* 1.9-10), and despite attempts to argue otherwise, Josephus is very clear and precise in his chronology for these events and cites several first-hand sources for them, while the manuscript tradition for the relevant details is completely sound, so there is no plausible case to be made that he

---

[9] For further analysis see "Was Quirinius Sharing Command with a Previous Governor?" (quirinius.html#dual).

is mistaken.[10] Likewise, as mentioned earlier, evidence from coins corroborates all of this, including the reigns of Herod's successors, Philip, Antipas and Archelaus. The reign of Archelaus is further corroborated by Cassius Dio (*Roman History* 55.27.6).

Josephus also mentions a lunar eclipse soon before Herod's death, and astronomers note there was such an eclipse in 5 B.C. and 1 B.C. Inerrantists therefore want Herod to have died in or shortly after 1 B.C. However, not only is all evidence against such a notion, but the Jewish *Scroll of Fasting* records the calendar day of Herod's death, and it preceded that of the eclipse of 1 B.C., but not that of 5 B.C. Since Josephus says his death followed (not preceeded) an eclipse, the eclipse Josephus mentions was probably that of the year 5. In the end, there is simply no evidence Herod died later than the year 4, and no plausible case to be made that he did.

1.7 FOURTH ATTEMPT: Inventing Another Census

There is no reasonable case to be made that Quirinius ever "governed Syria" before 6 A.D. Yet inventing such a fantasy contrary to all evidence and precedent is not even enough to eliminate the contradiction between Matthew and Luke. A census of Judaea before 6 A.D. must *also* be invented, contrary to all evidence and precedent. This is because Luke's description establishes three facts: the census affected Judaea (2:4-5), it was conducted under the administration of Syria (2:2), and it was specifically a *Roman* census (2:1). These three facts rule out every attempt to argue that Luke meant some other census or event than the one recorded for 6 A.D.

Before 6 A.D. Judaea was a nominally free kingdom, not a Roman province. Having sided with Augustus in the civil war that established him as emperor, Judaea was granted a favorable treaty assuring relative independence. This is proven by the coin evidence that Judaea continued to be governed by its own kings and rulers,

---

[10] Several wholly implausible arguments for rewriting the chronology in Josephus have been offered by Jack Finegan in his *Handbook of Biblical Chronology* (1998, revised edition). Finegan's errors consist of faulty math, implausible and unsupported conjectures, and relying on incompetent manuscript analysis. These gaffes are barely worthy of attention. Nevertheless, I address them in detail under "Was Herod Alive in 2 B.C.?" in my complete Secular Web article (quirinius.html#alive).

not Roman officials, until 6 A.D., and extensively confirmed by Josephus and Cassius Dio. Though such "allied kingdoms" were kept under a tight leash and informally controlled and meddled with, all evidence regarding the legal and political practices of Roman emperors in the first century and before confirms that these states were not subject to direct Roman administration, taxation or levies. That was, in fact, the very *point* of not annexing them as provinces: not only to reward friendly states (and thus encourage other states to be friendly), but to avoid the headache and expense of taking over a region that was already pacified, subservient, and paying sufficient dues.

Therefore, it is historically impossible that a Roman census was conducted under a Roman provincial governor when Judaea was still an allied kingdom. But it was typical and logical that immediately upon annexing a new territory a census would be taken of it. This was necessary to begin direct taxation and levies. So when Josephus describes Archelaus being removed from office, then Judaea being annexed to Syria and placed under the Roman command of Quirinius and his prefect Coponius, and then a census being conducted for the specific purpose of taking account of what Archelaus had left them, this description makes complete historical sense. In contrast, no other hypothesized "census" scenario makes any historical sense at all.

As Josephus reports, and as all logic and precedent entail, Judaea was not being directly taxed by Rome nor administered by Romans before the year 6, and therefore there would be no purpose for Augustus to order a census there (Luke 2:1). Since forcing such a census on an allied kingdom in violation of its honor and its treaties would be such an astonishing and devastating insult contrary to all known precedent, there is no way it wouldn't have been noticed by historians like Josephus, nor any reason the Romans would undertake such a pointless and dangerous task. They would have nothing to gain by it, and plenty to lose, and Augustus was not so reckless as to think otherwise.[11]

Nevertheless, inerrantists must have the impossible in order to save their bible from error. So these are the arguments they have attempted:

---

[11] For more on the basic problems of inventing an earlier census see "Was There a Roman Census in Judaea Before Quirinius?" (quirinius.html#III).

1.7.1 Luke Meant "Before Quirinius"?

The word translated "first" in Luke 2:2 can in certain contexts mean "before." But for various reasons such a meaning would not be grammatically correct in this case. Luke can only have meant, and all his readers would only have understood his sentence to mean, the first Augustan census that happened under Quirinius. And that is how all translators correctly interpret it.[12]

1.7.2 Romans Subjected Allied Kingdoms to a Census?

Since the very idea of Romans conducting a census of an allied kingdom is wholly implausible and unprecedented, inerrantists have tried to invent evidence of it. For example, the same *Lapis Venetus* discussed above is cited as "evidence" that the free state of Apamea was subject to an official Roman census. However, neither that census nor the inscription itself is dated, and as noted before there is no reason to believe the inscription refers to any other census than that of 6 A.D. Regardless, since no city named "Apamea" was free after 12 B.C. and Quirinius was not of consular rank before that year, it is impossible that the Apamea referred to in that inscription was an independent kingdom at the time. The only other "evidence" offered is a census revolt put down by legions in Cappadocia in 36 A.D. (Tacitus, *Annals* 6.41). But since Cappadocia was annexed as a Roman province in 17 A.D. (*Annals* 2.42, 2.56) this census was clearly not of an allied kingdom.[13]

1.7.3 Jesus Born During Census of 8 B.C.?

There is a modern myth that the Romans regularly conducted a census of their empire every 14 years. This is not true. There was little coordination between censuses of Roman citizens and censuses of provincial inhabitants, and rarely any fixed period of years between censuses, not even for citizens. Though Egypt continued to maintain a 14-year census cycle that the Romans

---

[12] For a complete discussion of the grammatical point, see "Did Luke Mean 'Before' Quirinius?" (quirinius.html#Word).

[13] For more on all this see "Was Apamea a Free City?" (quirinius.html #Apamea).

inherited from the previous Ptolemaic government, this was not extended to or consistently coordinated with any other province. Other provinces were assessed when they could be, often at various different times from each other.[14]

Nevertheless, this myth of a 14-year cycle is often used to support a claim that it would have been the census of 8 B.C. when Jesus was born, during the governorship of Saturninus rather than Quirinius. Why? Because some claim Tertullian said Jesus was born during the census of Saturninus (*Against Marcion* 4.19). But Tertullian doesn't say that. He says "censuses were conducted in Judaea by Sentius Saturninus" that confirm Jesus had brothers. Since these brothers had to have been born *after* Jesus, Tertullian cannot be referring to any census during which Jesus was born. There was in fact another Sentius Saturninus who was governor of Syria from 19 to 21 A.D. (the son of the former Sentius Saturninus) and it's almost certain this is whom Tertullian means.[15]

So there is no support for linking Luke's census with any census of 8 B.C. Though we know there was a universal census conducted in that year, it was only of Roman citizens, not the provinces. It therefore could not have been the census Luke describes, which clearly affected non-citizen inhabitants of Judaea. Indeed, Judaea was not even a Roman territory in the year 8, nor was Quirinius governing Syria then.

1.7.4 Herod's Census?

Since all those arguments fail, the last resort is to claim that it wasn't really a Roman census but a census conducted by Herod the Great. The immediate problem with this is that Luke does not say any such thing. He is quite clear that he means a census ordered by Augustus, not Herod, and carried out under Quirinius, specifically in connection with Syria, not under Herod independently. Judaea

---

[14] For a full analysis and discussion of the evidence and scholarship on the nature of Roman census-taking see "How Often Was the Census Held?" in my complete article online (quirinius.html#census).

[15] For this and several other attempts to argue that Luke "only" got the governor wrong see "Was 'Quirinius' a Mistake for Someone Else?" (quirinius.html#Tertullian). On the passage in Tertullian: C.F. Evans, "Tertullian's References to Sentius Saturninus and the Lukan Census," *Journal of Theological Studies* [n.s.] 24.1 (April 1973): 24-39.

was annexed to Syria under Quirinius in A.D. 6 and immediately subjected to a census. Obviously that's the census Luke means.

Nevertheless, the desperate plea is made that Luke "really meant" an unknown Herodian census. Apart from resting on no evidence at all, this claim is implausible for a number of reasons. Herod had no need of conducting a census, for the tribute owed him and that he owed Rome was a fixed annual sum. It didn't matter how many people were paying. Yet a census entails a vast outlay of expenses to cover administration and recordkeeping, and ties up a considerable amount of manpower. It also entails a significant inconvenience to the population, as even Luke's description makes clear. The Jews also had a tradition of cultural and moral hostility to a peacetime census. For example, 2 Samuel 24:1-17 and 1 Chronicles 21:1-17 depict the very idea of a peacetime census as sinful and Satanic, and when the Romans finally started subjecting Judaeans to a census in the year 6, many violently rebelled (Acts 5:37 and Josephus, *Antiquities of the Jews* 18.1-8 & 20.102 and *Jewish War* 2.433-34 & 7.252-54). For all these reasons, Herod had nothing to gain and plenty to lose by conducting his own census. To go ahead and do it anyway would have been so remarkable and unprecedented it could not have been omitted by historians like Josephus. Yet somehow no one noticed this remarkable census. And since Herod's involvement would be the most remarkable thing about it, it's inexplicable why Luke never mentions this, but only links the census to Roman decrees, Roman magistrates, and Roman provinces.[16]

1.7.5 Herod's Oath?

Stymied again, inerrantists resort to the last ditch effort of claiming Luke didn't really mean a "census" but an "oath-taking." And since according to Josephus (*Antiquities of the Jews* 16.136, 17.34-43, 17.89) Herod commanded his subjects in Judaea to swear an oath of loyalty to Rome in or around 8 B.C., "obviously" that's what Luke meant.

This is an indefensible thesis. Luke says "census," not "oath." Nor does he describe a situation where Herod is commanding people to take oaths, but of Augustus commanding people to be

---

[16] For more detail on all these points see "Was it a Census Conducted by Herod the Great?" (quirinius.html#Herod).

assessed. Moreover, the only possible rationale for Joseph's travel (Luke 2:3-5) is a tribal census register or the possession of taxable property in Bethlehem subject to a census. In contrast, an oath could be sworn anywhere and did not require traveling, nor is there evidence mass oaths even involved precise counting. And, again, Quirinius was still not governing Syria in 8 B.C.

Some claim Luke meant an oath Augustus had made to him every five years, but this oath was only made "by the consuls and priests" of Rome, not even all citizens, much less any provincials (*Res Gestae* 9). So this would never have involved Herod or Judaea. Some claim an annual oath was sworn by all the people subject to Rome on the anniversary of the emperor's accession, but even if that were the case, Judaea was not subject to Rome until 6 A.D., and an annual oath could not have involved constantly returning to one's ancestral city every year, or surely such an amazing inconvenience would be mentioned in the histories of the period. Others claim the event during which Jesus was born was when "the people of Rome" proclaimed Augustus "Father of the Nation" in 2 B.C., though that again requires reinventing the date of Herod's death, inventing an impossible second governorship for Quirinius, *and* ignoring what Luke actually says. And after all that, this event was only a vote made by Roman citizens anyway. So this would never have involved Judaeans.[17]

When everything above is considered, there is simply no way Luke Luke 2:1-6 could have meant or ever been read as referring to any national oath.

---

[17] For more see "Two Last Ditch Attempts" (quirinius.html#lastditch). On the plausibility of someone outside a province having to travel into a province for a census there, to an ancestral plot of land, see Lily Ross Taylor, "Quirinius and the Census of Judaea," *American Journal of Philology* 1933: 120-33 and S.R. Llewelyn, *New Documents Illustrating Early Christianity* 6 (1992), pp. 112-32. Evidence of such practices is also discussed in F. Kenyon and H. Bell *Greek Papyri in the British Museum* 3 (1907), p. 125; George Milligan, *Greek Papyri* (1910), pp. 72-3; Michael Rostovtzeff, *Studien zur Geschichte des römischen Kolonates* (1910), pp. 305ff.; and most recently, Klaus Rosen, "Jesu Geburtsdatum, der Census des Quirinius une eine Jüdische Steuererklärung aus dem Jahr 127 n.C.," *Jahrbuch für antike Christentum* 38 (1995): 5-15.

1.8 Conclusion

There is no reasonable way to get Matthew and Luke to agree with each other on the year Jesus was born. Luke clearly dates his birth in 6 A.D. and Matthew clearly dates it before 4 B.C. (possibly as early as 8 or 6 B.C.). Everyone concedes Matthew's narrative cannot be fudged to fit 6 A.D. And all attempts to force Luke to fit Matthew require groundless assertions contrary to all evidence and precedent, and always require declaring that in one way or another Luke didn't mean what he said. Not one of these proposed "solutions" rests on any evidence other than complete fabrications or distortions.

Ample evidence supports the conclusion that Luke meant no other year than A.D. 6, and no clear case can be made that Luke had any other year in mind. There is no way Quirinius could have governed Syria in any earlier year, nor could he have co-ruled Syria or been holding any other office there that Luke would refer to. There is no evidence that Augustus ever did or even would order a census of a Judaean kingdom before its annexation to Syria in the year 6. And Luke can neither have meant nor been describing a national "oath." Neither the *Lapis Tiburtinus*, nor the *Lapis Venetus*, nor the Antioch Stones even remotely imply any other conclusion. The Vardaman coins are definitively bogus. No reasonable case can be made that Herod the Great was still alive after 4 B.C. It's grammatically impossible to read Luke 2:2 as saying "before Quirinius governed Syria." And there is no rationale for assuming a census of Roman citizens in 8 B.C. would ever have affected the lives of any Judaean, and no evidence that Herod ever did or even would order a census of his own people, nor is it at all reasonable to interpret Luke as referring to such a thing.

There is no escaping the conclusion. Matthew contradicts Luke on a question of historical fact, and this entails either Matthew or Luke reports something historically false. The Bible is in error.

16

MARK 16:9-20 AS FORGERY OR FABRICATION

Originally published at ErrancyWiki.com.
Research & writing funded by ErrancyWiki.
Revised. © 2009, 2014.

Contents

1. Introduction: Problem and Significance
2. The Ending(s) of Mark

    2.1 The Original (OE), Long (LE), and Short Ending (SE)

    2.2 The Very Long Ending (VLE)

    2.3 The Bobbio Ending (BE)

    2.4 Assessment of the Markan Endings

3. The Principal Scholarship
4. The Internal Evidence

    4.1 Transition Is Illogical

        4.1.1 The LE

        4.1.2 The Terry Thesis

        4.1.3 The SE

    4.2 Style Is Not Mark's

        4.2.1 Deviations of Narrative Style

        4.2.2 Deviations of Lexical & Grammatical Style

        4.2.3 The Terry Thesis Revisited

        4.2.4 Agreements of Style

4.3 Content Betrays Knowledge of the New Testament

    4.3.1 The LE's Use of the NT
    4.3.2 Testing the Reverse Thesis
    4.3.3 The Robinson Thesis
    4.3.4 The SE's Use of the NT

4.4 Assessment of Internal Evidence

5. The External Evidence

   5.1 The Manuscripts: Textual Evidence

      5.1.1 In Greek
      5.1.2 In Syriac
      5.1.3 In Coptic
      5.1.4 In Ethiopic
      5.1.5 In Latin
      5.1.6 In Georgic and Armenian
      5.1.7 In Gothic
      5.1.8 The SE-LE Sequence and the Robinson Thesis
      5.1.9 Assessment of Textual Evidence

   5.2 The Manuscripts: Physical Evidence

      5.2.1 Ariston the Presbyter
      5.2.2 Accidental or Deliberate Transfer

   5.3 The Patristic Evidence

      5.3.1 Papias
      5.3.2 Justin
      5.3.3 Tatian
      5.3.4 Tertullian
      5.3.5 Irenaeus
      5.3.6 Hippolytus
      5.3.7 Origen, Clement, and Other 3rd Century Authors
      5.3.8 Vincentius (via Cyprian)

      5.3.9 Other Dubious Witnesses Before the 4th Century

      5.3.10 Eusebius

      5.3.11 Aphraates, Ephrem, Ambrose

      5.3.12 Jerome and Later

   5.4 Assessment of External Evidence

6. Conclusion

---

1. Introduction: Problem and Significance

Honest Bibles will tell you (in a footnote at least) that in the Gospel according to Mark all the verses after 16:8 are not found in "some of the oldest manuscripts." In fact, it is now the near unanimous agreement of experts that all those verses were either forged, or composed by some other author and inserted well after the original author composed the Gospel (for convenience I'll call that original author "Mark," though we aren't in fact certain of his name).

   The evidence is persuasive, both internal and external. In fact, this is one of the clearest examples of Christians meddling with the manuscripts of the canonical Bible, inserting what they wanted their books to have said (and possibly even subtracting what they didn't want it to have said, although I won't explore that possibility here). For the conclusion that those final verses were composed by a different author and added to Mark is more than reasonably certain.

   If Mark did not write verses 16:9-20, but some anonymous person(s) later added those verses, pretending (or erroneously believing) that Mark wrote them (as in fact they must have), then this Gospel, and thus the Bible as a whole, cannot be regarded as inerrant, or even consistently reliable. Were those words intended by God, he would have inspired Mark to write them in the first place. That he didn't entails those words were not inspired by God, and therefore the Bible we have is flawed, tainted by sinful human forgery or fallibility.

Even the astonishing attempt to claim the *forger* was inspired by God cannot gain credit.[1] For it is so inherently probable as to be effectively certain that a real God would have inspired Mark in the first place and not waited to inspire a later forger. The alternative is simply unbelievable. And in any case, a lie cannot be inspired, nor can a manifest error, yet this material is presented as among that which is "according to Mark," which is either a lie or an error.

This has a further, even greater consequence. Since we are actually *lucky* the evidence of this meddling survived, we should expect that other instances of meddling have occurred for which the evidence *didn't* survive, calling into doubt the rest of the New Testament (hereafter NT). Since the survival of evidence is so unlikely for changes made before c. 150 A.D. (fifty to eighty years after the NT books were supposedly written; Mark being most commonly dated around 70 A.D.), and in some cases even for changes made before c. 250 A.D. (well over a hundred more years later)—as we have few to no manuscripts of earlier date, and none complete, and scarce reliable testimonies—we can expect that many other changes could have survived undetected.[2]

And yet alterations in the earlier period are the most likely. For when the fewest copies existed, an emender's hope of succeeding was at its greatest, as well as his actual rate of success. Such was the case for all other books, so it should be expected for the Gospels. As Helmut Koester says, "Textual critics of classical texts know that the first century of their transmission is the period in which the most serious corruptions occur," and yet "textual critics of the New Testament writings have been surprisingly naive in this respect," despite the fact that they all agree "the oldest known

---

[1] Yes, some Christians actually defend the *forgery* as inspired (mainly Pentecostals who desperately need the snake handling pronouncement to be true), because they confess the evidence that it *is* a forgery is simply beyond any reasonable challenge (a noteworthy confession indeed): e.g. John Christopher Thomas and Kimberly Ervin Alexander, "'And the Signs Are Following': Mark 16.9-20: A Journey into Pentecostal Hermeneutics," *Journal of Pentecostal Theology* 11.2 (2003): 147-70.

[2] For other evidence of this same point see Chapter 14 ("Pauline Interpolations"). For even more examples of forgeries and interpolations in the NT, see the relevant sections of Bart Ehrman's *Jesus, Interrupted* (2009), *Misquoting Jesus* (2005) and *The Orthodox Corruption of Scripture* (1993).

archetypes" we can reconstruct from surviving manuscripts "are separated from the autographs by more than a century."³

The interpolation of the Markan ending thus refutes Biblical inerrancy. As Wilbur Pickering put it:

> Are we to say that God was unable to protect the text of Mark or that He just couldn't be bothered? I see no other alternative—either He didn't care or He was helpless. And either option is fatal to the claim that Mark's Gospel is 'God-breathed'.⁴

The whole canon falls to the same conclusion. This dichotomy is entailed by the fact of the Markan interpolation. It forces us to fall on either of two horns, yet on neither of which can a doctrine of inerrancy survive. If God *couldn't* protect His Book from such meddling, then he hardly counts as a god, but in any case such inability entails he can't have ensured the rest of the received text of the Bible is inerrant (since if he couldn't in this case, he couldn't in any), which leaves no rational basis for maintaining the inerrancy of the Bible, as then even God could not have produced such a thing. On the other hand, if God *could* but did not *care* to protect His Book from such meddling, then we have no rational basis for maintaining that he cared to protect it from any other errors, either, whether those now detectable *or not*.

Since the Bible we now have can only be inerrant if God wanted it to be, and the evidence proves he didn't want it to be, therefore it can't be inerrant. It does no good to insist the Bible was only inerrant in the originals, since a God who cared to make the originals inerrant would surely care to keep them that way. Otherwise, what would have been the point? We still don't have those originals.

Only the most convoluted and implausible system of excuses for God can escape this conclusion, and any faith that requires such a dubious monstrosity is surely proven bankrupt by that very fact.

---

³ Helmut Koester, "The Text of the Synoptic Gospels in the Second Century," in William Petersen, ed., *Gospel Traditions in the Second Century: Origins, Recensions, Text, and Transmission* (1989), pp. 19-27.

⁴ Quoted by Daniel Wallace, "Inspiration, Preservation, and New Testament Textual Criticism," *Grace Theological Journal* 12.1 (1992): 21-50 [44].

2. The Ending(s) of Mark

There are more variants for the ending of Mark than is commonly known. I'll discuss those that most bibles bother to mention, then those that most bibles conspicuously don't mention.

2.1 The OE, LE, and SE

Presently in the New American Standard Bible (NASB) the Gospel of Mark ends as follows (Mark 16:1-20, uncontested portion in bold):

> **[1] When the Sabbath was over, Mary Magdalene, and Mary the mother of James, and Salome, bought spices, so that they might come and anoint Him. [2] Very early on the first day of the week, they came to the tomb when the sun had risen. [3] They were saying to one another, "Who will roll away the stone for us from the entrance of the tomb?" [4] Looking up, they saw that the stone had been rolled away, although it was extremely large. [5] Entering the tomb, they saw a young man sitting at the right, wearing a white robe; and they were amazed. [6] And he said to them, "Do not be amazed; you are looking for Jesus the Nazarene, who has been crucified. He has risen; He is not here; behold, here is the place where they laid Him. [7] But go, tell His disciples and Peter, 'He is going ahead of you to Galilee; there you will see Him, just as He told you'." [8] They went out and fled from the tomb, for trembling and astonishment had gripped them; and they said nothing to anyone, for they were afraid.**
> [9b] Now after He had risen early on the first day of the week, He first appeared to Mary Magdalene, from whom He had cast out seven demons. [10] She went and reported to those who had been with Him, while they were mourning and weeping. [11] When they heard that He was alive and had been seen by her, they refused to believe it. [12] After that, He appeared in a different form to two of them while they were walking

along on their way to the country. [13] They went away and reported it to the others, but they did not believe them either. [14] Afterward He appeared to the eleven themselves as they were reclining at a table; and He reproached them for their unbelief and hardness of heart, because they had not believed those who had seen Him after He had risen. [15] And He said to them, "Go into all the world and preach the gospel to all creation: [16] He who has believed and has been baptized shall be saved; but he who has disbelieved shall be condemned. [17] These signs will accompany those who have believed: in My name they will cast out demons; they will speak with new tongues; [18] they will pick up serpents {in their hands}, and if they drink any deadly poison, it will not hurt them; they will lay hands on the sick, and they will recover."

[19] So then, when the Lord Jesus had spoken to them, He was received up into heaven and sat down at the right hand of God. [20] And they went out and preached everywhere, while the Lord worked with them, and confirmed the word by the signs that followed.

What is commonly called (and hypothesized to be) the 'Original Ending' of Mark (OE) is presented in bold above. The material not in bold is called the 'Longer Ending' of Mark (LE).[5] There is

---

[5] Many manuscripts omit the phrase "in their hands" in verse 18, so I have placed those words in brackets, as having a 50/50 shot at being either a later addition or original to the LE. One very late manuscript even omits the entire reference to serpents, but that was later doctrinal meddling; the original LE certainly included it. Some rare manuscripts containing the SE say "Jesus himself *appeared* [and] sent out" the word or "Jesus himself *appeared to them* [and] sent out" the word, but all scholars agree these are later interpolations (the added words are missing from almost all mss., especially the oldest and the best). There are numerous other manuscript deviations of little importance (in the OE, SE *and* LE), but discussing them further is unnecessary for the present thesis. Note also that some scholars confusingly call the OE the SE. Here the terms will be consistently employed as I have defined them. But that doesn't mean I'm certain the OE was in fact the way the Gospel originally ended, only that among biblical experts it is most commonly (but not universally) thought to be.

another ending in some manuscripts, completely replacing or preceding the lengthy text above, which reads:

> [9a] And they promptly reported all these instructions to Peter and his companions. And after that, Jesus Himself sent out through them from east to west the sacred and imperishable proclamation of eternal salvation. Amen.

This is called the 'Shorter Ending' of Mark (SE). Some manuscripts have neither SE nor LE (and thus have only the OE), and one manuscript contains only the SE (and that is among the oldest) while others give indications that many other such manuscripts once existed, but most (a great many in each case) have either the LE alone or both the SE *and* the LE (always with the LE following the SE, not the other way around, unlike the order shown in the NASB).[6] The SE and LE are logically and narratively incompatible, however, and thus cannot have been composed by the same author.

2.2 The VLE

There is also a third ending found in one surviving manuscript (and already known to Jerome in the 4th century), which you generally never hear of, but which I shall call the 'Very Long Ending' (VLE), as it is an extension of the LE, adding to the beginning of verse 16:15 (after Jesus "reproaches" them in verse 14):

> [15] And they defended themselves saying, "This world of lawlessness and unbelief is under Satan, who does not allow the unclean things that are under the spirits to comprehend God's true power [*or* truth and power]. Because of this, reveal your righteousness now." They said these things to Christ, and Christ replied to them, "The term of years of the authority of Satan has been fulfilled, but other dreadful things are drawing near, even to those for whose sake as sinners I was delivered

---

[6] Only one extant ms. clearly contains the SE alone (the Latin Codex Bobiensis: see section 2.2 of this chapter). Others that may have are ambiguous as to their original condition.

up to death so they might return to the truth and no longer sin, and might inherit the spiritual and incorruptible glory of righteousness which is in heaven. But go into all the world and preach the gospel to all creation."[7]

Such are the various endings of Mark.[8] All scholars now reject the VLE (if they even know of it) and now regard verse 16:8 to have been the OE, even though it is an odd way to end a book—though it is not without precedent, and does make more literary sense than is usually supposed.[9] The VLE, by contrast, is unmistakably a

---

[7] For "God's true power" the ms. literally reads "truth power" (both words framing "to comprehend God's"), which is ungrammatical and thus corrupt. Some suggest "and" has been dropped ("to comprehend God's truth [and] power") but the word order makes this less likely than a corruption of *alêthinên* into *alêtheian* (hence "true power"). The full Greek of the VLE reads:

> *Kakeinoi apelogounto legontes hoti ho aiôn houtos tês anomias kai tês apistias hupo ton Satanan estin, ho mê eôn ta hupo tôn pneumatôn akatharta tên alêtheian tou theou katalabesthai dunamin, dia touto apokalupson sou tên dikaiosunên êdê. ekeinoi elegon tô Christô, kai ho Christos ekeinois proselegen hoti peplêrôtai ho horos tôn etôn tês exousias tou Satana, alla eggizei alla deina kai huper hôn egô hamartêsantôn paredothên eis thanaton hina hupostrepsôsin eis tên alêtheian kai mêketi hamartêsôsin, hina tên en tô ouranô pneumatikên kai aphtharton tês dikaiosunês doxan klêronomêsôsin. alla [poreuthentes eis ton kosmon hapanta kêruxate to euaggelion pasê tê ktisei].*

The last bracketed clause is identical to the LE text.

[8] Unless otherwise noted I rely on the critical edition of the Greek text provided by Barbara Aland, Bruce Metzger, et al., *The Greek New Testament*, 4th Revised ed. (1983). See pp. 189-92 for the endings of Mark (and p. 191, n. 6 for the VLE, on which also see C.R. Gregory, *Das Freer-Logion* [1908]). This includes an apparatus distinguishing which endings appear in which manuscripts (hereafter mss.), although in other cases I have found the apparatus of this edition frequently omits variants that I have personally seen even in the mss. they attest to using, which means such omissions may also exist here (so we should not assume their apparatus is complete). A more (but still not entirely) complete apparatus is available in Reuben Swanson's *New Testament Greek Manuscripts: Mark* (1995), pp. 264-71.

[9] A fact well summarized by Daniel Wallace in Black, *PEM*, pp. 33-38; cf. also Darrell Bock [*PEM*], pp. 134-37. (*PEM* and other abbreviations are identified in section 3 below.)

forgery, so its existence further proves that Christians felt free to doctor manuscripts of the Gospels.

2.3 The BE

The same point is proven further by the fact that, in addition to the endings just surveyed, there is at least one known interpolation *within* the OE itself (expanding verse 16:3), extant in one ancient manuscript, which can be considered yet another 'ending' to Mark (making five altogether), the addition here given in bold:

> [3] They were saying to one another, "Who will roll away the stone for us from the entrance of the tomb?" **Then all of a sudden, at the third hour of the day, there was darkness over the whole earth, and angels descended from heaven and [as he] rose up in the splendor of the living God they ascended with him, and immediately it was light.** [4] Looking up, they saw that the stone had been rolled away, although it was extremely large.

This is from Codex Bobiensis, a pre-Vulgate Latin translation, which also deletes the last part of verse 8 before attaching the SE (thus eliminating the contradiction between them: see section 4.1.3 below). The manuscript itself physically dates from the 4th or 5th century, but contains a text dated no later than the 3rd century, and some evidence suggests it ultimately derives from a lost 2nd century manuscript.[10] No one accepts this Bobbio Ending (BE) as having any chance of being authentic, yet it must be quite ancient. It was also manifestly forged.

2.4 Assessment of the Markan Endings

Some scholars theorize that Mark's original ending did indeed extend beyond the OE but was lost (accidentally or deliberately) and then replaced by the SE and LE in different manuscripts (hereafter **mss.** [plural] and **ms.** [singular]), originating two separate traditions which were eventually loosely combined into a sixth 'Double Ending' (DE) in later manuscripts (even though they don't logically fit together), while in other mss. the LE was preferred or was expanded into the VLE, or the OE was expanded into the BE.

Though many of the arguments for a 'Lost Original Ending' (LOE) are intriguing, none are conclusive, nor can any produce the actual text of such an ending even if it existed, nor can scholars agree which ending it should be (some scholars find the original ending redacted in Matthew's Galilean mountain narrative, others in John's Galilean seashore narrative, yet others in Luke's Emmaus narrative, and still others in the SE or LE itself, and so on).

I will not discuss those debates, as they are too speculative and inconclusive. It is the sole task here to demonstrate that, regardless

---

[10] See Wikipedia on "Codex Bobiensis," with Metzger, *TNT*, p. 73. My translation is adapted from William Lane, *The Gospel according to Mark* (1974), p. 582, n. 3, and the original Latin. The Latin text of the BE reads:

> *Subito autem ad horam tertiam tenebrae diei factae sunt per totum orbem terrae, et descenderunt de caelis angeli et surgent in claritate vivi Dei simul ascenderunt cum eo, et continuo lux facta est. Tunc illae accesserunt ad monimentum.*

Literally this says the angels "descended from heaven and rose up in the splendor of the living God ascended with him" but that is oddly stated and grammatically incorrect. Almost certainly the middle verb has been corrupted in transmission, from a singular to a plural. The original must have had something like *surgente eo* rather than *sergent*, and my translation reflects this. The phrase *surgente eo* is the ablative absolute for "as he rose up" and such a construction and sense is entirely expected here, or possibly it was *sergente iu*, as the ablative *Iesu* was often thus abbreviated among the *nomina sacra* even in early Latin mss., while the Greek (if this interpolation derives from a Greek source) would have used the genitive absolute (with the very same abbreviation *iu*), in which case this verse said "as Jesus rose up."

of how Mark originally ended his Gospel, it was not the ending we have now (whether SE or LE; the DE, BE and VLE are ruled out heretofore). Quite simply, the current ending of Mark was not written by Mark.

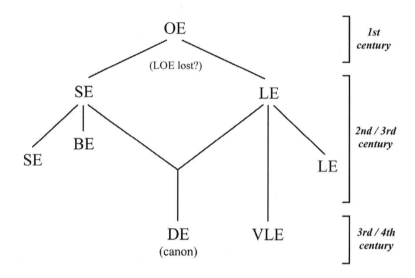

3. The Principal Scholarship

The literature on the ending of Mark is vast. But certain works are required reading and centrally establish the fact that the current ending of Mark was not written by Mark. They cite much of the remaining scholarship and evidence, and often go into more precise detail than I will here. So to pursue the issues further, consult the following (here in reverse chronological order):

> David Alan Black, ed., *Perspectives on the Ending of Mark: Four Views* (2008). **Hereafter PEM.**

> Adela Yarbro Collins, *Mark: A Commentary* (2007): pp. 797-818. **Hereafter MAC.**

Bruce Metzger and Bart Ehrman, *The Text of the New Testament: Its Transmission, Corruption, and Restoration*, 4th ed. (2005): pp. 322-27. **Hereafter TNT.**

Joel Marcus, *Mark 1-16: A New Translation with Introduction and Commentary* (2000): pp. 1088-96. **Hereafter MNT.**

James Kelhoffer, *Miracle and Mission: The Authentication of Missionaries and Their Message in the Longer Ending of Mark* (2000). **Hereafter MAM.**

John Christopher Thomas, "A Reconsideration of the Ending of Mark," *Journal of the Evangelical Theological Society* 26.4 (1983): 407-19. **Hereafter JETS.**

Bruce Metzger, *New Testament Studies: Philological, Versional, and Patristic* (1980): pp. 127-47. **Hereafter NTS.**

Bruce Metzger, *A Textual Commentary on the Greek New Testament*, 3rd ed. (1971): pp. 122-28. **Hereafter TCG.**

There are also a few online resources worth consulting (with due critical judgment). Most worthwhile is Wieland Willker's extensive discussion of the evidence and scholarship.[11] Though Willker is only (as far as I can tell) a professor of chemistry, and biblically conservative, he did a thorough job of marshaling the evidence. Much briefer but still adding points of note is the treatment of the problem at Wikipedia.[12] Other threads can be explored but will

---

[11] Wieland Willker, "A Textual Commentary on the Greek Gospels, Vol. 2b: The Various Endings of Mark," 6th ed. (2009) at www-user.uni-bremen.de/~wie/TCG/TC-Mark-Ends.pdf, which is part of Willker's extensive "Online Textual Commentary on the Greek Gospels" (www-user.uni-bremen.de/~wie/TCG).

[12] The best discussion at Wikipedia is "Mark 16:9-20 in the manuscripts and patristic evidence" in the entry for "Mark 16" (en.wikipedia.org/wiki/Mark_16).

only end up with the same results that all the above scholars document.[13]

4. The Internal Evidence

Internal evidence is what we can conclude from the reconstructed text, such as its internal logic and literary content and style. In order of physical creation, the 'internal' evidence is earlier and so will be treated here first. Other scholars usually treat it last, but the order of examination doesn't matter. Either way, the internal evidence still confirms the LE is not by Mark, in three different ways: the SE and LE are too incongruous with the OE to have been composed by its author (i.e. the transition from the OE to either the SE or the LE is illogical); the SE and LE are written in a completely different style from Mark (which proves a different author composed them); and the LE betrays (in fact assumes) knowledge of the Canonical New Testament, which did not exist when Mark wrote (and to a lesser extent the same can be said of the SE).

4.1 Transition Is Illogical

The transition from the OE to the LE violates logic and grammar, while the transition from the OE to the SE is grammatical but even more illogical. This alone greatly reduces the probability of common authorship.

---

[13] For example, the most extensive attempt to argue the LE was and is the original ending of Mark (and thus not a forgery) is still that of William Farmer, *The Last Twelve Verses of Mark* (1974), but his arguments have been refuted many times over by the scholars just listed. Some of his more egregious errors had already been noted in J.N. Birdsall's review of Farmer's book in *The Journal of Theological Studies* [n.s.] 26 (1975): 151-60. Similarly, a recent debate pitting scholars pro and con reads decisively in favor of the negative (*PEM*; see Bock's assessment therein, pp. 124-41). And other surveys come to essentially the same conclusion, e.g. Steven Cox, *A History and Critique of Scholarship Concerning the Markan Endings* (1993).

4.1.1 The LE

In the LE the transition from verse 8 to 9 is ungrammatical and thus cannot have been composed by the same author. In fact, this oddity suggests the LE actually derives from another text (possibly a 2nd century commentary on the Gospels) and was only appended to Mark by a third party. There is more evidence for this hypothesis in the manuscripts (which will be discussed later) and in every other element of this illogical transition (to be explored shortly).

For the present point, it is enough to note the internal evidence. First, the grammatical subject in verse 8 is "they" (the women), but in verse 9 it is "he" (Jesus). But the word "he" is not present in verse 9. Thus we have the strange transition, "For they were afraid and having risen on the first day of the week appeared first to Mary," which makes no sense. The pronoun "he" is expected (or the name "Jesus") but it is absent, creating a strange grammatical confusion. The oddity is clearer in the Greek than in English translation. In the Greek, verse 9 begins abruptly with a nominative participle with no stated subject, a strange thing to do when transitioning from a sentence about a wholly different subject.

The transition is not only ungrammatical, it is narratively illogical. Verse 9 reintroduces Mary Magdalene with information we would have expected to learn much earlier (the fact that Jesus had cast seven demons out of her). Instead it is suddenly added in the LE, completely out of the blue without any explanation, suggesting the author of the LE was trying to improve on the OE or wasn't even writing an ending to Mark but a separate narrative altogether (in which this is the first time Mary Magdalene appears in this scene or in which the story of her exorcism appeared many scenes earlier). Either entails that the same author did not write the OE. Indeed, it makes no sense to add this detail in the LE, as it serves no narrative function, adds nothing relevant to the story, and alludes to an event that Mark never relates. If the author of the LE were Mark, he would have added this exorcism story into the narrative of Jesus' ministry, and then alluded to it (if at all) when Mary Magdalene was first introduced in verse 15:40, or when she first appears in the concluding narrative (in verse 16:1). Furthermore, not only does the subject inexplicably change from the women to Jesus, but suddenly Mary Magdalene is alone, without explanation of why, or where the other two women have gone.

We should also expect some explanation of when these appearances occurred, yet we get instead an inexplicable confusion. Verse 9 says they happened after Jesus rose on the first day of the week, but it's then unclear as to how many days after. This single temporal reference would normally entail everything to follow occurred on the same day. But that would contradict the OE's declaration that Jesus had already gone ahead to Galilee and would appear *there*, as it would have taken several days for the women (or anyone else) to travel from Jerusalem to Galilee. It is unlikely Mark would produce such a perplexing contradiction or allow a distracting ambiguity like this in his story, as he is elsewhere very careful about marking relevant chronological progression (e.g. Mark 16:2, 15:42, 14:30, 14:12, 6:35, 4:35, etc.).

Mark also wouldn't repeat the declaration that it was "the first day of the week," as he already said that in verse 16:2. Instead, he would simply say "on the same day," or not even designate the day at all, as there would be no need for it (his narrative would already imply it), until the story entailed the passage of several days (perhaps either at 16:12 or 16:14). Apparently the author of the LE assumes the day hasn't yet been stated (and thus appears unaware of the fact that it was already stated in the OE only a few verses earlier) and then assumes all these events took place over a single day, and thus in and around Jerusalem, which contradicts Mark's declaration that the appearances were to occur in Galilee (16:7, 14:28; corroborated in Matthew 28:16-20), yet conspicuously agrees with Luke and John (a telling contradiction that will be discussed later).

All four oddities (the incorrect grammar, the strange reintroduction of Mary, the unexplained disappearance of the other women, and the chronological redundancies and contradictions) make the transition from the OE to the LE too illogical for the same author to have written both. On the hypothesis that the LE was written by another author in a different book and then just copied into Mark by a third party, all these oddities are highly probable. But on the hypothesis that Mark wrote the LE, all these oddities are highly improbable. Indeed, any one of them would be improbable. All of them together, very much so.

4.1.2 The Terry Thesis

Bruce Terry claims such odd transitions exist elsewhere in Mark and thus are not improbable, but his proposed grammatical parallels actually demonstrate what's so odd about this one, and he has no parallels for any of the other oddities.[14] To show this, I shall go through all his proposed parallels in order.

In Mark 2:13 we actually have a nested pericope in which the subject (Jesus) is already established at 2:1-2, and he remains the primary subject for the whole story, which story *includes* 2:12, which clearly explains the temporary transition of subject from Jesus to the man he healed: Jesus gives a command in v. 11, the man follows it in v. 12, then Jesus moves on in v. 13. There is no parallel here to 16:9, where Jesus has never been a subject of any prior sentence much less the whole pericope, yet suddenly he is the subject without explanation, whereas it is the *women* who have been the primary subject of the entire pericope up until now (beginning at 16:1), and yet even they inexplicably vanish, and suddenly all we hear about is Mary Magdalene alone. That is not a logical transition. Moreover, Mark's narrative in chapter 2 follows a clear structure of chronological stations, beginning when Jesus is introduced into the story (1:9), then sojourns in the desert (1:13), then returns to the seashore (1:14), then goes to Capernaum (1:21), then leaves (1:35) and goes through Galilee (1:39), then he returns "again" to Capernaum (2:1), where he heals the paralytic, then he returns "again" to the seashore (2:13). The structure and transitions are clear. There is nothing of the sort for 16:9. Hence the transitions in chapter 2 are logical and grammatical, but the transition at 16:8-9 is not.

A similar structure accompanies Mark 6:45: the subject is already established as Jesus at 6:34, then Jesus gives commands to his Disciples to deliver food to the multitude (6:37-39), and in result the multitude eat (6:40-44), thus temporarily becoming the subject, then Jesus gives another command to his Disciples (6:45). The nested structure already has the subject clearly established as Jesus. So there is no parallel here to 16:9.

---

[14] Bruce Terry, "The Style of the Long Ending of Mark," originally published as "Another Look at the Ending of Mark," *Firm Foundation* 93 (14 Sept. 1976), but available now at bible.ovu.edu/terry//articles/mkendsty.htm.

The same structure accompanies Mark 7:31: the subject is already established as Jesus at 7:6, then Jesus teaches and interacts with the crowd, then heads toward Tyre and enters a house (7:24), then a woman begs his aid and they have a back-and-forth conversation (7:25-30), in which the subject shifts entirely as expected from her (7:26) to him (7:27) to her (7:28) to him (7:29) to her (7:30), and then back to him (7:31). The woman has departed in verse 7:29, so obviously we expect the subject at 7:31 to pick back up with who the primary subject has been all along: Jesus. Mark even indicates this by telling us he "again" went toward Tyre (thus leaving no mistake who the subject is). Again, there is no parallel with 16:9.

In just the same way, at 8:1 we already know Jesus is the subject: he is the subject all the way up to 7:36, then we hear a brief audience reaction at 7:37, then Jesus is again the subject at 8:1, as we should already expect. In a comparable fashion, at 14:3 Jesus has already been the primary subject throughout chapter 13, then is temporarily the subject of *conversation* for just two verses (14:1-2), then becomes the primary subject again (14:3). There is no comparable nested structure at 16:9.

Moreover, all these alleged parallels show how different the style of the LE is, as Mark uses *kai* ("and") dozens of times to mark almost every transition in Mark 2 (19 out of 28 verses begin with *kai*), 6 (40 out of 56 verses begin with *kai*), and 7 (18 out of 37 verses begin with *kai*), yet the author of the LE shows no comparable fondness for *kai* (apart from two un-Markan transitions with *kakainos*, he begins only 1 of 12 verses with *kai*, and this despite the fact that the LE runs through no fewer than 9 comparable sentence transitions in just 12 verses), and more importantly, he doesn't use it to transition in 16:9, as we would expect if this is supposed to parallel the Markan style of 2:13, 6:45, 7:31, and 14:3 (which all transition with *kai*) as Terry claims.

Only verse 8:1 uses instead the device of a participle-verb construction similar to 16:9, yet *doesn't* transition with the particle *de*. The LE does. And again, the subject of 8:1 was already established two verses earlier, in an obvious nested structure not at all parallel to 16:9. Another stylistic oddity comes from another verse that Terry mistakenly considers a parallel: only once, he says, does Mark elsewhere *begin* a new pericope with a participle, and that's at 14:66, which he claims is a parallel for 16:9. But in fact 14:66 begins with a genitive absolute, which is indeed a very

Markan feature (it's also how he transitions in 8.1, another of Terry's alleged parallels). It's just that this is exactly what the author of the LE *doesn't* do at 16:9. Since 16:9 does not use the genitive absolute to mark its transition, but 14:66 does, even 14:66 fails to be a parallel, but instead shows just how different Mark's style was from the author of the LE.

4.1.3 The SE

The transition from the OE to the SE is smoother than for the LE, yet it is still too incongruous for the SE to have come from the original author. For the SE immediately contradicts the very preceding sentence (and without any explanation) by first saying the women told nothing to no one, then immediately saying they told everything to everyone, an error no competent author would commit.

This was so glaringly illogical that in at least one manuscript a scribe erased the contradiction by deleting the end of verse 16:8 before continuing with 16:9a, but that ms. (designated "k" = Codex Bobiensis, Latin, 4th/5th century) is actually known for many occasions of such meddling with the text (the BE itself being an example: see section 2.3 above).

The SE is thus even more illogical than the LE. Though otherwise a grammatically correct transition, the SE was clearly not written by Mark but by someone who could not accept his ending and had to change it, directly reversing what it just said. Mark would not have done that without explaining the incongruity (such as by mentioning a passage of time or otherwise indicating why the women changed their mind).

4.2 Style Is Not Mark's

That the LE was clearly written by another author is also sufficiently proved by its unique style. Some examples of this were already given in section 4.1.2 (above), but the evidence is far more extensive than that. It is nearly impossible for a forger to imitate an author's style perfectly, because there are too many factors to control and no one is cognizant of even a fraction of them (from the choice and frequency of vocabulary to average sentence length, grammatical idioms, etc.). And this is especially the case when the forger makes no effort even to try.

It is also very difficult for an author to completely mask his own style, especially since authors are always unaware of all the ways in which their style differs from anyone they may be emulating. And again, an author never even tries to do that unless he aims to.[15] Thus, if the LE was originally written in a separate work, and thus not even intended as an ending to Mark, it should exhibit a wildly different style, indicative of a different author. But if the LE was written by Mark, it should be the reverse, with far more similarities than deviations. This is not what we find.

4.2.1 Deviations of Narrative Style

In the LE the series of events is far too rapid and terse and lacks narrative development, which is very unlike the rest of Mark, who as an author would surely cringe at the obscure, unexplained jumble of the LE. Mark composes all his pericopes with clever and elaborate literary structure, nearly everything is present for a reason and makes sense (if you understand the point of it).[16] But the contents of the LE are simply rattled off like a laundry list without explanation or even a clear purpose.

There is nothing in the LE that resembles the way Mark writes or composes his stories. He never rapidly fires through a laundry list of ill-described events, as if alluding to half a dozen stories not yet written. So the whole nature of the passage is starkly uncharacteristic of Mark, being "a mere summarizing of the appearances" of the risen Jesus, "a manner of narration entirely foreign" to Mark's Gospel. Indeed, as Ezra Gould had already observed over a hundred years ago, the OE's narration of "the

---

[15] For a general discussion of the principles of stylistic forgery detection see: Donald Foster, *Author Unknown: Tales of a Literary Detective* (2000) and Robert Eagleson, "Forensic Analysis of Personal Written Texts: A Case Study," in John Gibbons, ed., *Language and the Law* (1994), pp. 362-73.

[16] See, for example, the studies of Randel Helms, *Gospel Fictions* (1988) and Dennis MacDonald, *The Homeric Epics and the Gospel of Mark* (2000). In chapter ten of *On the Historicity of Jesus* I summarize these and survey many other examples analyzed by other experts in the academic literature.

appearance of the angel to the women is a good example of his style" and yet it's in "marked contrast" to the LE.[17]

Even the cursory temptation scene (Mark 1:12-13) is no comparison. It still reads like a complete unit, for which we would not need or expect any further details had we not otherwise known of them (from the expansion made in Matthew and Luke). The LE, by contrast, is unintelligible without knowing the details alluded to, and is not a single event, but a long compressed series of them. Never mind that each one is of phenomenally greater narrative importance than the relatively trivial fact that Jesus was once tested by the Devil.

What remains inexcusably peculiar is the *great number* of events, compressed to so small a space—compressed so far, in fact, that each one bears even less detail than the temptation, and what details got added make no inherent sense (as will be shown in section 4.3.1). Moreover, Mark composed a unified Gospel from beginning to end, so if Mark had written the LE, we would expect the LE to mention Galilee: he has set this detail up twice already (in 14:28 and again in 16:7), anticipating an appearance in Galilee. So that he would drop this theme in the LE is inconceivable. Indeed, as observed in section 4.1.1 (above), the LE not only drops that theme, it contradicts it by evidently presuming a series of appearances in and around Jerusalem.

4.2.2 Deviations of Lexical & Grammatical Style

And if all that wasn't enough, the stylistic evidence is alone decisive. For the vocabulary and syntax of the LE could hardly be further from the style of Mark's Gospel. This has been known for over a hundred years, most famously demonstrated to devastating effect by Ezra Gould in 1896.[18] Unattributed quotations in the

---

[17] Ezra Gould, *Critical and Exegetical Commentary on the Gospel according to St. Mark* (1896), p. 303.

[18] Ezra Gould, *Critical and Exegetical Commentary*, pp. 301-03. Analysis of several of these stylistic incongruities has been repeated by several scholars since, generating an overall consensus: e.g. Paul Danove, "Determination of the Extent of the Text of the Gospel of Mark," *The End of Mark's Story: A Methodological Study* (1993): pp. 119-31; James Keith Elliott, "The Text and Language of the Endings to Mark's Gospel," *Theologische Zeitschrift* 27.4 (July-August 1971): 255-62.

present section are from Gould's seminal commentary (where also the evidence is given). Following is a mere selection of the style deviations demonstrating the LE was not written by Mark:

1. In the LE (a mere 12 verses), the demonstrative pronoun *ekeinos* is used five times as a simple substantive ("she," "they," "them"). But Mark never uses *ekeinos* that way (not once in 666 verses), he always uses it adjectively, or with a definite article, or as a simple demonstrative (altogether 22 times), always using *autos* as his simple substantive pronoun instead (hundreds of times).[19]

2. In the LE, *husteron* is used as a temporal ("afterward"), but never by Mark, who only uses cognates (the noun and verb) and only in reference to poverty (2 times), never to express a succession of events.

3. In the LE the contraction *kan* is used to mean "and if" but Mark only uses it to mean "even, just" (5:28 and 6:56, "if I touch *even just* his garment..."). Mark always uses the uncontracted *kai ean* to mean "and if" (8 times).

4. In the LE, *poreuomai* ("to go") is used three times, but never once in the rest of Mark (Mark only ever uses compound forms), which is "the more remarkable, as it is in itself so common a word," used 74 times in the other Gospels alone, and in Mark "occasions for its use occur on every page."

5. In the LE, *theaomai* ("to see") is used twice, but never once in the rest of Mark, who uses several other verbs of seeing instead, none of which are used in the LE. And this despite the fact that *theaomai* is normally a common word.

---

[19] The *kakeinon* used twice in Mark 12:4-5 is still a demonstrative, i.e. it references preceding nouns in each case: "he sent *another slave*, and *that one* they bashed in the head...he sent *another [slave]*, and *that one* they killed" (contrast Mark 14:2-3, where "he sent a *servant*...and *him* they beat up," using *auton* instead of *ekeinon*). The author of the LE uses *ekeinos* (by itself) as a synonym of *autos*. Mark never does.

6. In the LE, the verb *apisteô* ("to disbelieve") is used twice, but never once in the rest of Mark, who always uses nominal and adjectival expressions for disbelief instead (3 times).

7. The LE employs *blaptô* ("to hurt"), a word that appears nowhere else in Mark, nor even anywhere else in the whole of the NT (except once, and there very similarly: Luke 4:35); and *synergountos* ("working with," "helping") and *bebaioun* ("to confirm"), words that appear nowhere else in Mark, nor in any Gospel (but commonplace in the epistles of Paul); and *epakolouthein* ("to come after," "to follow"), a word that appears nowhere else in Mark, nor in any Gospel (but used in the epistles 1 Tim. and 1 Pet.); and several other words that appear nowhere else in Mark: *penthein* ("to mourn"), *heteros* ("other"), *morphê* ("form"), *endeka* ("eleven"), *parakolouthein* ("accompany"), *ophis* ("snake"), *analambanô* ("take up"), and *thanasimon* ("deadly thing," e.g. "poison"). Not all of these novelties are unexpected, but some are.

8. In the LE, the expression *meta de tauta* ("after these things") is used twice, but never once in the rest of Mark. Among the Gospels the expression *meta de tauta* (or just *meta tauta*) is used only in John and Luke-Acts. In fact, *meta tauta* is so commonplace in those authors as to be stylistically distinctive of them.

9. In the LE, the disciples are called "those who were with him," a designation Mark never uses, and employing *genomenos* in a fashion wholly alien to Mark (who uses the word 12 times, yet never in any similar connotation).

10. The LE says "lay hands on [x]" with the idiom *epitithêmi epi* [x], using a preposition to take the indirect object, but Mark uses the dative to do that, i.e. *epitithêmi* [x], with [x] in the dative case (4 times). He only uses the prepositional idiom when he uses the uncompounded verb (*tithêmi epi* [x], 8:25). Thus Mark recognized the compound idiom was redundant, while the author of the LE didn't.

11. The LE employs several other expressions that Mark never does: *etheathê hypo* ("seen by"); *pasê tê ktisei* ("in the whole

world"); *kalôs hexousin* ("get well"); *men oun* ("and then"); *duo hex autôn* ("two of them," an expression not used by Mark with any number, 'two' or otherwise); *par' hês* ("from whom"), which Mark never uses in any context, much less with *ekballô* ("cast out," "exorcise"), in which contexts Mark uses *ek* instead (7:27); and finally the LE uses *prôtê sabbatou* (16:9) where we should expect some variation of *tê mia tôn sabbatôn* (16:2).

12. The LE also lacks typical Markan words (like *euthus*, "early, at once" or *palin*, "again," and many others) while using Markan words with completely different frequencies, e.g. *pisteuein* ("to believe"), used only 10 times by Mark in 666 verses, in the LE is used 4 times in just 12 verses (a frequency far more typical of John, where the word appears nearly a hundred times). Any one or two of these oddities might happen in any comparably extended passage of Mark, but not so many.

In all, of 163 words in the LE, around 20 are un-Markan, which by itself is not unusual. What is unusual is how common most of these words normally are, or how distinctive they are of later NT writers or narratives, hence the concentration of so many of these words in the LE is already suspicious. But more damning are all the ways words are used contrary to Markan style, using different words than Mark uses or using Markan words in a way Mark never does. We also find 9 whole expressions in the LE that are un-Markan, which in just 12 verses is something of a record.

Certainly, any single deviation of style will occur at the hand of the same author in any passage or verse, sometimes even several deviations of different kinds, and unique words will be common when they are distinctive to the narrative. But to have *so many* instances of *so many* deviations in such a short span of verses (against a compared text of hundreds of verses) is so improbable there is very little chance the LE was written by the same author as the rest of Mark was. And the above list is but a sample. There are many other stylistic discrepancies besides the twelve just listed (and the others in section 4.1.2 above, which must be added to those twelve). James Kelhoffer surveys a vast number of them in *MAM* (pp. 67-122).

As Darrell Bock says, "it is the combination of lexical terms, grammar, and style, especially used in repeated ways in a short space that is the point." Hence appealing to similar deviations elsewhere in Mark fails to argue against the conclusion, which carries a powerful cumulative force matched by no other passage in Mark. This is emphasized by Daniel Wallace:

> First, the most important internal argument is a *cumulative* argument. Thus, it is hardly adequate to point out where Mark, in *other* passages, uses seventeen words not found elsewhere in his Gospel, or that *elsewhere* he does not write *euthôs* for an extended number of verses, or that *elsewhere* he has other abrupt stylistic changes. The cumulative argument is that these 'elsewheres' are all over the map; there is not a *single* passage in Mark 1:1-16:8 comparable to the stylistic, grammatical, and lexical anomalies in 16:9-20. Let me say that again: there is not a *single* passage in Mark 1:1-16:8 comparable to the stylistic, grammatical, and lexical anomalies that we find clustered in vv. 9-20. Although one might be able to parry off individual pieces of evidence, the cumulative effect is devastating for authenticity.

In fact, all the most renowned experts on this linguistic question conclude that the LE was not written by Mark and that the stylistic evidence for this is conclusive. Thus as J.K. Elliott puts it, "It is self-deceiving to pretend that the linguistic questions are still 'open'."[20]

The SE is even more incongruent with Markan style. Despite being a mere single verse, 8 of the 12 words in it "that are not prepositions, articles, or names" are never used by Mark—but half of them are found in the Epistles (and sometimes, among NT documents, *only* there).[21] The whole verse consists of just 35 words altogether, 9 of which Mark never uses, in addition to several un-Markan phrases (including, again, *meta de tauta*). Discounting articles and prepositions and repeated words, the SE employs only 18 different words, which means fully half the vocabulary of the

---

[20] Black, *PEM*, p. 133 (Bock), pp. 30-31 (Wallace), p. 89 (Elliott, who also emphasizes the fact that the peculiar features occur *repeatedly* in the LE, but comparable deviations do not occur 'repeatedly' in any other extended section of Mark).

[21] Marcus, *MNT*, p. 1089.

entire SE disagrees with Markan practice. Half the SE also consists of a complex grammatical structure that is not at all like Mark's conspicuously simple, direct style. You won't find any verse in Mark with the convoluted verbosity of "and after these things even Jesus himself from east and as far as west sent out away through them the holy and immortal proclamation of eternal salvation." The SE was clearly not written by Mark.

4.2.3 The Terry Thesis Revisited

Bruce Terry again claims there is nothing odd about so many unusual phrases, for even in Mark 15:42-16:6 "there are nine phrases" that appear nowhere else in Mark.[22] But that's not true. Terry chooses as 'phrases' entire clauses, which obviously will be unique, since authors tend not to repeat themselves. Hence he is either being disingenuous, or he doesn't understand what a 'common phrase' is. Phrases like "after these things," "those with him," "seen by," "whole world," "get well," "and then," "[#] of them," and "from whom" are entirely generic phrases that authors tend to use frequently, or certainly often enough to expect to see them at least a few times in over six hundred verses, unless they are not phrases the author uses. Which is exactly why their presence in the LE tells us Mark didn't write it. And this conclusion follows with force because there are so many of these oddities, and some go against Mark's own preferences, e.g. using *para* instead of *ek* in "cast out from," and using *prôtê sabbatou* instead of *tê mia tôn sabbatôn* to say "first day of the week."

In contrast, almost none of Terry's 'examples' are generic phrases—and what generic structure we *can* discern among them is often *confirmed* in Markan style elsewhere. For example, Terry claims "now evening having come" (*êdê opsias genomenês*) is a unique 'phrase' but what's actually generic in this phrase is *êdê [x] genomenos*, "now [x] having come," which Mark uses two other times (Mark 6:35 and 13:28). So this is *not* unique in 15:42. Likewise, Terry claims "know from" (*ginôsko apo*) is a unique phrase, but it's not, as Mark 13:28 has "learn from" (*apo mathete*), the exact same grammatical construction, just employing a different verb, while the same verb was not unknown to Mark (who used it at least three times, just never in a context that warranted the preposition).

---

[22] Terry, "Style."

Meanwhile, "roll on" (*proskulio epi*) isn't a generic phrase at all—it's just an ordinary verb with preposition, and Mark uses verbs with *epi* to describe placing objects on things quite a lot (e.g. Mark 4:5, 4:16, 4:20, 4:21, 4:26, 4:31, 6:25, 6:28, 8:25, 13:2, 14:35), so there is nothing unique about that here, either. And there is nothing generic whatsoever about "the door of the tomb" or "white robe." These are highly specific constructions, using established Markan words. For *leukos* ("white") and *stolê* ("robe") appear elsewhere in Mark, and *mnemeion* ("tomb") appears two other times in Mark (and the equivalent *mnêma* twice as well), and *thura* ("door") likewise appears four other times. Likewise, "be not afraid" (*me ekthambeisthe*) is not a generic clause, but a whole sentence (it is an imperative declaration), none of which is unusual for Mark, who routinely uses *mê* for negation and uses the exact same verb (*ekthambeô*) in 9:15. Similarly, "come very early" (*lian prôi erchomai*) is not a generic phrase, either, it's just a verb with a magnified adverb of time, nor is it an unusual construction for Mark, who has "go very early" (*lian prôi exerchomai*) in 1:35, and who otherwise uses *prôi* and *lian* several times, and *erchomai* often.

That leaves only two unusual phrases in verses in 15:42-16:6: *mia tôn sabbatôn*, literally "on the first [day counting] from the Sabbaths" (i.e. "first day of the week") and *en tois dexiois* ("on the right"). The former simply paraphrases the Septuagint (Psalm 24:1), which Mark is known to do (e.g. Psalm 22 all throughout Mark 15:16-34). Only the latter is very unexpected as Mark otherwise (and quite often) uses *ek dexiôn* to say "on the right." So these two phrases *are* unique to 15:42-16:6. It's just that 2 unique generic phrases in 12 verses is simply not enough to doubt their authorship (especially when one is a quotation). But 9 unique generic phrases definitely is, especially in conjunction with all the other deviations: the Markan vocabulary that's missing, the non-Markan vocabulary that's present, the un-Markan frequencies of Markan words, and the un-Markan idioms where Mark has established a completely different practice. It is all these oddities *combined* that makes for a vanishingly small probability of Markan authorship.

Indeed, if this is not enough evidence to establish the LE wasn't written by Mark, then we should just assume everything ever written in the whole of Greek history was written by Mark.

4.2.4 Agreements of Style

Though there *are* several Markan words and phrases in the LE, there are not enough to be peculiar. Most are words and phrases common to all authors and thus not unique to Mark. Excluding those, there are only a very few agreements with Markan style in the LE which can be considered at all distinctive. And yet there are as many agreements with the distinctive style of *all* the authors of the NT (including both the Gospels and Epistles)—very much unlike Mark.

Kelhoffer (in *MAM*, pp. 121-22, 138-39) lists over forty stylistic similarities with all four Gospels (and Acts). Notably those drawn from Mark show more deviation from Markan style, using different words and phrases to say the same things, while exact verbal borrowing from the other Gospels is frequent. It is thus more probable that the LE's author was influenced by NT style as a whole (see section 4.3 next), because the similarities to Markan style are no greater than similarities to the rest of the NT, whereas the *deviations* from Markan style are frequent and extreme. This aspect of the LE's style is very probable if the author of the LE knew the NT, but much less probable if the LE had been written by Mark.

Of course, such agreement can also be found by mere chance between any two authors. But it's even more likely when a later author has been influenced by the earlier one, and an author familiar with the whole NT could easily exhibit influence from all its authors, Mark included. This would be all the more likely if the author of the LE deliberately attempted to emulate Markan style (as a forger would be inclined to do), but if that was his intent, his effort was marvelously incompetent. For as we've seen, the *disagreements* of style are so enormous they far outweigh any agreement there may be. In fact, the deviations are so abundant and clear, they could argue against the original author of the LE intending it to be used as a forgery (if we assume a forger would do better). The 'forger' would then instead be some additional third party who attempted to pass off the LE as belonging to Mark. It's also possible the LE became attached to Mark by accident.

But the SE can only have been a deliberate forgery, yet it deviates as much or more from Markan style, so being a lousy forgery is evidently not a valid argument against forgery. Nevertheless, I have already presented evidence (in section 4.1

above) and will present more (in following sections) that, more probably, the author of the LE did not write it as an ending to Mark but as a harmonizing summary of the appearances in all four Canonical Gospels, originally in a separate book (quite possibly a commentary on the Gospels), which was simply excerpted and attached to Mark by someone else (whether deceitfully or by accident).

4.3 Content Betrays Knowledge of the New Testament

The NT didn't exist when Mark wrote, yet the LE not only betrays knowledge of the Canonical NT (all four Gospels *and* Acts), it assumes the *reader* is aware of those contents of the NT or has access to them. As noted in section 4.2.1, this makes no sense coming from Mark, and very little sense coming from anyone at all, *except* someone who already knew all the stories related in the other three Gospels (and Acts) and who thus set out to quickly summarize them, knowing full well the reader could easily find those accounts and get all the details omitted here (or would already know them).

Mark never writes with such an assumption. But a commentator writing a separate summary of the Gospel appearances in the NT would write something exactly like this. That the LE exhibits stylistic similarities with the whole NT, including the Epistles (as just surveyed in section 4.2), further supports the conclusion that the author of the LE knew the whole NT, and in fact was so influenced by it as to have adopted many elements of its diverse style. The author of the LE therefore cannot have been Mark.

James Kelhoffer (in *MAM*, esp. pp. 48-155) has already extensively proved the LE used the other three Gospels (and Acts) and has refuted every critic of the notion. I will only summarize some of the evidence here. But from this and all that Kelhoffer adds, it's very improbable these elements would exist in the LE unless the author of the LE knew the Canonical NT and intended his readers to have access to it themselves.

4.3.1 The LE's Use of the NT

As Joel Marcus observes, the LE looks like "a compressed digest of resurrection appearances narrated in other Gospels" (*MNT*, p. 1090), so compressed, in fact, it "would not make sense to readers who did not know" the other Gospels and Acts. Indeed. The entire content of the LE is a pastiche of elements drawn from the three other Gospels, stitched together in a new way that eliminates contradictions among their different accounts, and written in the writer's own voice (i.e. not copying the other Gospels verbatim, but rephrasing and paraphrasing, a technique specifically taught in ancient schools):

16:9b	Jesus appears (a) to Mary Magdalene (b) alone (c) on the first day of the week (Jn. 20:1, 14-18)
16:9c	from whom he had cast out seven demons (Lk. 8:2)
16:10a	she goes to tell the men (Lk. 24:9-10; Jn. 20:18)
16:10b	as they are mourning and weeping (Jn. 16:20; Mt. 9:15)
16:11	the men refuse to believe her (Lk. 24:11)
16:12	Jesus appears (a) in a different form (b) to two of them (c) on a road (Lk. 24:13-32)
16:13a	those two return and tell the others (Lk. 24:34-35)
16:13b	who still don't believe them (Jn. 20:24-25; Lk. 24:36-41)
16:14a	Jesus appears (a) to the Eleven (b) indoors (c) in a context of taking food (Lk. 24:33-43; and Jn. 20:19-29 w. 21:5-14)
16:14b	and remarks on their unbelief (Lk. 24:38-39; Jn. 20:26-29)
16:15	delivers the Great Commission (Mt. 28:19; Acts 1:8; Mk. 6:12; with direct verbal similarities in Mk. 14:9 & Mt. 24:14, 26:13)
16:16	emphasizes salvation and judgment (Acts 2:38, 16:31-33; Jn. 3:18-21)

16:16	and necessity of baptism (Acts 2:38-43; Mt. 28:19; Jn. 3:5)
16:17a	their powers will be a sign (Acts 2:43, 4:30, 5:12, 14:13)
16:17a	casting out demons in his name (Mk. 6:7, 6:13, 9:38-40; Lk. 9:1, 10:17; Acts 5:16, 8:7, 16:18, 19:12-17; Mt. 7:22)
16:17b	speaking with new tongues (Acts 2:4, 10:45-46, 19:6; 1 Cor. 14)
16:18a	picking up serpents (Lk. 10:19; Acts 28:2-6)
16:18b	laying hands on the sick (Mk. 5:23, 6:5; Lk. 9:1-2; Acts 5:16, 6:6, 8:7, 9:17, 14:13, 19:11-12, 28:8; James 5:14-15)
16:19a	Jesus ascends to heaven (Lk. 24:51; Jn. 20:17; Acts 1:2, 1:9-11)
16:19b	sits down at the right hand of God (Acts 7:55-56, 5:31, 2:33; Rom. 8:34; Eph. 1:20; Heb. 1:1; Col. 3:1; Mk. 12:35-37, 14:62)
16:20a	the disciples go out and preach everywhere (Mk. 6:12; Lk. 9:6, 24:47; Acts 1:4, 1:8, 2ff.)
16:20b	and Jesus confirms the word by the signs that followed (Acts 14:3; Heb. 2:2-4)

The only element of the LE that doesn't derive from the other three Gospels is the remark about 'drinking deadly poison' without effect. Papias claimed it was being said several generations after Mark that Justus Barsabbas (of Acts 1:23) drank poison without harm "by the grace of the Lord," the only (surviving) reference to such a power in the first two centuries.²³ How that would influence the LE is anybody's guess. But the LE's claim is more likely an inference from Luke 10:19, in which Jesus says "I have given you authority to tread upon serpents and scorpions, and over *all* the power of the enemy, and *nothing* shall in any way hurt you" (emphasis mine), which would certainly include poisons, especially given the juxtaposition of immunity to poisonous animals. Luke mentions scorpions *and snakes*; the LE, snakes *and poison*. Hence the substitution would be an easy economization of the whole thought of Luke 10:19 and a typical example of the composition skills ancient schools inculcated.

The LE thus looks unmistakably like a summary of Matthew, Luke, Acts, and John—particularly Luke-Acts and John (whose styles also influenced the vocabulary and grammar of the LE, as noted in section 4.2), which are notably the two last Gospels to be written, and only ever logically found together in the canonical NT. And conspicuously, *only* these four Gospels are aped here, not a single other Gospel, despite there being many dozens to choose from. None of the details or appearance tales referenced in the LE come from outside the NT. Which is practically a giveaway: the LE author is simply summarizing (and briefly harmonizing) the NT Gospels. Contrary to a common assumption, there is evidence that the traditional canon was assembled in codex form already by the mid-2nd century (even though not yet declared the official NT by

---

²³ Reported by Papias, according to Eusebius, *History of the Church* 3.39.9. This tale may have independently influenced the LE, but it does not reflect awareness of the LE—to the contrary, it entails ignorance of it (see section 5.3.1). Against Maurice Robinson's false claim that there are other elements of the LE not found in the Gospels (besides this one) see Bock's concise refutation in *PEM*, p. 134 (esp. n. 8), although even Bock erroneously claims the 'weeping and mourning' of 16:10 is novel (it is not: see table), and misses the fact that (a) Jesus' rebuke (and proffering of evidence) in Luke 24:35-46 entails the two from Emmaus were disbelieved (as even Bock seems aware in n. 8) and (b) four of the five signs *do* derive from the Gospels and Acts (see table), leaving only one novel fact: the immunity to poison drink (which, as will be argued, is a logical inference from Luke 10:19, and thus not really so very novel).

any particular authority).[24] But that's still long after Mark would have died.

One element is a near giveaway: the phrase 'two of them' (16:12) is verbatim: *duo hex autôn*, "two of them," in fact a very unusual way to say this, yet found verbatim in Luke 24:13, the very story being alluded two in the LE. That suggests direct influence from Luke's actual narrative. Kelhoffer (in *MAM*, pp. 140-50) adduces many more direct lifts from Luke-Acts and the other Gospels.

In fact, the LE would make no sense to a reader who had no access to the NT. Why is Mary suddenly alone? How did Jesus appear to her? Where? What did he say? Who are "the two men" and why are they traveling in the country? Where are they going? And what is meant by Jesus appearing "in a different form," and why does he appear in that way only to them? Why in fact are there only "the eleven"? It's commonly forgotten that Mark never narrates or even mentions Judas' death, nor specifically describes him as expelled from the group or in any other way less likely to see the risen Jesus (as 1 Corinthians 15:5 would imply he did), so if Mark were the author of the LE, his narrative would be inexplicably missing a major plot point. The LE clearly assumes familiarity with the NT explanations of Judas' death and thus his absence at the appearance to the Disciples (e.g. Acts 1:17-26; note that outside Acts and the LE, that Jesus appeared to "eleven" Disciples is a feature found only in Mt. 28:16 and Lk 24:9, 24:33), and is obviously alluding to the appearance of Jesus to Mary Magdalene in John (a story not told in Matthew or Luke) and to the appearance of Jesus in disguise to Cleopas and his companion on

---

[24] On the early (mid-2nd century) assembly of the NT: David Trobisch, *The First Edition of the New Testament* (2000) and "Who Published the Christian Bible?" *CSER Review* 2.1 (2007): 29-32. On there being over forty Gospels to choose from (over forty are known): Christopher Tuckett, "Forty Other Gospels," in Markus Bockmuehl and Donald Hagner, eds., *The Written Gospel* (2005), pp. 238-53. On how ancient schools taught students to summarize, paraphrase, and rewrite passages in their own voice: David Gowler, "The Chreia," in Amy-Jill Levine, Dale Allison, Jr., and John Dominic Crossan, eds., *The Historical Jesus in Context* (2006), pp. 132-48; Raffaella Cribiore, *Gymnastics of the Mind: Greek Education in Hellenistic and Roman Egypt* (2001); and see Dennis MacDonald, *The Homeric Epics and the Gospel of Mark* (2000), pp. 4-6, for a brief summary, and Thomas Brodie, *The Birthing of the New Testament* (2004), pp. 3-31, for a detailed summary.

the road to Emmaus in Luke (a story not told in Matthew or John). To a reader unfamiliar with those tales, the LE's narrative is cryptic and frustratingly vague, and essentially inexplicable. Why would anyone write a story like that? Only someone who knew the other stories—and knew his audience would or could as well.

The LE is not only a pastiche of the other Gospel accounts, it's also an attempt at harmonization. To make the narrative consistent, the LE's author did not incorporate every element of the canonical stories (which would have been logically impossible, or preposterously convoluted). He also deliberately conflates several themes and elements in the interest of smoothing over the remaining contradictions, giving the appearance of a consistent sequence of events—and forcing the whole into a narratively consistent triadic structure (examined below). This kind of harmonizing pastiche exemplified by the LE is an example of the very practice most famously exemplified in Tatian's *Diatessaron* (begun not long after the LE was probably composed), which took the same procedure and scaled it up to the entire Gospel (only copying words verbatim rather than writing in his own voice). Kelhoffer (in *MAM*, pp. 150-54) discusses other examples, demonstrating that the LE fits a literary fashion of the time.

4.3.2 Testing the Reverse Thesis

Confirmation of this conclusion comes from the fact that the thesis doesn't work as well in reverse. Though the LE clearly exhibits knowledge of the NT Gospels, the NT Gospels show no knowledge of the LE as a whole. Luke and Matthew follow Mark closely up to verse 16:8, but then diverge completely. What themes they share with the LE have no similar order or context between them, or with the LE. The LE harmonizes them, but they fail to retain any of the LE's harmony. Thus, we can prove the LE was aware of their divergent accounts (so as to harmonize them), but the same evidence argues against the NT being aware of the LE (because no element of that harmony was retained in them).

Instead, the LE appears to be a coherent narrative unit inspired by the NT. It depicts three resurrection appearances, in agreement with John 21:14, which says Jesus appeared three times. And all three appearances have a related narrative structure: all three involve an appearance of Jesus (16:9, 16:12, 16:14), followed by a report or statement of that fact, always to the Disciples (16:10,

16:13, 16:14), which the first two times is met with unbelief (16:11, 16:13), while the third time the Disciples are berated for that unbelief, when Jesus finally appears to them all (16:14). This running theme of doubt *also* appears in the other Gospels, but in entirely different ways, showing no cognizance of the LE (Matthew 28:16-17, Luke 24:10-11 and 24:36-41, and John 20:24-28). The author of the LE clearly intended to harmonize the three other accounts by merging them together in a semblance of a coherent sequence, a sequence that makes no sense except at the hands of someone who knew the three other Gospels and had in mind to unite and harmonize their accounts while glossing over their discrepancies.

One might hypothesize that this shared theme of doubt, as well as other shared themes (e.g. Mark 16:15-20 summarizes the "commission" theme present, but differently executed, in the other three Gospels: Luke 24:46-47, John 20:23, Matthew 28:18-20), indicates the LE was the source for the Gospels. But that does not fit. Those later authors must have each chosen coincidentally to drop entirely different elements from each other, and to completely rewrite the rest, all in a different order, and in consequence repeatedly and irreconcilably contradicting Mark. Which all makes far less sense than the opposite thesis, that the author of the LE was harmonizing their accounts after the fact.

The LE also lacks the details that are necessary to make sense of each story, and thus assumes those details were already in print. So the LE more likely abbreviates the Gospel narratives. Those narratives are far less likely to be embellishing the LE. Moreover, the LE summarizes the appearances and events in *all* of the Gospels, whereas none of those Gospels used all of the LE, but each (we must implausibly suppose) must have chosen different parts to retain. Instead, they seem unaware of the other appearances and events related in the LE.

It's thus improbable that the Gospels used the LE (but conveniently left out exactly those stories that the other Gospels left in, completely altered what they included, and sharply contradicted Mark in the process) but very probable that the LE used the Gospels (smartly changing or leaving out the details that contradict each other). The result, as noted, is a situation in which none of the Gospels follow the LE even in outline, while the LE follows all three Gospels, though only as closely as is logically possible, assembling all their diverse stories into a single narrative. The coincidence is unbelievable on any other theory.

4.3.3 The Robinson Thesis

Maurice Robinson attempts to argue the LE was composed by Mark because it employs the rhetorical storytelling devices of self-emulation by which Mark is well known to have composed his Gospel, e.g. as shown by Randel Helms in *Gospel Fictions* (1988). However, the triadic structure just revealed (in section 4.3.2) and the harmonizing pastiche of material using the sources tabulated (in section 4.3.1) explains far better all the details Robinson implausibly claims emulate earlier sections of Mark. Moreover, a forger could just as easily parody Mark as Mark himself could, thus even if correct, the Robinson thesis fails to independently establish that the LE was written by Mark.

In his first example (Mark 1:32-39, cf. *PEM*, pp. 68-69) many of the parallels Robinson adduces are specious (i.e. one must stretch the imagination to see a meaningful connection) and few make any literary sense (i.e. there is no intelligible reason for the parallels and reversals being alleged), while any connections we might expect to exist on his thesis (e.g. resisting serpents and poisons, the role of laying on hands, the significance of baptism, the theme of doubt, the first day of the week, appearing "in a different form," etc.) are all absent. Not that all of these would be expected, of course, but some at least should be, e.g. Robinson's claim of an earlier parallel use of exorcism and healing entails that the matching third component (immunity to poison) should be present. Otherwise the ending does *not* match the beginning. All we have are generic elements repeated throughout Mark and the whole NT.

There is a better case to be made that Mark 16:1-8 reverses 1:1-9 (which I outline in chapter ten of *On the Historicity of Jesus*), which would instead argue that verse 8 is the original ending—as framing a story this way (ending it by reversing the way it began) was a recognized literary practice of the era (called ironic *inclusio*), and would neatly explain many of the peculiar features of the OE (as a manifestation of irony, a device Mark uses repeatedly), making them intelligible, in exactly the way Robinson's theory does not make 16:9-20 any more intelligible in light of 1:32-39. This is not to argue here that Mark *did* end at verse 8, only that Robinson's thesis is less plausible than applying his own method to arguing Mark *did* end at verse 8.25.[25]

Similarly, Robinson's attempt to see parallels elsewhere in Mark (in *PEM*, pp. 70-72) are either contrived ("appointing the twelve" is supposed to parallel "appearing to eleven" even though neither verb nor number are the same; Mark 6:13 refers to healing by anointing with oil, not laying on hands, which actually argues *against* the connection Robinson claims), or simply erroneous (e.g. he mistakenly claims Mark 3:15 contains a reference to healing). The features he claims as parallels are also nonsensically out of order and lack any of the precise cues typical of Mark's practice of emulation. As with Robinson's first hypothesis, none of the features actually peculiar to the LE (e.g. immunity to poisons, damning the unbaptized, appearing "in a different form," etc.) are explained this way, whereas every feature (these and the ones Robinson singles out) are already explained (and explained much more plausibly, thoroughly, and accurately) by the triadic harmonization thesis.

I am normally quite sympathetic to the kind of analysis Robinson attempts (and I discuss how to employ such methods soundly in *Proving History*, pp. 192-204), but his applications fail on every single relevant mimesis criterion (order, density, distinctiveness, and interpretability). The patterns he claims to see simply aren't there. There are only generic elements ubiquitous throughout early Christian and NT literature. In fact, every feature Robinson identifies is not only explicable on the theory that Mark didn't compose the LE (but instead a harmonizer using Mark and the other Gospels did), but *more* explicable, particularly as the latter theory explains far more of the content of the LE (in fact, all of it).

---

[25] On this ironic *inclusio* in Mark see Richard Carrier, "The Spiritual Body of Christ and the Legend of the Empty Tomb," in Robert M. Price & Jeffery Jay Lowder, eds., *The Empty Tomb: Jesus Beyond the Grave* (2005), pp. 105-232 [163-64]. Mark's frequent use of irony is documented by Paul Danove, *The End of Mark's Story: A Methodological Study* (1993) and Jerry Camery-Hoggatt, *Irony in Mark's Gospel* (1992). For the OE as such: Adela Collins, "The Empty Tomb in the Gospel According to Mark," in Eleonore Stump & Thomas Flint, eds., *Hermes and Athena: Biblical Exegesis and Philosophical Theology* (1993), pp. 107-40.

4.3.4 The SE's Use of the NT

Now to revisit the SE. The SE is so obviously inept (since it immediately and inexplicably contradicts the sentence before it, and is implausibly brief) we can be certain it was not original. The SE also has an obvious apologetic function, of positively fixing Peter's primacy, and to 'complete' or 'answer' the OE. Its position in the manuscripts indicates it was intended to follow verse 8, not verse 16, hence it is the women who are the 'they' who inform Peter, which makes logical sense (it is clearly written by someone aware of the content of 16:7-8 and intent on completing the ending in a grammatically sound and intelligible way), and it clearly is meant to end the Gospel (it brings the story all the way to the exit of Jesus and beginning of the mission, and concludes with an 'amen'). Thus it had to have been forged by someone who didn't know of the LE (or any other ending), or someone who deliberately removed the LE (or some other ending) and replaced it with the SE. The former is more probable. For if such a forger knew the LE (or any LOE), he would far more likely alter it than replace it (see sections 5.1.4 and 5.1.8).

The SE is also far too brief to make sense from the pen of Mark: it seems to assume knowledge of the Book of Acts (e.g. Acts 1:8, and the subsequent missions to east and west depicted therein) and the Gospel of Luke (e.g. Luke 1:77). Otherwise it makes no sense, since Mark has never once mentioned 'salvation' before, much less what the 'message of salvation' is supposed to be that the Apostles then spread across the world (no such message is stated in Mark 16:5-8, for example). Likewise, Mark 16:7-8 anticipates, if anything, an appearance of Jesus, yet the SE lacks any—it simply says Jesus sent them, thus it assumes the reader is already familiar with what that means and how Jesus did that, and thus is already familiar with the NT appearance narratives in the other Gospels. This fact, combined with the lack of Markan style, condemns the SE as a forgery already from internal evidence alone.

4.4 Assessment of Internal Evidence

Already from the internal evidence it is clear neither the LE nor SE were written by Mark. As continuations of Mark's Gospel they are illogical, written in a completely different style, and betray knowledge of the Canonical NT and thus long-post-date the composition of Mark. Arguments to the effect that Mark would not likely have ended his Gospel at verse 16:8 are of no consequence to this conclusion, as they in no way entail or even imply the LE was the ending lost (there are several contenders more plausible: see section 2.4).

5. The External Evidence

When we turn our attention to the external evidence, this conclusion is confirmed. External evidence consists, first, of the evidence of the actual surviving manuscripts themselves, their evident dates and relationships, and the actual text they contain, as well as other physical evidence in them, such as scribal marks and marginal notes, and, second, the evidence of outside witnesses. In this case that means the Church Fathers, who are the earliest Christian writers outside the NT, several of whom quote or cite the Gospel of Mark, or even discuss what they saw in different manuscripts of Mark. The former is called the manuscript evidence, the latter is called the Patristic evidence.

5.1 The Manuscripts: Textual Evidence

A common misconception is that counting manuscripts decides what reading to regard as original. But a later reading will often have been copied many more times, precisely because it was more popular (and often for the very same reasons the emendation occurred in the first place). So often the original reading is actually the *rarest* in surviving manuscripts, not the most common. But occasionally the reverse is the case. So a more judicial analysis of the evidence is necessary.

And in this respect, ancient translations of the Bible afford an important source of information, as they can reflect the state of the text at the time the translation was first made, no matter how late the surviving copies of that translation are. Likewise, from many surviving copies of the original text we can often reconstruct what the manuscripts they were copied from contained, and even date when those 'source manuscripts' were made or copied from, even though those manuscripts are now lost (those would be the exemplars that existing mss. were copied from—we can sometimes also reconstruct more distant archetypes, hypothesized ancestral copies even further removed but shared in common by many extant mss.).

Meanwhile, some manuscripts carry far more weight than others, because they are the oldest, or used very early in contexts that entail their text held wide authority, or both.

5.1.1 In Greek

The oldest and most authoritative manuscripts of Mark are found in the Codex Sinaiticus (ℵ) and Codex Vaticanus (B), both of which lack the LE and the SE. There are a few older papyrus fragments of Mark, but none contain any part of chapter 16 and thus are of no help in determining the state of Mark's ending.[26] Both Sinaiticus and Vaticanus date to the mid-4th century and bear signs of having been treated as authoritative texts within the Church. Many of their readings agree with numerous other early mss. Both do leave a blank space at the ending of Mark, which some scholars believe may indicate awareness of a missing ending (although, of course, a lost ending may have simply been assumed). But the Vaticanus usually indicates known textual variants with a scribal mark, which is absent here, arguing against awareness of any lost ending; the space left is only large enough for the SE, which argues against awareness of the LE; and the Vaticanus leaves blank spaces after other books, demonstrating that such does not in fact indicate awareness of a lost ending.[27] Likewise, the Sinaiticus also leaves a blank space after Acts, thus such does not entail awareness of a lost ending to Mark, either.[28] And experts have determined the

---

[26] See the Wikipedia entries on these mss. for more infomation: "Codex Sinaiticus" (en.wikipedia.org/wiki/Codex_Sinaiticus) and "Codex Vaticanus" (en.wikipedia.org/wiki/Codex_Vaticanus). Both also have project websites devoted to them: see The Sinaiticus Project (www.codexsinaiticus.org) and The Vaticanus Project (www.csntm.org/Manuscript/View/GA_03).

[27] All demonstrated by Daniel Wallace in *PEM*, pp. 17-18. Maurice Robinson claims the Vaticanus scribe must have miscounted the number of words in the LE (in *PEM*, p. 52 n. 44), but that's just special pleading.

[28] See Wallace's discussion in *PEM*, p. 18 n. 42.

original form of Codex Sinaiticus also lacked enough room for the LE, which also argues against knowledge of the LE.[29]

J.K. Elliott asserts that Vaticanus and Sinaiticus were produced by the same scribe (in *PEM*, pp. 85-86), but as he adduces no arguments or evidence in support of that claim, I'm compelled to reject it as spurious. Even if they derive from the same scriptorium (a more plausible claim, although it's widely debated), Elliott himself admits such mss. can still derive from different exemplars (ibid., p. 83 n. 4), and we know for a fact these two must have, as their texts frequently do not agree. For example, Mark 1:40, 2:22, 10:26, and 15:44, all differ between the Vaticanus and Sinaiticus, and I just flipped to four random pages of the Aland text. Such disagreements between them number in the thousands.[30]

Moreover, expensive projects like these would not have relied on a single exemplar but been checked against several (e.g. the Vaticanus frequently indicates the existence of variant readings, and shows influence from both major text types, the Western and Alexandrian). Apologists like to denigrate the Vaticanus and Sinaiticus as aberrant texts, 'exceptions to the rule' (combining the fallacies of special pleading and poisoning the well) when in fact all early NT mss. are at least as deviant and flawed as they are (so cannot claim any greater authority over them on grounds of 'accuracy'), and yet these two were clearly very authoritative texts,

---

[29] Demonstrated in H.J. Milne and T.C. Skeat, *Scribes and Correctors of the Codex Sinaiticus* (1938), pp. 9-11; admitted reluctantly by Maurice Robinson in *PEP*, pp. 51-52 n. 43.

[30] See Wikipedia entries (cited above) for evidence and bibliography. On the debate whether they derive from the same scriptorium or even the same half of the century see Dirk Jongkind, *Scribal Habits of Codex Sinaiticus* (2007), pp. 18-21. Jongkind also demonstrates throughout his text that Vaticanus and Sinaiticus used different exemplars. This is now generally beyond dispute. The evidence that they nevertheless derive from the same scriptorium is much weaker. They do show many second-hand corrections aligning each other, and bear other similarities, but many of these corrections were made centuries later, some as late as the 12th century (and thus do not indicate origin in the same scriptorium), and their other similarities no more indicate a common scriptorium than a common fashion among all scriptoria of the period. Even shared decorative devices at best may indicate scribes trained in the same school, but such is not entailed, as such elements were commonplace. Moreover, Vaticanus and Sinaiticus bear significant differences (e.g. they do not contain all the same books), which argues against a common origin.

expensively produced by the church, based on multiple exemplars, and of the earliest date among all known mss. (some scholars estimate their exemplars dated as early as the late 2nd century; and no extant mss. date earlier than these mss. themselves). They are therefore far more authoritative than deniers would have it.

5.1.2 In Syriac

The SE and LE are also absent from the oldest Syriac manuscript (an erased palimpsest of the late 4th century), the Sinaitic Syriac. The LE finally appears in the Syriac tradition a century later, the earliest being the Curetonian Syriac (dated to the 5th century), which shows signs of revision from a Greek exemplar, unlike the Sinaitic which appears to be more original and, unlike the Curetonian, shows direct influence from (or upon) the *Diatessaron*, which rather supports the conclusion that the original *Diatessaron* also lacked the LE (see section 5.3.3).[31] The fact that other translations whose early representatives lack the LE were ultimately derived from the earliest Syriac confirms that the original Syriac tradition lacked the LE (see section 5.1.6).

5.1.3 In Coptic

In Coptic, all but one include the LE, but all surviving mss. date centuries after the translations were originally made, and the earliest version indicates it wasn't originally there. According to P.E. Kahle (see following note), the Coptic translation in the Sahidic dialect is the oldest (originating in the late 2nd century), yet "of the Sahidic manuscripts" that contain the LE "only one…regards 16:9-20 as part of the original text," while all "the other Sahidic manuscripts…contain evidence that some (older) manuscripts ended at 16:8."

---

[31] F. Crawford Burkitt, *Evangelion da-Mepharreshe: The Curetonian Version of the Four Gospels, with the Readings of the Sinai Palimpsest and the Early Syriac Patristic Evidence* (1904), pp. 215-17. See also the Wikipedia entries for "Syriac versions of the Bible" (en.wikipedia.org/wiki/Syriac_versions_of_the_Bible) and "Syriac Sinaiticus" (en.wikipedia.org/wiki/Syriac_Sinaiticus). The conclusions I summarize here are based in part on the critical apparatus provided in Aland & Metzger [n. 8].

And now we know one Coptic ms. indeed lacks the LE altogether (see below). Of the others, all but one include the SE and LE "but indicate by short notes that these are alternatives found [only] in *some* manuscripts" (many Greek mss. indicate the same, see section 5.2; as also the Ethiopic, see section 5.1.4). The same thing is observed in the only surviving Fayyumic ms. containing the ending of Mark (extant only in fragments, whose date is unknown but must be very ancient), despite having been translated from a different Western Greek text type than the Sahidic (no later than the early 4th century). Here, "in a short note after [the SE] it points out that [the LE] was not read by all the manuscripts before the translator."

Confirming these scribal notes, we have at least one Sahidic ms. (Codex P. Palau Rib. 182, from the 5th century) that clearly lacks the LE (ending with the OE), without any indication of knowing any other text, thus confirming the conclusion that the earliest Coptic translator did not know the LE. Only mss. containing the Coptic translation in the Bohairic dialect (rendered in the 3rd or 4th century) all contain the LE without comment, so either the LE was added to the Bohairic in the later 4th century or the Bohairic derives from a copy of Mark to which the LE had become appended in the 3rd or early 4th century—while the earlier Sahidic did not (it appears to have had it added later—unless it was dropped without comment by or before the Palau scribe, but even that entails the original Sahidic translator knew the LE was not in some mss., because then the original translation must have indicated this fact, as that indication is preserved in almost all subsequent copies surviving). Then the later Fayyumic was produced by a translator aware of the fact that some mss. lacked the LE (because he said so).[32]

All of these facts combined indicate the LE was a rare reading and not original to Mark when the earliest translations to Coptic were made, but became incorporated later.

5.1.4 In Ethiopic

The Ethiopic manuscripts all contain the SE and LE (or only the LE), but all date well after the 5th century when the translation was made. The earliest are the Garima Gospels, recently re-dated to the 7th century, which contain the LE alone, and beyond that the earliest surviving ms. dates no earlier than the 9th century.

And yet, as with the Coptic, evidence suggests the original Ethiopic translation lacked the LE. Of 65 Ethiopic mss. now extant, 18 contain the LE alone, while the other 47 contain the SE followed by the LE, and 13 of those indicate the LE was an addition (with symbols or terminations separating it from the SE,

---

[32] P.E. Kahle, "The End of St. Mark's Gospel: The Witness of the Coptic Versions," *Journal of Theological Studies* 2 (1951): 49-57; Gerald Browne, "The Gospel of Mark in Fayumic Coptic," *The Bulletin of the American Society of Papyrologists* 13.2 (1976): 41-43. See also the Wikipedia entry for "Coptic Versions of the Bible" (en.wikipedia.org/wiki/Coptic_versions_of_the_Bible). On the recent discovery of Codex P. Palau Rib. 182 lacking the LE see Kurt Aland & Barbara Aland, *The Text of the New Testament: An Introduction to the Critical Editions and to the Theory and Practice of Modern Textual Criticism* (2nd rev. ed., 1995), p. 202, and Hans Quecke, *Das Markusevangelium saïdisch: Text der Handschrift PPalau Rib. Inv. Nr. 182 mit den Varianten der Handschrift M 569* (1972).

Lectionary 1602 (8th century) has the Greek on one side, Sahidic on the other, and the Greek includes the LE, while the Sahidic ends with verse 16:6 (according to Aland & Aland, ibid., p. 203), but as I do not read Coptic I could not verify whether this was where the text ended or only where the damaged mss. ends. It appears to be the latter, so I consider its testimony inconclusive. Several Greek manuscripts likewise 'lack the LE' only because of lost pages and thus are of no use as evidence (minuscules 2386, 1420, 16; even 304, the commentary discussed in section 5.2.2, though not exhibiting actual ms. damage, nevertheless appears to be missing numerous concluding pages, exactly where a reference to the LE might appear).

or actual scribal notes declaring it).[33] Although a few of the oldest mss. (one dating as far back as the 7th century) have only the LE, the later mss. that indicate otherwise (i.e. that the LE was later appended and earlier mss. ended with the SE alone) likely derive from an even earlier tradition.

Since the original Ethiopic translation was made at the end of the 5th century, there had been plenty of time (around four centuries) for one tradition to append the LE and another tradition to append the SE (or the original translation may have simply begun with the SE). The second tradition then came to append the LE by influence from the first tradition. One might instead hypothesize that the original translation was derived from a Greek exemplar containing the DE *and* scribal indications of the LE being unknown in some mss. (which by the 5th century, when the Ethiopic translation was made, would be entirely plausible), but that would not explain the Ethiopic mss. that lack the SE. So one tradition must have contained the LE alone, and the other the SE alone, and then the SE tradition was merged with the LE tradition by adding the latter to the former. The reverse is far less likely, as it would require interpolating the SE *between* the OE and LE, which makes no logical sense, since the SE and LE contradict each other, and the SE adds nothing notable not already in the LE. And if the SE were appended as an alternative to an original tradition that ended with the LE, then the SE would more likely be placed *after* the LE, or in the margins. Even more likely, the SE would simply be rejected (and thus not appear at all), or else the LE would be replaced with the SE (see sections 4.3.4 and 5.1.8).

---

[33] Bruce Metzger, "The Ending of the Gospel according to Mark in Ethiopic Manuscripts," in John Reumann, ed., *Understanding the Sacred Text* (1972), pp. 167-80. See also: Rochus Zuurmond, *Novum Testamentum Aethiopice* 1.2 (1989): 44-52, and "The Ethiopic Version of the New Testament," in Bart Ehrman & Michael Holmes, eds., *The Text of the New Testament in Contemporary Research* (1994), pp. 142-56; and Martin Bailey, "Discovery of Earliest Illuminated Manuscript: Revised Dating Places Garima Gospels before 650," *The Art Newspaper* 214 (June 2010), which transmits the findings of J. Mercier, "La peinture éthiopienne à l'époque axoumite et au XVIIIe siècle," *Comptes-rendus des séances de l'Académie des inscriptions et belles-lettres* (2000): 35-71. Notably Mercier only tested two of the illuminated pages, not the leafs with the Gospel text, and the Gospels were rebound centuries after being compiled (with pages out of order) so it is still uncertain if the Garima texts of Mark are actually as old as the pictures inserted among them.

Consequently, the only plausible way so many Ethiopic mss. could have the SE followed by the LE (*and* for so many of those to clearly indicate that the LE was not original *and* for there to be so many Ethiopic mss. that contain only the LE and no hint of the SE) is if the LE was *not* in the original Ethiopic but came to be appended to some Ethiopic mss. sometime between the 5th and 7th centuries, while all other mss. in that period contained (or acquired) only the SE—and then these two traditions became combined in the later middle ages (exactly as would happen in the Greek, and possibly even inspired thereby). Thus if the Ethiopic translation began *without* the LE, all the evidence is easy to explain, but if it began *with* the LE, that same evidence is harder to explain. Therefore, the original Ethiopic tradition probably lacked the LE. And even if not, it must still have begun with explicit knowledge of the fact, by outright stating it, that many of the mss. it was translated from lacked the LE.

5.1.5 In Latin

The late-4th century Vulgate translation contains the LE, but the earliest Latin translation lacks it: the 4th century Codex Bobiensis contains only the SE (altered, as noted in section 2.3). This represents a translation dating at least as far back as the 3rd century and possibly even the late 2nd century (based on telltale evidence in the mss., according to experts who have examined it), which establishes that the absence of the LE predates the 4th century (and possibly even the 3rd). This demonstrates that the LE did not exist in the exemplar used by one of the earliest Latin translators.

Codex Vercellensis dates from around the same time, containing yet another Latin translation (thus originating from a different Greek archetype), yet it, too, lacked the LE. Vercellensis actually had a page containing the LE *tacked into it by a later scribe*. Experts have verified that the original leaves lacked the space to have ever contained the LE before this.[34] Thus the two oldest Latin mss. (which are in fact older than even most Greek mss.) directly attest the absence of the LE.

Other non-Vulgate Latin translations (collectively called Old Latin) contain the LE, but all extant mss. of these are of late date. The only early mss. in this category date from the 5th or even as late as the 6th century, exhibiting translations made in the 3rd or 4th century (though we still can't confirm the LE was in these original translations). There are only three of these: Codex Bezae, Codex Sangallensis 1394, and Codex Corbeiensis II.[35] All these Old Latin mss. are thus late enough that they could have had translations of the LE added onto them well after it had already become popular in Greek mss. (just as happened in every other translation tradition). Or any of them could have been translated from a copy of Mark containing the LE circulating in the 4th century (see section 5.3.10).

---

[34] Confirming this conclusion: C.H. Turner, "Did Codex Vercellensis (a) Contain the Last Twelve Verses of St. Mark?" *Journal of Theological Studies* 29 (1927-28): 16-18; with more supporting evidence in Kurt Aland, "Bemerkungen zum Schluss des Markusevangeliums," *Neotestamentica et Semitica* (1969): 157-80 [169-78]. See the remarks of Daniel Wallace in *PEM*, pp. 24-25 n. 6, and Bruce Metzger, *The Early Versions of the New Testament* (1977), pp. 312-13. See also the Wikipedia entry for "Codex Vercellensis" (en.wikipedia.org/wiki/Codex_Vercellensis).

[35] See Wikipedia entries on "Codex Bezae" (en.wikipedia.org/wiki/Codex_Bezae), "Codex Corbeiensis II" (en.wikipedia.org/wiki/Codex_Corbeiensis_II), "Vetus Latina" (en.wikipedia.org/wiki/Old_Latin_Bible), and "List of New Testament Latin Manuscripts" (http://en.wikipedia.org/wiki/List_of_New_Testament_Latin_manuscripts).

On Sangallensis see John Wordsworth, *Portions of the Gospels according to St. Mark and St. Matthew* (1886), pp. xxix-xxx.

Codex Bezae actually lost the page that would have contained the Latin text of the LE, and pages were added to the Codex centuries later replacing that loss with a borrowed translation from the standard Vulgate. My examination of the evidence in Frederick Scrivener, *Bezae Codex Cantabrigiensis* (1864) leads me to conclude that the Latin of Codex Bezae probably did contain the LE, but that this was derived largely from the Greek opposite, with knowledge of the Latin Vulgate, and thus is not an early Latin translation, but a late translation made from a late 4th century (or even later) Greek ms. containing the LE (such as we already know existed). See also Aland & Aland [n. 35], p. 189, and Bruce Metzger, *The Early Versions of the New Testament* (1977), pp. 317-18.

Otherwise, the Bobiensis and Vercellensis translations predate these, and they lacked the LE. Only a century or more later does the LE appear in any Latin translations (just as we see in the Syriac and Coptic traditions), and in every case these later translations either derive from a time after the LE was already being accepted as the ending of Mark (e.g. the Vulgate was translated by Jerome exactly when the LE was starting to become popular in the Greek: see section 5.3.12) or are suspect as later additions. As noted above, we can already see one case of the LE being surreptitiously 'inserted' into a Latin tradition. So we have good reason to suspect this is how the LE may have ended up in other Old Latin texts. Because the oldest Latin mss. and translations *lack* the LE.

5.1.6 In Georgic and Armenian

The oldest Georgic manuscript (dating to the 9th century) lacks the LE. The LE starts to appear in the Georgic tradition a century later. The Georgic translation is believed to have been made in the late 5th century, and not from the Greek but from the Armenian translation, which was made in the early 5th century by Mesrop Mashtots, itself originally from a Syriac translation, later corrected against the Greek. Although extant Armenian manuscripts are much later, most of them (nearly a hundred) lack the LE, including the earliest. Based on the trend already exhibited by the Latin, Syriac, and Georgic (and the trend evident in Coptic and Ethiopic), this suggests the LE was not known to Mesrop and only added later.

This agrees with the fact that most Armenian mss. lack the LE (the LE being added so late, it had less time to propagate) and the fact that the earliest Georgic mss. lack the LE (having derived from the original Armenian, which thus must have lacked the LE), which in turn confirms the Syriac began without the LE (as the Armenian translation was originally based on it), which further argues the *Diatessaron* lacked the LE (see sections 5.1.2 and 5.3.3).[36]

These translation traditions are very early and wildly diverse geographically and culturally, and in every case the absence of the LE is earlier. Though the Armenian and Georgic ultimately derive from the earliest Syriac translation of the late 2nd century, the Latin and Coptic and Ethiopic are all independent of that, and yet all of these attest the LE was not commonly known until the 4th century. That this is directly confirmed by two expert witnesses (Eusebius and Jerome, per sections 5.3.10 and 5.3.12) settles the fact. This supports the conclusion that the LE was a late addition to the text of Mark.

Corroborating this conclusion is the fact that an Armenian author, Eznik of Kolb, quotes the LE in the middle of the 5th century, a decade or two after the Armenian Bible was translated, yet he does not quote any known translation of the Bible, but composes his own, possibly from a Greek original, which verifies the Armenian translation originated without the LE. And since we already know there were Greek mss. of Mark containing the LE at that time, Eznik's awareness of it affords no proof of its originality.[37] Likewise, an Armenian translation of the Syriac of Aphraates a few decades after Eznik also attests the LE, but that *also* doesn't derive from the Armenian Bible, but a late Syriac copy of the *Diatessaron* (see sections 5.3.3 and 5.3.11).

---

[36] *TCG*, pp. 122-26; J. Neville Birdsall, "The Georgian Version of the New Testament," in Bart Ehrman & Michael Holmes, eds., *The Text of the New Testament in Contemporary Research* (1994), pp. 173-87 [178, 180]; Joseph Alexanian, "The Armenian Version of the New Testament," ibid., pp. 157-72 [157]. See also www.armenianbible.org and Ernest Cadman Colwell, "Mark 16:9-20 in the Armenian Version," *Journal of Biblical Literature* 56.4 (December 1937): 369-86. Colwell provides eight converging lines of evidence establishing that the LE did not exist in Mesrop's original Armenian translation, producing a fairly decisive case. This is further supported by the evidence in Albert Edmunds, "The Six Endings of Mark in Later Manuscripts and Catholic and Protestant Imprints of the Old Armenian Version," *The Monist* 29 (1919): 520-25.

[37] On Eznik's knowledge of the LE (from a source other than the Armenian Bible), see Colwell, "Mark," p. 384. The reference appears in Eznik, *On God or Sects* 112, quoting Jesus (first from Luke 10:19 and then from Mark 16:17-18), implying the Gospels were his source (though he doesn't specifically say so).

5.1.7 In Gothic

The only early translation that likely began with the LE is the Gothic. A 6th century Gothic ms. (the Speyer fragment of Codex Argenteus) attests the LE in a translation probably made by Ulfilas shortly after 348 A.D. in what is now Bulgaria (just north of Greece). But as we know there were mss. of Mark containing the LE by then (see section 5.3.10), this only confirms the rarity of source mss. containing the LE, as apparently only one early translation tradition began with one (apart from perhaps one or two Latin translations: see section 5.1.5).[38]

5.1.8 The SE-LE Sequence and the Robinson Thesis

The existence of the SE in numerous mss. (in several languages, including the original Greek) entails there were many root mss. that lacked the LE. The invention of the SE itself entails the LE was absent very early in the history of the text, necessitating the creation of the SE in order to address growing dissatisfaction with the OE.

An even more essential clue is that all the manuscripts that include both the SE and LE always place the SE *before* the LE, whether in Greek or any other language (see section 5.1.4). Since the SE was most likely created by an author unaware of the LE (thus all these mss. still attest that the LE did not exist in earlier copies of Mark), any manuscript that places the SE before the LE has clearly *added* the LE, i.e. their ultimate 'source manuscript' (or underlying archetype) must have contained only the SE, to which the LE was appended later. This is decisively confirmed in the physical evidence of the mss. (see section 5.2). It's also inherently obvious. No one would interpolate the SE before the LE anyway (see sections 4.3.4 and 5.1.4, and following).

A large number of manuscripts containing the LE thus attest to the previous absence of the LE in the very act of including it. This happens to include numerous Greek and Latin manuscripts, and most Ethiopic manuscripts, and the earliest Coptic manuscripts that even contain the LE at all. When all those examples are thus

---

[38] On the Gothic translation, see summary and bibliography in the entries at Wikipedia for "Ulfilas" (en.wikipedia.org/wiki/Ulfilas) and "Codex Argenteus" (en.wikipedia.org/wiki/Codex_Argenteus).

rightly excluded, the evidence from all the earliest mss. (and translations) strongly favors the LE being a late addition to Mark.

This evidence is fairly damning. Which is why Maurice Robinson desperately advances the claim that this universal sequence (SE followed by LE) is explained by a lectionary use of the SE as a forged "optional ending" (in *PEM*, pp. 58-59). Thus he can maintain the LE was the original ending. But his theory is too absurd to credit. Indeed, it's incredible five times over:

1. It's implausible to presume *all* extant mss. (even in the various translation traditions) derive from a lectionary (which at any rate would be special pleading, and that against all probability).

2. There is no evidence of such a practice (of providing an optional shorter ending to a whole story, much less interposed before the longer genuine one) in any lectionary. So his theory is not only wholly without precedent, it stands against all extant precedent; indeed, his own evidence of editing in lectionaries contains no instance comparable to what he is proposing: the insertion of an entire elaborate verse from whole cloth (cf. *PEM*, p. 59 n. 74).

3. It's self-defeating. Such a practice would entail Christians so little valued the canonical text of their scriptures that they felt free to substantially alter it just to suit lectionary convenience, and then let this error infect countless other Bibles in the whole of the world, and that without any marginal note explaining the fact, but instead passing off the alteration as "according to Mark," which fact if accepted undermines rather than supports the authenticity of the LE, as it ensures Christians would have no compulsion against inventing the LE for the very same reason Robinson alleges would motivate them to invent the SE. Moreover, Robinson's theory guarantees pervasive biblical errancy. It thus kills the doctrine of inerrancy in the very effort to save it.

4. It's directly refuted by the physical evidence in the manuscripts themselves, which uniformly declare a divergence of mss. and not a reliance on lectionary practice (see section 5.2), and by the testimony of Eusebius and Jerome (see sections 5.3.10 and 5.3.12), who would certainly not be so uninformed as

Robinson's theory requires them to have been—for if his theory were correct, we would have heard it from them. To the contrary, Eusebius and Jerome don't even know about the SE, and know only mss. with or without the LE. If the SE originated in texts with the LE, their testimony would be impossible. As their testimony exists, it's Robinson's theory that is impossible.

5. It suffers the final defect that the problem this egregious and implausible doctoring of the text is supposed to have solved (not wanting to end a daily reading at such a defeatist place as verse 8) would have been far more easily and plausibly solved by simply ending the lection at verse 10 (or even verse 6 or 7), a solution so vastly more probable that Robinson's theory fails even on the mere consideration of its prior probability. Indeed, as Darrell Bock notes, "The liturgical unit of Mark 15:43-16:8 is not long (13 verses). So why cut it off at v. 8?" (*PEM*, p. 133). Indeed. Why not just continue all the way to verse 20? Clearly Robinson so badly wants his theory to be true that he can't even see how ridiculous it is.

So Robinson's theory is to be rejected. We must conclude that the universal presence of the SE before the LE (where they appear together) argues against the authenticity of the LE.

5.1.9 Assessment of Textual Evidence

Combine the above fact with all the more direct evidence that the earliest mss. and traditions lacked the LE altogether, and we have a strong external case against the authenticity of the LE. There are only three theories that can explain all this evidence: (1) neither the LE nor the SE were in the original text of Mark (and are therefore forgeries, either of composition or insertion); (2) either the LE or SE was original to Mark but then lost by accident, and very early (and whichever was original, whether LE or SE, the other is not original and therefore a forgery); (3) either the LE or SE was original to Mark but then deliberately removed, and very early (and whichever was deleted, whether LE or SE, the other is not original and therefore a forgery). Thus, no matter which theory you adopt, you cannot escape the conclusion that Mark contains a forgery. Inerrancy is thus defeated.

On top of that, only the first theory is credible. Not only does all the other internal and external evidence confirm this, but the other two theories are deficient. The SE is not likely to have been accidentally lost, as it is much too short. Even the LE is too short. The loss of a codex page could destroy up to four whole columns of text, but the LE consumes not even two; the SE, a mere fraction of one. And early loss from a scroll is prohibitively improbable (the ending would be on the inside of the roll, attached to the cog, the least likely section to lose). The SE is also unlikely to have been *deliberately* removed, because it cannot possibly have contained anything anyone would want to remove.

Even the LE is unlikely to have been deliberately removed, for though it contains some content that might have been undesired by some (though its prevalence in the record suggests hardly anyone disliked its content, rendering that theory implausible from the start), most other instances of motivated deletion in the manuscript tradition involve excising only the offensive material, leaving the rest—or simply altering the material to be agreeable. This is particularly evident in how material in Mark was redacted by Luke and Matthew, and how passages in Mark were emended by later scribes.[39] Only occasionally did anyone delete whole sections of Mark, and not (so far as we can tell) because they were doctrinally offensive. Thus, for example, if the remark about handling snakes was offensive, we would more likely find manuscripts in which simply that one phrase or verse was removed (as indeed it was in one 15th century lectionary), or if Jesus upbraiding the Apostles was offensive, we would find altered manuscripts in which Jesus simply didn't upbraid them. If the transition was recognized as awkward, we would find manuscripts in which this was repaired by emendation. And so on. In other words, deliberate deletion cannot explain the loss *of the whole LE*. Hence the second and third theories are improbable, while the first theory is very probable. That it is fully corroborated in the remaining evidence (internal and external) only confirms this. Therefore, Mark did not write the SE or the LE.

---

[39] See Bart Ehrman, *The Orthodox Corruption of Scripture: The Effect of Early Christological Controversies on the Text of the New Testament* (1993).

5.2 The Manuscripts: Physical Evidence

Apart from the textual evidence of the manuscripts, the surviving manuscripts also contain physical clues to the late origin of the SE and LE. Annotations to this effect are actually found in numerous mss. Some mss. indicate the end of the Gospel after 16:8 by subscribing the title of the book there or placing some other symbol there (the same ways the ends of other Gospels were indicated), and then follow *that* with the LE (or SE and LE), demonstrating the scribe was aware of the fact that the LE (or even SE) was not originally the ending of Mark.[40] This practice is evident even in other languages, including the Coptic and Ethiopic (see sections 5.1.3 and 5.1.4) and the Armenian.[41]

The most likely explanation of this strange juxtaposition is that their ultimate 'source manuscripts' lacked the LE originally (and thus had the concluding subscription after 16:8), and then the LE (or SE & LE) was added by a second hand (i.e. a later scribe than the one who originally transcribed the ms.), and when this whole collage was copied out again it was simply copied verbatim in exactly that order (by a third scribe, transcribing either the ms. we have now or the archetype or exemplar from which ours ultimately derives). That entails each 'source manuscript' lacked the LE, and the LE was snuck in later on. We actually have examples of this process in the making: actual mss. in which the LE was clearly added later in a second hand.[42] We even have a medieval scribe confessing to doing this (see section 5.3.10).

Not only is the LE (or SE & LE) "often separated from 16:8 by scribal signs" like these but in some mss. there are actual "notations that state or suggest that what follows is not found in some witnesses," e.g. minuscule 199 (from the 12th century) says "in some of the copies this [the LE] is not found; rather, it stops

---

[40] Metzger & Ehrman, *TNT*, pp. 40-41; Collins, *MAC*, pp. 804-06.

[41] That all the same phenomena are observed in the Armenian manuscripts: Colwell, "Mark," pp. 375-78.

[42] See Willker, "A Textual Commentary," pp. 6-7 (see footnote 11 above) and Kelhoffer, "The Witness," pp. 104-09 (see footnote 70 below) and Edmunds, "Six Endings," p. 524 (see footnote 36 above).

here."⁴³ Some of these notes derive from common ancestors, but even counting archetypes there are numerous independent notations like this, and (as just noted above) many more indicators in other mss. besides these explicit scribal notations. This confirms that numerous root mss. lacked the LE. And though in some medieval mss. there are scribal notes claiming the LE is the older reading, by then it may have appeared to be—especially to medieval scribes, who only had a few mss. to compare and no knowledge of the modern science of textual criticism.

In addition to scribal markings in many mss. and scribal notes in many other mss., some mss. (like minuscule 274, and several Syriac and Coptic mss., and in a similar way even Codex Regius, commonly known as manuscript L) add the SE in the margins as an alternate ending.⁴⁴ This also suggests knowledge of other now-lost mss. in which Mark ended only with the SE. The scribe of L is the most explicit, concluding Mark at 16:8 with a dotted line in one column, and then using the other column for endnotes stating that "some" mss. "also" had the SE (by itself) and that others had only the LE (and in each note providing the text of the respective ending), which could even mean L's exemplar (or its ancestor) had neither, but at the very least it means some mss. had the SE by itself. Similarly, the 7th century manuscript 083 ends with the SE and then adds a note "there is also this, appearing after 'and they were afraid'" and appends the LE. The SE and LE are even found attached in some mss. to the ending of Gospels other than Mark (usually Luke or John).⁴⁵ This is most peculiar, and a fact that may be a clue to the origin of the LE.

---

⁴³ Marcus, *MNT*, p. 1089; Collins, *MAC*, p. 805; cf. Kurt Aland, "Der wiedergefundene Markusschluss? Eine methodologische Bemerkung zur Textkritischen Arbeit," *Zeitschrift für Theologie und Kirche* 67 (1970): 3-13.

⁴⁴ Metzger & Ehrman, *TNT*, p. 324. For the evidence of L see the facsimile in John Burgon, *The Last Twelve Verses of the Gospel according to S. Mark* (1871), p. 126 (with the scribal notes translated on p. 123). For the SE in the marginalia of several Syriac and Coptic (Bohairic) mss. see: Clarence Russell Williams, *The Appendices to the Gospel according to Mark: A Study in Textual Transmission* (1915), pp. 367, 372-73, 392-95, 441 (and for ms. 274, cf. p. 418).

⁴⁵ See Colwell, "Mark," pp. 378-81 (see footnote 36).

5.2.1 Ariston the Presbyter

In a 10th century Armenian ms. the LE is uniquely separated from the rest of the Gospel with a note saying "of Ariston the Presbyter." This note appears to have been added to that ms. by a later scholar in the 13th or 14th century, and thus could be a mere conjecture.[46] But it would be a strange thing to conjecture—in fact, the only plausible motive for anyone to scribble this in the margin would be their discovery that it was true. Although Metzger concludes "the probability that an Armenian" scribe of such late date "would have access to historically valuable tradition on this point is almost nil" (*TNT*, p. 325), that's not a sound argument, because it's even *less* probable that an Armenian scribe of *any* date would write such a note unless he *did* have a 'historically valuable tradition' confirming the very point being noted.

The name most likely refers to Aristion [sic], an early 2nd century Christian elder who may have written lost commentaries on the Gospels.[47] Some scholars conjecture instead that it refers to an Ariston [sic] believed to be an actual disciple of Jesus, and thus (the note would be claiming) the LE was written by an eyewitness.

---

[46] On this Armenian marginal note see Colwell, "Mark," pp. 383-84.

[47] Eusebius, *History of the Church* 3.39.14 says Papias "in his own book passes on other commentaries on the stories of the Lord from the aforementioned Aristion, as well as traditions from John the Elder," where the key phrase (*tôn tou kuriou logôn diêgêseis*) could actually be the title of a book (*Commentaries on the Sayings [or Stories] of the Lord*), or referring to such a book. Although Eusebius earlier quotes a passage (3.39.7-8) in which Papias implies he did not read the works of Aristion but asked other people about the things Aristion was saying (Aristion was evidently a contemporary), Papias only says he *preferred* the living word, not that he consulted it exclusively (i.e. that he preferred asking Aristion's disciples about Aristion's teachings does not mean he did not already know Aristion's teachings in writing, like the proposed *Commentaries*, just as Papias knew of some of the Gospels).

It has been suggested that this Armenian scribal note refers to the Aristion (who may or may not be the same Aristion) attesting in Papias to the Barsabbas story of surviving poison (see sections 4.3.1 and 5.3.1) but the note neither contains such a remark nor is placed anywhere near verse 16:18 (where such a remark would belong). The note precedes the whole LE, was added by a later scholar (not the copyist who produced the ms.), and is so brief, there is no plausible case to be made that some prior note about Barsabbas had become corrupted into this state.

Although passing his testimony off as Mark's would still be an act of forgery, it would also be foolish, since to pass off eyewitness testimony as instead the testimony of another author (Mark), whom everyone believed wasn't an eyewitness, would actually *diminish* that testimony's authority. There is thus no reason for any disciple to have done this, nor does the LE read at all like an eyewitness report (quite the contrary, as shown in section 4.3). This conjecture is thereby implausible. There is no evidence to support it anyway.

A 2nd century author is far more likely. There were two men of similar name around the same time (early-to-mid 2nd century): a certain Aristion the Elder, who (as noted above) may have written a commentary on the Gospels, and an Ariston of Pella, who composed a now-lost *Dialogue of Jason and Papiscus the Jew*, which was known to Origen and Jerome and which many scholars suspect was employed by Justin Martyr. Either would explain any use Justin may have made of the LE, i.e. if the LE originally appeared in either of those works (the *Commentaries* of Aristion or the *Dialogue* of Ariston), Justin could have employed it without having any idea of it being passed off later as the ending of Mark (see section 5.3.2).

5.2.2 Accidental or Deliberate Transfer

There is an actual commentary on the Gospels that does survive (from another author), on which Maurice Robinson observes (emphasis mine):

> [T]he primary matter [in ms. 304] is the commentary. The gospel text is merely interspersed between the blocks of commentary material, and should not be considered the same as a 'normal' continuous-text MS. Also, it is often very difficult to discern the text in contrast to the comments… [and] following *gar* at the close of [16:8], the MS has a mark like a filled-in 'o', followed by many pages of commentary, all of which *summarize the endings of the other gospels* and even quote portions of them [before continuing on].[48]

---

[48] Maurice Robinson as quoted in *The Encyclopedia of New Testament Textual Criticism*, entry for "Manuscript 304" (available online at www.skypoint.com/members/waltzmn/Manuscripts1-500.html#m304).

Note the eerie relevance of his remarks: it was often *difficult* to tell where the Gospel text ended and the commentary began, and commentaries on the Gospel of Mark naturally inspired commentators into *summarizing the endings of the other gospels*, a perfect description of the LE. Could someone have deliberately (or even accidentally) copied out a paragraph from such a commentary and inserted it into an actual copy of the Gospel? Like, say, a commentary by an Aristion whom at least one medieval scholar had some reason to believe originally wrote it?

Even Bruce Metzger has suspected something like this, concluding that "in view of the inconcinnities between verses 1-8 and 9-20, it is unlikely that the long ending was composed *ad hoc* to fill up an obvious gap; it is more likely that the section was excerpted from another document, dating perhaps from the first half of the second century" (*TCG*, p. 125). A brief summary and harmonization of all the actual appearance narratives (from the other three Gospels and Acts), is exactly the sort of paragraph we might expect to find in a *Commentary on the Stories of the Lord* (such as Aristion may have written), or even in Ariston's *Dialogue of Jason and Papiscus*, such as a summary of appearances from the extant Gospels placed in the mouth of the dialogue's Christian advocate Jason (which might even have been later mistaken as a quotation of the LE, once it had crept into some mss. of Mark). Its extraction and transfer to Mark would not be unheard of in ancient practice, particularly for someone keen on borrowing a more satisfying ending. This is all the more credible when we observe that the Western text, in which the LE first appears, typically placed Mark at the end of the Gospels, thus inviting the need to summarize (and harmonize) the appearances of the other Gospels that would all have just been read.[49]

This theory would explain every single oddity in the evidence:

1. It would explain the origin of the Armenian scholar's marginal note (only if he found the LE in its original context—whether an actual work by Ariston or Aristion, or by some later author who clearly indicated deriving it from there—would he be likely to have made a note attributing it to such an obscure author,

---

[49] Noted by Elliott in *PEM*, p. 92.

especially an author who wrote early enough to actually be the LE's author, which is otherwise a remarkable coincidence.

2. It would explain the fact that the LE mysteriously became appended to other Gospels, not just Mark (as if originally it was not associated with Mark alone but all the Gospels, as a commentary would be—in fact, the passage may have originally been appended to the Gospels as a whole and thus became attached to whatever Gospel ended each individual collection, which in the majority Western text was the Gospel of Mark.

3. It would explain the fact that the LE shows no awareness of having just followed verses 16:1-8 (as noted in section 4.1).

4. It would explain why the author of the LE made no notable effort to emulate Markan style (and yet exhibits influence from the style of all the texts of the NT, including Mark).

5. It would explain the LE's brief summarizing character and its evident harmonizing intent (the LE reads just like a paragraph taken out of context from a commentary on the Gospels, or even a dialogue in which their content was summarized).

6. It would explain the LE author's knowledge of the whole NT (and why he limits his summary of accounts to stories appearing only in the Canonical NT).

7. It would explain the LE author's manifest assumption that his readers must know or have access to the NT (especially if the LE appeared in a commentary on the Gospels or, as in the Western text, Mark was positioned at the end of them, for then those other stories would already be in the reader's hands—being, in fact, in the very same book).

8. It would explain why the OE-to-LE transition is both illogical and ungrammatical (which makes no sense for a deliberate forger of the LE but makes perfect sense if the LE was simply cut and pasted from another book).

9. It would explain why all the physical evidence in the mss. suggests the LE began as an appendix to Mark and not an actual continuation of Mark's narrative.

10. And, of course, it would explain why all indications are that the manuscript tradition for Mark originally and widely lacked the LE.

The LE therefore almost certainly derives from another work (whether of Aristion, Ariston, or someone else) and was transferred to the end of Mark and thus mistaken (or passed off) as Markan material.

5.3 The Patristic Evidence

That leaves only one more category of evidence: the Patristic. A major problem with relying on Patristic authority is that the manuscripts of the Church Fathers have *themselves* been doctored to reflect later canonical readings of the Bible. This is particularly a problem for the mss. of Irenaeus, which is thus a problem for the ending of Mark because Irenaeus is the *only* 2nd century author we have who clearly attests the existence of the LE. As experts have noted:

> The MS traditions of virtually all the church fathers show that later copyists tended to "correct" quotations of the Bible to the form of text prevalent in their own day. Consequently, Patristic writings that survive only in Medieval MSS or that are available only in uncritical editions, such as Migne's *Patrologia Graeca*, are of practically no value for establishing the original wording of the NT.[50]
>
> Before patristic evidence can be used with confidence, however, one must determine whether the true text of the ecclesiastical writer has been transmitted. As in the case of the New Testament manuscripts, so also the treatises of the fathers have been modified in the

---

[50] Bart Ehrman, *Didymus the Blind and the Text of the Gospels* (1986), p. 6 (cf. pp. 6-7 for discussion and references).

course of copying. The scribe was always tempted to assimilate scriptural quotations in the fathers to the form of the text that was current in the later manuscripts of the New Testament.[51]

Quotations in the Church Fathers also commonly contradict each other and are in other ways notoriously unreliable. We even have some confirmed instances in which later Christian redactors added entire sentences or paragraphs to an earlier Patristic text.[52]

While the manuscripts we have now exhibit several very different textual traditions of equal antiquity, only the Western Text of the New Testament (whose best extant representative is Codex Bezae, although it still deviates from the Western text-type in numerous ways) is most commonly used by early Patristic authors (especially Justin, Irenaeus, and Tertullian), "all of which are characterized by longer or shorter additions and by certain striking omissions," while other text-types, such as the Alexandrian, may be closer to the originals.[53] Patristic authors after the 4th century are also of no use in the present case, since we know the SE and LE were circulating as endings of Mark by then, and manuscripts containing them were growing more numerous thereafter, eventually eclipsing altogether the original text of Mark.

Keeping all these cautions in mind, only the following authors are of use in evaluating how Mark originally ended.

---

[51] Metzger & Ehrman, *TNT*, p. 12 (cf. pp. 126-34 for discussion and references).

[52] For a general survey of why Patristic evidence "involves the greatest difficulties and the most problems" see Bruce Metzger, "Patristic Evidence and the Textual Criticism of the New Testament" in *NTS*, pp. 167-88 (quoting p. 167), supported by Gordon Fee, "The Use of the Greek Fathers for New Testament Textual Criticism," in Bart D. Ehrman and Michael Holmes, eds., *The Text of the New Testament in Contemporary Research* (1994), pp. 191-207; and Miroslav Marcovich, *Patristic Textual Criticism* (Atlanta, GA: Scholars Press, 1994), s.v. "Interpolations" in the index.

[53] Metzger & Ehrman, *TNT*, pp. 308-09. For background see the Wikipedia entries on the "Western text-type" (en.wikipedia.org/wiki/Western_text-type) and the "Alexandrian text-type" (en.wikipedia.org/wiki/Alexandrian_text-type).

5.3.1 Papias

Papias (c. 130 A.D.) reported the miracle of Justus Barsabbas drinking poison and coming to no harm "by the grace of the Lord," which is sometimes cited as evidence Papias knew the LE (see section 4.3.1). But in fact this entails Papias *didn't* know the LE, which further argues the LE did not exist in the Gospel of Mark at that time (early 2nd century). For Papias claims he knew the Gospel of Mark.[54] Yet he credits all this information to oral tradition, not the Gospel of Mark, and shows no knowledge of Jesus having predicted it (which surely he would mention) or that this was in any way a *common* sign among apostles. Papias instead appears to have reacted to the Barsabbas story as though the effect were a surprise (uniquely "by the grace of God" and experienced by Barsabbas alone).

Though we do not have a full direct quote from Papias to confirm these conclusions, they seem undeniably apparent from Eusebius' account of them. This then stands as evidence *against* the authenticity of the LE, not in favor of it. To the contrary, the LE's inclusion of immunity to poison may have been inspired by stories like this, not the other way around (see section 5.3.6).

5.3.2 Justin

The earliest author usually cited is Justin Martyr (c. 160 A.D.), but he provides no real evidence of the presence of the LE in Mark. In only one passage (*Apology* 1.45.5) he uses together the same three words appearing in Mark 16:20, but does not indicate he is quoting *any* Gospel there, much less Mark. Where Justin mentions the OT had predicted "the powerful word that His Apostles preached everywhere after having left Jerusalem," the "preached everywhere after having left" is all that echoes the LE, just three words in Greek and not even in the same order (the LE word *logos* is also used by Justin elsewhere in the same sentence but is common and expected here and thus not telltale). In contrast, the LE does not have the words "Apostles" or "Jerusalem," nor does Justin mention

---

[54] Eusebius, *History of the Church* 3.39 contains both Papias' story about Barsabbas and Papias' declaring familiarity with the Gospel of Mark, as well as all the other details mentioned.

anything else that would suggest knowledge of the LE (such as the specific signs declared there, or even its appearances of Jesus).

The similarity between them thus appears to be coincidental, or at most evidence of an idiom in wide use that separately influenced both Justin and the author of the LE (the predicted sentiment is already inherent in Luke 24:47-52 and Acts 1:8, as well as Matthew 28:19). Moreover, even if we could consider this as evidence of the LE's influence on Justin, as noted in section 5.2, Justin may have only known the LE in a text other than Mark. For Justin doesn't in fact say he is citing a Gospel, and everyone agrees he is not quoting one.

Therefore, this passage cannot demonstrate the LE was in Mark at that time. Of course, even if it was, it could have been appended to copies of Mark in the early 2nd century, so even a direct quotation from Justin would be insufficient to establish the LE was *originally* in Mark. But we don't have any such quotation anyway.[55]

5.3.3 Tatian

It's possible that Justin's pupil Tatian incorporated the LE in his *Diatessaron* (or "Harmony of the Four Gospels") after 175 A.D. But we cannot confirm that this was originally the case, as we do not have Tatian's version of the *Diatessaron*.[56] We know the *Diatessaron* had additions and changes made to it over the centuries, few versions agree, and the texts we have now date centuries after Tatian. For example, a famous interpolation in John (on the adulteress, John 7:53-8:11) was evidently not originally in the

---

[55] James Kelhoffer makes the best case for this passage being evidence Justin knew the LE (*MAM*, pp. 170-75), but even his argument doesn't overcome the reasons just noted. Nevertheless, his case is equally compatible with the conclusion that Justin knew this material from *another* source, not Mark's Gospel.

[56] Kelhoffer is more confident than the evidence warrants (*MAM*, pp. 170-75). Note earlier dates are often given for the *Diatessaron*, but it was most likely composed in the East, and by all accounts Tatian did not go east after his conversion until the 170s. There is no evidence for an earlier date of composition.

Diatessaron, yet found its way in centuries later.[57] The LE may have done the same. In fact, different textual traditions have the LE incorporated into the *Diatessaron* in different ways. Other sections of the *Diatessaron* also differ among the various textual traditions.

So it does look like the LE was added later by different editors in different ways. At best, the earliest references to the LE being in the *Diatessaron* appear in the works of Aphraates and Ephrem in the mid-4th century (though these are to some extent questionable: see the footnote in section 5.3.11 below). But they also attest to many other interpolations in their copies of the *Diatessaron* (i.e. many passages that do not now exist—and certainly did not originate—in any of the four Canonical Gospels). Thus the *Diatessaron* had already become corrupt by then. It is therefore of little use in determining the origin of the LE. Moreover, even if Tatian incorporated the LE, that would only confirm that it had entered some mss. of Mark by mid-2nd century, which still would not establish that it was originally a part of Mark almost a hundred years earlier.

5.3.4 Tertullian

Supposed evidences of Tertullian's knowledge of the LE (c. 190 A.D.) are invalid because they can more easily derive from the other Gospel texts and Christian teachings that the LE itself drew upon. Passages from Tertullian exhibit no features distinctive of the LE, nor give any indication Tertullian is quoting anything, much less the Gospel of Mark.

Tertullian, *On the Soul* 25.8 (seven demons expelled from Mary) derives from Luke; *On the Cure for Heretics* 30.16 (Apostles given powers) derives from Acts and the Epistles; *On the Resurrection* 51.1 and *Against Praxeas* 2.1 and 30.5 (Jesus rising to sit at the right hand of God) obviously derive from Acts 1:11 (and Mark 12:36 and 14:62), not the LE; likewise, *On Fleeing Persecution* 10.2 (believers given power over demons) can just as easily derive from Mark 6:7 and elsewhere. See table in section 4.3.1 for obvious alternative sources. Other references are even less relevant, e.g. *On Baptism* 10.7 explicitly interprets a saying of John the Baptist, not Jesus, and conspicuously *lacks* reference to the Gospel of Mark; and

---

[57] See the Wikipedia entry on "Diatessaron" (en.wikipedia.org/wiki/Diatessaron).

Tertullian's remarks here otherwise don't resemble the LE at all, but merely echo standard Christian belief of the time.

In other words, we can't argue from any of this evidence that Tertullian knew the LE. To the contrary, the absence of any direct reference in any of these passages to what Jesus says in the LE argues Tertullian *didn't* know the LE. For a declaration of Jesus on these facts would have clinched Tertullian's point in almost every case, which makes the absence of the LE in these passages far more telling. Nor can we argue from any of these passages that Tertullian knew the LE was in Mark, for like Justin, even if we could prove Tertullian knew the LE (and we can't), that would not prove he knew it as the ending of Mark, rather than as a text in some other work (see section 5.2).

5.3.5 Irenaeus

The only other relevant author from the 2nd century is Irenaeus (c. 185 A.D.). He appears to provide the only reliable evidence that the LE was in any copies of Mark in the 2nd century. But the mss. of Irenaeus are notoriously corrupt and problematic. He only mentions the LE once, and that in a passage that only survives in Latin translation, yet the Latin texts of Irenaeus are among those most tampered with.

The claim has been made that Theodoret of Cyrrhus (c. 450 A.D.) quotes this passage in the original Greek, confirming that if it had been interpolated, it happened in the Greek before the Latin translation was made (which would certainly be possible). But this is not in fact true. Theodoret's actual quotation is from a *previous* section of Irenaeus, not this one.[58] It has also been claimed this passage is quoted in Greek in a marginal note added next to the LE

---

[58] The error originates from mistaking Rousseau's modern 'back translation' of the Latin into Greek for an actual Greek text—and then mistaking that as deriving from Theodoret. Kelhoffer, *MAM*, p. 170, even presents the Greek text of 'Theodoret' as if it came from him and not Rousseau, and posits theories from the text type! Probably one of the most embarrassing errors of his career. Alas, the Greek Kelhoffer quotes is Rousseau's. I verified this myself, consulting first-hand a copy of Adelin Rousseau & Louis Doutreleau, *Irénée de Lyon: Contre les hérésies livre III* (1974), vols. 1 (pp. 64-67, 79-82, pp. 144-48) and 2 (pp. 128, 137-39).

in a medieval Bible, but that's also not true.[59] The scholium in question only says "Irenaeus, who was near to the apostles, in the third book against heresies quotes this saying as found in Mark." It does not quote the text of Irenaeus. As that ms. dates to the mid-10th century (and the author of it's marginalia dates no earlier than the 5th century), this testimony confirms nothing, for the referenced passage could be an interpolation made anytime in the two hundred years or more after Irenaeus wrote—even in the Greek, yet for all we know this scholar could be referring to a Latin text of Irenaeus.[60] So we have no Greek text of this passage. It exists only in the medieval Latin.

Certainly, on its face we would still accept this passage as confirmation that Ireneaus' copy of Mark by the late 2nd century contained the LE. But there is a persuasive argument to be made that this passage was not written by Irenaeus but interpolated (at least within two or three centuries, or even later), quite possibly by accident. The passage looks like a marginal note added by a scribe intending to add to Irenaeus' arguments in that chapter. As there was no standard notation for distinguishing marginal notes from accidentally omitted text, we have countless examples of such notes being accidentally interpolated into the text of other manuscripts.[61] This could be one such case.

---

[59] In Minuscule 1582, per, e.g., Maurice Robinson (in *PEM*, p. 47 n. 26).

[60] Burnett Streeter, *The Four Gospels: A Study of Origins* (1953), p. 124. On the origin of this marginal note in the early 5th century or after (anytime from the late 5th to 9th century is possible) see K. W. Kim, "Codices 1582, 1739, and Origen," *Journal of Biblical Literature* 69.2 (June 1950): 167-75. The evidence is simply that of all the sources named by the annotator (in ms. 1582 where this citation of Irenaeus appears), the latest of them date to the early 5th century (which establishes the original author added these notes to the textual tradition behind 1582 either in the late 5th century or later), which could simply reflect the annotator's limited library or preference for venerable sources (so he could still be writing even as late as the 9th century). Moreover, the annotator who compiled the bulk of these notes is not necessarily the same one who added the note referencing Irenaeus. That could have been added by anyone at any time in the intervening centuries. An identical note appears in a different location in the 11th century manuscript 72, but we cannot deduce anything useful from this (72 might be lifting that note from any manuscript related to 1582 of any possible date).

[61] On the phenomenon of accidental interpolation see Chapter 19 ("Origen, Eusebius, and the Accidental Interpolation"), pp. 339-40.

To understand why the passage attesting the LE in Irenaeus may be an interpolation, the entire section must be quoted to reveal the flow of Irenaeus' argument, and why the LE does not appear to fit. Before this Irenaeus has spent an entire chapter arguing that Jesus is God and there is only one God in Jesus, extensively quoting the Old and New Testaments, every instance confirming his thesis that he can find. He then concludes (emphasis added):

> Wherefore also Mark, the interpreter and follower of Peter, does thus commence his Gospel narrative: "The beginning of the Gospel of Jesus Christ, the Son of God; as it is written in the prophets, 'Behold, I send My messenger before Thy face, which shall prepare Thy way. The voice of one crying in the wilderness, Prepare ye the way of *the Lord*, make the paths straight before *our God*.'" Plainly does the commencement of the Gospel quote the words of the holy prophets, and point out Him at once, whom they confessed as *God* and *Lord*, Him, the Father of our Lord Jesus Christ, who had also made promise to Him, that He would send His messenger before His face, who was John, crying in the wilderness, in "the spirit and power of Elijah," "Prepare ye the way of *the Lord*, make straight paths before *our God*." For the prophets did not announce one and another God, *but one and the same*, under various aspects, however, and many titles. For varied and rich in attributes is the Father, as I have already shown in the book preceding this, and as I shall show from the prophets themselves in the further course of this work. **Also, towards the conclusion of his Gospel, Mark says: "So then, after the Lord Jesus had spoken to them, He was received up into heaven, and sat on the right hand of God," confirming what had been spoken by the prophet: "The LORD said to my Lord, Sit Thou on My right hand, until I make Thy foes Thy footstool."** Thus God and the Father are truly one and the same: He who was announced by the prophets, and handed down by the true Gospel, whom we Christians worship and love with the whole heart, as the Maker of heaven

> and earth, and of all things therein. (Irenaeus, *Against All Heresies* 3.10.5.)

Note that before the sentence in bold, Irenaeus appears already to have concluded his argument. Yet then, out of the blue, he adds, as if an afterthought, "Also..." and quotes Mark 16:19 as verifying Psalms 110:1 (which had already been verified, and by Jesus himself, in Mark 12:35-37). Even more strangely, in none of this additional sentence does the word 'Father' appear, yet this passage is supposed to support Irenaeus's argument that "thus God and the Father" are one and the same—because this is the argument of the preceding sentence, *and* the conclusion declared in the *following* sentence. If the material in bold is removed, we have a consistent argument from premise to conclusion. But reinsert the material in bold and there is an illogical disconnect between the argument Irenaeus is supposed to be making, and the passage being quoted—because that passage does not support this argument.

So why is it here? It would make sense as an addition to the whole theme of chapters 9 through 12, but it makes no sense appearing exactly here. And even though his section 3.10.5 is where we would expect all his quotations from Mark to appear, this particular quotation still does not fit the specific argument Irenaeus is making. It would support only a different argument, albeit one that would reinforce his *overall* thesis, and thus should appear as a separate argument either before or after the present one, not inexplicably inserted in the middle of it. But a scholar who wished to add reinforcing evidence from Mark to Irenaeus' overall theme would certainly place it in the margins of section 3.10.5, if he would place it anywhere. Which would explain how it later came to be so arbitrarily inserted into the text.

In further support of this conclusion, Irenaeus knows that his argument from Mark 1:1-3 requires considerable elucidation (consisting of several sentences), but the comparably required elucidation of his supposed argument from Mark 16:19 is missing. As written, the text in bold actually refutes rather than supports Irenaeus, for it plainly says Jesus was a different entity from God (sitting next to him, not in his place, and addressing each other in the third person), and it is not explained how the Psalm quoted makes any different conclusion out of this. Irenaeus would have needed to explain the connections here: how the Psalm supports reinterpreting Mark 16:19 as a confirmation rather than refutation of the thesis that Jesus and God are one and the same. He would certainly have called into service Mark 12:35-37, and explicitly identified the links we are supposed to make between the different Lords named and God and the Messiah and why we are to presume David is speaking of the latter in Psalm 110:1. Yet none of this is present. A marginal note would easily consist of a single sentence, leaving the connecting arguments implied, but Irenaeus himself would not likely deliver such a presumptuous and unfinished argument, especially one so manifestly supporting his opponents (the heretics he is here engaged in refuting). The fact that it doesn't even support the argument it is attached to only confirms the conclusion that Irenaeus didn't write this. I conclude this testimony is probably spurious.

Another passage in Irenaeus is sometimes adduced as evidence he knew the LE, but the passage in question actually argues *against* such knowledge.[62] For it neither quotes the LE, nor uses the same vocabulary as the LE, nor even implies he is drawing any information from the Gospels at all—for he is providing his own description of current activity in the Church, which he lists not as exorcism, speaking in tongues, immunity to poison, and healing, but exorcism, prophecy, healing, and resurrecting the dead (and each described elaborately), thus showing no congruity with the LE. His list simply reflects common Christian practice and belief at the time.[63] And since his point is that these powers prove the Christian gospel true, the fact that *Jesus himself had said so* (16:17-18: "these signs shall accompany them that believe," thereby confirming the truth of the gospel) would so soundly secure his argument that for him to neglect citing it here is patently strange. This all but proves he did not know the LE.

---

[62] Irenaeus, *Against Heresies* 2.32.4.

[63] Heb. 6:2; 1 Cor. 12:8-11, 12:28-30 (cf. Mark 5:23, Luke 4:40); and Justin Martyr, *Dialogue with Trypho* 39. Notably, Irenaeus says Christians exhibit "in the name" of Christ the powers of God "in proportion to the gift each has received" and then lists four gifts; Justin says Christians prove the power of Jesus by "receiving gifts, each as he is worthy, illumined through the name of Christ" and then lists seven gifts; Tertullian says something similar (*Against Marcion* 5.8, conspicuously quoting only Paul as evidence); evidently this was a common mode of Christian preaching (most likely based on 1 Corinthians 12, cf. Romans 12:4-9, 1 Corinthians 7:8, 1 Corinthians 14, and Hebrews 2:4 and 6:4-6, etc.).

Similarly, Irenaeus mentions "speaking with all kinds of tongues" as a power Christians displayed, but only far away from this list, in a completely different book, showing no awareness that this was ever predicted by Jesus, much less in the same place as healing and exorcism. The phenomenon is already ubiquitously discussed in the Epistles (e.g. 1 Corinthians 14) and obviously still going on, so this passage does not attest knowledge of the LE. Indeed, again, this argues against such knowledge, since here as elsewhere he fails to associate the powers listed in the LE, and fails to mention that these powers were predicted by Christ himself. That he never shows any knowledge of "immunity to snakes and poison" being a power any Christians should or did have only confirms the point.

So from these passages as well it seems much more likely that Irenaeus did *not* know of the LE.

5.3.6 Hippolytus

Hippolytus (c. 210 A.D.) refers to eaters of the Eucharist becoming immune to poison, which is said to demonstrate knowledge of the LE, but it cannot be anything of the kind.[64] It neither quotes the LE, nor mentions snakes, nor even attributes the claim to Jesus, despite the supreme authority this would establish. And unlike the LE, Hippolytus associates the power with the eucharist, not baptism. Since other tales of immunity to poison were already circulating (see sections 4.3 and 5.3.1), the LE is not the only possible source of Hippolytus's claim. In fact, given the incongruities, it's the *least* likely source for it. Instead, unless the author of the LE was making that claim up out of whole cloth (and thus the claim is completely false, which then refutes inerrancy), the author of the LE must have been drawing on independent traditions regarding immunity to poison, which traditions could just as well be what informed Hippolytus. And even if there was no such tradition, an inference to this same conclusion from Luke 10:19 would be as obvious to Hippolytus as it was to the author of the LE (see section 4.3.1), so knowledge of

---

[64] Hippolytus, *Apostolic Tradition* 36.1 ("The faithful shall be careful to partake of the eucharist before eating anything else. For if they eat with faith, even though some deadly poison is given to them, after this it will not be able to harm them.").

the LE would not be required (and by his associating the power with the eucharist rather than baptism, his knowledge of the LE should even be rejected).

Other alleged references to the LE in Hippolytus are nothing of the kind, e.g. that Jesus sat on the right hand of God (*Treatise on Christ and Antichrist* 46) derives from Luke-Acts (and elsewhere). Thus, there is nothing in Hippolytus that confirms the LE even existed, much less was known as the ending of Mark.

5.3.7 Origen, Clement, and Other 3rd Century Authors

There are a large number of Christian authors from 100-300 A.D. who never mention the LE, which taken together is significant but not compelling (since many NT verses are likewise unattested but still certainly authentic). But most telling is the silence of Origen and Clement (c. 200-230 A.D.), who each left us a huge corpus erudite with discussions and quotations of the Gospels. Similarly other copious authors, like Tertullian and Cyprian, erroneously believed to have attested the LE, in fact very curiously did not. Likewise Lactantius, despite his having written extensive treatises on Christian abilities and beliefs. Though it is always possible they just never happened to strike upon an occasion to reference the LE, given the vast extent of their respective writings this at least approaches the improbable, the more so when combined with the silence of all other authors before the 4th century (apart from, at most, Irenaeus, although I am certain not even he mentioned it, per section 5.3.5).

Clement actually had credible occasions to quote the LE yet didn't (e.g. *Stromata* 4.6; *On the Rich Man* 34; *Comments on the Epistle of Jude*; etc.). So his silence is notable, even if still not conclusive. Tertullian might likewise be expected to cite the LE in several passages yet doesn't (e.g. *Against Marcion* 5.8; *Exhortation to Chastity* 4; and the passages noted in section 5.3.4). Cyprian, too (see section 5.3.8).

Origen also had occasion to quote or address the LE in his extensive treatise *Against Celsus* (e.g. 1.6, 1.67, 2.48, 2.56-70, etc.), but most especially where he had to rebut Celsus's claim that Mary was insane. Some now claim Celsus was there referring to Mary having once been possessed by demons (and hence he must be referring to Mark 16:9), but the context disproves this. In *Against Celsus* 2.55 Origen tells us Celsus said only two people saw the *wounds* Jesus had suffered, one woman who was *paroistros* ("driven frantic; beside herself" or "half-mad; practically insane") and one other man ("from among those engaged in the same charlatanry"). This is clearly the scene in John (the one man being Thomas), not the LE, which contains no reference to seeing wounds, nor any appearance to a single man. Origen assumes nothing else in his rebuttal (in 2.59-62). In fact, Origen's most direct rebuttal (in 2.60) is that Celsus's claim that Mary was insane is "a statement which is not made by the history recording the fact" but a calumny entirely made up by Celsus. That suggests neither Celsus nor Origen knew of Mark 16:9, which *would* be a historical record of the fact (directly declaring her an ex-demoniac). Moreover, Celsus would surely have lambasted the Gospel of Mark for including other material in the LE (such as its claim of immunity to poisons and snakes), compelling Origen to make a rebuttal. Yet instead all Celsus attacks is the account in John. So the silence here argues the LE was not known to Celsus, and it supports (though does not prove) the LE was not known to Origen.[65]

5.3.8 Vincentius (via Cyprian)

Cyprian reports that in 256 A.D. bishop Vincentius of Thibaris had said at a council that the Lord "commanded his apostles, saying, 'Go ye, lay on hands in my name, expel demons'. And in another place: 'Go ye and teach the nations, baptizing them in the name of the Father, of the Son, and of the Holy Ghost'." But the latter is an exact quotation of Matthew 28:19, while the former is *not* an exact quotation of Mark 16:17: the LE does not have Jesus giving this as a command (but rather promising it as a sign, and descriptively in the third person, not in the imperative; the imperative is only used for his command to go and preach the gospel two verses earlier), and in the LE Jesus does not link laying on hands and the expelling of demons, but connects laying on hands and healing (a whole verse later). Hence Vincentius must be quoting some other lost Gospel or agrapha, or some tertiary source that conflated the contents of the LE (which, as already noted in previous sections, could have originated in some source other than Mark, and probably in the early-to-mid 2nd century), or he is

---

[65] Kelhoffer, *MAM*, p. 171, n. 48 also refutes the specious suggestion that Celsus knew the LE.

conflating several passages from the NT (e.g. Mark 6:7-13 and 9:38-40 and Acts 14:3, cf. also Luke 10:17 and 9:49-50).

Since Vincentius does not say this passage is in Mark (or even a Gospel) and the quoted words do not match those of the LE, we can derive no conclusion from this that the LE was then in Mark. To the contrary, that none of the many dozens of bishops quoted on the role and importance of baptism in this text ever quote the LE is rather an argument *against* anyone knowing it as scripture even by the middle of the 3rd century.[66]

5.3.9 Other Dubious Witnesses Before the 4th Century

Other documents from the 2nd century have been proposed as witnesses to the LE, but none are credible. The *Epistle of Barnabas* 15:9, which quotes no Gospel, merely says Jesus ascended the day he rose, which claim derives from Luke. Similarly *Hermas* 102 (Parable 9.25.2) contains common phrases shared with Mark 16:15, but used in a different way, in no similar order or even together, and without any indication of deriving any of this from any source, much less a Gospel (to the contrary, it is there portrayed as a direct communication from an angel). Like the reference in Justin (see section 5.3.2), this only looks like a common set of idioms and phrases in Christian preaching (derived from Gospel passages other than the LE: see table in section 4.3.1), which independently

---

[66] Cyprian, *The Opinions of 87 Clerics at the Seventh Council of Carthage Concerning the Baptism of Heretics* 37:

> Vincentius of Thibaris said: "We know that heretics are worse than Gentiles. If, therefore, being converted, they should wish to come to the Lord, we have assuredly the rule of truth which the Lord by His divine precept commanded to His apostles, saying, 'Go ye, lay on hands in my name, expel demons'. And in another place: 'Go ye and teach the nations, baptizing them in the name of the Father, of the Son, and of the Holy Ghost'. Therefore first of all by imposition of hands in exorcism, secondly by the regeneration of baptism, they may then come to the promise of Christ. Otherwise I think it ought not to be done." Several other clerics at the same council likewise said heretics can only be accepted back into their church if they are exorcized by laying on hands and baptized.

> The notion that heretics must be exorcised by laying on hands and baptized before being accepted back into the fold is echoed by several other clerics at the same council, but conspicuously, none cite the Lord in support of their opinion.

influenced *Hermas*, Justin, and the author of the LE. Similarly, the last verses of the extant fragment of the Gospel of Peter (vv. 58-60) do not attest the LE but in fact contradict it, saying there were twelve, not eleven disciples, no appearance to Mary, and Jesus doesn't appear to the disciples indoors at dinner in Judea, but outdoors in Galilee. All the contents of this passage are more clearly adapted from John 21 (or a common source shared by John 21) and possibly other passages tabulated in section 4.3.1.

The 3rd century *Didascalia* has one passage that comes close to the LE, reading (in Syriac), "But when we had divided the whole world into twelve parts, and were gone forth among the Gentiles into all the world to preach the word, then Satan set about and stirred up the People to send after us false apostles for the undoing of the word." But this is clearly not a quotation of the LE (Jesus is not even the one speaking), and it conspicuously does not conform to Mark 16:15 or 16:20. It appears to merely embellish Matthew 28:19, or simply derives from Justin (see section 5.3.2).[67]

Several passages in the anonymous *Epistula Apostolorum* (originally composed mid-2nd century) likewise bear no demonstrable connection to the LE (deriving instead from the other Gospels), and we have no reliable text of the latter anyway, only distant translations of it.[68] And the extant portion of the *Acts of Pilate* that clearly employs the LE is unmistakably late. Some form of the Acts of Pilate may derive from the early 2nd century, but such cannot have been the text that cites the LE. Justin refers to the *Acts of Pilate* (in *Apology* 1.35.9 and 1.48.3), but the only part of the extant *Acts of Pilate* that could be of such early date is the appendix called *The Report of Pilate to the Emperor Claudius* which lacks any reference to the LE, yet contains all the material Justin claims to have found there. All other content of the extant *Acts of*

---

[67] *Didascalia* 23.(6.8), or p. 101 of the Connolly translation. See the Wikipedia entry for "Didascalia Apostolorum" (en.wikipedia.org/wiki/Didascalia_Apostolorum).

[68] See Kelhoffer, *MAM*, p. 171, n. 49.

Pilate dates from the late 4th century and later. So it is also of no use in answering the present question.[69]

5.3.10 Eusebius

So that leaves us with the 4th century and later. The next relevant author is therefore Eusebius (c. 320 A.D.). In his *Letter to Marinus* (a.k.a. *Ad Marinum*) Eusebius specifically addresses the authenticity of the LE. He says "it is not current in all the copies," and in fact not only do "the accurate copies" end at verse 16:8, but "nearly all the copies" do, the LE only "being rarely found in some copies."

Eusebius was a renowned publisher of Bibles, supervised a scriptorium, and had charge of the most extensive Christian library then in the world, whose members had actively sought the gathering of countless manuscripts of the Bible on an ongoing basis for over a century (from Origen to Pamphilus to Eusebius himself), and Eusebius's authority on the Biblical text was universally accepted by his peers and successors. So the fact that he observed the LE to be rare, and not present at all in the most trusted manuscripts, proves that the later mss. tradition, in which most copies contain the LE, is a later medieval development.

This testimony supports the conclusion that the LE is not original to Mark, but was interpolated in only a few mss. sometime before the 4th century. The Eusebian Canons also exclude the LE,

---

[69] See Kelhoffer, *MAM*, pp. 176-77; also "The Report of Pilate to the Emperor Claudius" at www.earlychristianwritings.com/text/reportpilate.html, as well as the entire "Acts of Pilate" resource page there (www.earlychristianwritings.com/actspilate.html), and the Wikipedia entry for "Acts of Pilate" (en.wikipedia.org/wiki/Acts_of_Pilate).

so Eusebius himself considered it non-canonical.[70] And there is no valid basis for rejecting his testimony. He had seen vastly more manuscripts of the first three centuries than any modern scholar could ever hope to, and thus we are in no position to gainsay him. No early witness contradicts his testimony. And even if he could be exaggerating, he can't be lying, since Jerome corroborates him (see section 5.3.12), and Jerome would know, having extensive experience with even more manuscripts than Eusebius. In fact, were the evidence any different Eusebius would have defended the LE's authenticity, not doubted it, much less have supported that doubt with a lie. We must conclude Eusebius has given us a sufficiently accurate report on the state of the LE text.

Eusebius shows no knowledge at all of the SE.

Eusebius's testimony alone is clear and authoritative, at least establishing the existence of the LE as of c. 300 A.D. Had it originated any later, Eusebius would have been aware of its recent appearance, but he shows no certainty as to its origin, so it can't have been composed and inserted later than the 3rd century. Accordingly, I find none of the later patristic attestations of any relevance. They merely repeat what we already know from Eusebius. Some even appear to have been using Eusebius as their source on the matter.[71] Kelhoffer even shows how a remark attributed (possibly pseudonymously) to the 6th century author Victor of Antioch deviously rewrites the same argument from *Ad Marinum* into an argument for exactly the opposite conclusion, thus betraying knowledge of the *Ad Marinum* in the very effort to gainsay it. This very same passage from Pseudo(?)-Victor then

---

[70] James Kelhoffer, "The Witness of Eusebius' *Ad Marinum* and Other Christian Writings to Text-Critical Debates concerning the Original Conclusion to Mark's Gospel," *Zeitschrift für die neutestamentliche Wissenschaft und die Kunde der älteren Kirche* 92 (2001): 78-112 [exclusion from Canons: 108]. This article also shows how what Eusebius reports was a rare reading in the 4th century became the most common reading in later medieval manuscripts; and it provides an English translation of the entire *Letter to Marinus* with accompanying Greek text. That Eusebius was well aware of Western readings (and thus Western manuscripts) and used them on occasion (while only tending to prefer the Alexandrian text) is shown by, among others, D.S. Wallace-Hadrill, "Eusebius and the Gospel Text of Caesarea," *The Harvard Theological Review* 49.2 (April 1956): 105-14, so it cannot be claimed his remarks apply only to manuscripts in the Alexandrian tradition.

[71] Kelhoffer, "The Witness," pp. 99-109.

confesses to having *added* the LE to manuscripts that lacked it! We can thus see how the LE came to proliferate in copies of Mark and the OE eclipsed.[72]

5.3.11 Aphraates, Ephrem, Ambrose

A certain Aphraates composed a collection of *Demonstrations* in Syriac, the relevant portion of which in 337 A.D. We don't have the originals, only much later copies, so we can't be sure he actually quoted the LE. Aphraates was employing the *Diatessaron* in some form. Ephrem the Syrian then composed a Syriac commentary on the *Diatessaron* about forty years later (c. 375 A.D.). Again we lack the originals and have only much later copies. Both seem to quote the LE and attest its presence in their copies of the *Diatessaron* (though one might still have doubts: see the following note). But we already know the LE had crept into copies of Mark by then (see section 5.3.10). So it could just as easily have also crept into the *Diatessaron* (see section 5.3.3 above). Neither author, therefore, affords any useful evidence regarding the origin of the LE.[73]

Ambrose (c. 375 A.D.) also unmistakably quotes the LE. But this again post-dates Eusebius, and Eusebius already attests the

---

[72] Kelhoffer, "The Witness," pp. 104-05 (cf. also Collins, *MAC*, p. 805).

[73] See introductions on Aphraates and Ephrem in the *Nicene and Post-Nicene Fathers* vol. 13. Aphraates quotes part of the LE (only a truncated version of vv. 16-17, the verses later found in the *Diatessaron*) in *Demonstrations* 1.17 (although a quotation of 16:15 is curiously absent from *Demonstrations* 1.8, where we would also expect it). For Ephrem see Carmel McCarthy, *Saint Ephrem's Commentary on Tatian's* Diatessaron*: An English Translation of Chester Beatty Syriac MS 709* (1993), p. 289 (section 19.15), where a compression of Mark 16:15 and Matthew 28:19 is quoted in a fashion resembling what we know was in some copies of the *Diatessaron* of that period (although again nowhere else is any material from the LE quoted or mentioned in the whole of Ephrem's commentary, and even here the only words that would derive from the LE consist of the brief and ambiguous expression "into the whole world" which is already implied by the "all nations" of Matt. 28:19). Unfortunately we know Ephrem's text has been compromised by later editors (McCarthy, pp. 31-34) and that Ephrem would have been well aware of other versions of the New Testament besides the *Diatessaron* (McCarthy, p. 15), so this attestation may be much less secure than is commonly supposed.

existence of the LE in some mss. of Mark.[74] Although Ambrose never specifies what document he knew the LE from (and though he quotes it many times, he only ever quotes exactly the same section: vv. 15-18), from the evidence of Eusebius we can assume Ambrose found it in a copy of Mark and regarded it as of that Gospel. This and all later examples in Patristic sources afford no further evidence, as they merely corroborate what has already been proved: that after the 3rd century some copies of Mark were circulating that ended with the LE.

5.3.12 Jerome and Later

The next relevant author is Jerome (late 4th century). In his *Letter to Hedybia* (*Epistles* 120.3) Jerome explicitly says essentially the same thing Eusebius did: the LE is not in most mss. and in none of the best (and he also shows no knowledge of the SE at all). He is almost certainly relying on Eusebius for this. But he would have known if Eusebius's observation was at all dubious, since Jerome's own acquaintance with the mss. was unrivaled in his day. So by approving what Eusebius said Jerome in fact corroborates him. Elsewhere Jerome says the VLE appears in some mss., especially in Greek mss., thus attesting the VLE was forged sometime in the 4th century (and thus barely one or two centuries after the LE itself was interpolated).[75]

Everything else after Eusebius is useless, only verifying what we already know: that by the 4th century the LE was circulating in some copies of Mark. The *Apostolic Constitutions* (*AC*) are of the late 4th century and thus of no use. Indeed, their primary source document, the 3rd century *Didascalia*, lacks any quotation of the LE (see section 5.3.9). Hence those elements were added to the *AC*

---

[74] Ambrose of Milan, *On the Holy Spirit* 2.13.(151), *On Repentance* 1.8.(35), and other works.

[75] Jerome, *Against Pelagius* 2.15.

later, exactly when the LE was circulating in copies of Mark.[76] Later in the 5th century, Hesychius appears to reject the LE without argument (though only in a vague context), while in the 6th century Severus (in a work once attributed to Hesychius) essentially just repeats what Eusebius said about it (see section section 5.3.10 above). Since unlike Jerome their vast knowledge of the mss. is not established, their testimony doesn't independently corroborate Eusebius. The same goes for all subsequent Patristic sources.[77] All other texts attesting to the LE (e.g. the late appendix added to the *Pistis Sophia*, which itself is in no way earlier than the late 4th century) are of such late date as to have no use in deciding the question. We know some copies of Mark ended with the LE in the 4th century, and this version began thereafter to gain in popularity. Hence further evidence only attests to what we already know. There is no other relevant evidence.

5.4 Assessment of External Evidence

From the Patristic evidence we can say with certainty that if the LE existed in the 2nd century, it was extremely rare and hardly anyone knew of it. And there is good reason to believe it was not then known as a part of Mark at all. The only evidence of such is a single passage in Irenaeus (which we have seen is of questionable authenticity) and its use in the *Diatessaron* (of which we have no 2nd century copies but only later corrupted ones). Only by the 4th century can we be certain it was clearly known, and known as an ending to Mark, yet even then it was explicitly known to be rare. Eusebius's account, paraphrased or gainsaid by many authors thereafter, is fairly damning: he certainly had access to numerous mss., and it was his observation that most mss. lacked the LE and

---

[76] Section 5.3.(14) of the *Apostolic Constitutions* clearly just summarizes Matthew, Luke and John, and in a manner conspicuously not conforming to the LE; but section 6.3.(15) directly quotes Mark 16:16 and section 8.1.(1) directly quotes Mark 16:17-18. None of these elements appears in the *Didascalia*. See also the Wikipedia entry for "Apostolic Constitutions" (en.wikipedia.org/wiki/Apostolic_Constitutions).

[77] Hesychius of Jerusalem, *Collection of Difficulties and Solutions* PG 93.1440 (5th century A.D.) simply assumes Mark ends at 16:8. Severus of Antioch, *Homily* 77 (5th/6th century A.D.) repeats Eusebius. See Kelhoffer, "The Witness," pp. 101-102.

that none of the mss. he trusted as the most reliable contained it. He does't even know about the SE.

Such was the state of the matter in the early 4th century. More than half a century later Jerome approvingly echoes Eusebius on this point. But we know Jerome also had access to numerous mss. and was a famous philologer and linguist (himself producing the Vulgate translation of the Bible still used by the Catholic Church and discussing in his letters many manuscripts and variants), so he would not have echoed Eusebius if he did not observe the same still to be true. Only in later centuries did the LE become increasingly more common, eventually eclipsing nearly all mss. that lacked it, even gradually leaking back into all foreign translations in the middle ages. The evidence of the manuscripts (particularly in the myriad early traditions of translation) corroborates this sequence (see sections 5.1 and 5.2). Hence "what became the majority reading in the Middle Ages started out as a minority reading," which indicates the LE was not in the original.[78]

Before the 4th century, none of the evidence that has been touted actually attests to the LE at all, much less as the ending of Mark, except one single reference in Irenaeus. Which by that very fact comes under suspicion. How could no one else ever show any awareness of Mark ending with the LE for nearly two whole centuries, except Irenaeus alone? Indeed, even more inexplicably, he is even represented as taking it for granted, as an undisputed fact, as if he knew of no mss. that lacked the LE and it therefore was in everyone's copy of the Bible—everyone who themselves failed to notice it. And that despite the fact that Eusebius informs us it was a rarely found reading a century later. It could be just luck that no one else who knew of it found occasion to reference it. But this and all other evidence still weighs against this reference in Irenaeus being authentic, and when we combine that fact with the actual evidence of that reference being a later interpolation (and thus not by the hand of Irenaeus after all), it carries force (as shown in section 5.3.5). And even if we accept that passage's authenticity, it can only establish that the LE had been appended to some copies of Mark by 185 A.D., not that it originated with Mark over a century earlier, much less was widely known as the ending of Mark. To the contrary, the most likely way no one else could know

---

[78] Quoting Daniel Wallace, in *PEM*, pp. 24.

of it *and* the majority of mss. a century later lack it is if it did *not* originate with Mark.

The correct theory must explain why so many diverse mss. lack the LE—which means not just the extant ones that do (section 5.1), but all the ones we know must have (5.2, corroborated by Eusebius and Jerome: sections 5.3.10 and 5.3.12). This includes the evidence of the large number of extant mss. that append the LE to the SE, or indicate it as an uncommon reading; the evidence of the many early translation traditions, which entail that several root mss. (the mss. on which the original translations were made) lacked the LE; the evidence of the earliest extant mss. (Vaticanus and Sinaiticus in the Greek, Bobiensis and Vercellensis in the Latin), which all lack the LE; the evidence of the earliest extant Gospel texts (Matthew and Luke both follow Mark closely up to verse 6:8 but then deviate wildly, confirming that even they didn't know the LE); and the evidence of Eusebius and Jerome who both attest directly to the fact that most mss. lacked the LE (again, sections 5.3.10 and 5.3.12). Though all of this is *possible* if the LE were original and lost very early, all of it would be far more *likely* if the LE was added later. When this conclusion is combined with the internal evidence, the case against the LE is decisive.

Either way, the LE has no sound Patristic support as being original to Mark. Meanwhile the SE has no support from the Church Fathers at all (Marcus, *MNT*, p. 1089).

6. Conclusion

Kelhoffer argues (in *MAM*) that the LE was composed between 120-150 A.D. and possibly originated in a text other than Mark and was transferred. Other scholars have concluded the same. I have also presented considerable evidence supporting this conclusion.

However, none of the evidence, even that Kelhoffer presents, establishes the conclusion that the LE had already been appended to Mark by the end of the 2nd century. As I have argued, even the testimony of Irenaeus and the *Diatessaron* are doubtful. However, it's still possible. The LE must have become appended to a copy of Mark at least by the end of the 3rd century, and there is no reason to suppose this can't have happened in the 2nd century. And whenever it occurred, all the same evidence confirms that this is indeed what happened: the LE was appended to Mark, a century or more after Mark was originally written.

The style, logic, and content of the LE all demonstrate against Markan authorship, indeed decisively even by themselves, the more so together (section 4). The manuscript evidence and even the Patristic evidence strongly confirm this conclusion in every respect (section 5). And all the leading experts agree (section 3). There is therefore no rational basis for believing the LE was written by Mark. Yet it is presented as such and appears as such in the canonical Bible.

The authenticity of the SE is even more indefensible. We have seen ample evidence to confirm it is a forgery, and all experts are now unanimous that it is. Thus, whether the LE or SE or both, canonical Mark contains a forgery. This conclusively proves the Bible is not inerrant but contains at least one egregious interpolation, falsely represented as original text, which can be neither true nor inspired.

The Troublesome Evidence for Jesus

17

THE NAZARETH INSCRIPTION

Originally published by The Secular Web in 2000.
© 2000 by Richard Carrier and Internet Infidels®.
Revision © 2014 by Richard Carrier.

Several authors over the years have advanced a particular stone inscription as early evidence of the empty tomb story in the Gospels (and thus also confirming the historicity of Jesus). I will not attempt to trace all uses of this argument (I have encountered several), but I will note the two most important examples: it was used most recently (relative to when I first wrote this) by Norman Geisler and Ron Brooks and most popularly by Josh McDowell.

In Geisler & Brooks we're told:

> A slab of stone was found in Nazareth in 1878, inscribed with a decree from Emperor Claudius (A.D. 41-54) that no graves should be disturbed or bodies extracted or moved. This type of decree is not uncommon, but the startling fact is that here "the offender [shall] be sentenced to capital punishment on [the] charge of violation of [a] sepulchre" (Hemer, *BASHH*, 155). Other notices warned of a fine, but death for disturbing graves? A likely explanation is that Claudius, having heard of the Christian doctrine of resurrection and Jesus' empty tomb while investigating the riots of A.D. 49, decided not to let any such report surface again. This would make sense in light of the Jewish argument that the body had been stolen (Matt.

28:11-15). This is early testimony to the strong and persistent belief that Jesus rose from the dead.[1]

McDowell adds:

> Michael Green [*Man Alive* (1968), p. 36] cites a secular source of early origin that bears testimony to Jesus' empty tomb. This piece of evidence "is called the Nazareth Inscription, after the town where it was found. It is an imperial edict, belonging either to the reign of Tiberius (A.D. 14-37) or of Claudius (A.D. 41-54). And it is an invective, backed with heavy sanctions, against meddling around with tombs and graves! It looks very much as if the news of the empty tomb had got back to Rome in a garbled form (Pilate would have had to report: and he would obviously have said that the tomb had been rifled). This edict, it seems, is the imperial reaction."[2]

How such an inscription makes it "look very much" like the empty tomb story made it to Rome is not immediately obvious to one who is familiar with Roman law: as we shall see in the second part of this essay, the inscription contains nothing new in it, and decrees like this were issued even by emperors as late as Severus (early 3rd century A.D.), thus the inscription bears on an old and never-ending problem, and repeats an old and traditional solution. It thus provides no evidence for any specific event.

---

[1] Norman Geisler and Ron Brooks, *When Skeptics Ask: A Handbook on Christian Evidences* (1990), p. 206. The exact same paragraph appears in Geisler's *Baker Encyclopedia of Christian Apologetics* (1998), p. 48. The link with the Jewish riots in Rome is imaginative but pure speculation. I will discuss those riots in Chapter 20. They had no connection to Christianity.

[2] Josh McDowell, *The New Evidence That Demands a Verdict* (1999). This is the 2nd ed. of the original *ETDAV* publ. in 1972, rev. in 1979. The Nazareth Inscription is mentioned in the 2nd ed., pp. 244-5, § 9.6A.2B.1C; and in the 1st ed., p. 218, § 10.4A.2B.1C. In both places the material is basically identical, except McDowell adds to his 2nd ed. the above quote from Geisler & Brooks (p. 67, § 3.3A.3B.2C.6D). These claims have since become part of the Wikipedia entry for this inscription (en.wikipedia.org/wiki/Nazareth_ Inscription).

THE NAZARETH INSCRIPTION

Green is also wrong when he says that Pilate *had* to report to the emperor: this presumes a level of bureaucracy that did not in fact exist in ancient Rome—until, at best, the time of Diocletian (late 3rd century A.D.), and even the government then is unlikely to have involved such a level of correspondence. Simply put, the Roman Empire lacked the personnel and the finances to handle such a load of paperwork. Rome depended on its governors making hundreds of independent decisions daily—for the emperor had quite enough to do.[3] Try to imagine every attorney general in the United States sending to the President a report on every legal case they had to tackle—even with today's monstrous government and efficient communications this would be absurd. In Rome's empire, governing personnel only referred unsolved problems to the emperor, or matters that bore on the safety of the empire. Though this did happen frequently, there is no evidence or even a claim that Pilate referred to the emperor either the issue of Jesus's execution or any matter of an empty tomb (the late forgery of the *Acts of Pilate* is the exception that proves the rule).

Therefore, there is absolutely nothing linking this inscription with Christianity apart from the town it was found in (even though Jesus was not buried in Nazareth), and its "possible" date (even though Green's dating admits that it may come from well before the time of Jesus's burial), and those details are too trivial to make much of a case (and are probably incorrect to boot). Worse, that same case is weakened by the presence of details in the inscription that have nothing to do with the empty tomb story, so that this decree cannot really be explained as the outcome of that event. These unexplained details are in bold type in the translation below.

To the right is a photograph of the inscription, on a stone slab of 0.6 x 0.375 meters (Photoplate from F. Cumont, *Revue Historique* [Jan-Apr. 1930], p. 243).

---

[3] Consult Fergus Millar, *The Emperor in the Roman World* (1977) and Andrew Lintott, *Imperium Romanum: Politics and Administration* (1993).

Translation

My translation follows, which reads awkwardly not only because I've rendered it literally and line-by-line, but also because its author badly translated the original Latin of the decree (even the Greek is misspelled in places), and appears to have omitted words or placed them out of order.

> Edict[4] of Caesar:
>
> It satisfies me that [regarding] the graves and tombs
> anyone makes **for the cult-worship** of ancestors
> or of children or household members,
> that those [graves and tombs] remain **unmoved**
> throughout their existence. And if anyone charges that
> anyone has either **destroyed them**, or in some other
> way made off with what's buried in them, or to another
> place with knavish malice
> has taken [them], for the purpose of **doing injury** to
> the buried, or [had] the **doorstone**[5] or
> [other] stones **switched**, against that
> man [who is accused] I order that a trial
> occur, just like [a trial] concerning [worship of] gods,
> [only] for the cult-worship of men.
> For it shall be much more necessary

---

[4] I write "edict," following the actual Greek word used, and I use this interchangeably with "decree" and "law" as synonyms throughout this essay, even though there is technically an important difference between an edict, decree, rescript, mandate, and *lex* ("law"). It is unclear whether the inscriber is using the technically correct nomenclature. But the difference doesn't greatly matter to the present discussion.

[5] The word here, *katochos*, means the stone that seals the tomb, but it can also mean the title stone—the stone that states who owns the tomb. Removing the latter is even more obviously a crime. The term is perhaps meant to include both. Zulueta (see below) raises the possibility that the scribe has accidentally added "or" between this word and the next (the mere generic "stone"). That's not an unlikely error for this scribe, and if so the law does not after all refer to just any stones, but *only* these stones specifically. In such a case, "title stone" may be a more likely meaning: what is being outlawed in such a case is theft of a tomb by swapping property markers.

to honor the buried:
[so] let no one at all move them.
Otherwise, that man I
want condemned to death for the charge[6]
of digging through tombs.

Note the details here that require explanation: (1) the law is prefaced by a reference to the importance of family *burial cult*, and thus the motivation for the law seems to have been a grievance against those who were depriving people of the right to pay cult to their dead ancestors, a circumstance that has little connection with the supposed case of the missing body of Jesus; (2) the first thing it aims at preventing is not the taking of bodies, but the *moving of entire tombs and graves*, which makes no sense as a concern that would arise from the mere theft of a body; (3) the second thing it prohibits is the *destroying* of tombs, which again makes no sense in the case of the empty tomb story; (4) the edict goes out of its way to mention a worry that body-snatchers are stealing bodies to *do injury* to them, which again makes no sense as a concern that would arise from the empty tomb account; (5) the law goes out of its way to prohibit *stealing a doorstone*, yet none of the empty tomb accounts mention the stone being carried off, and it is not clear what this would even have to do with that case; (6) then the law prohibits *switching stones*, which likely refers not only to doorstones but to all stones, since the actual word for doorstone is used in the previous section while the generic "stone" is used here, so this is very likely a law against taking a stone from a tomb's walls or alcoves in order to use it elsewhere, and perhaps putting in its place an inferior stone or leaving a gap, a worry that has no link at all with the story of Jesus's tomb, and thus begs for an explanation.

So there are six details in this edict that make no sense at all if it was inspired by the reported theft of Jesus's body, but which do make sense if something much more widespread and quite different was going on that called for such an edict, with so many specific crimes involved, and a central focus on preserving the observation of the proper burial cult for ancestral tombs, and, in

---

[6] There is an important legal distinction here lost on most commentators, but duly noted by Zulueta: the rule says the emperor *orders* a trial to occur (the Latin would be *sic iubeo*), but merely *desires* the death penalty (*sic volo*). In other words, capital punishment is a *recommendation* and not a requirement.

connection with this, preventing tombs from being relocated, and their stones from being stolen. Only in the midst of all this is the theft or abuse of bodies mentioned, and this is obviously connected with the general issue evident throughout the decree, and thus not with a specific theft event such as involved Jesus.

Analysis of the Inscription

An excellent summary of the history and nature of this inscription in English, complete with a list of all other work on it up to that time, is F. de Zulueta's article "Violation of Sepulture in Palestine at the Beginning of the Christian Era," *Journal of Roman Studies* 22 (1932), pp. 184-97, and this relies heavily on the most decisive research and commentary on the stone, available only in the French of F. Cumont's "Un Rescrit Impérial sur la Violation de Sépulture," *Revue Historique* (Jan-Apr. 1930), pp. 241-66. These tell us...

The Date: Zulueta concludes that the most extreme possible dates of the inscription, based on the style of lettering, are 50 B.C. to A.D. 50. He thinks it most likely in the middle, thus around the turn of the era, long before the death of Jesus. Cumont agrees, believing the edict to be of Augustus, although it may even be of Julius Caesar from the time of the Alexandrine War. Both arrive at this conclusion because the edict states simply "Caesar" and does not qualify with the specific successor's name, as is almost always the case. Thus, the claim that it dates to the reign of Tiberius or Claudius is not only unsupported by any evidence, but is all but contradicted by the evidence. A Claudian date was conjectured by Gaetano De Sanctis only because Galilee (where Nazareth is located) was not under the empire until the time of Claudius, but this is not very decisive for two reasons: first, allied states often voluntarily appealed to Julius Caesar or Augustus for a ruling in some issue (especially in time of war, when the power of Rome was the only effective law enforcement around); second, it is very doubtful that the inscription is actually from Nazareth.

The Location: The inscription's origin is not clearly known. It was found in the collection of a man named Fröhner when it was donated to the Paris National Library in 1925. His notes on the item state nothing more than "Dalle de marbre envoyée de Nazareth en 1878." That's it. This translates as "Slab of marble sent from Nazareth in 1878." Zulueta observes that this *does not* say "found" in Nazareth (*découverte à*), but *sent* from there, and it has been shown that Fröhner's "notes on the provenance of his treasures are very exact," thus he can be counted on to have chosen his words carefully.

In the late 19th century there were only two major market centers for all antiquities recovered in Palestine: Jerusalem and Nazareth. Thus, Zulueta makes the plausible conjecture that the slab was recovered either in Samaria or Decapolis and either purchased in or shipped out of the nearest possible place, which would be Nazareth. Indeed, Zulueta also observes that the text uses the plural form "gods" which would have been offensive to Jews, making the most likely origin the Hellenized district of Decapolis. In line with this is the constant emphasis in the decree on the cult worship of the dead, even as being on par with the religious worship of gods, a choice of words and phrases that would not have been much approved by Jews, no matter how much it might have been true, but would have made perfect sense in a community of Greeks. There is a historical event in Samaria that might have served as a cause of this decree. In 8 A.D. some Samaritans entered the Temple after midnight and tossed around corpses they had presumably illegally exumed elsewhere, possibly provoking the recall of the governor Coponius.[7] Even so, Zulueta leans in favor of Decapolis, since this edict seems to be unconnected with a Temple violation, and obviously aimed more at Greeks than Jews.

To this it can be added that a tiny village of no more than a few hundred inhabitants, none of whom are even remotely likely to have been literate (or even speakers of Greek), is not where such an inscription would be set up.[8] Jerusalem would have been a candidate, but not Nazareth, where the inscription would be useless

---

[7] Josephus, *Jewish Antiquities* 18.29. The passage is problematic. It's not clear what the Samaritans were up to, what the point was for Josephus to mention it, or whether something has become corrupt or omitted in his text here.

[8] It's still debated how widely known the Greek language was in Galilee during the time of Jesus. But pretty much everyone agrees it was not the norm. That does not mean Greek language and culture were wholly unknown there, only that we should not expect Greek inscriptions to have been erected in Galilee at this time—least of all without a translation into Hebrew or Aramaic. That would be like promulgating laws in Mexico in English.

and a pointless expense. Though the poor quality of the inscription demonstrates that it was put up by a private person, who either was or hired a scribe who was somewhat incompetent in Greek (but who apparently knew Latin), even this sort of person would not go to all this trouble and expense to put up a slab like this where no one would read it—though even if he did, its location would have nothing to do with the interests of the emperor or governor.[9] And again, since the tomb Jesus's body would have been stolen from was not in Nazareth or even Galilee, it would make no sense for an inscription responding to that incident to be erected there.

All of the above evidence decides fairly strongly against a Nazarene provenance, and in favor of an Augustan date.

Laws Against Graverobbing

Whatever the case, it was probably already a capital crime for non-Romans to disturb graves in the time of Julius Caesar. So this Nazareth Inscription cannot represent a new law, and therefore is even less likely to be connected with Jesus in any specific way, even if post-Augustan.

We know that at one point the law was as follows: Gaius, in a textbook on Roman law called the *Institutes* (c. 160 A.D.), speaking in the context of traditional law, says that as soon as a body is buried in a tomb by its owner, the tomb and body become *religiosus*, consecrated to the gods of the underworld. Violation of any such thing is an act of sacrilege (*Inst.* 2.2-10). When we examine the Nazareth Inscription, this is what we see happening: Roman law is being promulgated among Greeks. First, the Roman idea that trials concerning tombs of men are just like trials concerning the things of the gods is an explanation of the Roman legal principle of *religiosum*. The rest of the law is therefore an elaboration of the Roman crime of sacrilege, being applied to a previously non-Roman territory.

Marcian's *Institutes* (c. 310 A.D.) reports that:

---

[9] Zulueta notes that "Hellenistic sepulchral inscriptions are found which put civil and criminal prosecution side by side" (p. 190), citing F. Wamser, *De iure sepulcrali Romanorum quid tituli doceant* (1887), pp. 31-35. This may be one of those: a stone set up over someone's tomb to discourage (at least literate) thieves.

> It is laid down further in the mandates on sacrilege that provincial governors are to track down those who commit sacrilege, brigands, and kidnappers, and punish each according to the degree of his offense. And it is so provided in the constitutions, that those who commit sacrilege are to be punished with a fitting penalty *extra ordinem*.[10]

The trial and crucifixion of Jesus is an example of a trial *extra ordinem*. It essentially means the governor has a *carte blanche* when it comes to deciding guilt and punishment. Note, also, how in Roman legal texts sacrilege is equated with brigandage and kidnapping—it was thus always an extremely grave crime.

What penalties were typical? Ulpian's *Duties of the Proconsul* (c. 220 A.D.) states that "Many have been condemned to the wild beasts for sacrilege, some even burned alive, and others hanged on the gallows." Even the lightest penalty is "deportation to an island." (*Dut. Proc.* 7; cf. *Dig.* 48.13.7) and in his Praetor's Edict from the same period "the action for violation of a tomb entails *infamia*" (*Praet. Ed.* 2; *Dig.* 47.12.1), i.e. "disgrace," a formal legal term entailing loss of important rights as well as gaining a severely poor reputation—the criminal becomes "infamous" and loses the right to represent himself or others in any court of law, and the right to stand for or hold any office.[11] Ulpian continues that "by tomb we understand any place of burial" (*Praet. Ed.* 25; *Dig.* 47.12.3.2), and that Septimius Severus (between 193 and 211 A.D.) reinforced by decree that "corpses are not to be detained or molested" (ibid.; *Dig.* 47.12.3.3) and that "provincial governors are to take severe action against those who despoil corpses" (ibid.; *Dig.* 47.12.3.7).

---

[10] Marcion, *Inst.* 14; cf. *Digest of Justinian* 48.13.4.2 The latter is a collection of laws made in the 6th century A.D. by imperial order, drawing on laws from as early as the Republic. The editors were known to alter texts to make them coherent and contemporary, but in this case it's most unlikely that what I discuss was not already the law even in Republican times (hence pre-Christian). Imperial edicts often aimed at reinforcing already-existing laws, not merely creating new ones, and this is even more the case when Roman law was being applied to regions where it was not already standard. I rely on the translations of Alan Watson (1985), and shall abbreviate this work from now on as *Dig*.

[11] See Simon Hornblower and Antony Spawforth, eds., *Oxford Classical Dictionary*, 3rd ed. (1996), s.v. "*infamia*."

Though these sources are late, they are almost certainly reflecting and codifying laws and traditions that are very old. In fact, that Severus would have to reinforce the law about bodies by decree shows that emperors more than once had occasion to issue such decrees for reasons entirely unrelated to Christianity, and therefore the Nazareth Inscription can have no certain connection with Jesus. It also shows that no matter how severe the laws, people still broke them, and regularly got away with it, so much so that frustrated emperors had to keep issuing decrees—considering the near total lack of a system of criminal detectives in the ancient world, and the complete absence of forensic techniques, laws were notoriously difficult to enforce.

Ulpian then reports in the same passage that despoiling of corpses had granted a civil action since the time of Labeo, i.e. *before* Augustus and thus well before the date of Jesus. This civil action likely coexisted with the criminal action for sacrilege.[12] The loss of a civil suit very often resulted in *infamia* for the defendant—though this could be avoided by settling out of court.[13]

Finally, Macer's *Public Prosecutions* (c. 230 A.D.) reports that "the offense of violating a tomb can be said to come under the *Lex Julia de vi publica*...where it is provided that nothing shall be done to prevent the occupant from being entombed" (*Pub. Pros.* 1; *Dig.* 47.12.8). By definition, a *Lex Julia* was passed by Julius Caesar or Augustus, and therefore this law would have already been in place

---

[12] Zulueta assumes that the seemingly more popular recourse to a civil action entails that there was no criminal action until late, but this is not sound reasoning. It was quite common for a victim, just like today, to have simultaneous recourse to *both* a civil and a criminal action: see Barry Nichols, *An Introduction to Roman Law* (1962). Indeed, Zulueta's only evidence of the "popularity" of the civil action is its existence in what is reconstructed to have been the Praetor's Edict under the (pre-Christian) Republic, but since that edict *only* dealt with civil actions, we will not see in such a source any of the corresponding criminal actions that were available. He is thus falling victim to selection bias.

[13] On what these facts would mean regarding the accounts of Jesus' burial and allegations of his corpse's disappearance if Jesus *did* exist, see my discussions in *TET$_b$* and *TET$_t$* (with www.infidels.org/library/modern/richard_carrier/nazarethlaw.html#12 and #14 and www.richardcarrier.info/Carrier--ReplyToDavis.html#corpses).

in Jesus's day.[14] The particular law in question here is a law against the use of force in public, such as any act of breaking and entering entails, and like most felonies was a capital crime for non-citizens. Paul's *Views* (c. 220 A.D.) concludes that:

> Those guilty of violating tombs, if they remove the bodies or scatter the bones, will suffer the supreme penalty [i.e. death] if they be of the lower orders; if they be more reputable, they are deported to an island. Otherwise, the latter will be relegated [i.e. banished] and the former condemned to the mines. (*Views* 5; *Dig.* 47.12.11)

In Paul's day this distinction between higher and lower persons replaced what had formerly distinguished citizen and non-citizen (in Paul's day, all inhabitants of the empire were citizens, by imperial decree as of 212 A.D.).

All of this evidence favors the conclusion that the Nazareth Inscription was merely extending or explaining already-existing Roman law to an Eastern province, and is not a novel decree.

Conclusion

The Nazareth Inscription provides no evidence for Christianity or Jesus or the Gospels' claim of an empty tomb. It contains no new or unusual laws regarding graverobbing, the decree itself is not unique, and it has no references or direct links to Christianity of any kind. Moreover, its date is most likely pre-Christian, its origin is not likely to be Nazareth or even Judea, and its contents are not explainable even as a *muddled* imperial reaction to the theft of Jesus' body. Its contents refer to Gentile polytheistic religious practices and a broad range of criminal activities wholly unrelated to the Gospel narratives. To tie this to Christianity requires piling dozens

---

[14] Here is an occasion to point out how this differs from an edict or rescript (see note 4): this *Lex* would have been proposed by either Julius Caesar or Augustus, and then actually passed by popular vote of all the citizens of Rome. Thus, the Nazareth Inscription is not a *Lex*, since the people of Rome are not mentioned, though it may borrow entirely from, or expand upon, an existing *Lex* (or a *Senatus Consultum*, a kind of unofficial "law" passed by the Senate alone, a Republican precedent to the Imperial "decree") in order to transfer or advertise Roman laws to non-Roman peoples.

of conjectures onto scores of speculations, and the rejection of a good supply of contrary indications and evidence, none of which is either necessary or reasonable.

18

THALLUS AND THE DARKNESS AT CHRIST'S DEATH

This article first appeared in the Journal of Greco-Roman
Christianity and Judaism *8 (2011-2012): 185-91.
Copyright © 2012 Sheffield-Phoenix Press.
Reproduced with permission.*

It is commonly claimed that a chronologer named Thallus, writing shortly after 52 A.D., mentioned the crucifixion of Jesus and the noontime darkness surrounding it (which reportedly eclipsed the whole world for three hours), and attempted to explain it as an ordinary solar eclipse.[1] But this is not a credible interpretation of the evidence. A stronger case can be made that we actually have a direct quotation of what Thallus said, and it does not mention Jesus.

The darkness at Christ's death is first mentioned in the Synoptic Gospels, which all derive the claim from the same source: the Gospel according to Mark.[2] The Gospel according to John makes no mention of it (no reference to it appears in the account of Jesus' death in John 19 or elsewhere) nor does any other New Testament writer. For all that we know, the claim was invented by

---

[1] For typical (and, as will be shown here, often erroneous) views and further references, see Robert Van Voorst, *Jesus outside the New Testament: An Introduction to the Ancient Evidence* (Grand Rapids: Eerdmans, 2000), pp. 20-23; and Gerd Theissen and Annette Merz, *The Historical Jesus: A Comprehensive Guide* (Minneapolis: Fortress Press, 1996), pp. 84-85. [Note that for the present volume all dates have been converted from CE/BCE to AD/BC; see Chapter 4. Unicode Greek has also been converted to standard Roman transliteration.]

[2] Mk. 15.33; Mt. 27.45; Lk. 23.44-45. Some later (apocryphal) Gospels and texts (like the Gospel of Nicodemus) also borrow or even embellish the claim.

Mark, either to fulfill prophecy[3] or to symbolize Jesus' death as that of a great king.[4] The event was certainly unhistorical. The crucifixion by all accounts occurred on or near the Passover, which always took place during a full moon when a solar eclipse is impossible (the moon being then on the other side of the planet), and solar eclipses last only minutes, not three hours, and darken only a relatively narrow track along the earth, not the whole world. Such an impossible event would not fail to be widely recorded among the records and authors of the era. A more ordinary event (like a dense cloud-front passing over Jerusalem in just those three hours) is clearly not what was imagined by the Synoptic authors. Luke outright calls the event an eclipse of the sun, and Mark surely intended something as awesome.

It is in this context that the following quote is often cited, which was preserved by the ninth-century Christian chronologer George Syncellus from a now lost work by the early third-century Christian author Julius Africanus:

> This event followed each of his deeds, and healings of body and soul, and knowledge of hidden things, and his resurrection from the dead, all sufficiently proven to the disciples before us and to his apostles: after the most dreadful darkness fell over the whole world, the rocks were torn apart by an earthquake and much of Judaea and the rest of the land was torn

---

[3] Most likely Amos 8.9 ("I will cause the sun to go down at noon, and I will darken the earth in the clear day"; v. 8 even mentions an earthquake, duly inserted by Matthew in 27.51-53), but there were many to choose from, none of which were any stranger than others the New Testament authors regarded as prophecies of their Christ: e.g. Mic. 7.8; Amos 5.20; Joel 2.31-32; Ezek. 32.7-8; Isa. 60.1-2.

[4] It was common lore of the time that the sun would be eclipsed at the death of a great king: John Lydus, *Ost.* 70a; see, for example, Herodotus, *Hist.* 7.37; Plutarch, *Pel.* 31.3 and *Aem.* 17.7-11; Dio Cassius, *Hist. Rom.* 55.29.3.

down.[5] Thallus calls this darkness an eclipse of the sun in the third book of his *Histories*, without reason it seems to me. For the Hebrews celebrate the passover on the 14th day, reckoning by the lunar calendar, and the events concerning the savior all occurred before the first day of the Passover. But an eclipse of the sun happens when the moon creeps under the sun, and this is impossible at any other time but between the first day of the moon's waxing and the day before that, when the new moon begins. So how are we to believe that an eclipse happened when the moon was diametrically opposite the sun? In fact, let it be so. Let the idea that this happened seize and carry away the multitude, and let the cosmic prodigy be counted as an eclipse of the sun according to its appearance. [Phlegon reports that in the time of Tiberius Caesar, during the full moon, a full eclipse of the sun happened, from the sixth hour until the ninth. Clearly this is our eclipse!] What is commonplace about an earthquake, an eclipse, rocks torn apart, a rising of the dead, and such a huge cosmic movement? At the very least, over a long period, no conjunction this great is remembered. But it was a godsent darkness, because the Lord happened to suffer, and the Bible, in Daniel, supports

---

[5] Likewise mythical. The occurrence of a rock-splitting earthquake is claimed in only one source (Mt. 27.51-53, thus it is not even in Matthew's own source, Mark, nor corroborated by Luke or John) and is surely a fabrication: the complete absence of its social and material effects in the narrative of Acts is sufficient proof, but it likewise gets no notice in any other writer of the era, nor finds any archaeological support (yet material evidence of such a thing as Africanus describes would certainly be detectable now). The only earthquake confirmed for Palestine between 26 and 36 A.D. was 'not energetic enough to produce' visible effects of this magnitude, in contrast with another in 31 B.C. already noted by Josephus and extensively confirmed in surviving physical evidence (including cracked rocks and damaged human structures), according to Jefferson B. Williams, Markus J. Schwab and A. Brauer, "An Early First-Century Earthquake in the Dead Sea," *International Geology Review* 54.10 (May 2012), pp. 1219-28.

that seventy spans of seven years would come together up to this time.[6]

From this it is not clear what Thallus actually said. All we are told is that "Thallus calls *this* darkness an eclipse of the sun in the third book of his *Histories*," which does not actually say Thallus mentioned Jesus. That inference may derive from Julius Africanus. The fact that he felt free to make such an inference from Phlegon (who, as we shall later see, did not say the eclipse lasted three hours, or that it occurred during a full moon, nor placed it anywhere near Palestine—yet the remark here assumes he said all three) leaves us free to assume he did much the same with Thallus. Unless, as seems likely, this entire reference to Phlegon is an interpolation,[7] but even if so, the interpolator was making the same loose inferences, and thus so might Africanus have been. If Thallus connected an eclipse with a destructive earthquake in the same year Africanus had just calculated the crucifixion must have occurred (which year he derives prophetically from Daniel, rather than from a historical source), that would be enough to lead Africanus to conclude Thallus was talking about 'this' same darkness (the one Africanus had just mentioned, which also occurred alongside a destructive earthquake). We cannot claim to be certain Africanus meant anything more than that.

---

[6] Julius Africanus, *Chron.* 18.2 (as preserved in George Syncellus, *Chron.* 391). For a thorough and still essential and illuminating discussion of this passage, see Felix Jacoby, *Fragmente der griechischen Historiker* (Leiden: Brill, 1954), § 256 (Thallus) and § 257 (Phlegon). For a translation and commentary of Jacoby's § 256, see Richard Carrier, "Jacoby and Müller on 'Thallus'," *The Secular Web* (1999) at www.infidels.org/library/modern/richard_carrier/jacoby.html. The passage quoted here from Julius Africanus is presented and discussed by Jacoby in § 256 F1.

[7] That it is likely an interpolation was astutely noticed by Martin Routh, *Reliquiae Sacrae* (1814), II, pp. 335-38. Hence I put it in brackets to show how it breaks the flow of argument and to indicate that it is uncertain from the hand of Africanus. There are various telltale signs (grammatical and rhetorical), but most indicative is the fact that Africanus is making the point that the conjunction of events (eclipse, earthquake, resurrections) is what is remarkable, yet doesn't think to mention that Phlegon also reported a conjunction (of eclipse and earthquake), thus this remark is disconnected from the argument being made. It looks like an accidental interpolation of a later marginal note, on which phenomenon, quite common in manuscript transmission generally, see [Chapter 19, pp. 339-40].

That alone is enough to alert us that this reference may be unreliable in the study of early Christianity and its sources and claims. But the problems multiply.

Dating Thallus

We do not know when Thallus wrote. Claims are boldly made that it must have been shortly after 52 A.D., but that is based solely on a conjectural emendation of a corrupted text.[8] In an Armenian translation of the *Chronicle* of Eusebius, a list of references is given (not preserved in the Greek) in which Eusebius says he used "three volumes of Thallus, in which he made a summary in abbreviated fashion from the sack of Troy to the 167th Olympiad," which would mean from the twelfth century B.C. until 109 B.C., concluding much too early for Thallus to have covered events in the first century A.D.[9] But this passage must be referring to the same Histories cited by Africanus, since if Thallus had written other books on chronology or history the reference in Eusebius would have been more specific (that he just says "the three volumes of Thallus" means he was certain no one would be confused as to which treatise was meant, or which Thallus), and Africanus says he found the reference to an event at the time of Christ in the third volume of Thallus, which perfectly fits a three volume work that concluded its timeline in the first (or second) century. So it seems most likely that the Armenian text has become corrupted, and the concluding date was something other than 109 B.C.

---

[8] The 'corroborating' claim that a Thallus is mentioned by Josephus as living in the reign of Tiberius is not only false (the text [of Josephus] does not present the name Thallus), it is irrelevant (as no mention is made there of this person being a writer, and the name Thallus, even were it there, was common). This has long been known (see Horace Rigg, "Thallus: The Samaritan?" *HTR* 34 [1941], pp. 111-19), so no historian today should still repeat these claims. For further discussion of this problem, see P. Prigent, "Thallos, Phlégon et le Testimonium Flavianum témoins de Jésus?" in Frederick Bruce (ed.), *Paganisme, Judaïsme, Christianisme: Influences et Affrontements dans le Monde Antique* (Paris: Bocard, 1978), pp. 329-34; and Ida Miévis, "A propos de la correction 'Thallos' dans les 'Antiquités Judaïques' de Flavius Josèphe," *Revue Belge de Philologie et d'Histoire* 13 (1934), pp. 733-40.

[9] Jacoby, *Fragmente*, § 256 T1.

Indeed that is what most scholars have concluded. However, it is typically claimed that the most likely correction to the text brings us a closing date at the 207th Olympiad, or 52 A.D., but there is no solid basis for this conclusion. That is simply one suggestion made by one textual critic (and that two hundred years ago). In actual fact, any number of corruptions were possible (far beyond those that have happened to be suggested), and some are even more likely than this one. Apart from probability there is no principled way to choose between them—while choosing on the grounds of probability would sooner indicate an original reading of the 217th Olympiad, which ends in 92 A.D., or even the 227th or 237th Olympiads, which end in 132 or 172 A.D. respectively.[10] In other words, the date 52 A.D. may not be right at all. The correct logic would hold that Thallus most likely wrote in the second century, since pagan notice of the Gospels is unattested before that century, and any given author is more likely to be typical than wholly exceptional. If, that is, Thallus was responding to the Gospels. But that is very unlikely.

What Thallus Said

The *Chronicle* of Eusebius quotes Phlegon verbatim, the text of which is attested in Syncellus in the original Greek, but also in the Latin of Jerome, a Syrian epitome, and the Armenian. Translating from the Greek:

> Jesus Christ, according to the prophecies which had been foretold, underwent his passion in the 18th year of Tiberius [32 A.D.]. Also at that time in other Greek

---

[10] An analysis is provided in Carrier, "Jacoby." The conjecture that produces an end-date of 52 A.D. requires transforming the Greek numeral ρχζ into οζ, while the conjecture that produces an end-date of 92 A.D. requires transforming ρχζ into οιζ, either way two errors (or even three in the former case), while a likelier error (on grounds of orthography) would be to mistake ρχζ for σκζ, which brings us an end date of the 227th Olympiad, which concludes in 132 A.D., or even to mistake ρχζ for σλζ, which brings us an end date of the 237th Olympiad, which concludes in 172 A.D. These are just the most likely. Any number of other errors could have occurred, giving us virtually any conceivable date. And this end date is also not necessarily the publication date (Thallus may have brought his chronology only up to a certain year, possibly decades before his own time).

compendiums we find an event recorded in these words: "the sun was eclipsed, Bithynia was struck by an earthquake, and in the city of Nicaea many buildings fell." All these things happened to occur during the Lord's passion. In fact, Phlegon, too, a distinguished reckoner of Olympiads, wrote more on these events in his 13th book, saying this: "Now, in the fourth year of the 202nd Olympiad [32 A.D.], a great eclipse of the sun occurred at the sixth hour [i.e. noon] that excelled every other before it, turning the day into such darkness of night that the stars could be seen in heaven, and the earth moved in Bithynia, toppling many buildings in the city of Nicaea."[11]

We know Eusebius used a chronology of Thallus as a source, and that it was almost certainly the very same *Histories* cited by Africanus. The implications of this are decisive: if the *Histories* of Thallus mentioned the eclipse in connection with Jesus, Eusebius would certainly have quoted Thallus here to that very effect. Instead, Eusebius knows only a passage in Phlegon (the one also referenced in the extant text of Africanus, although here, notably, quoted verbatim, even though it *does not* mention Jesus, proving how more certainly Eusebius would have quoted *Thallus* verbatim if *he* had mentioned Jesus) and "other Greek chronologers." The latter must mean Thallus, as well as, if we take the intention to be plural, some others who repeated the same exact line—possibly compilers who, like Eusebius now, were just quoting Thallus—because Eusebius says they all recorded the event *kata lexin tauta* "with this phrase."

It is even possible (in fact, more than merely possible) that Eusebius originally wrote *en thallou men hellênikois hypomnêmasin* rather than *en allois men hellênikois hypomnêmasin*, since only two errors are required to alter the one to the other (the loss of a theta, and a confusion or 'emendation' converting an upsilon to iota-sigma, thereby transforming *thallou* into *allois*). In fact, the plural *allois*, even if original, can mean the singular ("*a* Greek compendium"), since the adjective modifies the noun, and the noun is always plural (e.g. Thallus's book is the *Histories*, plural), and therefore Eusebius might in fact be quoting a single treatise, the *Histories* of Thallus, just

---

[11] George Syncellus, *Chron.* 394.

without bothering to name him. This conclusion requires no conjectured error in the text (it can be what the text as we have it literally means). But arguing for a corrupted text (and that Eusebius actually named and was originally *explicitly* quoting Thallus) is the fact that it seems odd to say "another Greek compendium" before you have named even one. Replace "another" with "Thallus's" and the passage makes much better sense. But even if Eusebius really said (and meant) 'other' Greek writers, he must have meant Thallus among them.

This conclusion follows from three undeniable premises: Eusebius is quoting some number of unnamed Greek chronologers who wrote the same line; Eusebius was using Thallus, a Greek chronologer, as a source, and almost certainly the very same book by Thallus that Africanus cited; and Eusebius does not reference or quote Thallus here in any other respect, even though he certainly would have (and thus certainly is). For if he bothered to do this for Phlegon and other 'unnamed' authors who mention the same event, he could hardly have omitted Thallus (*especially* if Thallus actually mentioned Jesus, since none of these other authors did). So we must assume he is not omitting Thallus, but including him among the several 'others' (or the one 'other') he quotes a line from. Therefore we can conclude that to a very high probability the passage in the third book of the *Histories* of Thallus that Julius Africanus was referring to said only this: "The sun was eclipsed; Bithynia was struck by an earthquake; and in the city of Nicaea many buildings fell." This means Thallus probably made no reference to Jesus, nor showed any knowledge of the Gospels (e.g. the eclipse is not said to have occurred in Palestine; and Bithynia is in Turkey, nowhere near Palestine). This would also argue for the conclusion that Thallus wrote after Phlegon (whose work is usually dated between 120 and 140 A.D.), as the line being quoted from Thallus appears to be an abbreviation of Phlegon, repeating the exact same sequence of eclipse of the sun, earthquake in Bithynia, and collapsed buildings in Nicaea, just with the details stripped away.

The curtness and brevity of this line is also what would be expected from a treatise that covered the history of the entire world over the enormous course of twelve centuries in only three scrolls. Whereas, by contrast, refutation of claims made in the literature of obscure cults is what would *not* be expected from such a treatise, there being neither room nor purpose for such a thing.

Therefore the *Histories* of Thallus probably contained no such thing. And from the evidence of Eusebius, we can be virtually certain that it did not. Therefore Thallus should be removed from lists of writers attesting to Jesus, and Thallus's most probable floruit should be revised to the middle or late second century.

19

ORIGEN, EUSEBIUS, AND THE ACCIDENTAL INTERPOLATION IN JOSEPHUS, *JEWISH ANTIQUITIES* **20.200**

This article first appeared in the *Journal of Early Christian Studies* 20.4 (Winter 2012): 489-514.
Copyright © 2012 by Johns Hopkins University Press and the North American Patristics Society.
Reproduced with permission.

SUMMARY: Analysis of the evidence from the works of Origen, Eusebius, and Hegesippus concludes that the reference to "Christ" in Josephus, *Jewish Antiquities* 20.200 is probably an accidental interpolation or scribal emendation and that the passage was never originally about Christ or Christians. It referred not to James the brother of Jesus Christ, but probably to James the brother of the high priest Jesus ben Damneus.

There are two mentions of Jesus Christ in the extant manuscripts of Josephus's writings: 1) a full paragraph at Jewish Antiquities (*AJ*) 18.63–64, now called the Testimonium Flavianum (TF), that most commentators agree has been deliberately meddled with (if not wholly forged) by Christian scribes, and 2) a brief mention at *AJ* 20.200 in association with the execution of a certain James, which notably does not refer back to the other passage. The TF has already generated a vast literature and I will not treat the subject here except to say that I side with those scholars who conclude that the entire passage is an interpolation and that there was no mention of Jesus in the original text of *AJ* 18.¹ Here I address the second passage, arguing that there was no mention of Jesus Christ in *AJ* 20 either. This instance was not a deliberate interpolation, but an accidental one that occurred in a manuscript transcribed and held in the Christian library of Caesarea sometime between the death of Origen and the writings of Eusebius, most likely between 254 and 315 A.D.²

---

¹ For detailed surveys and discussion of the scholarship on this passage see James Carleton Paget, "Some Observations on Josephus and Christianity," *Journal of Theological Studies* 52 (2001): 539–624, esp. 546–54, which treats the scholarship on the passage in *AJ* 20.200. See also Alice Whealey, *Josephus on Jesus: The Testimonium Flavianum Controversy from Late Antiquity to Modern Times* (New York: Peter Lang, 2003), and Robert Van Voorst, *Jesus Outside the New Testament: An Introduction to the Ancient Evidence* (Grand Rapids, MI: William B. Eerdmans, 2000), 81–104. Paget argues for some part of the TF being original, but concedes this can only be based on conjecture and that it is entirely possible there was none. There are many reasons to doubt any part of the TF was originally there, but two in my opinion are decisive and even argue against the "emended" versions some scholars propose. First, the paragraph that follows the TF begins with, "About the same time also another sad calamity put the Jews into disorder..." (*AJ* 18.65), thereby indicating that Josephus had just ended with the sedition resulting in a public massacre described in *AJ* 18.60–62, and leaving no logical place for the unrelated digression on Jesus and the Christians (*AJ* 18.63–64). Second, the fact that the next story about a controversy involving Judaism and Isis cult is told at great length (*AJ* 18.65–80—a narrative eight times longer than the TF, but on a much more trivial affair) suggests that Josephus would have written a great deal more about the Jesus affair had he written anything about it at all, whereas a forger would have been limited [or believed he was] by the remaining space available on a standard scroll (hence explaining the TF's bizarre brevity, in comparison with the preceding and following narratives, and in light of its astonishing content, which normally would require several explanations and digressions, which are curiously absent). Both facts strongly demonstrate that there cannot have been here any reference to Jesus in the original *AJ*, even one differently worded than we now have. [UPDATE: I now consider the case to be closed: the TF is wholly a forgery. See note 11.]

² Many scholars have already proposed that the reference in *AJ* 20 is an interpolation; see G.A. Wells, *Did Jesus Exist?* (Amherst, NY: Prometheus Books, 1975), 11; K.A. Olson, "Eusebius and the Testimonium Flavianum," *Catholic Biblical Quarterly* 61 (1999): 305–22, at 315; and Paget, "Some Observations," 546–47 (even Paget himself entertains the possibility: 552 n. 45). I will not merely propose it; I will come as near to proving it as extant evidence will allow. [UPDATE: for the present volume all dates have been converted from CE/BCE to AD/BC; see Chapter 4.]

On the General Notion of
Accidental Interpolation

As manuscripts were copied by hand, it often happened that text became accidentally skipped over or left out. When this error was noticed upon proofreading (when no erasure or "do over" was practical), the omitted text would be written in the margins or between the lines, sometimes with a mark indicating its place (in much the same way modern editors indicate corrective insertions even now). But scribes and scholars also often scribbled the equivalent of "footnotes" (and glosses and passage labels and other notes and commentary) in the margins or between the lines of manuscripts, sometimes again with a mark indicating its place (to which the note refers). As there was no standard notation for distinguishing marginal notes from accidentally omitted text, we have countless examples of such notes being accidentally interpolated into the text of other manuscripts. A later scribe simply mistook the marginal note as accidentally omitted text and, upon creating a copy, "rectified" the error by "reinserting" it, thus creating an altered sentence that appears to be what its author originally wrote, but is not.

According to manuscript specialist F.W. Hall, "the casual jottings of readers and correctors are often imported into the text" in this way, hence he dedicates an entire section in his manual on textual criticism to "insertion of interlinear or marginal glosses or notes" as a common cause of erroneous interpolation in manuscripts.[3] Robert Renehan agrees that "marginal confusions… occur frequently in mss.," giving several examples (e.g. §35 shows several "marginal scholia which have been incorporated into the text" of Epicurus's letters, in some cases, entire sentences).[4] In his own brief survey, Miroslav Marcovich documents at least thirty-three examples of this kind of mistake in the works of the early church fathers, and he was not even trying to be

---

[3] See F.W. Hall, *A Companion to Classical Texts* (Oxford: Clarendon Press, 1913), 193–97, quoted at 194.

[4] Robert Renehan, *Greek Textual Criticism: A Reader* (Cambridge, MA: Harvard University Press, 1969), 36 (§32).

comprehensive.⁵ The standard manual on textual criticism by Maas thus includes this as a common error to look for.⁶

Once such a note was made, any reader could interpret it as omitted text and thus even quote that text with the note interpolated. And when a copy was made (as when an aging or damaged manuscript was renewed, or an additional copy was produced for distribution), the interpolation would be included without any mention of the fact that the text had ever read any other way. From then on, the reader would be unable to know where the inserted text originated from or even that it had been inserted. All subsequent copies would appear likewise. All along, however, it would just have been an innocent mistake.

ON THE ORIGIN OF EUSEBIUS'S
MANUSCRIPTS OF JOSEPHUS

Around 231 A.D., Origen established a Christian library in Caesarea, which was passed to Pamphilus and then to Eusebius.⁷ Eusebius was thus in all likelihood using the very same manuscripts of Josephus that Origen had been using, or else copies thereof. The extant text of the TF is virtually identical in both all surviving manuscripts and multiple quotations of it by Eusebius (e.g., *Evangelical Demonstration* 3.5 and *Ecclesiastical History* 1.11). As already noted, many scholars agree that that version is not original to Josephus, but underwent considerable (and deliberate) Christian revision (or outright insertion).

---

⁵ Miroslav Marcovich, *Patristic Textual Criticism* (Atlanta, GA: Scholars Press, 1994), s.v. "Interpolations" in the index.

⁶ Paul Maas, *Textual Criticism*, trans. Barbara Flower (Oxford: Clarendon Press, 1958), 34–35 (§33) and 14 (§16). See also Martin West, *Textual Criticism and Editorial Technique Applicable to Greek and Latin Texts* (Stuttgart: B. G. Teubner, 1973), 28. I have personally verified numerous examples of whole sentences accidentally interpolated into the *Weights and Measures* of Epiphanius (which I presented in a paper "Scribal Error and the Destruction of the Library of Alexandria" at the Repetition and Error conference sponsored by the Department of Classics, University of California at Berkeley, on March 12, 2005), and those are confirmed cases where we have earlier versions of the text and can verify additions to the original.

⁷ For a full account of this library and Eusebius's use of it, see Andrew Carriker, *The Library of Eusebius of Caesarea* (Boston: Brill, 2003).

In fact, the TF in that precise form was almost certainly not known to Origen, as there are several passages where it is almost certain he would have remarked upon it, even quoted it, had he known of it.[8] For example, at *Against Celsus* 1.47, Origen is tasked with proving that contemporaries or near-contemporaries of Jesus attested to his affairs (the very task he sets forth in *Against Celsus* 1.42, in response to the several challenges made by Celsus at *Against Celsus* 1.37–41), yet his only pieces of evidence are Josephan passages attesting John the Baptist and James. We would expect Origen to have used the TF at many other points in *Against Celsus* to attest to Jesus' ministry and wisdom in order to dismiss Celsus's argument that Jesus was a charlatan, to corroborate Jesus' resurrection on the third day in order to challenge Celsus's insistence that this is merely a Christian claim, and to confirm that Jesus had fulfilled prophecy, a major concern of Origen's and one for which the TF would have provided priceless attestation.

To explain away Origen's silence (Paget surveys several attempts) would require adopting at least one baseless hypothesis (e.g., that Josephus had written something wildly different, which the TF then replaced), illogical hypothesis (e.g., if the original TF had treated Christians negatively, Origen would have been more likely to respond, not less so, since he would not want Celsus or any other critic to cite Josephus, whose authority Origen praises, against him—without a preemptive apologetic), or irrelevant hypothesis (e.g., explaining Origen's silence by supposing that Josephus said something else about Jesus in the current location of the TF). These *ad hoc* and faulty hypotheses only affirm the present conclusion: the TF as contained in all extant manuscripts of the *AJ*, if at all, cannot have been known to Origen, yet it is identical to what was known to Eusebius.

We must conclude that all extant manuscripts of the *AJ* almost certainly derive from the manuscript used by Eusebius, which was likely a copy of the manuscript used by Origen. Other authors' *quotations* of the TF, however, may or may not derive from this

---

[8] In fact, not a single writer before Eusebius refers to it, but Origen most conspicuously. On both points (and all related arguments), see Paget, "Some Observations," 555–65, and Whealey, *Josephus on Jesus*, 6–18.

same manuscript tradition. This is endlessly debated,[9] but I must issue a major caution in using this data (echoed by both Paget and Whealey). A continual problem is that quotations often deviate from the originals (not just when Josephus is being quoted; Eusebius himself, or his later copyists, frequently introduce deviations in his quotations, even when repeating the exact same quotation). Copyists can have their own agendas (many of which Paget surveys) or commit errors in reproducing a text—not only in producing the manuscripts an author quotes (which thus may yet derive from the same manuscript used by Eusebius, only with deviations introduced deliberately or by error), but in copying the author who does the quoting, i.e. we do not have the originals, so we cannot be certain their quotations did not more closely correspond to the Eusebian (and Josephan) text. These problems magnify when we are dealing not with quotations of the original Greek, but with translations in other languages (as most of these external quotes happen to be). We have countless examples of intentional and unintentional distortions entering the textual tradition of other quotations in ancient and medieval manuscripts; we have no reason to expect any more fidelity in the case of Josephus. As Paget warns, the variants of the TF in quotation are so numerous, chaotic, and inconclusive that textual criticism can make little headway with them.

For example, Whealey has argued that the original Eusebian TF quotation read "he was *believed to be* the Christ," rather than "he *was* the Christ," and that somehow all subsequent manuscripts of the *AJ*, as well as all Eusebius manuscripts that contain the quotation, were emended to agree with the corruption.[10] That all *AJ* manuscripts would so perfectly agree with a *later* corruption that somehow simultaneously occurred in *all* the texts of Eusebius (a corruption that, by Whealey's argument, must have occurred after the 4th century) is rather improbable. More likely some early copy

---

[9] See Paget, "Some Observations," 554–624, and Olson, "Eusebius," 319–22; but most importantly, Alice Whealey, "The Testimonium Flavianum in Syriac and Arabic," *New Testament Studies* 54 (2008): 573–90, which persuasively argues that even the previously touted Arabic version of the TF actually also derives from Eusebius, through a Syriac intermediary, and thus does not derive from a manuscript of Josephus.

[10] This is the main argument of Whealey, *Josephus on Jesus*, and (in more detail) Whealey, "Testimonium Flavianum."

of Eusebius's *History* alone was "improved" by a scribe intending to restore a more plausible quotation from a Jew (thus producing "he was *believed to be* the Christ"), and it is *this* that we see in Whealey's cited examples. It is inherently less likely that all manuscript traditions of all the texts of Eusebius *and* all manuscript traditions of Josephus were conspiratorially emended in the same way, than only one manuscript tradition of a single text of Eusebius being emended the *other* way, and thus (as one would then expect) only occasionally evidenced in quotation (which, as Whealey shows, is what we observe). Whealey's evidence, then, more likely corroborates the conclusion that even extant *quotations* of the *AJ* descend (ultimately) from the same manuscript used by Eusebius. And even if they do not, the *manuscripts* of the *AJ* obviously do.

Not only do all extant manuscripts of the *AJ* likely descend from the manuscript quoted by Eusebius, which was itself a descendant of the manuscript used by Origen, but we can also be reasonably certain that this "copy" was made with deliberate revisions to the TF (if not its outright inclusion) in the intervening years between Origen and Eusebius. As discussed above, the TF as we have it (and as Eusebius quotes it) was not likely in Origen's copy, but was obviously in the copy read by Eusebius, which he found in the very same library. So Eusebius must have been using a *copy* of the *AJ* manuscript used by Origen and not the manuscript actually consulted by Origen, and a copy in which emendations had already been made (as the presence of the TF proves). This makes sense, since it was more than possible that Origen had procured what was already an old manuscript—for example, if it came from the first generation of manuscripts produced, his copy would be over a hundred years old already (the *AJ* was published in or shortly after 93 A.D., according to *AJ* 20.267), and approaching two hundred years old around the time the copy would have been made. And, it should be noted, that manuscript (from which

Eusebius's copy derived) would have included any marginal notes made by Origen himself.[11]

ON THE PROPOSED INTERPOLATION IN *AJ* 20.200

The current manuscripts of Josephus read as follows:

τὸν ἀδελφὸν Ἰησοῦ τοῦ λεγομένου Χριστοῦ, Ἰάκωβος ὄνομα αὐτῷ, καί τινας ἑτέρους ...

---

[11] A case has been made that Eusebius himself forged the TF, but this conclusion is debated: Olson, "Eusebius," vs. Alice Whealey, "Josephus, Eusebius of Caesarea, and the Testimonium Flavianum," in *Josephus und das Neue Testament: Wechselseitige Wahrnehmungen*, ed. Christfried Böttrich and Jens Herzer (Tübingen: Mohr Siebeck, 2007), 73–116. Paget likewise discusses this debate ("Some Observations," 554–619), siding in the negative. However, in both cases this ruling is largely based on other quotations of the TF, which is a flawed method, as I explained previously. I consider the question unresolved.

[UPDATE: After my article went to press, a much stronger case appeared that has me persuaded: Ken Olson, "A Eusebian Reading of the Testimonium Flavianum," in *Eusebius of Caesarea: Tradition and Innovations* (Harvard University Press, 2013), pp. 97–114, supplemented by Ken Olson, "The Testimonium Flavianum, Eusebius, and Consensus," *The Jesus Blog* (13 August 2013) at historicaljesusresearch.blogspot.com/2013/08/the-testimonium-flavianum-eusebius-and.html. Olson's evidence now entails that if Eusebius is not the forger of the TF, then his teacher and predecessor Pamphilus almost certainly is. We have almost none of what was written by Pamphilus, so we can't check directly, but all the evidence Olson finds of Eusebian authorship of the TF could easily be remnants of vocabulary, idioms, and ideas Eusebius inherited from his teacher. And the timeline fits. Pamphilus had custody of the manuscripts employed by Eusebius and would have directed any copying made after Origen, precisely when the present article finds the interpolation occurred. Meanwhile it has been demonstrated that the TF is derived from the Gospel of Luke: G.J. Goldberg, "The Coincidences of the Testimonium of Josephus and the Emmaus Narrative of Luke," *Journal for the Study of the Pseudepigrapha* 13 (1995): 59-77. When these facts are combined with my observations in notes 1 and 9, the case for the entire TF being a Christian forgery should be considered decisive. I add more to the point in *OHJ*.]

> The brother of Jesus (who was called Christ), the name
> for whom was James, and some others ...[12]

These are the men whom the newly appointed high priest Ananus the Younger charged with unspecified crimes and had stoned, without following the appropriate procedure of involving the authorities in charge of the law. For this outrage, many leading Jews protested to the authorities, and Ananus was duly deposed (after only a few months in office) and replaced with Jesus ben Damneus.

There are five reasons to suspect that the phrase, "who was called Christ" (τοῦ λεγομένου Χριστοῦ), is an interpolation, and that the original text said simply "the brother of Jesus, the name for whom was James, and some others . . . ," or perhaps, as I discuss below, "the brother of Jesus ben Damneus, the name for whom was James, and some others. . . ."

First, "the one called Christ" is exactly the kind of thing a scholar or scribe would add as an interlinear note to remind himself and future readers that—so the scribe believed—the Jesus here mentioned is Jesus Christ, as we would do today with an informative footnote or marginal note. These kinds of marginal "passage identifiers" are common in extant manuscripts; for instance, one manuscript of Tacitus has similar marginal comments that highlight the mention of Christ for the benefit of Christian readers skimming for passages of interest.[13]

Second, the words and structure chosen here are indeed the ones that would commonly be used in an interlinear note, e.g., a participial clause—remarkable brevity for something that would sooner otherwise spark a digression or cross-reference, had Josephus actually written those words. Indeed, there would very likely be a reference to the TF, if it existed (perhaps even identifying the book in which it appeared, so that the reader would know which scroll to pick up to find out or remind themselves who or what this "Christ" is and why he is mentioned, or at the very least mentioning that he had previously discussed this person), especially since the reference is so obscure. For example, the extant

---

[12] Ed. Benedikt Niese, *Flavii Iosephi opera* (Berlin: Weidmann, 1892), 4:310; my translation.

[13] Adjoining Tacitus, *Annals* 15.44, as is evident in the right margin of folio 38r of Codex Laurentianus Mediceus 68 II, cf. *Codices Graeci et Latini Photographice Depicti* 7.2 (Leiden: A. W. Sijthoff, 1902).

TF neither mentions Jesus having a brother nor explains why his brother would be a target of prosecution, much less a person defended by other leading Jews. It does not even mention *any* persecution of Christians, but rather emphasizes their unimpeded thriving "to this day." Thus there would be much to explain here even if the TF had existed: in the same narrative, Josephus refers back to his previous discussion of the Sadducees when he mentions *them* (*AJ* 20.199, probably referring to *AJ* 13.293–98) and explains why mentioning them is relevant to his present story, yet surely "Christ"—more obscure than the Sadducees, as they are mentioned several times previously in the same book (*AJ* 18.16)— would merit at least the same treatment, and an explanation or cross-reference to the TF would be even more natural (e.g. "the one called Christ whom I mentioned before"). After all, Josephus provided both a reference to the Sadducees *and* an explanation of their significance; likewise when he mentions Judas the Galilean in *AJ* 20.102, Josephus employs the phrase, "as I mentioned before," and an additional explanation. Even if there was no TF, we would certainly find here an explanation of why this Jesus was called "Christ," what that word meant (at the very least explaining its connection to "Christians" and James's being one, if that is even what is meant—since James is not said to be a Christian here, or in the TF, the text requires an assumption that only a Christian would make, further suggesting that this is not from Josephus's hand), and why Josephus thought it important to mention either, since the passage as written leaves no stated reason why either Jesus or his moniker Christ is mentioned at all. Any inferences to such a reason would only occur to a Christian, not to Josephus or his intended readers, who would know nothing about the obscurities of Jewish laws or religion, which is why he always explains such things when they come up elsewhere.[14] In short, while Josephan authorship is not impossible, it is far more probable that such omissions were the result of the passage being an accidental interpolation.

---

[14] Josephus otherwise never uses the word "Christ" (even where it appears in the TF it is widely regarded as an interpolation; see Van Voorst, *Jesus*, 91–92; as noted earlier, I find Whealey's attempt to defend it implausible) and Josephus often refers readers to his previous discussions of obscure persons and subjects (Paget, "Some Observations," 553–54). These and other considerations against this passage's authenticity are discussed in Olson, "Eusebius," 314–19.

Third, the completed phrase is (apart from a necessary change of case) identical to Matt 1.16, Ἰησοῦς ὁ λεγόμενος Χριστός (which happens to be a passage about Jesus' family). This is not a phrase that Josephus would likely use in the same way as a Christian annotator would. Again, while not impossible for Josephus to construct on his own, it is far more probable that the phrase came from a later, Christian hand.

Fourth, the execution of Christians makes little sense in the context of the story, not only because the reason for the executions is not mentioned, but also because the executions outrage many influential Jews, who then seek and procure from Jewish and Roman authorities the punishment of Ananus. If he were executing members of the hated and illegal Christian sect, punishing Ananus makes little sense. Indeed, writing for a Roman audience in the era of Domitian, Josephus would be describing an inexplicable course of events, where the execution of Christians was considered a legal matter of course, not an act warranting outrage and dismissal from office.[15] In fact, we get no sense from the story that there was any popular animosity toward this James and his affiliates. On the contrary, the story directs all this animosity against their killers. Regardless of what Josephus himself may have thought about Christians, it is more likely he would feel compelled to explain this strange course of events to his Roman audience than to simply gloss over it. However, if this is not a passage about Christians, then its content is not improbable at all.[16]

Fifth, apart from the execution by stoning (the most common form of execution employed by Jews, and therefore not at all peculiar to or indicative of Christian victims), this story does not agree with any other account of the death of James the brother of Christ (a point to which I will return).

All five reasons, even combined, are grounds only for a very strong suspicion, not a conclusive proof. One can advance expla-

---

[15] See, for example, a comparable course of events and the elite reaction to it in Pliny the Younger, *Ep.* 10.96–97 as well as Tacitus's remarks about popular sentiment during the events of 64 A.D. at *Annals* 15.44 and (if we are to trust its account) the representation of elite Jewish reaction to Christianity in Acts. [UPDATE: I now consider the reference in Tacitus not to be a reference to Christians. See next chapter.]

[16] That the *AJ* was written specifically for a Gentile audience, see Josephus, *AJ* 1.pref.5–10.

nations on all counts. The issue then becomes which explanation is the most probable.[17] I will not delve any further into that debate. At this point I mean only to have established the thesis and the credible grounds on which it stands. In advancing these five preliminary arguments, I am selecting, collecting, and perfecting the best arguments previously made for this conclusion (from among those advocates listed in Wells, Olson, and Paget, as cited earlier), and thereby rejecting others as untenable.

For example, most previous proponents of interpolation have argued for a deliberate interpolation, or that more was interpolated than just the phrase, τοῦ λεγομένου Χριστοῦ. I will not defend these two theses here, as they require more assumptions, and therefore are less probable; simply put, they do not provide the best explanation of the surviving evidence. The thesis that I defend is immune to all the arguments against interpolation in *AJ* 20.200 summarized in Olson and Whealey, since they are only directed against a deliberate interpolation, with the single exception of citing Origen's quotation of *AJ* 20.200, which I shall demonstrate is not true.[18] In fact, in addition to the five arguments for interpolation just summarized, there is a most decisive sixth argument, which derives from that very evidence in Origen.

From Origen to Eusebius

Origen is presumed to quote *AJ* 20.200 once in his *Commentary on Matthew* and twice in *Against Celsus*, yet upon close examination, it becomes clear that Origen did not note the phrase, "who was called Christ," as original to Josephus, or claim that he was even quoting

---

[17] Because the mere ability to explain things away does not make for a valid rebuttal. According to the logic of evidence, as long as any element of the evidence E is merely *more probable* on hypothesis A than hypothesis B, then E still necessarily argues for A and against B, and the only question is *how strongly* for and against. But if there are several such items (as is the case here), their cumulative effect can be quite strong, the more so the more probable any E is on A than on B. It then depends on prior considerations (i.e. how probable you consider hypotheses like A or B to be in general). See references and discussion in Richard Carrier, *Proving History: Bayes's Theorem and the Quest for the Historical Jesus* (Amherst, NY: Prometheus, 2012).

[18] See Olson, "Eusebius," 314; and Whealey, *Josephus on Jesus*, 2–5.

Josephus at all. It is only with Eusebius's quotation of Origen that this presumption is made. And therein lies an important clue. In his rebuttal to Celsus, Origen wrote,

> For in the eighteenth book of his *Jewish Antiquities*, Josephus bears witness to John as having been a Baptist [or, "a baptizer"] ... and the same writer, although not believing in Jesus as the Christ, in seeking after the cause of the fall of Jerusalem and the destruction of the Temple ... says nevertheless (being, although against his will, not far from the truth) that these disasters happened to the Jews as a punishment for the death of James the Just, who was a brother of the Jesus who was called Christ, since they killed him despite his being supremely just.[19]

Origen goes on to say, of course, that Josephus should have said the real cause was the execution of Jesus.

Several things must be noted here before proceeding. First, Josephus neither says, in *AJ* 20.200 or anywhere else, that James's execution caused the fall of Jerusalem nor mentions any James named "the Just" or describes any James as just. Josephus actually says the fall of Jerusalem was a punishment for (and natural consequence of) the execution of Ananus the Younger (the very Ananus who executed this James in *AJ* 20.200). He explains in detail that Jerusalem was defiled by the killing of a former Temple high priest and the sacrilegious discarding of his body, and that this defilement brought God's final wrath upon the city. The Jews had also doomed themselves, he says, by killing the one man eloquent enough to persuade both sides toward an amicable peace (*Jewish War* 4.314–25), nicely paralleling a divine with a natural explanation side-by-side, so readers could pick the one they liked the more according to their own religious beliefs about the nature of things. Josephus, then, could hardly have contradicted himself elsewhere by (inexplicably) laying responsibility on the execution of an unknown James. That would make no narrative sense. No James is significant enough in any of Josephus's accounts to explain how his death could have caused the fall of Jerusalem. Instead, Josephus

---

[19] Origen, *Against Celsus* 1.47 (ed. M. Borret, *Origène. Contre Celse*, SC 132 [Paris: Éditions du Cerf, 1967], 198–201; trans. *ANF* 4:800–801).

clearly identified the killing of Ananus as the cause (and even then, not because Ananus was "supremely just"). So why does Origen say Josephus blamed the destruction of Jerusalem on the killing of James, much less a "James the Just," a name nowhere found in Josephus?

Second, contrary to previous assumptions, Origen does not say that Josephus said this in the *AJ*. He refers to a passage in Josephus attesting John the Baptist in *AJ* 18 (and, notably, not a passage that attests to Jesus in that same book, one of the many instances in which we must conclude Origen cannot have known the TF, which now also appears in *AJ* 18), and only then says, "the same writer says" this thing about James the Just. Notably, he does not say Josephus says it in the same book, or even in the same work. Origen must have had an entirely different treatise in mind. We will return to this point, but here it is worth noting that Jerome (*On Illustrious Men* 13) mistook this passage in Origen as saying that this report (about the execution of James as the cause of Jerusalem's destruction) appeared in *AJ* 18, when certainly it does not (neither this report, nor the execution of any James, nor the phrase "brother of Jesus who was called Christ," appear in *AJ* 18). That Jerome would make this mistake, from the mere juxtaposition of this report and an unrelated mention of *AJ* 18 in this same passage by Origen, is notable for reasons we will see in a moment (all the more, as Eusebius quotes all of these passages in succession, and Eusebius's works are known to have been consulted by Jerome).

Third, Origen is certainly not quoting Josephus here (neither does any sentence correspond verbatim to anything in Josephus nor does Origen specifically identify any of these words as being a quotation), but we do see ὃς ... ἀδελφὸς Ἰησοῦ τοῦ λεγομένου Χριστοῦ, "the brother of Jesus who was called Christ," a nearly identical wording to that found in *AJ* 20.200, yet in the middle of a differently constructed sentence and with reference to a different story. These words appear to be Origen's. Since he is referring here to a supposed passage in which Josephus credits the fall of Jerusalem to the execution of a James the Just, this in fact *cannot* be a quotation of *AJ* 20.200, which neither mentions the causes of the fall of Jerusalem nor identifies any James as "the Just."

Further confirmation of this comes from the fact that the only element of *AJ* 20.200 that would be a telltale sign of quotation is Josephus's idiomatic construction Ἰάκωβος ὄνομα αὐτῷ, "the name for whom was James," and that *following* rather than *preceding* the name of Jesus. Origen never quotes that clause or employs the same order, but always uses his own clause and order ("James the Just, the brother of . . ."). The material that they share is biblical (deriving from Matt 1.16) and thus Origen already has a non-Josephan source. Once we take away "who was called Christ," all they share in common is "brother of Jesus" and the name "James," wholly commonplace words and phrases and not distinctive to Josephus at all. Origen thus shows no awareness of the specific wording or context of *AJ* 20.200 (wherein James is only obliquely named, not identified as "Just," not linked with the fall of Jerusalem, and not killed with the consent of "the Jews"). Combine this with the fact that Origen clearly does not refer to any of *AJ* 20.200's content but to something entirely different, and we must conclude there is no quotation of *AJ* 20.200 here or anywhere in Origen.

Later in the same treatise Origen says, "Titus destroyed Jerusalem, on account, as Josephus wrote, of James the Just, the brother of Jesus who was called Christ, but in reality, as the truth makes clear, on account of Jesus Christ the Son of God."[20] Again, Josephus never wrote any such thing, so we must ask why Origen thought he did. But note that Origen gives the same line verbatim as appeared in the earlier passage (τὸν ἀδελφὸν Ἰησοῦ τοῦ λεγομένου Χριστοῦ) and attaches it to Ἰακώβου τοῦ δικαίου ("James the Just") —exactly as it was in his earlier passage (*Against Celsus* 1.47). Again, Origen says that Josephus wrote this, but not where.

Now we come to Origen's *Commentary on Matthew*, where he writes this:

> And to so great a reputation among the people for righteousness did this James rise, that Flavius Josephus, who wrote the *Antiquities of the Jews* in twenty books, when wishing to exhibit the cause why the people suffered such great misfortunes that even the Temple was razed to the ground, said that these things happened to them in accordance with the wrath of God in consequence of the things which they had dared to do against James the brother of Jesus who is called Christ. And the amazing thing is that although he

---

[20] Origen, *Against Celsus* 2.13 (SC 132:324–25; trans. *ANF* 4:846).

did not accept Jesus as Christ, he yet gave testimony that the righteousness of James was so great, and he says that the people thought that they had suffered these things because of James.[21]

Several things here must be noted. First, Origen does not identify his source as *AJ* 20 or even the *AJ* at all; he only notes that Josephus wrote the *AJ* in twenty books. It is thus strange that the connection between a James and this "Jesus who was called Christ" happens to appear in *AJ* 20. Origen never claimed it did. Could a mistake have inspired a scribe to expect a connection between a James and "Jesus who was called Christ" in *AJ* 20, one similar to Jerome's when he incorrectly expected it to be in *AJ* 18?

Second, Origen clearly thinks both that Josephus claimed not only that the execution of James the Just was the cause of Jerusalem's fall, but also that the Jewish "people" themselves had thought this, and that Josephus had given "testimony that the righteousness of James was so great" as his reputation held. Yet none of these three claims are anywhere in Josephus's works, nor could they have been, since they contradict what Josephus himself states in the *Jewish War*, as noted earlier. They are not even plausible things for him to say: there is no significant figure named James anywhere in his writings about the war, and the execution of a mere criminal (from the perspective of Josephus and his Roman patrons) would never have contributed to or been the sole cause of Jerusalem's destruction, especially since the only offense Josephus reports here was procedural, and it was duly and quickly redressed.

Third, this passage contains another verbatim repetition of τὸν ἀδελφὸν Ἰησοῦ τοῦ λεγομένου Χριστοῦ, "brother of Jesus who was called Christ," again connected to a James the Just and to an especially elaborate account that is not (nor could have been, contrary to Origen's statement) in *AJ* 20.200. In other words, despite this clause's striking similarity to *AJ* 20.200, Origen is certainly not quoting it here or any of the three other places where the phrase appears.

So here we can compare Origen—Ἰακώβου τοῦ δικαίου ὃς ἦν ἀδελφὸς Ἰησοῦ τοῦ λεγομένου Χριστοῦ (*Against Celsus* 1.47);

---

[21] Origen, *Commentary on Matthew* 10.17 (ed. Robert Girod, *Origène. Commentaire sur l'évangile selon Matthieu*, SC 162 [Paris: Éditions du Cerf, 1970], 216–19; trans. *ANF* 10:702).

Ἰάκωβον τὸν δίκαιον **τὸν ἀδελφὸν Ἰησου του λεγομένου Χριστοῦ** (*Against Celsus* 2.13); Ἰάκωβον [sc. τὸν δίκαιον] **τὸν ἀδελφὸν Ἰησοῦ τοῦ λεγομένου Χριστοῦ** (*Commentary on Matthew* 10.17)—with Josephus—**τὸν ἀδελφὸν Ἰησοῦ τοῦ λεγομένου Χριστοῦ** Ἰάκωβος ὄνομα αὐτῷ (*AJ* 20.200). The *AJ* does not begin the line with "James the Just," but lacks the "Just" and places the name of James after the "brother of Jesus," not before, and with a peculiar and distinctive idiom ("the name for whom was James"), which we only find in *AJ* 20.200, but not in Origen. Finally, the story to which Origen refers is nothing like the content of *AJ* 20.200. If Origen is quoting anyone other than himself, he is quoting something other than the *AJ*, and probably a work not written by Josephus at all.

We next find Eusebius quoting Origen on this point:

> Josephus, at least, has not hesitated to testify this in his writings, where he says, "These things happened to the Jews to avenge James the Just, who was a brother of Jesus, who is called the Christ. For the Jews slew him, although he was a most just man." And the same writer records his death also in the twentieth book of his *Antiquities* in the following words . . . [here Eusebius quotes *AJ* 20.200 verbatim].[22]

Three things must be noted. First, here Eusebius quotes "Josephus" as if deriving this quotation directly from one of his writings, when in fact he is quoting Origen: apart from the trivial difference of two dropped articles, the passage is entirely identical (in the Greek) to Origen, *Against Celsus* 1.47.

Second, and like Origen, Eusebius does not claim to know where Josephus said this. Eusebius states only that the following quotation (which neither blames Jerusalem's fall on James's execution nor mentions any "James the Just") is in "the twentieth book of his *Antiquities*." Yet both passages contain the same phrase, τὸν ἀδελφὸν Ἰησοῦ τοῦ λεγομένου Χριστοῦ, "the brother of Jesus who was called Christ." But, as we have just seen, Origen cannot have been deriving this from *AJ* 20.200. So how did both

---

[22] Eusebius, *Ecclesiastical History* 2.23.20–21 (ed. G. Bardy, *Eusèbe de Césarée: Histoire ecclésiastique*, SC 31 [Paris: Éditions du Cerf, 1952], 86–90; trans. *NPNF*[2] 1:206–9).

passages come to contain the exact same phrase, six identical words in identical order, despite being completely different stories?

Third, Eusebius actually quotes *AJ* 20.200 whereas Origen never did. It would certainly seem as if Eusebius found a reference to Christ in *AJ* 20.200 unknown to Origen. Indeed, Eusebius quotes the entire passage in *AJ* 20.200 complete with context, but when he quotes the mysterious "other" Josephan passage to which Origen referred with respect to James, Eusebius gives no additional content, but reproduces Origen's words. Thus Eusebius did not even know what Josephan work or passage Origen was using or what its context was. All he could do was simply quote Origen and pass this off as a quotation of Josephus—and then supplement this with a quotation of a "surprise" new finding in the actual *AJ*, one that Origen himself never quotes or refers to, despite his clear familiarity with the *AJ*.

The reference to Christ in *AJ* 20.200 would thus seem to have appeared in the *AJ* manuscripts sometime between Origen and Eusebius, and the interpolated material seems to derive from a quotation of another, non-Josephan work, but falsely attributed to Josephus by Origen, in which entirely different things are said about a certain James the Just. How such an interpolation would have come about I will explore in a moment, but first we must understand what the original text would have been that later acquired a reference to one "who was called Christ."

What Josephus Originally Said

As previously noted, many features of *AJ* 20.200 are inexplicable if Josephus was actually writing about the execution of Christians. Among them is the fact that, had he discussed the "Christ" person elsewhere, or even mentioned him, he would more likely have provided a cross-reference. If he did not mention him, Josephus would have digressed to explain what this name meant or why he was bothering to mention it, as both Tacitus and Pliny did in *their* explanations of Christ as the personal name of a god or leader followed by Christians and why this led to their being executed. However, if "who was called Christ" are not Josephus's words, but rather an accidental interpolation, then all the inexplicable features of this passage vanish. We are left with the mere statement, "the brother of Jesus, the name for whom was James, and some others," and in that case, without a cross-reference or explanation as to who this Jesus was (who wasn't being executed but whose brother was), readers would expect such a reference to be to a Jesus mentioned in the same story already being told. And indeed there is such a one: at the end of this very same narrative (*AJ* 20.203), Josephus discusses the man named high priest in 62 A.D., Jesus ben Damneus.

This is rendered more probable by the fact that the narrative is about Ananus's misuse of office and the outcry at his illegal execution of James, the brother of a certain Jesus. The fact that the response to this abuse, his very "punishment," was to depose him and replace him with this Jesus, is the only reading of events that makes the story intelligible: Ananus was persecuting his rival for office by attacking his brother, and the authorities achieved justice by punishing Ananus, and redressed his offense by giving the office to his enemy, the very man whose brother he had killed. This hypothesis explains both an otherwise unexplained reference to a mysterious Jesus and the odd designation of the punished man as "the brother" of a certain Jesus, and adding, as if an afterthought, that his name was James. Hence this James's death is only mentioned because of the importance to the story of his brother Jesus. If Jesus ben Damneus is the Jesus meant, then all of this makes sense. Otherwise, where does Josephus explain the central importance to the story of his brother Jesus? Why is "Jesus" the primary subject in the execution of James, rather than James, the one actually executed? Even the TF provides no explanation inasmuch as it makes no mention of the subsequent persecution of Christians, its rationale (legal or otherwise), or of the fact that Jesus' brother was a Christian.

Hence the story ends that when the Roman governor Albinus found out about this illegal execution: "Albinus wrote in anger to Ananus, and threatened that he would bring him to punishment for what he had done, at which point king Agrippa took the high priesthood from Ananus, when he had ruled but three months, and made Jesus, the son of Damneus, high priest."[23] This concludes a long narrative about the reasons different high priests succeeded each other; naturally, we should expect here a reason why Jesus ben

---

[23] Josephus, *AJ* 20.203 (trans. William Whiston, *Flavius Josephus: The Second Jewish Commonwealth: From the Maccabean Rebellion to the Outbreak of the Judaeo-Roman War*, ed. Nahum Glatzer, revised by A. R. Shilleto [New York: Schocken Books, 1971], 519).

Damneus replaced Ananus. The only reason implied here is that Ananus illegally executed his brother, and as punishment, the authorities replaced Ananus with the brother of the man Ananus unjustly killed. Thus, what Josephus meant was that this James was the brother of Jesus ben Damneus, not the brother of Jesus Christ. In effect, Josephus was saying, "Ananus illegally executed the brother of Jesus, which got a reaction; for his crime, he was deposed and replaced by Jesus." This is not merely a coincidence of names; it is probable that *this* is what Josephus intended to convey, and even more probably if "son of Damneus" *also* fell out of the text at this point, perhaps by replacement (a possibility that I will address later).

This conclusion is supported by fact that the execution of this James in *AJ* 20.200 corresponds in no way (except for the method of execution as stoning) to accounts of the death of James, the brother of Jesus.[24] The only contemporary example of such a narrative, deriving from the late second-century author Hegesippus, is particularly relevant.[25] To that we will next turn, but first it is worth noting a supporting argument for this conclusion, namely, the fact that Luke-Acts lacks any mention of this event.

THE SILENCE OF LUKE-ACTS

In Acts, only one James is killed; king Herod Agrippa ordered the execution and it was enacted by sword, not stoning (Acts 12.1–2). Acts does not know of a James "brother of Jesus Christ" killed by a high priest, by stoning, and not supported *but opposed* by king

---

[24] As discussed in Paget, "Some Observations," 546–54.

[25] Other references to James's death allude only to peculiarities in the account found in Hegesippus (e.g. Clement of Alexandria, see following note) or are not clearly independent of it (e.g. the Coptic and fragmentary *Second Apocalypse of James* looks to be an elaborate redaction of the same legend in Hegesippus, and has nothing more in common with Josephus). Note that some scholars (e.g., Paget, "Some Observations," 547) incorrectly cite the *Clementine Recognitions* 1.66–70 as containing an account of James's death when in fact it does not, but a separate incident decades earlier, in which of course he is not killed. In fact there is no record of his death in the *Clementine Recognitions*.

Herod Agrippa.[26] Several experts have argued that Luke used the *AJ* as a source, since he frequently draws material, personages, vocabulary, and context from it.[27] His neglect of this very attractive passage would be very hard to explain, unless it was not present in the *AJ* in Luke's time; without the phrase "who was called Christ," Luke would have no reason to think the James in *AJ* 20.200 was a Christian (since, additionally, he was not aware of any story about "James the Just" as Origen was—that legend likely developed in the following century).

In fact, this conclusion holds even if Luke did not use the *AJ*, but rather sources that he had in common with Josephus.[28] Luke always depicts the Romans as protecting or rescuing Christians from the excesses of Jewish persecution or other dire fates (e.g., Gallio at Acts 18.12–23, Lysias and Festus at Acts 23–24, and the

---

[26] Accordingly, it was then and is now assumed that the author of Luke-Acts meant, and thus only knew, of a *different* James's death (as is claimed, for example, by Clement of Alexandria in the eighth book of his lost *Outlines*, as quoted by Eusebius, *Ecclesiastical History* 2.1.3–4, which also shows that Clement reached this conclusion from comparing Acts with the account in Hegesippus, and *not* Josephus, of which Clement shows no knowledge).

[27] Richard Pervo, *Dating Acts: Between the Evangelists and the Apologists* (Santa Rosa, CA: Polebridge Press, 2006), *The Mystery of Acts* (Santa Rosa, CA: Polebridge, 2008), and *Acts: A Commentary* (Minneapolis, MN: Fortress Press, 2009); David Trobisch, "Who Published the Christian Bible?" *Committee for the Scientific Examination of Religion Review* 2 (2007): 29–32; Steve Mason, *Josephus and the New Testament* (Peabody, MA: Hendrickson, 1992), 185–229; Heinz Schreckenberg, "Flavius Josephus und die lukanischen Schriften," in *Wort in der Zeit: Neutestamentliche Studien: Festgabe für Karl Heinrich Rengstorf zum 75. Geburtstag*, ed. Wilfrid Haubeck and Michael Bachmann (Leiden: Brill, 1980), 179–209; Max Krenkel, *Josephus und Lucas: Der schriftstellerische Einfluss des jüdischen Geschichtschreibers auf den christlichen* (Leipzig: H. Haessel, 1894).

[28] Even scholars who do not agree (or are uncertain) that Luke used Josephus tend to agree that they must have employed common sources, since this is the only other probable explanation of their many agreements; see G.J. Goldberg, "The Josephus-Luke Connection," *Journal for the Study of the Pseudepigrapha* 13 (1995): 59–77; Hans-Josef Klauck, *Magic and Paganism in Early Christianity: The World of the Acts of the Apostles* (Edinburgh: T & T Clark, 2000), 41–43; Heinz Schreckenberg, *Jewish Historiography and Iconography in Early and Medieval Christianity* (Minneapolis, MN: Fortress Press, 1992), 1:42–53; Gregory Sterling, *Historiography and Self-Definition: Josephos, Luke-Acts, and Apologetic Historiography* (Leiden: Brill, 1992), 365–69.

Roman guards at Acts 16.19–40, 27.42–44). He also depicts some of the Jewish elite as less negatively disposed toward Christians (e.g., Gamaliel at Acts 5.34–42 and even Herod Agrippa at Acts 25–26).[29] In its present form, *AJ* 20.200 has all of this. Indeed, it hands Luke a rhetorical coup: Romans (and Agrippa himself) *punishing* Jews for persecuting Christians. There is no possible way Luke would have passed up an opportunity to include this in his account.

We can be certain, if Luke was using the *AJ*, that the original form of *AJ* 20.200 did not contain a reference to Christ. Even if Luke wrote before Josephus, the story now extant in *AJ* 20.200 would have been unknown (since Luke makes no mention of it, yet would have all the same compelling reasons to do so). Because it would be virtually impossible for a Christian of the time to know less than Josephus about the fate of "James the brother of Jesus Christ" (particularly a Christian claiming to have researched the history of his church [see Luke 1.1–4]), we would then have to conclude the story now extant in *AJ* 20.200 must be a fabrication of either Josephus or a post-Luke, Josephan source (the only way it could not be known to Luke, but still known to Josephus)—*unless* it never mentioned Christ. Since neither Josephus nor any of his sources would have any evident reason to fabricate such a story, it is likely that the passage did not mention Christ. The story probably predates Luke, but it has nothing to do with Christ or Christians, which explains why Luke does not use it while Josephus does.

HEGESIPPUS

We now return to the question of where Origen got this story about "James the Just," since it certainly did not come from *AJ* 20.200. A Christian hagiographer named Hegesippus wrote five books of *Commentaries on the Acts of the Church* fifty years or so before Origen flourished. These texts do not survive, but quotations from them survive in various authors, most extensively Eusebius. Among Eusebius's quotations of Hegesippus is a passage on the death of James, positioned between several Josephan passages, including *AJ* 20.200. This account of James is rife with

---

[29] See, for example, the analysis of Sterling, *Historiography and Self-Definition*.

implausibilities and dramatic absurdities and looks like other apocryphal gospels or acts from the same period. It is surely legendary, and as we shall see, this legend must be Origen's source. To offer clarity on both counts, I provide all of the relevant passages from Hegesippus as Eusebius preserves them:

> Now some persons belonging to the seven [Jewish] sects existing among the people, which have been before described by me in the *Commentaries*, asked James: "What is the door of Jesus?" And he replied that he was the Savior. In consequence of this answer, **some believed** that Jesus is the Christ. But the sects before mentioned did not believe, either in a resurrection or in the coming of one to requite every man according to his works; but those who did believe, believed because of James. So, when many even of the ruling class believed, there was a commotion among the Jews, and scribes, and Pharisees, who said, "A little more, and we shall have all the people looking for Jesus as the Christ."
>
> They came, therefore, in a body to James, and said, "We entreat you, restrain the people: for they are gone astray in their opinions about Jesus, as if he were the Christ. We entreat you to persuade all who have come here for the day of the Passover, concerning Jesus. For we all listen to you; since **we, as well as all the people, bear you testimony that you are just**, and show partiality to none. Therefore, persuade the people not to entertain erroneous opinions concerning Jesus: for all the people, and we also, listen to you. Take your stand, then, upon the summit of the Temple, that from that elevated spot you may be clearly seen, and your words may be plainly audible to all the people. For, in order to attend the Passover, all the tribes have congregated here, and some of the Gentiles also."
>
> The aforesaid scribes and Pharisees accordingly set James on the summit of the Temple, and cried aloud to him, and said, "**O just one**, whom we are all bound to obey, forasmuch as the people are in error, and follow Jesus the crucified, do tell us what is the door of Jesus, the crucified." And he answered with a loud voice, "Why ask me concerning Jesus the Son of Man? He Himself sits in

heaven, at the right hand of the great power, and shall come on the clouds of heaven."

And, when many were fully convinced by these words, and offered praise for the testimony of James, and said, "Hosanna to the son of David," then again the Pharisees and scribes said to one another, "We have not done well in procuring this testimony to Jesus. But let us go up and throw him down, that they may be afraid, and not believe him." And they cried aloud, and said, "Oh! Oh! **The just man** himself is in error." Thus they fulfilled the Scripture written in Isaiah: "Let us away with **the just man**, because he is troublesome to us: therefore **shall they eat the fruit of their doings**." So they went up and threw down **the just man**, and said to one another, "Let us stone **James the Just**." And they began to stone him, for he was not killed by the fall; but he turned, and kneeled down, and said, "I beseech Thee, Lord God our Father, forgive them; for they know not what they do."

And, while they were thus stoning him to death, one of the priests of the sons of Rechab, the son of the Rechabites, to whom testimony is born by Jeremiah the prophet, began to cry aloud, saying, "Stop! What are you doing!? **The just man** is praying for us." But one among them, one of the fullers, took the staff with which he was accustomed to wring out the garments he dyed, and hurled it at the head of **the just man**.

And so he suffered martyrdom; and they buried him on the spot, and the pillar erected to his memory still remains, close by the temple. This man was a true witness to both Jews and Greeks that Jesus is the Christ. **And immediately Vespasian besieged them.**[30]

This story has several notable features. Hegesippus repeatedly refers to this James as "the Just" and once explicitly calls him "James the Just" (indeed, as if originating the appellation, even deriving it from a scriptural prophecy about this very event). Hegesippus also strongly implies that Jerusalem's destruction was the result of this execution, not only by the passage's last line, but

---

[30] Eusebius, *Ecclesiastical History* 2.23.3–18 (SC 31:86–90; trans. *NPNF²* 1:207–8, modified; my emphasis).

also by his quotation of a prophecy (foreshadowing the last line) predicting the Jews would "eat the fruit of their doings."

Additionally, beyond the fact that both mention a man named James who was stoned (a name and mode of execution that were tremendously common), there are no parallels to *AJ* 20.200: according to Hegesippus, James's execution has nothing do with a high priest of any stripe, it is not a punishment for a crime that resulted from a trial, it is a solitary affair (i.e. no one else was killed along with him), and it immediately precedes Jerusalem's destruction, without the Romans or Agrippa punishing the Jews first by deposing and replacing the high priest. This passage also presents "the people" as bearing "testimony" that this James was extraordinarily "just" (the very thing that Origen had said *Josephus* reported), refers to others "believing" that Jesus is the Christ (rather than the text simply declaring him the Christ, thus implying the authorial distance that Origen credits to Josephus), and has one of the priests attempt to stop his execution, recognizing it was wrong. Finally, the people recognize his unjust death with a monumental burial, an acknowledgment that they had indeed done wrong, immediately before the destruction came. Thus one could infer that they recognized the cause of their fate, as Origen also implies Josephus had said. Eusebius himself makes this inference, stating immediately after quoting Hegesippus's passage that "the more sensible even of the Jews were of the opinion that this was the cause of the siege of Jerusalem, which happened to them immediately after his martyrdom for no other reason than their daring to act against him."[31] Though this may have been inspired by his reading of Origen (whom he then quotes), it is also possible that Hegesippus went on to say this, which Eusebius here only paraphrases. Christians had long assumed that such anti-Christian acts had thus doomed the Jews (e.g. 1 Thess 2.14–16).

Could Origen have mistakenly opened and read a scroll from Hegesippus's *Commentaries* thinking he was reading a work by Josephus?[32] Then, when he wanted to find the passage again to cite it, he was unable to do so because the passage was not from the *AJ*. Instead, he merely repeated what he thought he knew, without

---

[31] Eusebius, *Ecclesiastical History* 2.23.19 (SC 31:90; trans. *NPNF*² 1:208).

[32] The authors Josephus and Hegesippus were indeed confused in some later manuscripts, and some scholars have indeed suspected that this is what happened here; see Paget, "Some Observations," 550–51 (cf. n. 43).

specific attribution. This explains every odd feature of Origen's claim that Josephus said all the same things that Hegesippus coincidentally says, despite the fact that Josephus never does and almost certainly never would have said those things, having credited the Jews' fate to the death of Ananus, and that for very different reasons than Hegesippus. I myself have made mistakes like this in my recollection of who said what. I usually take the care to confirm a citation before publishing, but then I have better technological resources than Origen did: a computer text-string search of my notes and files will set me straight—Origen had no such luxury. Moreover, Origen is already known for making errors of memory. For example, he confused the *Protevangelium of James* §23 as having been in Josephus, and thus incorrectly cited Josephus as his source.[33] It is therefore not implausible that he could repeat a similar error.

Origen also probably had a copy of Hegesippus in his library. Eusebius, who used that same library, frequently refers to Hegesippus, and even quotes this very passage, which precedes Eusebius's quotation of Origen's inadvertent paraphrase of it, which in turn precedes Eusebius's quotation of *AJ* 20.200. It is far more probable that Origen made this mistake than it is that he quoted a lost Josephan text, whose content contradicts other known statements of Josephus yet precisely matches with Eusebius's quotation of Hegesippus.

Other hypotheses are also improbable. That Origen conflated the two passages is too complicated: such a theory requires us to assume that Origen forgot the Josephan passage in a way that contradicts and hardly illumines what Origen says, but accurately remembered the details in Hegesippus. The simpler explanation is that he is following Hegesippus. That someone else conflated these

---

[33] Paget, "Some Observations," 550–51, and Whealey, *Josephus on Jesus*, 18. The error appears in an excerpt of one of the lost portions of the Greek original of Origen's *Commentary on Matthew* (fragment 25), preserved in a twelfth-century catena; see Erich Klostermann, *Origenes Werke*, vol. 12 (Leipzig: J. C. Hinrichs, 1941), 190, § 457 II. This remark does not appear in the Latin translation of Origen's commentary, but this was probably a result of abbreviation; cf. Klostermann, *Origenes Werke*, vol. 11 (Leipzig: J. C. Hinrichs, 1933), 42. That the Latin often gives an abbreviated version of the original text (and thus such a loss of detail in it is typical), see Hermann J. Vogt, *Origenes. Der Kommentar zum Evangelium nach Mattäus III* (Stuttgart: Hiersemann, 1993), 1–8, with the remarks in C. P. Bammel's review of same in *The Journal of Ecclesiastical History* 46 (1995): 549–50.

two passages before Origen, a conflation that he later employed, is also too complicated: this theory requires us to invent an unattested source that Origen does not mention and assume that the same improbable errors were made in that source. Again, it is more likely that Origen would be using a source that simply confused Hegesippus for Josephus. The fact that Origen does not quote any sentence from Josephus in this matter confirms the point: he uses only four words (with their expected articles) shared by Josephus, which constitute a construction already known to Origen, but none that are unique to Josephus, to construct a sentence that says exactly what Josephus does not say (but Hegesippus does). The conclusion is unavoidable: it is very unlikely that Origen draws upon Josephus, but very likely that he paraphrased Hegesippus and confused the attribution.

Conclusion

That Origen mistook Hegesippus for Josephus is more than adequately convincing. The only passage to which Origen refers when he mentions James "the brother of Jesus who was called Christ" comes from Origen's paraphrase of Hegesippus, not Josephus; he could never have been quoting *AJ* 20.200. He mistakenly recalled Hegesippus's text as Josephus's. We cannot use Origen as an attestation of a mention of Christ in *AJ* 20.200, and indeed, its absence in Origen's text speaks against its authenticity.

Where, then, did it come from? We have already seen that Origen quotes his own paraphrase, using the exact same six words, on three different occasions. However, none refer to [or quote] the *AJ* or Hegesippus. These words are probably his own, inspired (as noted earlier) by the biblical wording of Matt 1.16, a passage that discusses Jesus' family and lineage. It would be natural for Origen to use the Matthean wording, particularly if this thought originated in his *Commentary on Matthew*, where it appears. That Origen was fond of repeating the phrase suggests a familiar idiom.[34] The phrase also appears in Matt 27.17 and 27.22, though there it is uttered by Pilate (as opposed to Matt 1.16, where it is uttered by the narrator), but a similar idiom appears in John 4.25. This implies that it was a common Christian or Jewish designation for the messiah; the author probably intended irony by having Pilate repeat it. Notably, Matthew's source, Mark 15.9 and 15.12 does not have this phrase: Pilate there only refers to Jesus as the "King of the Jews," which is clearly intended to be ironic (since Pilate did not actually regard Jesus to be the "King of the Jews," yet the reader is supposed to understand that he was precisely that and that a Roman official just inadvertently declared it so). Like Matthew and John, Origen appears to treat the phrase as a common designation for the messiah, which he associated with his paraphrase of a source that he mistook as having authorial distance ("although he did not accept Jesus as Christ"—always a true description of any Jewish author, and, as we saw, an inference that could also have been made by a reader of the James narrative in Hegesippus, if he mistook which author he was reading). Certainly, as we have established, Origen does not quote Josephus.

We also have reason to believe that Origen looked long and hard for this passage in Josephus when he wanted to use it: the phrase appears twice in close proximity to references to the *AJ*, and yet Origen conspicuously avoids stating where *this* material was to be found. His repeated use of oblique references like "the same writer says," and "who wrote the *Antiquities of the Jews* in twenty books," suggests annoyance at not identifying the precise source. It is likely that what he found in *AJ* 20.200 was a reference to an execution by stoning of a certain "brother of Jesus" named James a few years before the war. Origen perhaps scribbled "who was called Christ" in the margin, or above the line, perhaps even marking the text immediately after "brother of Jesus," since, altogether, this would form his own phrase, "brother of Jesus who

---

[34] Apart from the gospel passages to be discussed, the same idiom appears in the *Clementine Homilies* 18.4.5 and Justin Martyr, *Apology* 1.30.1 (in contrast with *Dialogue with Trypho* 32.1, where it is used derogatorily by a Jew). The phrase is frequently quoted from the gospels throughout Origen's works (e.g., *Against Celsus* pref.2.12; *Commentary on the Gospel of John* 1.5.29, 1.21.126, 13.26.title; *Series of Commentaries on the Gospel of Matthew* 255; *Scholia on Matthew* 17.308) and is used in a related fashion in Origen, *Homilies on Jeremiah* 16.10 and *Against Celsus* 4.28.

was called Christ" (all the more likely if he had deceived himself into thinking his own words came from Josephus). A later scribe in his library could then have mistaken this as an intended correction, thereby inadvertently producing the interpolation.

Such a scribal note, though, need not have been Origen's. The natural juxtaposition, producing the same six-word line as Origen wrote, in a passage about a brother of Jesus named James being executed by stoning a few years before the war, in the very book "twenty" of the *AJ* that Origen could have been mistaken as implying contained a reference to James the brother of Jesus being executed, would be enough to inspire a scholiast to make this marginal note. Perhaps it was even a conjectured omission (a frequent occurrence in scribal annotation) with the scholiast thinking that surely Josephus must have meant to say this (especially if the scholiast had already read what Origen wrote about what Josephus was supposed to have said), or else as merely a note to himself that this must be a passage pertaining to that event. Either way such a note could then have become accidentally incorporated into the text thereafter. "Certainly," Paget concludes, "we should not exclude the possibility of a Christian gloss becoming a part of the text."[35] I think that it is more than a possibility: from all the evidence surveyed, the probability is high enough to merit near certainty.

In fact, the text may have originally said, "the brother of Jesus ben Damneus, the name for whom was James, and some others." Since "Jesus ben Damneus" appears again a few lines later (and as I have argued, it is more likely that Josephus actually meant this Jesus), a scribe who saw a marginal note "who was called Christ" (τοῦ λεγομένου Χριστοῦ) scribbled above "ben Damneus" (τὸν τοῦ Δαμναίου), regardless of how or why it came to be written there, may have inferred a dittography. This is a common scribal error where a copyist's eye slips to a similar line a few lines down (by mistaking which "Jesus" he had left off at), then realizes he had picked up at the wrong place, but corrected himself and then wrote a superlinear phrase intended to replace the erroneous material. A later copyist would then interpret the earlier copyist's correction as calling for the erasure of "ben Damneus" as a dittograph, omit the words, and replace it with the gloss, "who was called Christ." This was a frequent occurrence in manuscript transmission, resulting

---

[35] Paget, "Some Observations," 552 n. 45.

from scribes correcting a perceived error, but in the process, implanting their own error into the text. It is even possible, though not necessary to presume, that Origen himself believed this dittograph to have occurred (convinced by his faulty memory that Josephus mentioned James the brother of Jesus, and this being the only passage he could find), and that, when he annotated the *AJ* passage, he intended for (and may even have directed) a copyist to correct the text accordingly.

By any sequence of events, had this process taken place some time in the sixty years separating Origen from Eusebius, Eusebius would have found in the Caesarean library a Josephan text that said, "the brother of Jesus, who was called Christ, the name for whom was James," and quoted it, immediately after quoting Origen and repeating Origen's error of attributing the phrase to Josephus. Eusebius himself could have been the copyist who made this emendation, believing that he was restoring the original text because he read what Origen wrote about Josephus and James the Just. A marginal note made by Origen, then, could have led Eusebius to emend the text that he then quoted, an error repeated in all subsequent copies of the manuscripts of the *AJ*, such as we have now. Either error could have also occurred at the hand of other scribes in the same library during the two generations between Origen and Eusebius.

All, or any combination, of these scenarios are possible. In terms of probability, each possible scenario can be likened to a card drawn from a deck: the odds that one of two specified cards will be drawn are double the odds of drawing just one specific card; that is, the probability of drawing an ace or a king is higher than the probability of drawing only an ace, while the probability of drawing an ace or a king *or a queen* is higher still, and so on as the options increase. Given that there are many ways that the same result could have been produced, with each way fitting our evidence, the odds that one of them did indeed occur is increased, and all the more with multiple paths to the same result. The plethora of possible scenarios thus increases rather than reduces the probability of the conclusion that τοῦ λεγομένου Χριστοῦ is an accidental interpolation, a conclusion that has already been rendered probable by all the other evidence.

It is more probable that the phrase, "the brother of Jesus, who was called Christ, the name for whom was James," originated in an accidental interpolation in the Caesarean library than that it came from Josephus's hand. Without "who was called Christ," we have no reference to this passage in Origen at all, and we have no evidence that the phrase was ever in Josephus, as the silence of Luke-Acts, Origen, and every other author, including Hegesippus (whose account shows no knowledge of the events related in *AJ* 20.200) suggests. Origen does not quote Josephus when he, in three places, uses the phrase "the brother of Jesus, who was called Christ," because in none of these places does he quote or refer to other Josephan material (be it a distinctive construction like "the name for whom was James," or content particular to *AJ* 20.200). Rather, he uses a story clearly found only in the Christian author Hegesippus, who also relates a story unknown to Luke and, therefore, probably a second-century invention, as its internal absurdities further suggest.

Origen never claims that his material originated from the *AJ*, and Eusebius could not find it anywhere in Josephus's writings either, so he simply quoted Origen, but passed it off as a Josephan quotation. Eusebius is the first to notice any mention of Christ in *AJ* 20.200; unlike Origen, he is the first to quote it; he is the first to declare it a reference to the same James. It seems highly likely, then, that τοῦ λεγομένου Χριστοῦ ("who was called Christ") is an accidental scribal interpolation or innocent emendation, and never appeared in the original text of Josephus.

Since all the *AJ*'s extant manuscripts probably descend from the same manuscript that contained this interpolation (for the reasons argued earlier), we would not see direct manuscript evidence of this interpolation, even if manuscripts of the *AJ* are found or examined that have not been included in current editions. Nevertheless, the circumstantial evidence has been shown to be sufficiently strong. We can no longer proceed with confidence that Josephus referred to Christians here.

The significance of this finding is manifold, but principally it removes this passage from the body of reliable evidence for the fate of Jesus' family, the treatment of Christians in the first century, or Josephus's attitude toward or knowledge of Christians. Likewise, future commentaries on the relevant texts of Origen and Josephus must take this finding into account, as must any treatments of the evidence for the historical Jesus. Most pressingly, all reference works that treat "James the brother of Jesus" must be emended to reflect this finding, particularly as this passage is the only evidence by which a date for this James' death has been derived.

20

THE PROSPECT OF A CHRISTIAN INTERPOLATION IN TACITUS, *ANNALS* 15.44

This article appeared in *Vigiliae Christianae* 68 (2014): 1-20.
Copyright © 2014 by Koninklijke Brill NV, Leiden.
Reproduced with permission.

SUMMARY: Some scholars have argued that Tacitus' reference to Christ in connection with the burning of Rome under Nero is a 4th century (or later) interpolation. It is here argued that their arguments can be met with no strong rebuttal, and therefore the key sentence in Tacitus referring to Christ should be considered suspect.

Throughout the years a few scholars have argued that some or all of Tacitus' report about Christians in connection with the burning of Rome under Nero is a 4th century (or later) interpolation and not original to Tacitus.[1] Building on their arguments, I find that an interpolation of a single key line in this passage is reasonably likely, and therefore that line should be considered suspect. Though we

---

[1] For surveys see Robert Van Voorst, *Jesus Outside the New Testament: An Introduction to the Ancient Evidence* (Grand Rapids, Michigan: William B. Eerdmans, 2000), pp. 42-43; and Herbert W. Benario, "Recent Work on Tacitus (1964–1968)," *The Classical World* 63.8 (April 1970), pp. 253-66 [see pp. 264-65] and "Recent Work on Tacitus (1974–1983)," *The Classical World* 80.2 (Nov.–Dec. 1986)], pp. 73-147 [see p. 139]. The two most recent (and most important) examples are Jean Rougé, "L'incendie de Rome en 64 et l'incendie de Nicomédia en 303," *Mélanges d'histoire ancienne offerts à William Seston* (Paris: E. de Boccard, 1974), pp. 433-41; and Earl Doherty, *Jesus: Neither God nor Man: The Case for a Mythical Jesus* (Ottawa: Age of Reason Publications, 2009), pp. 596-630.

can't be certain, the evidence suggests it probably is an interpolation, and Tacitus did not refer to Christ. That suspect line is *auctor nominis eius Christus Tiberio imperitante per procuratorem Pontium Pilatum supplicio adfectus erat*, "The author of this name, Christ, was executed by the procurator Pontius Pilate in the reign of Tiberius."[2] With this line included, I shall call the whole account of the persecution of "Christians" in Tacitus the "Testimonium Taciteum" (Tacitus, *Annals* 15.44).

The Base Rate of Interpolation in Christian-Controlled Literature

Spanning the first three centuries the number of non-Christian references to Jesus numbers fewer than 10 and the number of interpolations among them numbers at least 1, for a base rate of interpolation equal to more than 1 in 10. The apparent rate is actually an astonishing 1 in 3, but I will assume that this evident rate is highly biased by the small sample size, and conclude instead that the highest rate of fabrication reasonably possible was 1 out of every 10 references to Jesus in non-Christian sources.[3] We could err even more on the side of caution and say that that rate may have been twenty times lower, and thus as low as 1 in 200 (meaning one out of every two hundred non-Christian references to Jesus would be an interpolation). From the evidence we have I believe it would be implausible to conclude the rate was any lower than that.

---

[2] Translations are my own where not otherwise noted.

[3] Van Voorst, *Jesus Outside the New Testament*, pp. 19-134 adduces only nine, and two of those are not certain to contain mentions of Jesus (Suetonius and Mara bar Serapion), one is non-existent (Thallus; we almost certainly have a direct quotation of his original words, from which we can confirm Thallus did not mention Jesus: see [Chapter 18]), and two are certain to have suffered some degree of interpolation (Josephus: the longer passage in whole or in part: Van Voorst, *Jesus Outside the New Testament*, pp. 81-103 and James Carleton Paget, "Some Observations on Josephus and Christianity," *Journal of Theological Studies* 52 [2001]: 539–624; and the shorter passage, in relevant part: see [Chapter 19]). That leaves only six passages, two of which have suffered interpolations, for an apparent base rate of interpolation equal to 1 in every 3 passages. The survey of non-Christian references to Jesus in the first three centuries in Gerd Theissen and Annette Merz, *The Historical Jesus: A Comprehensive Guide* (Minneapolis: Fortress, 1996), pp. 63-124, does not expand on the list in Van Voorst.

Consider the rate of interpolation in Christian books, for example. Even counting just one instance per book (even though there are often more), the New Testament contains at least five known interpolations in all its 27 books, for a base rate of interpolation of no less than 1 in 5 ($^5/_{27} = {}^1/_{5.4}$), if we measure by book. But we should measure by verse, not book, and count all interpolations, not just one per book. There are close to 8,000 verses in the New Testament, of which at least 20 are known interpolations (and that's counting only the most unquestionable cases in standard textual apparatuses; there are actually many more), for a base rate of 1 in 400.[4] The rate could appear much higher in non-Christian sources due to the fact that the New Testament already extensively favors what Christians want to have been said, and thus there was less need of inventing witnesses to Jesus there, whereas the temptation to or interest in finding witnesses in non-Christian authors was more compelling and thus would have been more frequent. If it was even just twice as frequent, we would have a rate of interpolation of 1 in 200, my minimum estimated rate; while my maximum estimated rate is 1 in 10, based on observation. So the suggestion of an interpolation in Tacitus is not out of bounds, but within the range of plausible events known to happen.

Evaluating the Evidence: Pliny the Younger

For context it is important to note that Pliny the Younger attests to a pervasive ignorance of Christians and Christian beliefs among even the most informed Roman elite at the time of Tacitus (be-

---

[4] Mk. 7:16, 9:44, 9:46, 11:26, 16:9-20; Mt. 12:47, 17:21, 18:10, 21:44, 27:49b; Lk. 17:36, 22:43-44, 23:17, 23:34a; Jn. 5:4, 7:53-8:11; Acts 8:37, 15:34, 28:29; Rom. 16:24. And this list is a definite undercount (especially for Luke-Acts, and especially considering known interpolations often not included in standard textual apparatuses). So the actual rate was certainly higher than 1 in 400 and arguably nearer 1 in 200 (if for every example listed here we can add one other) or even 1 in 100 (if for every example here listed we can find *three* others that probably should be listed as well).

tween 110-120 A.D.).[5] Notably, Pliny was not only a contemporary of Tacitus but his good friend and regular correspondent.[6] Pliny the Younger tells us he had never attended a trial of Christians and knew nothing of what they believed or what crimes they were guilty of. To redress his ignorance, Pliny's procedure involved no independent fact-checking (beyond an interrogation of local Christians), and from his behavior and attitude we can conclude that this would have been typical, and thus Tacitus is unlikely to have done more.

Pliny had been governing Bithynia for over a year already, before even learning there were any Christians in his province, and before that he held the post of consul (the highest office in the Roman Empire, short of being Emperor). He had also been a lawyer in Roman courts for several decades, then served in Rome as Praetor (the ancient equivalent of both chief of police and attorney general), and then served as one of Trajan's top legal advisors

---

[5] Pliny, *Letters* 10.96. See Van Voorst, *Jesus Outside the New Testament*, pp. 23-29; Theissen and Merz, *The Historical Jesus*, pp. 79-83; and Bradley Peper and Mark DelCogliano, "The Pliny and Trajan Correspondence," in Amy-Jill Levine, Dale C. Allison, Jr., and John Dominic Crossan, eds., *The Historical Jesus in Context* (Princeton, N.J.: Princeton University Press, 2006), pp. 366-71.

[6] Pliny and Tacitus exchanged many letters (not just the ones in which Tacitus asks for information to add to his history in Pliny the Younger, *Letters* 6.16; also 6.20, note this was a quite personal question, and 7.33), had worked side-by-side in the Senate (*Letters* 2.11.2), and on political campaigns in which they were on intimate terms (*Letters* 6.9); they had several intimate friends in common (*Letters* 1.6, 4.15.1, and 7.20.6); Pliny admired Tacitus's oratorical skills (*Letters* 2.1.6) and writing (*Letters* 9.23.2) and talked them up to everyone; Pliny indicates he often visited with Tacitus, was always keen to be informed of his well-being, and trusted him with personal favors that he normally discussed with him "in person" and which he surely would never ask some distant acquaintance (*Letters* 4.13); Pliny wrote Tacitus letters about events in his personal life and gave him advice (*Letters* 1.6) and seeks and trusts his advice in turn (*Letters* 1.20); Pliny also sent intimate but admiring letters to him (e.g., *Letters* 9.14); they shared and discussed each other's poetry (*Letters* 9.10); and Tacitus asked Pliny to read advanced drafts of his histories and mark them up with advice and criticism, while Pliny asked the same of Tacitus (*Letters* 7.20 and 8.7); finally, Pliny outright calls Tacitus his friend (*Letters* 6.16.22) and says "the tale will everywhere be told of the harmony, frankness, and loyalty of our lifelong friendship" (*Letters* 7.20.2) and "our love should be still the warmer" because of all their friends and work in common (*Letters* 7.20.7).

for several years, before he was appointed to govern Bithynia.⁷ And yet, he tells us, after all that, he still knew next to nothing about Christians and had never witnessed a trial of them. This verifies that Christians were extremely obscure, and their beliefs and origins entirely unknown to the highest and most experienced Roman legal authorities. Tacitus is not likely to have been any better informed, indeed insofar as he was informed at all it would most likely have been through his very friend and correspondent, Pliny.⁸ Otherwise, from having completed a similar career, Tacitus would likely know only as much as Pliny did before his interrogations—which is only that Christians existed and were in some vague fashion criminals.

Evaluating the Evidence: Pliny the Elder

There were several eyewitness historical accounts written about Nero's reign that have become lost. Cluvius Rufus, Nero's herald, is known to have written an eyewitness account of Nero's reign sometime in the 70s A.D. As did Fabius Rusticus, an author we know Tacitus used.⁹ But the most extensive account was that of Pliny the Elder (killed during the eruption of Vesuvius in 79 A.D.), who had written a monumental 31 volume history beginning in the 30s, dedicating an entire volume to each year, including every year of Nero's reign, and this Tacitus also employed as a source.¹⁰

---

[7] For summary and bibliography: A.N. Sherwin-White and Simon Price, "Pliny (2) the Younger," in Simon Hornblower and Antony Spawforth, eds., *Oxford Classical Dictionary*, 3rd ed. (New York: Oxford University Press, 1996), p. 1198.

[8] Tacitus was even governing the neighboring province of Asia when Pliny interrogated Christians in Bithynia (and we know Tacitus consulted with Pliny on information to include in his histories: see earlier note), making communication between them on the Christian matter very likely: see "Tacitus (1)," in Simon and Spawforth, *Oxford Classical Dictionary*, pp. 1469-71; and Stephen Benko, "Pagan Criticism of Christianity During the First Two Centuries A.D.," *Aufstieg und Niedergang der römischen Welt* II 23.2 (1980), p. 1063.

[9] Tacitus, *Annals* 13.20, 15.61; *Agricola* 10.3.

[10] Tacitus, *Annals* 1.69, 13.20, 15.53; *Histories* 3.29; Pliny the Younger, *Letters* 6.16.

Pliny's history would certainly have included his own account of the burning of Rome in 64 A.D. and subsequent events. Most likely a resident of Rome at the time, his information would have been first hand. He would surely have recorded how it degenerated into the execution of scores if not hundreds of Christians for the crime of burning the city of Rome, surely the single most famous event of that or any adjacent year. If that in fact happened. And such an account would surely have included any necessary digressions on the origins of Christianity. We know, for example, Pliny believed Nero had started the fire deliberately, lamenting in his *Natural History* that it destroyed ancient trees invaluable to botanical science.[11]

However, it is unlikely Pliny mentioned Christians in his account of the fire. Because his nephew and adopted son Pliny the Younger was an avid admirer and reader of his uncle's works and thus would surely have read his account of the burning of Rome, and therefore would surely have known everything about Christians that Pliny the Elder recorded. Yet in his correspondence with Trajan, Pliny indicates a complete lack of knowledge, making no mention of his uncle having said anything about them, or about their connection in any way to the burning of Rome (and yet, whether believed to be a false charge or not, that would surely be pertinent to Pliny's inquest, in many respects). Corroborating this conclusion is the fact that no one else ever mentions, cites, or quotes Pliny the Elder providing any testimony to Christ or Christians (as likely Christians or their critics would have done, if such an invaluably early reference existed). Indeed, his history would likely have been preserved had that been the case (since mentions of Christ seem to have been a motive for preserving texts in general: the works of Josephus and Tacitus may have survived the Middle Ages for precisely that reason).

And if Pliny the Elder, of all people, did not mention Christians in connection with the fire, no other historian is likely to have. Which conclusion is corroborated again by the fact that no one ever mentions, cites, or quotes any of *them* providing any testimony to Christ or Christians, either (as likely Christians or their critics would have done, if any such existed).

---

[11] Pliny the Elder, *Natural History* 17.1.5.

Evaluating the Evidence: Suetonius

Suetonius attests to a persecution of Christians under Nero, but is evidently unaware of this having any connection to the burning of Rome.[12] Among a list of various, briefly-mentioned legal crackdowns during the reign of Nero, Suetonius includes the remark that *afflicti suppliciis Christiani, genus hominum superstitionis novae ac maleficae*, "punishments were inflicted on the Christians, a class of men given to a new and wicked superstition," but not, apparently, for the crime of arson, legitimate or contrived, much less the atrocity of burning down Rome.[13]

One could conjecture that this line originally read *Chrestiani* (later 'corrected' in transmission), and thus referred to the Jewish rioters that (as we shall see) Suetonius reported had begun to make trouble under Claudius. It's also possible that this line was an accidental interpolation of a marginal note summarizing the Testimonium Taciteum.[14] But I shall not explore either possibility here. I will simply assume the passage is authentic as we have it. As such, it confirms that Suetonius, a prominent and erudite Latin author and imperial librarian, knew nothing of any connection between Christians and the burning of Rome. He knew only that Nero had executed some Christians in Rome, possibly for sorcery (*malefica superstitio*), as part of his overall plan to enforce a stricter moral order in the city (which is the overall context of the remark).

Elsewhere, Suetonius says of the emperor Claudius that *Iudaeos impulsore Chresto assidue tumultuantis Roma expulit*, "since Jews con-

---

[12] See Van Voorst, *Jesus Outside the New Testament*, pp. 29-39; Theissen and Merz, *The Historical Jesus*, pp. 83-85.

[13] Suetonius, *Nero* 16.2.

[14] Argued by Stephen Dando-Collins, *The Great Fire of Rome: The Fall of the Emperor Nero and His City* (Cambridge: Da Capo Press, 2010), p. 6; and Doherty, *Jesus: Neither God nor Man*, pp. 616-18. The language of the line as we have it is certainly not in Suetonian style and reflects a Latin idiom that arose after his time: see K. R. Bradley, "Suetonius, *Nero* 16.2: '*afflicti suppliciis Christiani*'," *The Classical Review* 22.1 (March 1972): 9-10. Although Bradley argues that this means the text was corrupted and should be restored to align with a paraphrase of Orosius and the known style of Suetonius, an interpolation would explain the same evidence. And if we must emend this passage, as Bradley says, to guarantee its authenticity, we could just as soon emend Christians to Chrestians as well.

stantly made disturbances at the instigation of Chrestus, he expelled them from Rome," in a section listing various brief examples of how Claudius treated foreigners.[15] Such an expulsion of all Jews from Rome would have been a near impossibility. There would have been tens of thousands of Jews in Rome at the time, complete with extensive real estate, synagogues, businesses, as well as countless Jewish slaves in both private and public hands that would have been indispensable to the urban economy, not to mention an enormous challenge to locate and drive out.[16] In fact, we learn from Cassius Dio that "as for the Jews, who had again increased so greatly that by reason of their multitude it would have been hard without raising a tumult to bar them from the city, Claudius did not drive them out, but ordered them, while continuing their traditional mode of life, not to hold meetings," which is a far more plausible report.[17] It's still possible some select Jews were expelled (or left of their own accord), as Suetonius does not actually say *all* Jews were expelled, but only that "Jews" were. But a total expulsion cannot really be believed.[18]

Neither Suetonius nor Dio show any knowledge of this decree (or the riot inspiring it) being in any way connected to Christians; nor, apparently, did Tacitus—since if the Testimonium Taciteum is

---

[15] Suetonius, *Claudius* 25.4. See commentary in J. Mottershead, *Claudius / Suetonius* (Bristol: Bristol Classical Press, 1986), pp. 149-57 (Appendix 2).

[16] Various estimates of the Jewish population of Rome are made in E. Mary Smallwood, *The Jews under Roman Rule: From Pompey to Diocletian* (Leiden: Brill, 1976) and Harry Leon, *The Jews of Ancient Rome*, updated edition (Peabody, Mass.: Hendrickson Publishers, 1995).

[17] Dio Cassius, *Roman History* 60.6.6 (translation by Earnest Cary, Loeb Classics edition). The fifth century Orosius, in *A History against the Pagans* 7.6.15-16, claims Josephus reported this expulsion, but there is no mention of this in Josephus' extant works (Orosius is probably confusing this with an expulsion incident under Tiberius, which *is* mentioned by Josephus); see Leonard Victor Rutgers, "Roman Policy towards the Jews: Expulsions from the City of Rome during the First Century C.E.," *Classical Antiquity* 13.1 (April 1994): 56-74. Orosius also produces *Christus* instead of *Chrestus* in his quotation of Suetonius here, and thus assumes Suetonius was speaking of riots over Christianity.

[18] Acts 18:2 is alone in saying "all the Jews" were expelled, but its reliability on this point is doubtful: see Richard Pervo, *Acts: A Commentary* (Minneapolis: Fortress Press, 2009), pp. 446-47.

authentic, it was clearly the first reference Tacitus had made to Christians, therefore he cannot have mentioned Christ or Christians in connection with this riot or decree under Claudius. In fact not even Acts (cf. 18:2) shows any awareness of this expulsion being connected to Christians, yet the author of Acts would certainly have made use of the fact that the Jews were making trouble for Christians in Rome and were duly punished for it by the emperor, so we can be fairly certain no such thing occurred (and thus no such rhetorical coup was available to the author of Acts). Suetonius clearly wrote that the riots were instigated by Chrestus himself (*impulsore Chresto* means "because of the *impulsor* Chrestus," an *impulsor* being a man who instigates something, not the reason for instigating it), and so it cannot plausibly be argued that this meant *Jesus*, who was neither alive nor in Rome at any time under Claudius.[19] Note, also, that Acts 28:22-24 depicts Jews at Rome knowing little about Christianity (and nothing bad, other than that people spoke against it), which hardly makes sense (even as an authorial invention) if it was known the whole Jewish population of Rome had rioted over it just a decade before. Likewise that Paul saw no need to address this in his letter to the Romans further suggests no such thing had occurred.

Moreover, if the other passage in Suetonius has been soundly transmitted (documenting the Neronian persecution), then Suetonius knew the difference between Christians and Jews, and would have commented on the fact had Christians (much less Christ) been in any way the cause of these riots. Many scholars nevertheless try to press this evidence in that direction, but from the parallel passage in Dio, and the reports of Acts and the silence of Romans (and the evident silence of Tacitus), it's simply not likely. This incident was more likely city-wide violence ginned up by a Jewish demagogue named Chrestus (a common name in Rome at the time), as many scholars agree. And that was likely a man well known to Suetonius and his peers, thus explaining why he did not

---

[19] The use of "Chresto" in place of "Christo," though a linguistic possibility (as well as a possible corruption in transmission), is nevertheless not a necessary conjecture, as Chrestus was a common name. See Stephen Benko, "The Edict of Claudius of A.D. 49 and the Instigator Chrestus," *Theologische Zeitschrift* 25 (1969): 407-408; and Dixon Slingerland, "Chrestus: Christus?" in A.J. Avery-Peck, ed., *New Perspectives on Ancient Judaism*, Vol. 4: *The Literature of Early Rabbinic Judaism* (Lanham, MD: 1989), pp. 133-44.

digress to explain who he was. This is significant because it informs the possible meaning of the passage in Tacitus, to which we now turn.

Evaluating the Evidence: Tacitus

In our present text of the *Annals* of Tacitus, we learn that Nero scapegoated the Christians for burning down most of the city of Rome in 64 A.D.[20] The text now reads:

> Nero found culprits and inflicted the most exquisite tortures on those hated for their abominations, whom the people called Chrestians [*sic*]. The author of this name, Christ, was executed by the procurator Pontius Pilate in the reign of Tiberius, and the most mischievous superstition, thus checked for the moment, again broke out not only in Judea, the source of this evil, but even in Rome, where all things hideous or shameful flow in from every part of the world and become popular.
>
> Accordingly, arrests were first made of those who confessed; then, upon their information, an immense multitude was convicted, not so much for the crime of burning the city as because of the hatred of mankind. Mockery of every sort was added to their death. ... *[Tacitus then describes their torments]* ... Hence, even for criminals who deserved the most extreme punishments, there arose a feeling of compassion; for it no longer appeared that they were being destroyed for the public good, but rather to satisfy the cruelty of one man.

The key line here is "the author of this name, Christ, was executed by the procurator Pontius Pilate in the reign of Tiberius." This is

---

[20] Tacitus, *Annals* 15.44. See Van Voorst, *Jesus Outside the New Testament*, pp. 39-53; and Theissen and Merz, *The Historical Jesus*, pp. 79-83.

the first clear reference to a historical Jesus outside the New Testament, dating to around 116 A.D.[21]

If that key line is authentic. The first clue it might not be is that our one manuscript containing this passage had originally spelled the persecuted group as the "Chrestians," not the Christians, and this was subsequently corrected by erasure.[22] To explain this, it is more likely that Tacitus originally wrote *chrestianos*, "Chrestians," than that this was produced by subsequent error from "Christians" and then corrected back again.[23] And if that's the case, it's not believable that Tacitus would have explained the name "Chrestians" using the name "Christus." Instead, obviously, he would use "Chrestus." Which may also have been the original reading here, corrected earlier in the text's transmission history.[24] I think it's more likely that Tacitus had already explained who the Chrestians were in his account of the Chrestus riots (those also recorded by Suetonius), which would have appeared in his section of the *Annals* for the early years of the reign of Claudius, now lost.[25] If that is the case, then what would become the Testimo-

---

[21] On the date: in Tacitus, *Annals* 2.61 and 4.4-5 allusions are made to Trajan's annexation of Parthian territories in 116 A.D. but not their loss a year or two later. On this being the earliest reference to Jesus: the two references to Jesus in Josephus would be earlier (dating to just after the year 93 A.D.), if they were authentic, but that is doubtful (see [Chapter 19]).

[22] This was most extensively demonstrated in Harald Fuchs, "Tacitus über die Christen," *Vigiliae Christianae* 4.2 (April 1950): 65-93 (who also brings up other stylistic difficulties with the passage, to no certain conclusion); see also Heinz Heubner, "Zu Tac. Ann. 15, 44, 4," *Hermes* 87.2 (August 1959): 223-30. I had my own doubts until they were met by Erík Zara, whose personal report on the condition of the manuscript in question, "The Chrestianos Issue in Tacitus Reinvestigated" (2009), can be accessed at www.textexcavation.com/documents/zaratacituschrestianos.pdf.

[23] This is also the opinion of leading experts on the matter: see Van Voorst, *Jesus Outside the New Testament*, pp. 43-46.

[24] Robert Renehan, "Christus or Chrestus in Tacitus?" *La Parola del Passato* 122 (1968): 368-70.

[25] Dio dates the associated decree to the year 41 A.D. A date of 49 has alternately been suggested, based on an unreliable report in Orosius, but Tacitus makes no mention of such an incident in his treatment of that year (which we have), yet surely he would have, so it more likely appeared in his treatment of the year 41, which is lost.

nium Taciteum was originally about the sect of Jewish rebels first suppressed under Claudius, who were at that time led by their namesake Chrestus and were thereafter named for him (whether he was still alive or not). Several scholars have suggested this possibility.[26]

In that event, Tacitus originally wrote that Nero put the blame on *quos per flagitia invisos vulgus Chrestianos appellabat repressaque in praesens exitiabilis superstitio rursum erumpebat, non modo per Iudaeam, originem eius mali, sed per urbem etiam*, "those whom the people called the Chrestians, who were [*i.e. already*] despised for their shameful deeds; and though this despicable superstition had been suppressed for a time, it had erupted again, not only in Judea, the origin of this evil, but also in the city." The entire line in between ("the author of this name, Christ, was executed by the procurator Pontius Pilate in the reign of Tiberius") would then be a later Christian interpolation, attempting to convert this passage about the Chrestians into a

---

[26] See Erich Koestermann, "Ein folgenschwerer Irrtum des Tacitus (*Ann.* 15, 44, 2ff.)?" *Historia: Zeitschrift für Alte Geschichte* 16.4 (September 1967): 456-69; Josef Ceska, "Tacitovi Chrestiani a apokalyptické císlo," *Listy Filologické* 92.3 (Sept. 1969): 239-49; and Charles Saumagne, "Tacite et saint Paul," *Revue Historique* 232.1 (1964), pp. 67-110 and "Les Incendiaires de Rome (ann. 64 p. C.) et les lois pénales des Romains (Tacite, *Annales*, XV, 44)," *Revue Historique* 227.2 (1962), pp. 337-360. Saumagne argues that the line about Christ being crucified under Tiberius was later transferred here from a now-lost section of the *Histories* of Tacitus that, he proposes, actually *was* about Christians, which passage Saumagne presumes to have been the source for a later account found in Sulpicius Severus (*Chronicle* 2.30.6-7), on which possibility see, more recently, Eric Laupot, "Tacitus' Fragment 2: The Anti-Roman Movement of the 'Christiani' and the Nazoreans," *Vigiliae Christianae* 54.3 (2000): 233-47. Although I believe the material in Severus more likely derives from another source shared by Orosius (*History against the Pagans* 7.9.4-6), not Tacitus (Orosius concluded his history twenty years after Severus, yet clearly drew the same information Severus employs from a source unfamiliar with the account in either Severus or Tacitus). Although if at all Tacitean, it is possible the original passage referred to the *Chrestiani*, and Severus has again only assumed Tacitus meant Christians.

Neronian persecution of Christians. This, too, has been proposed before.[27] And there are good arguments in its favor.

First, the text flows logically and well with the line removed. Second, the notion that there was "a huge multitude" (*multitudo ingens*) of Christians in Rome to persecute, though not impossible, is somewhat suspect; whereas, by contrast, Jews were present by the tens of thousands, and there were already enough Chrestus-followers under Claudius to result in a city-wide action against them. Third, it is not clear why Tacitus, much less the general public (as he implies), would regard the Christians as "criminals who deserved the most extreme punishments" merely for being in thrall to a vulgar superstition (which was actually not even a *crime*, much less a capital one).[28] But if these were the *Chrestians* who were already hated for their previous urban violence (which Tacitus would have recounted in an earlier book, when he treated the Chrestus

---

[27] Most convincingly by Jean Rougé, "L'incendie de Rome," and in a different respect by Saumagne (see previous note). Earl Doherty, an undergraduate in classics, also details a respectable argument to the same conclusion, in line with Rougé (see first note). A similar case for interpolation, suggesting it may have begun as a marginal gloss later inserted accidentally, has also been made online by Roger Viklund, "Tacitus as a Witness to Jesus – An Illustration of What the Original Might Have Looked Like," *Jesus Granskad* (2 October 2010) at rogerviklund.wordpress.com/2010/10/02. On accidental interpolation as a general phenomenon see [Chapter 19, p. 339].

[28] Christians came to later be policed for violating general laws against illegal assembly and, ultimately, treasonously refusing to bless the emperor's guardian spirit (the Roman equivalent of a Pledge of Allegiance), as reported in Pliny the Younger, *Letters* 10.96-97 (compare 10.34). See also: W.H.C. Frend, "Martyrdom and Political Oppression," in Philip Esler, ed., *The Early Christian World*, vol. 1 (2000): pp. 815-39; Naphtali Lewis and Meyer Reinhold, *Roman Civilization: Selected Readings*, 3rd ed., vol. 2 (1990): § 51-52 (see also § 169 and n. 37 in § 68); and Timothy Barnes, "Legislation Against the Christians," *Journal of Roman Studies* 58 (1968): pp. 32-50. Even then there is no reliable evidence they were ever prosecuted for such crimes in the first century (the book of Acts, for example, evinces the contrary, never depicting Romans prosecuting Christians at all and even rejecting their prosecution, e.g. Acts 18:12-17, 23:26-35, 26:24-32, although that could be a fabrication), and Tacitus does not mention either as being their crimes in this case. The only crime the victims in this account are charged with is arson; Tacitus indicates they were *also* widely believed to have been guilty of crimes deserving of the worst possible punishments, which would have to be crimes more severe than mere illegal assembly or want of allegiance.

riots also mentioned by Suetonius), their deserving of extreme punishments would be a more intelligible sentiment. Fourth, Tacitus says the people "called" them Chrestians, *vulgus Chrestianos appellabat*, notably the past tense.[29] Why would he not use the *present* tense if he believed the group was still extant, as Christians were? In fact, Tacitus makes no explicit mention of this group still being extant in his own day (notably unlike the Testimonium Flavianum, which does).[30] So it would appear this was a group that Tacitus believed no longer existed (probably having been expunged or disbanded since the Jewish War, if not already decisively ended by Nero's mass executions).[31]

But fifth, and most convincingly, there is no evidence that this event happened. The burning of Rome itself is well attested, by

---

[29] It's also not credible that Christians would be so well known then that "the people" (*vulgus*) would already have named them and formed popular beliefs about them; whereas if Tacitus was referring to present beliefs, he would use the present tense. Christianity was surely far too obscure in 64 for the *vulgus* even to know of them (we must remember that the population of Rome at the time approached a million people), much less have named them or known anything about them, given that it was barely any less obscure to Pliny the Younger almost *half a century later*, as we previously saw. If Pliny knew nothing about Christians, neither would "the people" in Rome a whole lifetime before him (see Candida Moss, *The Myth of Persecution: How Early Christians Invented a Story of Martyrdom* [New York: HarperOne, 2013], pp. 138-39). This conclusion is not mitigated by the legend recounted in Acts 11:26 (on the origination of the name "Christian" in Antioch), even if that legend is true (Pervo is skeptical: *Acts: A Commentary*, pp. 294-95), because it does not refer to the people of Rome (or any population near Rome), nor does it say the appellation was used by the general populace, or even widely known, in Antioch or anywhere else (only that it was then coined).

[30] The Testimonium Flavianum is the longer passage in Josephus, *Jewish Antiquities* 18.63-64, which is almost certainly an interpolation (see earlier note), but in any event concludes "and even until now the tribe of Christians, so named from this man, has not gone extinct."

[31] I do not credit the argument, however, though sometimes made, that calling Pilate a "procurator" is evidence of Christian authorship. There is abundant evidence that Pilate was *both* a procurator *and* a prefect (that in fact most equestrian governors were), and Tacitus would have a sufficient rhetorical reason to prefer the former (it was more embarrassing to be executed by a mere business manager). Though this is inessential to my argument here, for anyone who wishes to know more, summaries of the evidence and scholarship supporting it is available in [Chapters 6 and 7].

both literary and physical evidence.[32] But no one seems to have ever known Christians were in any way connected with it, until late in the 4th century. The *Letters of Seneca and Paul* (a late 4th century forgery), epistle 12, is the first mention of the event in such a connection, claiming *Christiani et Iudaei quasi machinatores incendii - pro! - supplicio adfecti, quod fieri solet,* "Oh! Christians and Jews have even been executed as contrivers of the fire, like usual!" This account does not align with Tacitus in any other specifics, beyond common tropes and lore, so its source is uncertain. As a forgery this text could simply be reflecting a circulating legend of the time, and embellishing freely. But it is also possible that this is the origination of the legend, which then inspired the interpolation in Tacitus at a later date. That this remark assumes it was already "usual" to blame Christians for such things confirms its late date (as it presumes a centuries long history of persecution), and also suggests a precedent for inventing it.[33]

The first *direct* attestation to the Testimonium Taciteum is usually said to be the 5th century text of Sulpicius Severus, *Chronicle* 2.29-30, which certainly draws on this passage from Tacitus, but notably it does not attest the suspect line. So it is possible Sulpicius simply assumed "Chrestians" meant Christians (just as Orosius assumed the Chrestus of Suetonius was Christ), and thus he might not even have been looking at an interpolated manuscript. Before these two texts, there is no evidence anyone had ever heard of Nero persecuting Christians in connection with the burning of Rome. And that is extraordinarily peculiar.

---

[32] Dio Cassius, *Roman History* 62.16-18 recounts the event of the fire but omits any mention of who was punished or blamed (other than Nero); Pliny the Elder, *Natural History* 17.1.5 mentions Nero burning the city and assumes he was to blame for it. For other evidence (including epigraphic and archaeological) see: Edward Champlin, *Nero* (Cambridge, Mass.: Belknap Press of Harvard University Press, 2003), pp. 122, 125, 178-200, with corresponding endnotes.

[33] For example, Paul's threat to Nero in *Acts of Paul* 11:3 (a late second century text that was predominately fictional) that God would burn the world with fire, resulting in Nero burning Paul's companions instead, is a possible inspiration. Knowledge that in fact Jews (the Chrestians) were burned for burning Rome would then explain the insertion of Christian victims among them.

Evaluating the Evidence: Unlikely Silence

We are faced with only three possibilities: (1) no such persecution happened and Tacitus invented it (perhaps by deliberately conflating a separate persecution with his account of the fire, to further darken the reputation of Nero), or (2) no such persecution happened and Tacitus never connected Christians with the fire, but only the Jewish sectarians inspired by Chrestus, in the manner I just proposed (which might explain why the *Letters of Seneca and Paul* say Nero punished Christians *and* Jews for the fire), or (3) the persecution happened, in connection with the fire, and Tacitus recorded it (even if exaggerating).

The third of these possibilities can be ruled out on the grounds that there would very likely have been a strong and widely-referenced Christian tradition deriving from it, widely enough in fact to be evident in extant literature. But no such Christian tradition exists. It is wholly unheard of in all extant Christian memory, until the later 4th century, and there only in a patent forgery (and we shall explore this argument from silence in a moment). The first possibility can be ruled improbable on the same grounds. Although ignorance of a fabricated tale in Tacitus might be more likely than ignorance of a genuine event, it's still unlikely. Such a thesis would have an even lower probability because it requires the *ad hoc* supposition of specifically deceptive behavior from Tacitus. These considerations together would render it no more or less likely than the third option, so I will treat the first and third options as two versions of the same one thesis: the Testimonium Taciteum was actually written by Tacitus as we have it.[34]

Refuting the third option (that the event happened), we have elaborate Christian accounts of Nero's persecution of Christians, resulting in the deaths of Peter and Paul, as related in the *Acts of*

---

[34] A fourth possibility, a modification of the third, is that the story was invented by Christians and simply "bought" by a gullible Tacitus. This can be discounted on the grounds that the story would then be more widely evidenced throughout extant Christian literature (since such a tale so widely disseminated among Christians that even Tacitus would have heard of it, and even believe it, could not fail to appear *somewhere* in extant Christian literature before the late 4th century). It is therefore at least as improbable as the first and third options.

Paul and the *Acts of Peter*.³⁵ Even though those are certainly fabrications (their narratives are wildly implausible in almost every conceivable detail), surely even a fabricator would use the existing memory of the monstrous false persecution for arson that the present text of Tacitus describes, and thus the story of the fire and subsequent scapegoating would feature prominently in their tales, a ripe context for condemning Nero and wallowing in its horrific details, as Christian martyrologies regularly enjoyed doing. But instead, neither the *Acts of Peter* nor the *Acts of Paul* show any knowledge of the fire or its connection to either the Christians, the deaths of Peter and Paul, or Nero's persecution of Christians generally. How is that possible? It is not believable that Tacitus would know of such an enormous persecution event, but all subsequent Christians have no knowledge of it for over two hundred years.

That makes the third option too improbable to credit. The more so when we consider the whole of Christian literature up to the 4th century. In all such literature surviving, the only persecutions known under Nero are always those of Peter and Paul (and some of their companions), as relayed in their respective *Acts*; never any connection to the burning of Rome, or any kind of elaborate, mass-scale event like that described in the extant text of Tacitus. And from this evidence we can rule out the first option, too (that Tacitus invented it). For example, Tertullian, a Latin author we know was familiar with the works of Tacitus, says only to "consult your histories: you will there find that Nero was the first who assailed with the imperial sword the Christian sect, beginning especially at Rome," and "at last it was Nero's savagery that sowed the seed of Christian blood at Rome," in both cases in a context referencing the fates of Peter and Paul (Paul having been beheaded, Peter crucified upside down, but neither in any mass persecution).³⁶ In asking why Christians are still persecuted, Tertullian says that "under Nero [Christianity] came to be condemned," yet, he says, this policy is continued even though every other policy

---

[35] Peter: Oscar Cullmann, *Peter: Disciple, Apostle, Martyr*, new ed. (Waco, Tex.: Baylor University Press, 2011), pp. 71-157; Paul: Dennis MacDonald, *The Legend and the Apostle: The Battle for Paul in Story and Canon* (Philadelphia: Westminister, 1983).

[36] Tertullian, *Apology* 5.3 and 21.25. That Tertullian knew the works of Tacitus is demonstrated in Tertullian, *Apology* 16 and *Ad Nationes* 1.11 and 2.12.

of Nero's has itself been condemned.[37] Tertullian gives no details. But it's strange that he makes no mention of the unjust charges it was then based on: arson, a charge that could no longer be applied to Christians of Tertullian's day, a point he obviously would have made, had he known such a thing (and as a reader of Tacitus, he would have—unless he did not see any mention of Christians in his copy of the *Annals*).

Tertullian also gives us more detail elsewhere:

> We read the Lives of the Caesars: at Rome Nero was the first to stain the rising faith with blood. That's when Peter is girded by another, when he is fastened to the cross. That's when Paul, the Roman citizen, gets his nativity, when there he is born again by the nobility of martyrdom.[38]

Here it is clear his only real source is the martyrdom tales of Peter and Paul—and perhaps the line about Nero persecuting Christians in the *Lives of the Caesars* of Suetonius, if such was present in his copy. But as we saw, that, too, fails to show any apparent knowledge that this persecution was linked with the burning of Rome, even though Suetonius also covered that fire in some detail (although he does not mention *any* scapegoats, Chrestians or Christians). Not only would Tertullian (and as we shall see, Lactantius; and we must add to this *all* Christian authors in Latin, extant and not) have remarked upon and made use of any such tale told or invented by Tacitus, he (no less than they) would have publicized its existence among the Christian community generally—hence such a valuable Christian gem of a passage would almost certainly be more widely known than only among the usual readers of Tacitus. It would have entered Christian lore and joined and influenced its growing body of martyrdom literature. Yet it didn't.

In Greek, we have Eusebius, who surveys all the persecutions he knew the church had suffered, and he says he is aware of many treatises refuting the false accusations of such persecutors as Nero. So he very likely would have known of the arson charge, had it existed, as well as the whole tradition of the Neronian persecution in

---

[37] Tertullian, *Ad Nationes* 1.7.8.

[38] Tertullian, *Antidote for the Scorpion's Sting* 15.

connection with the fire, yet he never mentions either. Even when he relates the persecutions under Nero, this never comes up.[39] He is completely ignorant of the event. Like Tertullian, Eusebius only knows of the martyrdoms under Nero of Peter and Paul (and with them, at most, a few of their colleagues).

Then there is the famous professor of Latin literature, learned Christian and tutor to Constantine, Lactantius, who surely cannot have been ignorant of the works of Tacitus (that would be impossible for any 4th century professor of Latin). He wrote an entire book on the emperors who persecuted Christians, and their fates, in which he details, again, the persecutions under Nero, yet shows, again, no knowledge of the burning of Rome being involved with it, or anything at all resembling what our text of Tacitus reports.[40] Yet again, he only knows of the martyrdoms of Peter and Paul (and some Christians attending them). This is all but impossible—unless at that time the text of Tacitus did not say Christians were the scapegoats for the fire, and the suspect line about Christ's execution under Pilate was not yet present.

This becomes all the more certain a conclusion when we look at what Lactantius says regarding the persecution by Galerius (his contemporary), in the late 3rd century:

> Galerius ... sought in another way to gain on the emperor. That he might urge him to excess of cruelty in persecution, he employed private emissaries to set the palace [in Nicomedia] on fire; and some part of it having been burnt, the blame was laid on the Christians as public enemies; and the very appellation of Christian grew odious on account of that fire. It was said that the Christians, in concert with the eunuchs, had plotted to destroy the emperors; and that both of the emperors had nearly been burnt alive in their own palace.
>
> Diocletian, shrewd and intelligent as he always chose to appear, suspected nothing of the contrivance, but, inflamed with anger, immediately commanded that

---

[39] Eusebius, *History of the Church* 2.25 (where he cites Tertullian as a source); cf. also 2.22, 3.1, and 4.26 (for Eusebius' knowledge of other sources).

[40] Lactantius, *On the Manner in Which the Persecutors Died* 3 (translation by William Fletcher, *Ante-Nicene Fathers* edition).

> all his own domestics should be tortured to force a confession of the plot. He sat on his tribunal, and saw innocent men tormented by fire to make discovery. All magistrates, and all who had superintendency in the imperial palace, obtained special commissions to administer the torture; and they strove with each other who should be first in bringing to light the conspiracy. ... Presbyters and other officers of the Church were seized, without evidence by witnesses or confession, condemned, and together with their families led to execution. In burning alive, no distinction of sex or age was regarded; and because of their great multitude, they were not burnt one after another, but a herd of them were encircled with the same fire; and servants, having millstones tied about their necks, were cast into the sea ... tortures, hitherto unheard of, were invented.[41]

For this passage, Rougé enumerates numerous parallels with the account of the Neronian fire in Tacitus, and rightly concludes literary dependence is certain. The coincidences would otherwise be too improbable. Lactantius' account of the burning of Nicomedia employs Tacitus' account of the burning of Rome as a model. For example, both accounts mention agents being tasked with starting the fire, and their attempts to start additional fires. Lactantius likewise adapted the theme of rounding up scapegoats for the fire, and the barbaric and innovative tortures applied to them, and the immense number of victims, and the notion of a prejudicial hatred being attached to the "name" of 'Christian', all features of Tacitus' account.

This makes it likely that Tacitus wrote his account as we have it (and Lactantius knew it well), but without any mention of Christ or Christians. Otherwise, Lactantius would have certainly used that fact in his account earlier in this same book of the persecution under Nero, and might even have drawn explicit parallels to it when developing his account of Galerius. Instead, it appears that Lactantius only knew of a narrative in which Tacitus related the scapegoating of the Chrestians, a belligerent band of Jews, and then

---

[41] Lactantius, *On the Manner in Which the Persecutors Died* 14-15 (translation by William Fletcher, *Ante-Nicene Fathers* edition).

used this as a model to *invent* (or embellish) a scapegoating of *Christians* under Galerius. Eusebius also relates the same tale of the Nicomedian fire, and he may have been adapting Lactantius as a source, though he shows no specific knowledge of the Neronian story or any similarities to it.[42]

In similar fashion, no other Christian literature before the late 4th century shows any knowledge of the Neronian persecution being as exaggeratedly elaborate as Tacitus describes, or being in any way connected with the burning of Rome, even when discussing Nero's treatment of Christians.[43] The book of Revelation also appears to have no knowledge of this. Nero's burning of Rome is almost certainly alluded to throughout Rev. 18, complete with the belief that he tasked agents with starting the fire on purpose (Rev.

---

[42] Eusebius, *History of the Church* 8.6.

[43] References to it are absent also from the Acts of the NT (despite that being written most likely in the late first or early second century: Richard Pervo, *Dating Acts: Between the Evangelists and the Apologists* [Santa Rosa, CA: Polebridge, 2006] and *Acts: A Commentary* [Minneapolis, MN: Fortress Press, 2009]). Nor is there any mention of it in 1 Clement, despite that traditionally being written from Rome itself within decades of the supposed event. 1 Clement chs. 5-6 discuss martyrdoms or persecutions only vaguely, naming only Peter and Paul, mentioning various unnamed others, and giving no specifics that confirm knowledge of the event described in the Testimonium Taciteum or even any particular involvement of Nero. 1 Clem. 1:1 mentions a plurality of misfortunes and setbacks delaying the letter, but being in the plural and without details we cannot connect that with any particular event such as we now find in the Testimonium Taciteum. Nor is there any specific mention of it in the Christian redaction of the *Sibylline Oracles*, despite their summary of Nero's crimes in 5.140-46. The Christian redaction of the *Ascension of Isaiah* 3:13-4:22 also refers to Nero executing some of the apostles and persecuting Christianity in general, but once again makes no specific mention of the atrocity in the Testimonium Taciteum.

17:16).[44] Though this narrative says Rome will remain desolate forever, that didn't happen, so that is either a metaphor, or an adapting of the known event to fantasize about Rome's expected apocalyptic future. But either way, the text shows no knowledge of Christians being persecuted for it, or after it. To the contrary, it depicts the burning of Rome as a punishment by God for Nero's *previous* persecution of Christians (Rev. 19:1-4; 17:12-14). Such an interpretation would be wholly exploded if that fire were known to have been followed by Rome redounding its wrath back upon Christians—without some apologetic or apocalyptic interpretation being added to it. That none was, means no such event was known to the author of Revelation, yet that author knew well the event of the fire and lived not long after it.

Conclusion

In the final analysis, given the immensity of the persecution Tacitus describes, its scale in terms of the number of victims, its barbarity, and the injustice of it being based on a false accusation of arson to cover up Nero's own crimes, what are the odds that no Christian would ever have heard of it or made use of it or any reference to it for over three hundred years? By any reasonable estimate, quite low. Not even prolific and erudite professors of Latin like Tertullian or Lactantius? Lower still. That for nearly three centuries no Christian martyr tradition would develop from either the event or Tacitus' account of it? Lower still. That no known legends, martyrologies, or tales would adapt or employ it as a motif in any way, not even in the various stories and legends of the persecutions and martyr-

---

[44] That Nero is the target of Rev. 17-19: Elaine Pagels, *Revelations: Visions, Prophecy, and Politics in the Book of Revelation* (New York: Viking, 2012), pp. 31-34. Rev. 17:10-11 says there were five dead emperors, one living, and one to come who will stay awhile, and then one of the five dead will return as an eighth (meaning Nero resurrected, as we know from later legend). The five dead would most likely be Augustus, Tiberius, Claudius, Nero, and Vespasian; Titus would then be the one "now living," and Domitian the next to come "and rule for a while." As typical for apocalypses, this would be written as if predicting what in fact had already occurred, which dates this text to the reign of Domitian, hence 80-96 A.D. Corroborating that conclusion is the fact that the eruption of Vesuvius, which occurred in 79 A.D., is probably the basis for Rev. 8 (see Pagels, *Revelations*, pp. 20-21); and the fact that Irenaeus, in *Against Heresies* 5.30.3, says that Revelation was written in the reign of Domitian.

doms under Nero that we know did develop and circulate? Lower still. And on top of all that is the additional unlikelihood that all other pagan critics of Christianity (like Suetonius and Pliny the Younger, but even such critics as Celsus) would also somehow not have heard of the event or never make any mention of it.

Lowering the probability further is the way Tacitus describes the event. Tacitus treats the persecuted group as unusually large, and no longer existing, and at the time widely and inexplicably regarded as composed of the most vile criminals, who could credibly have committed arson—three features that do not fit "Christians" that well, but would have fit followers of the instigator Chrestus. It is certainly *less likely* that Tacitus would say these three things about the Christians in Rome in the year 64 than that he would say them of the Chrestians.

For all these reasons in combination I believe we should conclude the suspect line was probably not written by Tacitus, and was most likely interpolated into its present position sometime after the middle of the 4th century A.D. More likely Tacitus was originally speaking of the Chrestians, a violent group of Jews first suppressed under Claudius, and not the Christians, and accordingly did not mention Christ. We should so conclude because alternative explanations of the evidence require embracing a long series of increasingly improbable assumptions. So the line should be rejected as spurious, or at least held in reasonable suspicion. And this conclusion should now be taken into account when assessing the evidence for Christ and Christianity, and also when translating and interpreting Tacitus and the events following the burning of Rome under Nero. The whole passage in *Annals* 15.44 should instead be considered as possible evidence supplementing Suetonius on the matter of "Chrestus the instigator" and Jewish unrest at Rome.

Bayesian Model

The editors of *VC* were a bit mathophobic and did not want to deal with logical representations of the argument justifying my conclusion of "most likely." So it was removed at their request and the colloquial argument left in its place. Here I shall restore it. I justify and explain the method here employed in *Proving History* (Prometheus: 2012).

In the first section of this chapter I found that the base rate of interpolated references to Jesus in non-Christian literature could not reasonably have been lower than 1 in 400 (and in fact it could easily have been much higher, possibly as high as 1 in 10, but I think most likely close to 1 in 200). This makes the prior probability at least 1 in 400 (0.0025) that any randomly selected reference to Jesus in non-Christian literature is an interpolation (arguing *a fortiori* in favor of authenticity) or at most 1 in 10 (0.10, arguing *a fortiori* in favor of interpolation), but most plausibly 1 in 200 (0.005, arguing *a judicantiori*).

The hypotheses being compared are that Tacitus did not write the line about Christ (that it was interpolated by Christian scribes in the 4th century, whether accidentally or deliberately) or that he did (and no interpolation occurred). The prior probability favors that he did. It's nearly four hundred times more likely (0.9975:0.0025 = 399:1)—and even at worst, nine times more likely (0.90:0.10 = 9:1). But one must then consider the evidence specific to the case.

How likely is the evidence surveyed in this chapter, if the Testimonium Taciteum (TT) did *not* originally mention Christ (h)? And how likely is that same evidence if it did ($\sim h$)? There is no evidence increasing the likelihood of $\sim h$. But there is evidence increasing the likelihood of h. I surveyed five bodies of evidence:

(A) The fact that the TT had no influence on any of the several stories and reports of Neronian persecution that we actually have before the 4th century. We should expect those stories and reports to at least be aware of the event related in the TT if that event happened at all, and certainly if it happened and even Tacitus (a pagan) knew and wrote about it.

(B) The fact that until the forgery of the Paul-Seneca correspondence in the late 4th century, no other Christian tales or traditions arose embellishing or drawing on the event found in the TT at all. The complete absence of *any* martyrdom tradition resulting from that event for almost three hundred years is very unexpected.

(C) The fact that there is no evident knowledge of the TT, or the event it records, in Tertullian, Lactantius, or *any other Latin author* (Christian or otherwise), or in Greek for that matter, before the forgery of the Paul-Seneca correspondence over three hundred years later (and over two hundred years after Tacitus supposedly wrote about it). We should expect at least *someone* to have mentioned it, and certainly these authors, who knew and used the works of Tacitus and wrote on related matters frequently.

(D) The fact that features in the entire account of *Annals* 15.44 fit Chrestians (the violent partisans of Chrestus, a Jewish agitator in Rome under Claudius) better than Christians (the nonviolent worshippers of Christ, a Jewish holy man executed in Judea under Tiberius). We should sooner expect the reverse (pp. 378–83, 391).

I consider (A) to be very improbable. It surely can't be any more likely than 1 in 20. I consider (B) and (C) to be at least improbable. Surely neither can be any more likely than 1 in 5. One could swap the odds between (A) and (B), since realistically I find both very improbable, but I consider the silence of stories we actually have to be more improbable than the absence of stories we should expect to have, even though the latter is also quite improbable in this case. Meanwhile, I think (D) *could* be accidental, but as such, it's still not exactly what we expect, so it's likelihood cannot be 100%. It is surely not even 80% expected. So it can't be any more likely than 4 in 5.

Assigning higher likelihoods to any of these would be defying all objective reason. Whereas given the selective survival of evidence, which was highly decimated and under exclusive Christian control for over a thousand years, (A)–(D) are all exactly what we'd expect if the line about Christ was interpolated sometime in the 4th century and not originally in the *Annals* of Tacitus. The likelihood of (A)–(D) on that account is 100%. So the odds favoring interpolation are 20:1 for (A), 5:1 for (B), 5:1 for (C), and 4:5 for (D).

This gives us a total odds ratio of 4 in 2500 ($1/20 \times 1/5 \times 4/5 = 4/2500$), or 1 in 625, *against* authenticity. So when we consider how likely the evidence is on either hypothesis, we have an odds ratio against this line about Christ having been written by Tacitus equal to 625 to 1, and that's *at best*. I think the actual ratio could easily be twice that. But no reasonable argument can be made that it is lower. This represents the unlikelihood of the enumerated cumulative silence in the record (and the oddities of Tacitus's account) if the suspect line were authentically in Tacitus' original, relative to what the likelihood of that same silence (and those same oddities) would be if the suspect line did not appear in the *Annals* until at least the mid-to-late fourth century. In the latter case, all these silences and oddities are completely expected; in the former case, very much less so.

This means that even if the prior probability of interpolation is as low as 1 in 400, the probability that the TT did *not* originally refer to Christians is still $1/400 \times 625/1 = 625/400 = 1.5625/1$, or more than 60% ($0.39 \times 1.5625 \approxeq 0.61$). It is thus probably an interpolation. And a prior of 1 in 400 against this hypothesis is actually unrealistic. If we accept the more plausible prior of 1 in 200 (if we can reasonably expect that 1 in every 200 references to Jesus in non-Christian sources before the 4th century would have been interpolated) then the probability of interpolation is $1/200 \times 625/1 = 625/200 = 3.125/1$, or more than 75% ($0.2424 \times 3.125 \approxeq 0.7575$). It's then over three times more likely this is an interpolation than not. And if we are more pessimistic (as perhaps we should be; we should certainly allow the possibility), and accept that the prior is closer to 1 in 10, then the probability of interpolation is $1/10 \times 625/1 = 625/10 = 62.5/1$, or more than 98% ($0.0157 \times 62.5 \approxeq 0.981$). Interpolation is then over sixty times more likely than authenticity. These probabilities will also increase substantially if we more pessimistically adjust any of the likelihoods of (A)–(D) as well.

ABOUT THE AUTHOR

Richard Carrier, Ph.D., is a philosopher and historian of antiquity, specializing in contemporary philosophy of naturalism and Greco-Roman philosophy, science, and religion, including the origins of Christianity. He blogs regularly and lectures for community groups worldwide. He is the author of *Sense and Goodness without God: A Defense of Metaphysical Naturalism*, *Proving History: Bayes's Theorem and the Quest for the Historical Jesus*, *On the Historicity of Jesus: Why We Might Have Reason for Doubt*, *Why I Am Not a Christian: Four Conclusive Reasons to Reject the Faith*, and *Not the Impossible Faith: Why Christianity Didn't Need a Miracle to Succeed*, and now, *Hitler Homer Bible Christ: The Historical Papers of Richard Carrier 1995-2013*. He has also authored chapters in several other books (p. ix), and articles in academic journals and for his namesake blog and beyond. He also happens to be an ex-construction worker, a veteran of the U.S Coast Guard, and an alumnus of UC Berkeley and Columbia University. He now lives in the California Bay Area with his wife, Jennifer, and their cat, Paiwacket. For more about Dr. Carrier and his work see www.richardcarrier.info.

Printed in Germany
by Amazon Distribution
GmbH, Leipzig